AF262958

PATRIOT PLEA

THE J6 JOURNEY OF A POLITICAL PRISONER IN THE DIVIDED STATES OF AMERICA

JOHN STRAND

FOREWORD BY ERIC METAXAS
AFTERWORD BY SIMONE GOLD, MD, JD

Skyhorse Publishing

Copyright © 2026 by John Strand
Foreword copyright © 2026 by Eric Metaxas
Afterword copyright © 2026 by Simone Gold, MD, JD

All rights reserved. No part of this book may be reproduced in any manner without the express written consent of the publisher, except in the case of brief excerpts in critical reviews or articles. All inquiries should be addressed to Skyhorse Publishing, 307 Fifth Avenue, 4th Floor, New York, NY 10016.

Skyhorse Publishing books may be purchased in bulk at special discounts for sales promotion, corporate gifts, fund-raising, or educational purposes. Special editions can also be created to specifications. For details, contact the Special Sales Department, Skyhorse Publishing, 307 Fifth Avenue, 4th Floor, New York, NY 10016 or info@skyhorsepublishing.com.

Skyhorse® and Skyhorse Publishing® are registered trademarks of Skyhorse Publishing, Inc.®, a Delaware corporation.

Visit our website at www.skyhorsepublishing.com.
Please follow our publisher Tony Lyons on Instagram @tonylyonsisuncertain.

10 9 8 7 6 5 4 3 2 1

Library of Congress Cataloging-in-Publication Data is available on file.

Cover design by Jonathan Torino
Cover photo credit: Ira Veridiano

Print ISBN: 978-1-5107-8698-1
Ebook ISBN: 978-1-5107-8699-8

Printed in the United States of America

To the love, honor, and enduring memory of

Jack and Claire
my original patriot heroes
#FORZA

and

Simone
my "partner in crime" and the ultimate advocate
of courage and compassion
#AHAVAH

Then his disciples remembered this prophecy from the Scriptures:
"Passion for God's house will consume me."
—John 2:17

"We in America do not have government by the majority—we have government by the majority *who participate*. . . . All tyranny needs to gain a foothold is for people of good conscience to remain silent."
—Thomas Jefferson

"As a citizen, you are an equal partner in the American enterprise, a democratic constitutional republic; and *there are no silent partners in democracy*."
—John Strand

CONTENTS

FOREWORD

Sometimes you realize that what you believe—or what you believe *most deeply*—has personal roots that make what you believe life-changing. It's no longer just an intellectual assent to something. It's part of you, something that touches your heart and mind and soul all together. So when you merely know *intellectually* of a certain injustice, it might bother you and motivate you to action to some extent, but when you know that that injustice has been done to someone you know *personally*, someone you have come to love and admire, your sense of the injustice is multiplied infinitely. Your sense of having to do something about that injustice leaps to the forefront of your being. You cannot avoid thinking about the injustice because it is tied to someone in your life. For me that someone is the author of this book, John Strand.

When all hell was breaking loose in this country a few years ago, when well-meaning medical professionals like Dr. Simone Gold—who is a major part of this story—were being silenced and punished for speaking out, many of us knew we had entered an existential crisis in America. We never dreamt anything like this could happen, but it was happening and we had to face it and fight it with everything we had. And we suddenly began to see that anyone who was in this fight with us was our ally and friend. Those of us trying to make sense of the madness and vile lies looked to those allies and friends to help us. We knew we were in this together. We knew that whatever new community was forming in these new friendships was the way forward, was at the essence of why any of us had any hope that we could get through it.

I remember the day in a parking lot in California when I had the privilege of meeting John Strand, along with Dr. Gold. We embraced as though we had known each other for years, because knowing that we were all together in standing against the evil we saw meant that our connection was even deeper than many of the relationships we had had with people over years and decades, many of whom had cut off their relationships with us precisely because we were standing against the evil that they were complicit with in their silence.

My friendship with John deepened over the months that followed that meeting, but when I knew he was being sentenced to prison for the events he describes in this extraordinary memoir, something in me changed forever. I realized that someone I had come to care about deeply was going to suffer for speaking the truth when most people I had known had refused to speak the truth or even be allied with those who spoke the truth. Knowing John and meeting his family during the time of his despicable incarceration made everything dramatically personal for me, as I say, and made it completely unthinkable that I could ever look away from the injustices being done, not just to John and so many others, but to every single lover of truth and freedom.

During that time it was my privilege to pray for John, and to know that like Dietrich Bonhoeffer, he was facing something evil and unjust, but that God had chosen him for this privilege and would use John's story to bring redemption and healing to a broken and confused nation. Whenever we trust God with our sufferings, we know that He will vindicate us and redemptively bring something beautiful out of that suffering. This book is part of that vindication and redemption.

That John was able to write this book and tell the world of what he suffered is a major part of God's answer to the injustices and lies. So this book is a big part of the way forward. When you read it, all of these things will become personal to you too. You will therefore become part of that army of truth tellers standing against the evils of our time. May God bless you and speak to you as you read it and share it with others.

—Eric Metaxas is the author of *BONHOEFFER: Pastor, Martyr, Prophet, Spy*, and host of *Socrates in the City* and *The Eric Metaxas Show*

INTRODUCTION

Ciao!

My name is John Strand, and I am an actor.

I introduce myself this way not so much from a vocational perspective, but from a human one. While film and television work is on my résumé and a favorite of my many passions, it's just one of the eclectic slices that make up my rather "maverick" professional pie. Yet those experiences have shown me that, in truth, we are all actors—in the sense that all of us have been enabled to act; not the AI-driven automation of a machine, but the organic, self-determined will of a unique conscious mind. No, most of us do not have the aptitude or interest for memorizing lines and endlessly repeating scripted scenes to earn a paycheck—but all of us are, essentially, improv actors on the grand stage of our lives. Each passing year offers an expanding view—not only of our own roles, but of the backstory, the landscape, the diverse cast, and perhaps a glimpse of the approaching climax scripted into this dramatic story we all inhabit.

It's with that spirit of discovery and enlightenment that I endeavor to share some background, along with a few pivotal scenes recently playing out in my own personal "Act I."

Like any compelling drama, it includes battles and betrayals, love and loss, suffering and triumph . . . with a few plot twists no screenwriter could have dreamed up. As a California kid working in Los Angeles,

I've always been drawn to the hope of a "Hollywood ending"—that iconic finale of victory and redemption. This yearning, I believe, still burns in all of us. Whether smoldering or snuffed out, I invite you to rekindle that flame and join me as *the hero of your own story*. We embark now in pursuit of true love and greater glory, in search of that which is real and good and beautiful—in hope of that which we need most: to fulfill our destiny.

Let's fly! *Maverick, over and out.*

—JS

WELCOME TO THE DARK SIDE

This was it.

The step I had prepared to take—the stand I had declared I would make. This was the moment I had known was coming since that pivotal day in January more than two and a half years earlier. A moment steadily approaching with the agonizing anticipation of a collision course with a freight train viewed in slow motion.

That fateful day was January 18, 2021—Martin Luther King Jr. Day, a celebration of our nation's marquee civil rights activist and political prisoner of conscience. It was like God Himself had scripted the scenes with poetic irony. The FBI SWAT team raid exploded out of nowhere—my life shattered and changed forever by a day that eventually brought me to this moment of truth: standing at the entrance of a prison.

Today was July 25, 2023, and I was about to leave the world I had always known, to interrupt the life I had always lived, to cross over from the light of liberty into the darkness of captivity . . . and in a sense, it was quite voluntary. This moment was a culmination of that other fateful day of infamy, endlessly lied about and weaponized, which had occurred only twelve days prior to my MLK Day arrest: **January 6**. Back in 2020, in the wake of an unprecedented civil rights catastrophe—with rampant government abuse and totalitarian controls becoming universally accepted under the guise of "public health"—a resistance movement was born. Lockdowns were my last straw: undisguised tyranny unleashed in the supposedly free nation of the United States of America. I knew this was existential, so I went public . . . and ended up torching my Hollywood career. In the early months of 2020, I ventured to the front lines, leading a freedom rally in Los Angeles and declaring support for "MAGA" and President Trump—right in the heart of the propaganda power center. It was an act of open rebellion against an emerging empire of oppression sweeping the nation. Demagogues spun lies and weaponized fear to implement a global reset of control before the Constitution could even catch its breath.

Choosing to be a rebel—in the sacred American tradition of peacefully protesting for constitutional rights—made me a target. When I dared to stand tall and do my job by joining a fellow civil rights advocate on January 6, the government hit that target—arresting me for the crime of protecting my colleague in a crowd, and for defending the civil liberties of all citizens. And now, standing on the shoulders of Martin Luther King Jr., I found myself stepping beyond personal comfort and volunteering to become a literal "political hostage"—all because I chose to refuse a DOJ plea that I knew was a poisonous lie. That plea deal was a deadly weapon, wielded by government gangsters waging an opaque war against their own citizenry—powered by the dark forces of an unseen, and very real, galactic empire of immeasurable evil.

And now, I was about to come face to face with it.

There was an invisible darkness in the brilliant morning sunshine as the blacked-out Frontline Doctors SUV rolled across southern Florida. We drove past the endless palm trees and nondescript strip malls, finally pulling into the deceptively pleasant-looking entrance of FCI Miami. My soul sighed with a bittersweet resolve to meet this moment girded with purpose, and with poise.

Easier said than done, I was soon to discover.

"Well . . . I guess this is it," Dr. Simone Gold turned toward me and said with resignation. "Are you okay? Are you ready?"

Her eyes met mine with the deep love and concern of a close friend—but quickly drifted, heavy with inescapable anguish at the imminent pain I was about to bring upon all of us. I swallowed hard as the SUV came to a stop in front of the Receiving and Discharge entryway.

"Yes, I'm okay. And I'm ready. God is in control."

I believed it . . . but I still felt very strange inside.

We turned to share a final embrace there in the vehicle. My stomach clenched even as my arms held close my dearest friend—a woman I revered—never imagining in that moment, as she promised to visit me in the next week, that it would be the last glimpse I would have of her or any of my friends and family for more than eight excruciatingly painful months. Months marked by horrific isolation and the crushing despair of being denied any sight or sound from my loved ones, with no knowledge of when, or if, it would ever end . . . a hell I couldn't have fathomed until I was writhing in it.

But in that moment, mercifully blind to the future, I stepped calmly into my present assignment: a sacred duty to sacrifice comfort in service to my country by self-surrendering my liberty—my life—to the custody of the United States Federal Bureau of Prisons.

Today, that was the price of defending freedom.

The steamy south Florida air walloped my navy-blue Ted Baker suit as I walked toward the facility. I paused briefly to turn back and wave a last farewell, whispering "I love you" to Dr. Gold and the other team members watching from the car glinting beneath the dazzling Miami sun. The tropical scene was another of God's ironies—it belied the ominous storm I was deliberately encountering as I turned toward the prison entrance once more, walking away from the light . . . and stepping into the "Dark Side."

Chapter 1

IT'S A CONTROL THING

In the end, it always comes down to one thing: control.

Who has it?

When do we fight to keep it—or let it go?

What are the consequences of losing it?

And . . . why does it matter?

Life doesn't always offer clean or obvious answers. Most of us are trying to make sense of things we can't explain, fix, or escape—things we can't control. That leaves us with a choice: Do we keep looking for answers, or tune out the noise and try not to care?

This dilemma is symbolized by the iconic "red pill or blue pill." Truth versus illusion. Like Neo in *The Matrix*, I chose the red pill—and that choice ignited a "Red Pill Revolution." I'm committed to seeking the truth—at all costs—because that search is the only path to freedom.

This book is that story—a personal journey, but also a challenge for us all to choose truth and "Uncomfortable Courage." If you join me on this journey, you'll have demonstrated my opening thesis: exercising control over your mind by continuing to read. That matters more than you might think.

Because here's the hardest truth of all:

There are things we can control—and many more we can't.

Knowing the difference is step one. Only then can we rise to the next, paramount challenge: using our limited control to achieve limit-less victory.

And victory is key, because another vital truth is we're all caught in a cosmic war. This battle is also shown in *The Matrix*, and it's what I was referring to in a tweet used by the federal prosecutor, Mr. Jason Manning, as the very first words of the government's opening statement against me in my January 6 trial:

THIS. IS. WAR.

Yes, Mr. Manning—(read this in the voice of Hugo Weaving's brilliant performance of Agent Smith, hissing hypnotically to Neo: "Mr. Anderson . . .")—this most certainly is a war. And though you may be unwitting as a pawn of the evil empire that is our deeply corrupted federal government, you are no less culpable as an enemy combatant in this clash:

A war between the Power and the People.

A war between good and evil.

A war to seize control of the human mind—and, ultimately, the human soul.

Elon Musk said it this way: "It's a war between the humanists and the extinctionists. Once you see it, you can't unsee it."

But once you see it—what will you *do* about it?

Discovering you're caught in the crossfire of a war waged by once-trusted institutions is a tough pill to swallow—but it is lifesaving medicine. The inescapable reality is this: The war is real—spiritual as much as political and cultural; global and yet simultaneously individual. It is an ongoing battle to control the mind—and there are only two sides in the fight.

I'm fighting for the good guys, whom I have officially named "Team Reality." We believe in absolute truth and rally around its source, to defend the ultimate human reality:

We are all divinely designed to be sovereign individuals.

This creed is a death cry to the enemy; sovereignty and individuality are intolerable to tyrants. And it is tyranny that tells you who is essential and who is not. It is despotism that dictates who is permitted to work, and where; who is approved to travel, and when; who is accepted to worship, and how; who is allowed to speak—and what they're allowed to say before the signal is cut. So, while you were created to be free—to control your own mind and shape your destiny—the enemy has other plans.

It doesn't take long to look around and see the chaos erupting in every corner of the world, always paired with a political figure perfectly positioned to offer "the solution." And it doesn't take a rocket scientist—with all due respect to Elon—to recognize the endgame . . . and how little time remains to rescue freedom from the jaws of modern slavery. This war is raging—whether we like it or not, whether we see and acknowledge it or not. It is the most existential and consequential thing there is, and not a single human—past, present, or future—can escape the fury of its final outcome.

Every moment counts—and every move will be counted.

Everything good, true, and beautiful now hangs in the balance. The resounding question is:

Are you going to fight for what's right?

Are you going to stand for what's real?

Or will you sit on the sidelines, sedated by social media swipes and convenient coping—avoiding controversy and tough choices—until you've surrendered your heart, mind, and soul?

It's time to take control.

CHAPTER 2

SIT BEFORE YOU STAND

If you stand for nothing, you'll fall for anything. That's what they say—and these days, it seems more relevant than ever. A lot of people are quick to "take a stand" for something—a cause, a trend, a movement. But what are they standing *on*? What anchors their convictions? What's the foundation beneath the slogans?

Nobody seems to be asking that question.

I remember a talk show host from my youth named Mike Rosen, who gave a challenge to callers with strong opinions: "Tell me where you sit before you tell me where you stand." In other words—what's your worldview? Your framework? That simple idea has never felt more necessary than in today's chaos of clickbait headlines, algorithmic manipulations, and filtered outrage.

That challenge stuck with me. My brother Michael—one of the most thoughtful people I know—wrote something similar while I was incarcerated. In one of his letters, he said, "It seems like there are more and more experts, but fewer people who see the big picture."

He called it a "loss of context." A world of narrow views and disconnected knowledge.

He was right.

And now with technology accelerating everything—especially artificial intelligence—we're not just losing the big picture. We're losing the ability to think clearly at all. My brother added, "There are too many people looking at a tiny square millimeter of the intellectual landscape—and not enough people asking what it all adds up to." That also stuck with me. And I believe it explains a lot of what's going wrong.

The famous author G. K. Chesterton never earned a university degree, yet he produced an impressive body of work—essays, books, poetry—and brought sharp wit and insight to nearly every subject he touched. He had a label for modern specialists—"heretics." Not because their ideas were (necessarily) wrong, but because they existed in isolation—cut off from their context. He warned of those who lock themselves inside "the clean, well-lit prison of one idea."

It's a striking image—and a real warning.

My childhood pastor used to say: "A text without context is no text." Our modern era has brought us to such an extreme acceleration—not just in how we speak, but in how we think—that we now routinely process and communicate our beliefs in fragmented sound bites and TikTok stories without any connection to the bigger picture, much less the root causes of things. We're not just losing the context. We're losing the ability to even *recognize* that context matters.

We need to press the pause button—and consider where we "sit" in our understanding of the world. In other words, we need a stable intellectual framework—a philosophical baseline—on which to anchor and analyze our ideas and experiences. Even if people don't agree on the framework itself, the fact that such a framework exists—and can be named—is what makes real dialogue possible. Without context, even well-intentioned messages dissolve into adversarial static—blustering winds of confusion, division, and ultimately, hatred.

Ideas break down. Noise takes over.

This chaos now spills into almost every public debate. Even casual dialogue feels charged—like one wrong word could spark a shouting match. For many, that tension is a deterrent. Why bother engaging if it only leads to frustration or rejection?

It's no wonder people are retreating. There's a growing sense that meaningful conversation is, at best, pointless, and at worst—dangerous.

Does anyone today still believe that "left and right" can sit down and work things out as fellow Americans?

How, exactly, have we devolved from the United to the Divided States of America? For that is certainly where we "stand" today. We don't just disagree on policies. We don't agree on *reality.* We are no longer unified by the fundamental principles of our republic. Even the facts of our nation's founding are now up for debate—revised, removed, or simply forgotten. In their place: slogans, distortions, and a collective amnesia that widens the cracks in our foundation.

It seems that in today's world, we're constantly stumbling into stupid ideological skirmishes—that bloody battle in the middle—without realizing what was right or wrong at the beginning.

The middle is meaningless without the beginning . . . and hopeless without the end.

The poet and explorer Richard F. Burton summarized the peril of humanity's "heretical" tendency when he wrote:

"The truth is a shattered mirror strewn in myriad bits, and each believes his little bit the whole to own."

It's a beautiful line—and a warning of the danger posed by *omission bias.* Telling part of the truth while hiding the rest isn't "telling the truth." It's telling a particularly ominous lie.

That's why history matters. Not the curated version, not the approved talking points—but the full picture. Without it, we're distracted—and deceived—by the fragments.

The more our history is erased, twisted, or ignored, the more our understanding of reality unravels. It becomes harder to know what's true—and harder to find a place to stand. But honest history gives us something solid.

John Dos Passos describes the importance of seeking honest, accurate history in *The Ground We Stand On* (1941):

"In easy times history is more or less of an ornamental art, but in times of danger we are driven to the written record by a pressing need to find answers to the riddles of today. We need to know what kind of firm ground other men . . . have found to stand on . . . they managed to meet situations as difficult as those we have to face, to meet them sometimes lightheartedly, and in some measure to make their hopes prevail.

"We need to know how they did it.

"In times of change and danger when there is a quicksand of fear under men's reasoning, a sense of continuity with generations gone before can stretch like a lifeline across the scary present and get us past that idiot delusion of the exceptional Now that blocks good thinking."

That phrase—"*find answers to the riddles of today*"[1]—ties into our red or blue pill dilemma. We think our era is so unique, so unlike anything before. But often, the answers we seek have already been lived and written.

Dos Passos believed those answers are worth finding. I agree—but my next question is: What is history? Ornamental in easy times, fundamental when the chips are down, but in either case, I think we can say history is the study and preservation of . . . reality. And in a time like ours, reality is under attack.

To explain, let me ask you another question—and this isn't an abstract hypothetical, but a situation we all face on a regular basis:

---

1. Throughout this manuscript, I use italics and bolding to emphasize words within quotes.

When you've got a problem, would you rather listen to someone who speaks in polished phrases but never solves the issue . . . or someone who shows up and fixes the damn problem?

If you prefer the problem-solver, I'd say you've picked "Team Reality" for yourself. Most people claim to want solutions. But when it comes time to act, many still choose sides, assign blame, and distract themselves from doing the hard work that's necessary.

Fear and hate have filled that vacuum. They've become the default language of our public square. And fueling them both is ignorance. Not a lack of intelligence—but a lack of truth. That ignorance feeds on pride—the "original sin" that places self above everything else. . . even God.

As we noted from the start: It's a control thing.

Love is considered the opposite of hate—but it's really the cure for pride. Not the vague, feel-good kind of "love" that gets tossed around on bumper stickers. Real love tells the truth. It carries weight. It humbles the self. That's the kind of love I hope to offer as I tell this story—not to preach, but to clear the air. To push back the haze of confusion and discover something beautiful.

I've found that one of the best ways to make sense of this chaos is by understanding how thinking works. That's where my take on *Cognitive Theory* comes in. It's a simple maxim I've developed to describe how belief becomes behavior—and how words, over time, shape history.

MAVERICK COGNITIVE THEORY

WORDS develop your THOUGHTS, which direct your ACTIONS, which define your CHARACTER, which determines your DESTINY
The sequence matters. And it may surprise you that words come before thoughts. But they do. "Word" in Greek is *logos*—a term for truth, for reason, for meaning itself. Words are the boundary marker or limiting edge of a specific idea. Without them, everything would mean

everything, and then nothing means anything at all ("love is love"). To have meaning implies the existence and *mutual recognition* of boundaries.

We also understand this as a "rule"—a limitation *on* something, but also a pathway *to* something.

Cognitive Theory is about direction. It shows how meaning builds. How language leads to choice, and choice to consequence. If we skip the early steps—or get them wrong—we risk veering off course before we even know we've started.

We instinctively understand that, as living humans, we are "in motion." But motion without direction leads to collision. That's how people clash. Their actions may conflict—but the real disconnect often started much earlier, with a word or a thought left unexamined.

As earlier noted, the middle is meaningless without the beginning.

This brings us to **Control Theory**—another simple but powerful idea. If Cognitive Theory shows how change happens, Control Theory shows who's responsible for it.

MAVERICK CONTROL THEORY

To reach a meaningful destination, follow three steps:

1. **Acknowledge** that God does something—His original control. He created. He commanded. He holds ultimate authority.
2. **Activate** your ability to do something—your self-control. You have free will. You can respect God's design—or reject it.
3. **Accept** both what God has done and what He will do—His ultimate control. Your destiny reflects both divine authorship and your response to it.

   1 + 2 + 3 = Your God-given, self-directed destiny.

It might sound abstract at first. But once you grasp it, it's intuitive. I've come to see these patterns everywhere—in nature, in relationships, in decisions that shape lives and nations. I believe you'll start to see them too, as we move forward together.

Next, I'll tell you how my own framework developed—my view of the world, and of myself. Not to convince you of anything right away, but to show you where I sit, before I tell you where I stand.

Once you understand that . . . you may understand why I "chose" a felony and years in prison.

And why I'm sounding this alarm—my Patriot Plea.

CALIFORNIA DREAMIN'

Colorful, unconventional, curious, and yes, even ridiculous—my still-unfolding journey resembles a "Technicolor dreamcoat" of bold choices, wild pursuits, and some unpredictable turns.

Rock & Roll singer?

Check.

Construction worker?

Check.

Editorial contributor for a national newspaper?

Check.

Hollywood actor?

Check.

Hollywood cocktail lounge host—*uh, wait, isn't that the same thing?*

Double-check.

Event production staff manager?

Check.

Civil rights activist?

Check.

Social media news anchor?

Check.

Creative director and filmmaker?

Check.

Armed security guard?

Checks credentials on security badge . . . **Check.**

International fashion model—dude, are you serious right now?!

Check—and check.

See what I mean? It's like I flipped through the career catalog and signed up for everything adventurous, competitive, and exhausting. My poor mom! There was never a dream too daring in my eyes—and I am nothing if not a hopeless romantic and a "consummate dreamer."

"Love, Liberty, Rock & Roll" has been my lifelong motto—and for better or worse, I've lived it with fearless abandon through every act of this ongoing drama.

The biblical story of Joseph—a legendary consummate dreamer—always struck a chord with me. His visions, betrayals, and ultimate purpose felt oddly familiar. But I never could have predicted how closely my own path would echo his, or how dark those echoes might become. It's been a roller coaster of blessings and bruises—and I'm still deep in the plot. I don't think I've even hit the intermission yet . . . but like we said, the middle is meaningless without the beginning.

So to the beginning we go.

My genesis was the fruit of another hopelessly romantic dream. My parents left an East Coast Italian family to chase a vision of life aboard a sailboat on the Pacific—the quintessential "California Dreamin'," which became the birthplace of a dreamer named John Strand. Even with those idyllic aspirations, my father was a practical man. He was the first of eight children born to my grandfather, a Marine Corps artillery officer who served in both the Korean and Vietnam wars. Following those patriotic footsteps, my father joined the Naval Reserve at age seventeen.

He eventually served as navigator and conning officer on a destroyer escort, qualified as a salvage diver, and supervised the dry-docking of ships as large as aircraft carriers. His Navy-issue leather flight jacket sparked my Maverick spirit from an early age, especially when he introduced me to Top Gun with real military authority. Though his arena was vastly different from mine, my father had crafted a technicolor dreamcoat of his own—and I am surely my father's son. He passed down a work ethic that drove me to chase big goals and fight hard to reach them.

And yet, I've never forgotten the day my father pulled me aside to describe the full panorama of his adventures and achievements, only to conclude with a piercing truth: All the vibrant colors of his dreamcoat paled in comparison to his highest calling. He found true fulfillment in his God-given roles as a husband and father, with a sacred responsibility to provide for his wife and children, and to connect with them.

"Relationships," my dad told me time and time again, "relationships are what will matter to you after the lights dim, the applause fades, and the gear gets packed away. The way you treat people—and the time you invest in their lives—will determine the value of the life you're able to achieve."

I've spent the rest of my life discovering how true that was, along with much of his wisdom—especially one principle tied to that insight: **priorities**. He often reminded me to weigh the true importance of my goals and values. More than just work ethic, I owe him gratitude for instilling the core virtues of honor, humility, courage, and service. Those became the rebar in the concrete foundation I've built my life on.

I also inherited his love of analogies. He had a gift for them. "It's a control thing" was a classic Jack-ism, a phrase I heard countless times growing up to describe power struggles. He brought the rebar-and-construction metaphor to life when he and my mom began remodeling our home, enlisting the participation of both me and my "other half," my brother Bobby. "Like oil and water" is how he always described the two of us—nearly twins in our inseparable closeness, but opposites in temperament. I was loud and boisterous; Bobby was quiet and observant.

Still, when asked if we wanted to "help Daddy build a garage," we were equally thrilled. It felt like a rite of passage—providing for our mother and sister, building something real with our own hands and minds. We were still shy of our teens when that project began, but we already understood what mattered most: We were building it with the ultimate man in our lives—our dad.

It's what I call "triumphant masculinity."

In a world full of crises and scoundrels, my father was my first true hero—and remains one of my greatest. Of all the gifts he gave me, the most important was the revelation of God's Word, the Bible, as the standard of absolute truth. He taught me it wasn't just a book of stories, but the primary source of knowledge, wisdom, and direction to guide the battleship of our lives through a storm-tossed world.

Years after those lessons, I scrawled this scripture on hotel stationery and set it on the witness stand in a Washington, DC, courtroom, stepping into the most intense battle of my life:

"Be strong in the Lord and in His mighty power. Put on the full armor of God so that you will be able to stand firm against all strategies of the devil. For we are not fighting against flesh-and-blood enemies, but against evil rulers and authorities of the unseen world, against mighty powers in this dark world . . ."

—Ephesians 6:10–12

It's a dark world indeed—and at times, it seems to grow darker still. But the Bible offers more than comfort. It offers clarity. And it's no accident that our Founding Fathers considered it essential to everything they built.

Their belief in Scripture wasn't subtle. It was the cornerstone of their philosophy, their law, and their view of human nature:

"The Bible contains more knowledge necessary to man . . . than any other book in the world. . . . *It is the only correct map of the human heart that ever has been published.*"

—Benjamin Rush

"The first and almost the only book deserving such universal recommendation is the Bible."

—John Quincy Adams

"The teachings of the Bible are so interwoven and entwined with our civic and social life that it would be literally . . . impossible [to imagine our life without them]."

—Theodore Roosevelt

"The Bible is the best gift God has given to men."

—Abraham Lincoln

"I suggest a nationwide reading of the Holy Scriptures . . . for a renewed and strengthening contact with those eternal truths and majestic principles which have inspired such measure of true greatness as this Nation has achieved."

—Franklin Delano Roosevelt

"Resolved, that the United States in Congress assembled . . . recommend this edition of the Bible to the inhabitants of the United States."

—Continental Congress, 1781

"[The Bible] is 'the rock' on which our Republic rests."

—Andrew Jackson

These weren't fringe beliefs. They were foundational convictions—shared across political parties for generations—that recognized the Bible as the moral bedrock of liberty. And it was that same legacy, passed from father to son, that prepared me for the battles I would face.

President Jackson clearly understood a Bible verse my parents reflected in our family remodel. It underscores the need to build virtue and character by anchoring our lives in the immovable truths of Scripture:

> "Anyone who listens to my teaching and follows it is wise, like a person who builds a house on solid rock. Though the rain comes in torrents and the floodwaters rise and the winds beat against that house, it won't collapse because it is built on bedrock. But anyone who hears my teaching and doesn't obey it is foolish, like a person who builds a house on sand. When the rains and floods come and the winds beat against that house, it will collapse with a mighty crash."
>
> —Matthew 7:24–27

Those are dramatic words—almost cinematic—and they come straight from Jesus Christ: the only man to live a perfectly righteous life and, simultaneously, the one true God. Yes, that's a very uncomfortable thing to say—and that's exactly why I believe it's important for me to say it. It's either true or it isn't. If it is, then it's the cornerstone of reality.

This dual identity makes Jesus the ultimate master builder. Through Him, all good things were created—including the most significant: our free will. That agency enables us to be self-aware and self-determining—in other words, we have a measure of control. It's what makes us human. And it's what allows us to know our Father God by name—Yahweh—and to discover His character, through His Word and His fingerprints across creation.

The life of Jesus—fully virtuous, fully human—also makes Him the highest example of how to live a courageous, meaningful life. The Founders didn't hesitate to acknowledge this. Their words are clear:

"I have sometimes thought there could not be a stronger testimony . . . than for men who occupy [the government] and are rising in reputation and wealth publicly to declare their [deficiency by their own merit alone] by becoming fervent advocates in the cause of Christ."

—James Madison

"I subscribe to the entire belief of the great and leading doctrines of the Christian [faith], such as the being of God; the universal defection and depravity of human nature; the Divinity of the person and the completeness of the redemption purchased by the blessed Savior [Jesus]; the necessity of the operations of the Divine [Holy] Spirit; of Divine faith accompanied with a habitual virtuous life."

—Richard Stockton

"I have a tender reliance on the mercy of the Almighty, through the merits of the Lord Jesus Christ."

—Alexander Hamilton

"Christ Jesus . . . is the only Savior of sinners, in opposition to all false religions . . . as He Himself says (John 14:6): 'I am the way, and the truth, and the life: no man cometh unto the Father but by Me.'. . . If you are not reconciled to God through Jesus Christ—if you are not clothed with the spotless robe of His righteousness—you must forever perish."

—John Witherspoon

These aren't the platitudes of fringe fanatics—they're the sober convictions of the men who built America. And they weren't afraid to name their source.

"I am a real Christian, that is to say, a disciple of the doctrines of Jesus, imbuing genuine benevolence and a firm reliance on divine justice."

—Thomas Jefferson

"Significantly, Jefferson spent decades of his life studying the moral teachings of dozens of famous national teachers from across the centuries, including Ocellus, Timaeus, Pythagoras, Aristides, Cato, Socrates, Plato, Epicurus, Cicero . . . and many others . . . Jefferson read the moral teachings of each of these leaders and compared them against those of Jesus, finding Jesus' teachings to be far superior in every case."

—*The Founders Bible: The Origin of the Dream of Freedom*
(David Barton, editor)

Some modern critics claim Jefferson disbelieved the divinity or miracles of Jesus. But the actual record tells a different story:

". . . you can safely reject the claims of today's ill-informed or mal-intentioned writers who argue that Jefferson excluded such passages. Both of his works are still available today, and reading either of them will quickly disprove modern revisionist claims. . . . Long ago, Jefferson told his close evangelical friend and fellow signer of the Declaration of Independence, Dr. Benjamin Rush: 'My views . . . [are] very different from that anti-Christian system imputed to me by those who know nothing of my opinions.' That declaration remains unchanged today."

—*The Founders Bible*

The truth is simple: the Bible and the Gospel was central to the Founders' worldview. That context matters, as we emphasized in chapter two—*always go back to the beginning.* Verify the actual source statements or documents related to any controversy, in their entirety, and be sure you are discovering *the truth, the whole truth, and nothing but the truth, so help me God.*

> "America was born a Christian nation—America was born to exemplify that devotion to the elements of righteousness which are derived from the revelations of Holy Scripture."
>
> —Woodrow Wilson

> "This is a Christian Nation. In this great country of ours has been demonstrated the fundamental unity of Christianity and democracy."
>
> —Harry Truman

These are just a few of the many declarations made by the Founders and the leaders who followed them—clear affirmations of the truth and central importance of God's revelation in Scripture, particularly the life, death, and resurrection of Jesus. It was the teachings of Christ that inspired and sustained the men and women who risked everything to build the world's greatest constitutional republic—the extraordinary nation we are blessed to call home.

It's no exaggeration to say I'm keenly aware—every day—of the priceless gift my parents gave me in their unwavering commitment to these foundational truths. I thank both God and my parents for that gift. It was a vital investment in my development—one that demanded energy, patience, and courage. They persevered through constant obstacles and the scorn of an increasingly secular culture.

That investment paid lifelong dividends, ensuring my life-house has remained on solid rock—along with plenty of roll—ever since.

Before you flinch—or protest—at my direct statement of belief in the divinity of Jesus Christ and the truth of the Bible, let me add this: My father isn't a gullible man. He holds two college degrees, including a Master of Science in mechanical engineering. He worked in senior roles at companies like Ball Aerospace and Hewlett-Packard. He's an engineer. A man of science and reason.

His life was grounded in cold, hard facts—in the Navy, *very* cold and *very* hard. Logic wasn't optional. That's why his journey to Christianity wasn't based solely on emotion or "blind faith." It was rational. After encountering the Gospel during college, he faced a personal crisis when his Christian beliefs seemed to conflict with his scientific training—specifically the dogma of Darwinian evolution, long treated as unquestionable fact or "settled science" (a blue pill oxymoron often used by those seeking to squelch further inquiry).

Darwinian theory was said to pose a serious threat to the credibility of the Bible—or so my father thought. But that view unraveled when he found a growing body of scientists and scholars identifying major flaws in both Darwinism and materialism. They exposed glaring fallacies in the theory that all the complexity of life on Earth could be explained by "random mutation and natural selection"—not to mention its failure to account for how life could emerge from non-life in the first place. Over time, the evidence convinced him: Darwinism wasn't just flawed. It was absurd. And the claims of atheism, built on that foundation, collapsed under the weight of their own contradictions.

We both came to see a deeper pattern: The more humanity discovers—through science and every other discipline—the more it ends up confirming what the Bible has shown from the start. That kind of consistency would be impossible if it were merely human in origin.

The Bible remains the solid, unfailing rock on which our nation was built.

History shows that clear knowledge of Yahweh God—the specific origin of all things—was widely understood long before Charles Darwin's flawed "origin" story appeared in 1859. Even the most skeptical minds among the Founders recognized what many today refuse to admit: Science, at its core, reveals design—not chaos. And where there is design, there is a designer:

"Our Founding Fathers were well acquainted with these [atheistic] writings [of antiquity] and the theories of evolution long before Darwin synthesized them in his famous book. The Founders spoke openly about the creation issue and consistently took the side of the Bible.

"This was true even for Thomas Paine, certainly the most [irreligious] individual among the Founders. In a 1798 address to leaders in France, Paine pointedly denounced their educational system for teaching students that man was the result of prehistoric cosmic accidents and had developed from some other species:

"It has been the error of schools to teach astronomy and all the other sciences and subjects of natural philosophy as accomplishments only, whereas they should be taught theologically, or with reference to the Being who is the Author of them, for all the principles of science are of Divine origin. Man cannot make, or invent, or contrive principles; *he can only discover them, and he ought to* **look through the discovery to the Author**.

"When we examine an extraordinary piece of machinery, an astonishing pile of architecture, a well-executed statue, or a highly finished painting . . . our ideas are naturally led to think of the extensive genius and talent of the artist. . . . How, then, is it that when we study the works of God in creation, we stop short and do not think of God? *The evil that has resulted from the error of the schools in teaching natural philosophy as an accomplishment only has been that of generating in the pupils **a species of atheism**.* Instead of looking through the works of creation to the Creator Himself, they stop short and employ the knowledge they acquire to create doubts of His existence. . . ."

—*The Founders' Bible*

Paine's observation is remarkable—not just for its clarity, but for how it dismantles the folly of atheistic materialism. Most strikingly, he insists that the proper function of knowledge is to "look through the discovery to the Author." This concept—that true sight requires seeing not just facts, but meaning—would be echoed generations later by C. S. Lewis:

"But you cannot go on 'explaining away' forever: you will find that you have explained explanation itself away. You cannot go on 'seeing through' things forever. *The whole point of seeing through something is **to see something** through it.* . . . To 'see through' all things is the same as not to see."

—*The Abolition of Man*

Is it just me, or do more and more people these days "look" with sneering pride—and see nothing but lunacy?

Many other American Founders echoed Paine's reasoned belief in a divine Creator evidenced by intelligent design:

"The belief in an uncreated, self-existent, intelligent First Cause takes possession of our minds whether we will or not, because if man could not create himself, nothing else could; and matter, if it were not external, could produce nothing but matter; *it could never produce thought nor free will nor consciousness.* There must have been, therefore, a time when this globe and its inhabitants did not exist. The question then arises, what gave it existence? We answer: God, the great First Cause of all things."

—Daniel Webster

"The movements of the heavenly bodies, so exactly held in their course by the balance of centrifugal and centripetal forces; the structure of our earth itself with its distribution of lands, waters, and atmosphere; animal and vegetable bodies examined in all their minutest particles; insects—mere atoms of life—yet as perfectly organized as man or mammoth; the mineral substances, their generation and uses; it is impossible, I say, for the human mind not to believe that there is in all this design, cause, and effect up to an Ultimate Cause—a Fabricator of all things, from matter and motion—their Preserver and Regulator . . . and *their Regenerator into new and other forms.*"

—Thomas Jefferson

Thomas Jefferson's reference to a "Regenerator" touched on a spiritual truth I was raised with—but would experience at a deeper level in my Patriot Plea journey. Today I describe it as "spiritual alchemy"—a transformation we'll discover to be the destiny of humanity.

"[S]hould I go about to prove this first principle: the existence of a Deity and that He is the Creator of the universe . . . *what all mankind in all ages have agreed in.* I shall therefore proceed to observe that He must be a being of infinite wisdom (as appears in His admirable order and disposition of things), whether we consider the heavenly bodies . . . or the admirable structure of animate bodies of such infinite variety . . . so exactly that the highest and most exquisite human reason cannot find a fault."

—Benjamin Franklin

"It is so obvious to every reasonable being that he [man] did not make himself, and the world which he inhabits could as little make itself, that the moment we begin to exercise the power of reflection, it seems impossible to escape the conviction that there is a Creator."

—John Quincy Adams

Long before the Founders reached this conclusion, the Apostle Paul had already declared it in stark terms:

"But God shows his anger from heaven against all sinful, wicked people who suppress the truth by their wickedness. They know the truth about God because He has made it obvious to them. For ever since the world was created, people have seen the earth and sky. Through everything God made, they can clearly see his invisible qualities—his eternal power and divine nature. So they have no excuse for not knowing God. Yes, they knew God, but they wouldn't worship Him as God or even give Him thanks. And they began to think up foolish ideas of what God was like. As a result, their minds became dark and confused. Claiming to be wise, they instead became utter fools."

—Romans 1:18–22

Make no mistake—it is these very "*utter fools*" within our nation who, over the last century, have schemed to erode the validity of God's Word. In doing so, they've weakened the natural "nuclear" family—unraveling the moral fabric of society and tearing us apart . . . into *the Divided States of America.*

My father shared with me the details of his faith crisis—and the insights he gained through it. He passed on the solid, rational evidence he'd found for the existence and character of God—and for the truth of the Messiah, Jesus Christ. He also introduced me to many excellent books that substantiated these truths. If I could recommend just one title (besides this one, of course), it would be *Is Atheism Dead?* by my dear friend Eric Metaxas, who graciously wrote the foreword to this book.

It's one of the most enjoyable—and important—books I've ever read. Once you see that all the most recent, cutting-edge discoveries (and indeed, the vast sweep of evidence humanity has gathered across history) point directly to a specific, personal, intelligent Creator, you can no longer rationally ignore the implications. Who is that God? What did He say—and what has He done about it? And how should that shape what *we* say and do?

It certainly shaped my parents' choices. They traded their dream of an endless-summer sailboat cruise for a family of six kids (little did they realize then just how stormy a sea they'd chosen to sail). This new voyage brought the gales of responsibility—and the endless treasure—of investing in God's kingdom here on Earth.

Building God's kingdom begins with building a family.

So my story begins in sunny California, near the Pacific beaches where golden rays, iconic palms, and shimmering waves made an indelible mark on my soul. I've come to describe California as "*the Leading Edge of America's Destiny.*" For years, it's been the frontier of the American dream—offering some of the most alluring and consequential opportunities to shape the future of our nation.

But our ultimate destiny depends on how we pursue it. The choices we make—who we chase, what we believe, and whether we reclaim our pledge to be "*One Nation Under God*"—will determine the climax of our national story, from Los Angeles to New York City and everywhere in between.

Even my name carried a kind of destiny. "Strand" comes from a European word that means "the leading edge of a land"—essentially, a beach of consequence. Something about my birthplace always echoed in me—like a calling I couldn't escape. No matter where else life took me—naval bases on both coasts, school years in Colorado—I never felt those other places were truly home. It felt like my soul had cast an anchor off the Santa Monica Pier, and only the mystic haze of Los Angeles could bring my lungs a fully satisfying breath of air. California touched my heart—and it would give rise to many of my brightest dreams . . . and my darkest heartaches.

My early years were filled with light: building sandcastles on beautiful beaches, swimming and surfing the ocean waves, camping and skiing in the mountains, riding bikes as a family through the neighborhood and nature beyond. There were father-son fishing trips, big family reunions, holiday feasts, spaghetti-and-meatball Sundays, and cozy Christmas getaways in rustic log cabins at the YMCA campgrounds.

One early memory stands out. I heard a booming "OH-ho-ho!" echo through the house and sprinted out, my brother and sister close behind, to discover . . . Santa Claus himself, right there in our living room! He was seated next to Mom by the Christmas tree—eyes twinkling, belly jiggling, in all of his red-robed glory. I believed it really was him—until he spoke. That warm New Jersey twang gave him away—it was my Italian grandfather.

"I didn't know Pop-Pop was Santa Claus!" I gasped.

It was no less magical. Holiday traditions were important throughout the year, marked by delicious flavors, joyful activities, and warm fellow-ship—always connecting people with a spirit of peace and generosity. My parents practiced a remarkable hospitality that beckoned people near and far to come and find rest for their souls—and authentic Italian refreshment for their bodies. Our house was rarely empty. It overflowed with laughter, conversation, and the joy of shared encouragement.

The Christmas season was especially rich with spiritual meaning. Nativity scenes were memorable, including a hand-carved set from Italy, passed down with the timeless retelling of the Gospel story. There was even a tasty gingerbread nativity that my talented mother crafted each year. Student musicals and drama productions gave me my first taste of acting—and sparked a love for the stage. Mom had majored in English literature and worked in the costume department of a Southern California theater company. Her love for books, art, and culture brought creative depth to our home, balancing my father's military background. It gave our learning environment both structure and imagination.

Home is, as they say, where the heart is. And while California always held a strong pull on mine, a child's heart finds true shelter in a loving marriage between a man and a woman. Next to the unshakable truth of God and His Word, this is the most important lesson my parents taught me. It still lights my path today.

Standing for traditional—biblical—marriage as the natural and necessary foundation of a healthy family has become politically incorrect, precisely because the nuclear family exposes the destructive folly of moral relativism. It debunks the trendy slogan of "love is love" (which, logically, reduces love to nothing—and makes it meaningless). The undeniable success of traditional marriage in producing responsible, functional adults dismantles the WOKE myth of "white privilege" in what is, for all its flaws, the most liberated and prosperous nation in human history.

There is no privilege like the two-parent privilege of a strong father and a nurturing mother.

While never easy and sometimes under duress, my parents made a conscious decision to prioritize their marriage and their children—with one very dependent on the other. Even their struggles proved this. One memory seared into my soul was a period of tension and arguments between them, ending with my mother suddenly leaving the house to take a drive alone. It rattled me and my siblings.

During those pensive hours, I experienced an action lesson I will never forget. My father quietly pulled out his ladder and tools, allowing me to help, and we carefully tacked up white Christmas lights to form letters across the garage. They spelled a glowing message to the street—and to my mom:

I LOVE YOU CLAIRE

Tears fill my eyes even now as I write this, remembering my father's example. He owned his mistakes and chose humility. He turned around, repaired the damage, and led our family back to peace. That moment remains etched in my soul.

I'm sure it was uncomfortable for him—but it healed our home. During that process, our local Bible-based church became a lifeline. It wasn't just a place we attended; it was a community that actively supported my parents as they worked to restore their marriage. The church was full of families from all walks of life—different professions, different politics—but united in a way that was powerful and deeply attractive. That unity was built on a foundation of shared values—lived out with the belief that broken families could be restored and despairing souls redeemed. I saw it happen again and again. These families pursued virtue in everyday life while leaning on the grace and power of God's salvation through the Gospel. That resulted in people of good character, and they blessed my family with generosity, compassion, and practical support.

There is no knowledge more powerful than what you've lived first-hand. I have seen and felt this truth myself, and I still reap the rewards of that community built on virtuous bedrock: the clarity of knowing Yahweh as Almighty God, and recognizing His Word—the Bible—as our blueprint for a meaningful life. The richness of sacrificial love, the joy of a father-and-mother-led family, and the strength of a healthy spiritual community are truly priceless treasures. Nothing could entice or compel me to surrender them—after all, that's the stuff dreams are made of.

LIGHTS, CAMERA, ACTION!

———

Dreams are tricky things—take it from Joseph. Humanity's most legendary dreamer saw his wild, improbable visions come true in an epic of astonishing success—but not before enduring horrific betrayals, entrapment, and political intrigue.

Hmmm . . . that sure sounds an awful lot like—But wait, I'm getting ahead of myself.

Joseph's story begins, like mine, with a cherished son raised by godly parents. A boy full of dreams and grand ambition, wrapped in a stylish *dreamcoat* of dazzling color—prehistoric Versace, perhaps. It mirrored the spirit of my own journey, as I began to explore and excel across a wide range of interests.

My love for learning—especially literature—began early at home. I was reading by five and soon skipped ahead to third-grade classes at a local school to match my insatiable curiosity . . . and my "bouncing off the walls" energy. That energy soon found a natural outlet in gymnastics.

My parents quickly realized the traditional school system was both flawed and inflexible—especially for a hyperactive boy already acting out some Maverick tendencies. Thankfully, they rejected the growing trend to medicate such kids with a bogus ADD "diagnosis." After visiting a college bookstore and finding the Education Department textbooks saturated with WOKE ideology, my parents made a life-altering decision—initially protested by my grandparents but later celebrated—to leave the public school matrix entirely. They fully embraced their parental responsibility and switched to homeschooling.

It was the right call. My siblings and I thrived in the creative flexibility of that environment. We studied, helped in the family garden, completed household chores—cleanliness was next to godliness, and next to my mother as well—and spent time outside, learning through hands-on experiences.

We also learned there are many options for blending homeschooling with traditional school programs, and I expanded into baseball, swimming, tennis, and varsity basketball. This formative period depended on yet another politically incorrect value: a mother choosing homemaking and child-rearing as her full-time vocation. My mother and I can now say from personal experience—there's no higher calling for a woman, and no greater reward.

My schooling included civics education alongside other homeschool families, featuring mock elections with campaign speeches, advertisements, and debates. From the start, the Bible and America's founding documents formed the core curriculum—alongside biographies of the Founding Fathers and other notable patriots. Classical history—both world and American—was a critical foundation.

Homeschooling gave us access to real history, free from political distortion.

Further civics training included student conferences at state capitols, where our homeschool group partnered with governors and legislators—many of whom were delighted to meet youth capable of adult conversation, let alone those who grasped the mechanics of American governance.

For my part, I was deeply impressed by the Founding Fathers—true patriots, men of intellect and grit, surrendered only to God, sober in mind and will, and fiercely devoted to what is righteous, true, and beautiful. I was fascinated by the inner workings of the constitutional republic they built more than two centuries ago—in which we can still thrive today. But it was the unique power of the arts, especially the wizardry of music, that truly captured my soul.

Rock & Roll cast a permanent spell on me—captivated by dreams only music can reveal. The avenues of that inspiration would later branch out into an emerald city of artistic expression—from fashion and film to journalism and branding. But melody and rhythm remained the language and heartbeat of every discipline I pursued. If we see in color, then we hear, feel, and hope in even more vibrant tones: the infinite shades of sound and sentience—the amazing Technicolor coat of our dreams. Sound allows us to perceive what our eyes can't see—it is the vision of the heart.

My entrance to the magical kingdom of music began with a piano. When I was ten—interested in everything but focused on nothing— my intuitive mother asked if I'd like to play. I said yes. She promptly found the best piano we could afford: a $100 garage-sale special. More important, she found the best teacher we could find—who became like a second mother to me. After my parents, Christine Schumann's invest- ment in my development shaped my life more than nearly anyone else.

An esteemed musician in her own right—now known as Chris James—she has spent decades generously sharing her unique gifts and extraordinary patience with countless students. A cornerstone of her philosophy is the joy of creativity. From nearly the first lesson, she gave me the space and tools to discover that I, John Strand—a ten-year-old dreamer just starting to hammer out chords and scales—could create a piece of magic that never existed before. That I could touch a human soul where nothing else could reach.

That creative environment swelled a river of dreams I hadn't realized was flowing inside me—a wellspring of color and melody that spilled into every part of life. My skill and passion for piano—and music itself—blossomed with speed and focus. Classical performance led to state-level competitions and university recitals before I reached middle school.

Soon I began composing—with a prize-winning ensemble piece performed at a historic theater, and my original piano solo, *Lily Pond,* published as a sheet music performance piece. The "sun, moon, and stars" of Joseph's early visions had begun to shine in my own story. The bright lights of the performative arts flooded the stage of my unfolding youth. That effect was soon amplified by my discovery of Rock & Roll: a moment so sonically explosive, I still tingle at the memory.

My mother had brought Bobby and me into a bookstore to find a greeting card. We wandered the aisles while she browsed. Up to that point, most of the music we listened to at home was classical or gospel—two musical pillars our culture has sadly abandoned. I'm grateful my parents did not follow that trend.

I drifted to the music section, drawn by pop artist posters. I saw demo stations with headphones for sampling albums. Feeling a strange premonition, I grabbed a headset, skipped the volume check, and hit play. Instantly, my senses were detonated by 110 decibels of blistering '80s synths, electric guitars, and thunderous reverb, just then climaxing in Michael W. Smith's soaring chorus:

I will be here for you
Somewhere in the night, somewhere in the night
I'll shine a light for you
Somewhere in the night, I'll be standing by . . .
I will be here for you

I stood frozen. When the final chord faded, it felt like someone pressed the pause button on the entire universe. I thought I'd found a vortex straight into heaven. I'm not kidding—I'd never experienced anything like it. Colors and sounds washed over my dreamscape in spectrums I never knew existed. My life changed in that moment—a spiritual metamorphosis I didn't yet understand.

I dragged Bobby over to hear it. He would later dig out Dad's old acoustic guitar, teach himself to play, and start jamming with me on the keys. After relentless lobbying, we finally wore Mom down and secured a few "parentally acceptable" pop albums. From there, we devoured every bit of Rock & Roll inspiration we could find. One album Mom initially resisted proved especially influential: *Jesus Freak* by dc Talk—a hybrid vocalist group we began to emulate. We never guessed they'd later personally connect to our musical journey.

The first song we ever wrote—still a cherished part of Strand family lore—came when Mom asked us to modify the lyrics to an old Western movie theme she felt was too violent. Bobby had taught himself the theme and kept jamming it on the guitar. So, I grabbed a pen, scribbled new lyrics, and just like that, "Gunfighters" became "Faithfighters." A new story was born—and perhaps even a prophecy.

Within a week, we'd composed a dozen original songs. Within a few months, nearly a hundred. Our writing matured, and the "Strand" Rock & Roll band took flight. Before my parents could say "Plan B" to suggest a backup career, we'd already envisioned radio singles, nationwide tours, blockbuster soundtracks, and Grammy aspirations. To their credit, they soon recognized we were committed: writing, recording, and performing wasn't a phase—it was our calling. And in our own unexpected ways, Bobby and I would answer that call . . . but not without a few detours on the road to glory.

Mom and Dad were both our biggest fans and toughest critics. They cheered from the audience when they could—but offstage, they urged disciplined rehearsals, frequent performances, and forward-thinking business strategies.

Preparation. Execution. Persistence.

My parents understood the value of economic wisdom—as found in *The Wealth of Nations* by Adam Smith. This foundational book on free-market supply and demand, driven by competition and specialization, became a blueprint for the architects of America. Our Founders didn't just build a government; they created an economic engine that powered the greatest leap in human history for both industry and artistry. It shaped the fate of not only our nation but the entire world, offering a roadmap for unprecedented global prosperity.

Alongside a career in the arts, my dad encouraged me to pursue a trade or practical college degree—something with market value (definitely *not* gender-theory grievance studies). He offered to pay for my college education—a real sacrifice, especially with our family doubling in size—on the condition that I contribute at home and maintain the band's performance goals. Together, we mapped out a strategic plan.

I began college courses and pursued a degree in Business Administration. I earned a 4.0 GPA and made the Dean's List every semester I attended. When faculty noticed I had a knack for explaining algebra to struggling classmates, I secured my first formal employment. Students who had been failing began to pass.

True to form, I gave my public speaking class a homeschool-style twist. The speech was about my Italian family heritage and culinary traditions—"illustrated" with a full-course Italian feast my amazing mom made from scratch and delivered to campus: from antipasto to cannoli. The entire class enjoyed it as I delivered my final assignment. Needless to say, I got an A . . . and a memory I'll never forget.

My parents also supported other interests. I served in the Civil Air Patrol, an auxiliary of the United States Air Force, attaining the rank of Staff Sergeant and engaging in community search-and-rescue training. I also participated in debate conferences and civic leadership events. One year, I worked a full cycle on state senator Kevin Lundberg's campaign, a respected figure in the homeschool arena. I made hundreds of calls, polled voters, and learned firsthand how messaging and policy connect with the public. The experience led me to agree with our second president, John Adams:

"I do not curse the day when I engaged in public affairs . . . I cannot repent of anything I ever did conscientiously and from a sense of duty."

—John Adams

The Lundberg campaign also brought an early exposure to an age-old cancer—diagnosed by my favorite patriot hero, Thomas Jefferson:

"There is a natural aristocracy among men. The grounds of this are virtue and [merit]. There is, also, an *artificial aristocracy*, founded on wealth and birth, without either virtue or [merit]. . . . I consider as the most precious gift of nature . . . these natural aristoi into the offices of government."

—Thomas Jefferson

My parents and pastors always emphasized virtue as the "golden prize"—a mark of true strength and beauty. Jefferson's observation held true. Over time, I saw it taking shape: the *Artificial Aristocracy*, propped up by wealth, connections, and entitlement—and poisoned by greed and vice. They infect every branch of government like a disease—and this "American Cancer" has evolved into the permanent bureaucracy we now call the "Deep State." Our Founders warned us repeatedly that our greatest threat was not foreign enemies, but domestic subversion. As usual, they were right.

Still, that first campaign experience deepened my enthusiasm for the public discourse protected by the First Amendment. It showed me the far-reaching consequences of political affairs—and suggested potential opportunities in public life. But another stage had already taken hold of my imagination. A different spotlight. A louder rhythm. The siren song of Rock & Roll was serenading my heart . . . and it would prove entirely irresistible.

The indie-rock band Bobby and I formed—eventually named Celeste ("Sky Blue" in Italian, evoking a "dream expanse")—was gaining real momentum. We played every local venue that would have us, won several band competitions, and drove—barely legal behind the wheel—to Nashville for meetings with record labels and publishers. It was clear we were ready to level up. So, with my parents' counsel and blessing, I made a bold move: I paused my college program to take an internship with my friend and mentor Taylor Mesplé at his music production studio. While there, Bobby and I wrote and recorded our debut record, *Every Thought I Ever Had.*

The lights of Rock & Roll stages were soon followed by cameras—fashion industry cameras, in a totally unexpected twist. Photographers at Celeste shows snapped some shots that gained the attention of modeling agency scouts. Bemused and intrigued by their invitations to model, I soon found success with runway shows and magazine shoots. A new dream had been airbrushed into view. Expecting little at first, I embraced fashion and fitness modeling as a serious craft—developing through the lens of celebrity fashion photographer Tony Duran, among others. I also embraced a vigorous training regimen, which eventually grew to four hours a day—including a daily 2,000-yard swim, spin and yoga, strength training, and the quintessential Hollywood jog at Runyon Canyon. My diet evolved until I became fully "OMAD": one meal a day, now termed *intermittent fasting*, consuming all solid food during the evening dinner period. I signed with agencies across the United States and abroad, including the flagship agency Wilhelmina Models, working markets from New York City and Los Angeles to New Delhi, Las Vegas, Miami, and more. An unusual career path, running parallel to music, was coming into focus.

And with the "lights" and "camera" came "action!" as agents and managers urged me to pursue acting work. This led to early roles in Nicki Minaj and David Guetta's *Turn Me On* and Far East Movement's *Like a G6*. My band Celeste faced the usual turmoil—lineup changes, financial pressure—but we kept writing, and eventually released our second album: *The Rivalry EP*, a title echoing the creative tension that shaped it. We released it independently on iTunes, Apple Music, and Spotify.

Then came a shock: the tech recession hit, and my dad lost his job—and couldn't find work for a year. But he didn't respond as a victim. Dad focused on what he *could* control: his attitude and his response to adverse circumstance. He diligently pursued every avenue to fulfill his responsibility as a provider. He also asked me to find paid work to help avoid foreclosure on our home. I gave up my internship and plunged into twelve-hour days of backbreaking construction work—building custom houses and bringing my paycheck home to the family. That framing job was the hardest I have ever worked in my life.

Well, until writing this book.

It was also one of the most gratifying seasons of my life, illustrating one of the Ten Commandments, "the first commandment with a promise":

"Honor your father and mother. Then you will live a long, full life in the land that Yahweh your God is giving you."

—Exodus 20:12

God came through for us. The house was saved, and our faith was increased. Supporting my family through that season taught me responsibility, loyalty, and perseverance. I discovered the quiet strength and dignity of hard work, especially in service of our first duty: to worship God and provide for our own.

Divine providence became a torchlight of hope, and it would guide me through future adversity—storms of darkness I never could have seen coming, just beyond that still-glowing horizon.

Dramatic fade of center-stage light . . . and, "Cut!"

TRAGEDY IN PARADISE

———

Surprising to probably no one but me, romance was the next twist of fate woven into my dreamcoat. Despite my intention to wait for the right time and place to compose a fairytale love story, I was swept up in an impromptu rendition of Cupid's chorus. A man's greatest strength often doubles as his greatest weakness, and the strength—and particularly the speed—of my exuberance would prove costly as I fell in love hard . . . and very fast.

Anticipating the arrival of Cupid's arrows, my dad—who had recently regained steady work and given his blessing for me to shift back from construction to music (while still living at home)—posed the classic question:

"Is there a special Ms. Someone in your life? Any possibilities?"

I assured him there weren't. At the time, it was true. I was laser-focused on building a career as an artist and had no plans for romantic distraction. But a few months later, I stumbled right into falling in love—and my calculation was turned upside down:

"We can make our own plans, but the Lord Yahweh gives the right answer. . . . We can make our plans, but Yahweh determines our steps."

—Proverbs 16:1, 9

43

This naturally raises the age-old question: "Do we really have free will? Or is God pulling the strings, leaving us victims of His divine dictates?"

The truth is: We are victims only if we choose to be.

God truly has given us free will. We can choose our attitude (the direction of our heart) and our action (the direction of our body) in each moment. But the outcome of our choices plays out within the "laws of nature" God created—what I call #TeamReality. God controls that world. We control how we move through it.

The question I had to ask myself a short time later was: "Did God want me in a relationship that would bring so much heartache and disruption? Did He intend to divert—or derail—my dreams?" These are painful questions to acknowledge, and they can be difficult to answer. Living life is as much art as science, and in that mystery lies the magic—and, too often, the misery as well. But God answers for Himself with this encouraging promise:

> "'For I know the plans I have for you' says the Lord Yahweh. 'They are plans for good and not for disaster, to give you a future and a hope.'"
> —Jeremiah 29:11

This declares that God's dreams for us are fundamentally good. While He does allow disasters in our lives for reasons we often can't see or imagine, they are not His desire for us. And they won't define our future . . . *if* we control our response to pleasure and pain—both of which cannot fully function without the other. Yes, pain has a purpose—but we tend to overlook it, especially in the myopia of the moment. Unexplained suffering remains one of humanity's most painful mysteries . . . yet those opaque threads, woven into the tapestry of our lives, often shape our individual character—and even our collective destiny.

"Though he experienced years of bondage and misery, Joseph's character was refined and strengthened by his trials. Eventually he rose up to become a prime minister of Egypt who saved thousands of lives and even his own family from starvation. If God had not allowed Joseph's years of suffering, he never would have been such a powerful agent for [justice] and spiritual healing.

"Whenever I preach on this text, I hear from many people who identify with that narrative. Many people have to admit that most of what they really needed for success in life came to them through their most difficult and painful experiences. Some look back on an illness and recognize that it was an irreplaceable season of personal and spiritual growth for them. . . . Though none of these people are grateful for the tragedies themselves, they would not trade the insight, character, and strength they had gotten from them for anything. With time and perspective most of us can see good reason for at least *some* of the tragedy and pain that occurs in life. Why couldn't it be possible that, from God's [infinitely wider] vantage point, there are good reasons for all of them?"

—Tim Keller

I read this reflection on suffering while in prison, from a man who had been betrayed, imprisoned, and crushed many times over:

"Nothing in any life, no matter how well or poorly lived, is wiser than failure or clearer than sorrow. And in the tiny, precious wisdom that they give to us, even those dread and hated enemies, suffering and failure, have their reason and their right to be."

—Gregory David Roberts

Tragically, our responses to suffering often bring—or worsen—disaster. As my friend and pastor Rob McCoy preaches, Western culture has come to despise the pain God designed to balance and preserve life. Instead, we isolate pleasure, worship it, and eliminate pain at all costs—drugging ourselves into the zombie status of the living dead. But because God is *not* dead—and remains captain of #TeamReality—our actions still carry consequences. And when we reject the purpose of pain, we often compound it, inviting disruption that could have been avoided. This tragedy deepens when we realize self-inflicted pain rarely stops with us—it spreads to others, often touching the innocent in ways we never intended.

The *Butterfly Effect* can radiate through both healing and harmful frequencies—and God has given us the power to choose the channel.

In my case, a dramatic fusion of pain and promise came from a whirlwind sequence: meeting a young woman introduced by the band's drummer . . . discovering mutual romantic interest . . . sharing this new development with my parents (who were predictably blindsided, given how recently I'd declared total focus on building an artistic career with my brother) . . . misreading my parents' concerns for disapproval—and greatly confusing the poor girl . . . and then—just barely past my teenage years—plunging into marriage.

All within a year.

The relationship issues hidden by that haste soon surfaced, bringing deep suffering into the marriage—and rippling outward to both our families. Still, we labored to make it work for five difficult years.

Marriage is the most sacred and consequential promise a person can—and should—make. It's the foundation of civilization itself. And we took it seriously, carrying doubts and anguish in our shared desire to honor that vow. There were good times and hard times—and there were desperate and dark times. A heavy depression seeped in, foreign to my naturally positive spirit. It was worsened by adrenal fatigue and recurring illness, and it began to consume my soul. At times, it cast me into a very real pit of despair . . . and I would remember the story of Joseph, wondering why my dreams had grown so dim—some of them seemingly shattered altogether.

That season forced me down a hard road of struggle as I pressed toward the vision still etched on my horizon. Bobby and I juggled odd jobs while keeping up a relentless rehearsal and performance schedule. Thankfully, his own romantic path led to a far happier outcome. His marriage—shortly after mine—would become a steadfast blessing for our entire family. We also served as worship leaders during those years, performing for churches, conferences, weddings, memorials, and regional worship concerts. Those experiences shaped us spiritually, sharpened us professionally, and gave us the chance to serve the community with our gifts.

Meanwhile, my work as a fashion model and commercial talent continued steadily. Magazine covers, print ads, and agency representation began to stack up. That visibility, combined with our need to expand the band's audience, made it clear: We had to break into a major market. The three core members of Celeste agreed it was time to leave the rural Midwest and head to the coast. To me, Los Angeles was the obvious choice—a destined homecoming. But Bobby and our drummer, who had ties to the Pacific Northwest, were drawn to Portland's indie rock scene. I couldn't sway them, and I wasn't about to fracture our unity with an ultimatum—so we moved to Portland.

We didn't get far before disaster struck.

Months of planning and grueling prep, housing logistics, day jobs, and an exciting tour schedule I'd somehow managed to book—all gone in an instant. Our drummer abruptly announced that he and his girlfriend were bailing to move back.

The psychological whiplash was brutal. Refusing to abandon our childhood calling—the world of lights, cameras, and action we believed was our destiny—Bobby and I scrambled to survive. We fought to sustain momentum, but confusion and exhaustion took their toll. Eventually, we were pulled apart by the torrents of instability and disappointment. The band stalled. My marriage was already fraying. And now, all of it began to drown me.

I was facing a full-blown crisis—of my health, my family, my career . . . an existential crisis of faith.

Where was God in all this darkness? Why did the vibrant dreamcoat woven into my soul now feel like it was unraveling at the seams? I prayed, and I wept during worship—week after week, month after month—as I searched every darkening corner of my soul.

But I heard no answer.

Still unwilling to let go of the dream—but nearly a decade into the band, without the momentum our early success had promised—I felt a shift was needed. After months of prayer and family discussion, I made the call: We would leave Portland and return to California, the land of my earliest roots and technicolor memories. Bobby was happier in Portland than I was, but I still hoped he might one day join me in the music mecca of Los Angeles. In the meantime, I set my sights on the bright lights of Hollywood.

I've often looked back at that moment—a choice to exercise control in response to disaster—and wondered if I chose rightly. I still don't have a satisfying answer. What I've learned, slowly and painfully, is that our hero's journey is often a tragedy in this former paradise of a broken world. It's marked by hard choices, setbacks, and suffering— some inevitable, some tragically avoidable. The road forks often, and sometimes without clarity. Virtue should always be a hero's guide, and God's Word his North Star—but even then, painful detours and disappointments still come. It's in those dark places, at the edge of despair, where I've had to cling to the lifeline of Christ—a truth I stand on when everything else gives way:

"For we know that God works all things together for the good of those who love God and are called according to His purpose for them."

—Romans 8:28

The qualifiers here are vital: "God works (has control of) *all* things"—every tragedy and every triumph—and ultimately brings them to a good conclusion. But only for those who love Him. And that love isn't a feeling. It's a decision to trust Him and live in alignment with His design. In short: it's **acting with virtue**.

Holding on to that promise, I launched into the next stage of my journey. My wife and I drove down the Pacific Coast Highway and straight into the heart of the City of Angels. Armed with the courage of God's promises—and a dreamer's bold faith flirting with the danger of the unknown—we navigated to the epicenter of LA's creative chaos—the West Hollywood Whole Foods—without even knowing where we would sleep that night. That Maverick approach—and even the moniker itself—would come to define my career. I improvised and adapted, grinding from heartbroken dreamer to heart-breaking model and actor. I clawed my way up from the bottom of a vast and volatile barrel, learning the ropes of the Hollywood jungle while taking hits from predators eager to exploit the vulnerable.

My acting coach taught me to "leap, and the net will appear"—and I applied that in the most Maverick way possible.

Returning to Southern California's sunshine and sea breeze did wonders for my health. It helped regulate my hormones, lift the fog of depression, and push me to peak performance in an ultra-competitive industry. We also hoped this healing would extend to our faltering marriage. And for a while, we made new friends and some beautiful memories. But eventually, we agreed it was best to let go—to give each other a second chance. It was one of the hardest and most humbling moments of my life, requiring the full measure of God's promises to forgive, to heal, and to make "His mercies new every morning" (Lamentations 3:23).

The pain and complexity of this season was a deep wound. But with time, we have both found a measure of peace. I remain grateful for the support of my family, who bore that pain with me—especially my gracious mother. From my first breath, she poured every ounce of her petite five-foot frame into nurturing me. And to this day, she continues to show me the love and service of Jesus Christ in living color.

I would need every ounce of that love and grace in the years ahead. The heartbreak lingered, even as I threw myself back into work. Purpose became my therapy. It required focus and discipline—and while acting and modeling brought some success, fame and fortune proved unreliable companions.

That wasn't a surprise. I hadn't grown up focused on those things. My dad was one of eight kids, my mom one of five, and I was one of six siblings. Add in about forty first cousins, and you get the picture: a big Italian-American family marked by hard work, patriotism, military service, and Christian tradition—and largely of humble means. Truth mattered. So did integrity. And I'd always been taught that chasing money, status, or fame at the expense of honoring God was idolatry. That wasn't abstract—it was the first of the Ten Commandments and the foundation of truth itself. That's how critical priorities are. I understood the true "pursuit of happiness" was the pursuit of God's purpose—and though imperfectly, I've always lived with a commitment to that Divine Order.

Still, keeping those priorities straight, especially in places like Hollywood or Washington, is no easy task. And yet, the scripture I brought to the witness stand doesn't suggest retreat from conflict. It commands us to stand and fight—while adequately armored by virtue, which is only forged in a "strong" relationship with God:

> "Be strong in the Lord and in his mighty power. Put on all of God's armor so that you will be able to stand firm against all . . . mighty powers in this dark world. . . . Therefore, put on every piece of God's armor so you will be able to resist the enemy in the time of evil. Then after the battle you will still be standing firm. *Stand your ground*, putting on the belt of truth and the body armor of God's righteousness. For shoes, put on the peace that comes from the Gospel so that you will be fully prepared. In addition to all of these, hold up the shield of faith to stop the fiery arrows of the devil. Put on salvation as your helmet, and take the sword of the Spirit, which is the word of God."
>
> —Ephesians 6:10–17

There's a growing trend in modern Christianity to retreat—to isolate from the world under the guise of holiness. People misuse Scripture to justify apathy and all manner of escape from the duties we are called to fulfill as citizens—both of our earthly country and our heavenly kingdom. But that's not biblical. It's selfishness and cowardice posing as religion. Jesus didn't call us to isolate. He called us to love—and love requires engagement and sacrifice:

> "'You must love **Yahweh** your God with all your heart, all your soul, and all your mind.' This is the first and greatest commandment. A second is **equally** important: 'Love your neighbor as yourself.'"
>
> —Matthew 22:37–39

His parable of the Good Samaritan defines a "neighbor"—and it's not just proximity or profession, but action. When Jesus taught His disciples how to pray, he began with: "Our Father in heaven, holy is your name; your kingdom come, *your will be done **on earth*** as it is in heaven." God's will matters *here*—He's not disinterested in this world, nor is He abandoning it. In fact, quite the opposite. His first instruction to mankind was "*fill the earth and govern it.*" Jesus' final instruction was just as active: "Go and make disciples of all the nations." Faith isn't about escape. It's about truth, love, and courageous action. We are designed—and commanded—to engage in our world. To "wrestle" in pursuit of truth and goodness on this earth. And yes . . . to fight against evil.

We're meant to be Faithfighters.

In my own journey, I've wrestled—and not just with evil, but also with God. Somewhat like Joseph's father, Jacob, who was renamed *Israel* after his struggle with the divine. That wrestling—a "struggle with God"—is the literal meaning of the name Israel, which God gave to Jacob, and by extension, an entire nation. I've also "wrestled" with my parents, brothers, and spiritual mentors—trying to discern how to interpret and manifest my dreams. But dreams are tricky things—you can take it from me as well—and finding clarity through the mirage of life's confusion and chaos has been a continual struggle.

"'Human beings are remarkable—at what we can learn to live with,' Father told me. 'If we couldn't get strong from what we lose, and what we miss, and what we want and can't have . . . then we couldn't ever get strong enough, could we? What else makes us strong?'"
—John Irving, *The Hotel New Hampshire*

I kept wrestling—with both dreams and demons—as I pushed forward in my career, from the City of Angels to the streets of New York City, the mecca of the modeling world. Manhattan became my second home, and I settled into a bicoastal rhythm: spring and fall in New York for fashion week, winters back in Los Angeles to chase auditions.

The tales of those years could fill another book, but a panoramic sweep gives a dizzying range of highs and lows. I spent time in some of the most lavish penthouses and palaces on earth—and there were nights I found myself sleeping on a sidewalk, literally homeless.

Feast or famine—that was the nature of modeling and acting. The two industries were interwoven in a bizarre dance: One week I'd be in designer menswear on a TV show, the next I'd be smashing a wedding cake with a baseball bat—while wearing a tux—for a bridal magazine. Some jobs had me in swimsuits or underwear for runway shows and fashion editorials that veered into the bizarre and avant-garde (that's a polite way of saying you might raise an eyebrow if you browse my work history online).

Despite the glamour people associate with fashion or film, the reality was grueling. It was unpredictable, exhausting, and often thankless. No one was handing out prizes or support. Motivation to strive against setbacks and extreme competition could only be pulled from deep inside. I had to keep swimming upstream against a mighty current of doubters, haters, and constant ridicule.

But then again . . . that's what being a Maverick is all about.

I traveled constantly, living out of a suitcase for most of my adult life—embracing both the risks and rewards of an unpredictable, nomadic career. I suffered multiple thefts, including the costly musical gear I'd collected over years of hard work. Once, my luggage was stolen—packed with about ten thousand dollars' worth of rare fashion pieces I'd earned through grit and hustle. That one stung.

I initiated and produced many of my own fashion editorials, earning national and international magazine features to build an extensive portfolio. I worked for elite clients like Armani, Valentino, and Ermenegildo Zegna, along with more exotic fare—romance and action novel covers, living art installations—and practical jobs like Jeans.com and Champion sportswear.

But not every chapter was glamorous. I fell victim to several predators, including a deranged stylist who turned out to be a clinical psychopath with arrest warrants for theft and fraud across the country. That episode wiped out every dollar I had along with my car, wrecked my credit, and forced me to rebuild my life from scratch—yet again. I survived this episode only with the help of my soon-to-be talent manager, Russell Stuart, who remains one of my closest allies.

Better times found me working on TV shows ranging from the glitzy *Vanderpump Rules* to the quirky *Breaking Amish* to the ominous *True Crime* (my favorite joke for prison inmates asking about my background: "No, I'm not actually a criminal—but I do play one on TV!"). In Manhattan, I created and hosted a weekly tastemaker's event by the Plaza Hotel and a Los Angeles Rams fan club at American Whiskey gastropub (love you, Hoosh!) in New York's Fashion District. I also built a multi-platform social media following that neared a quarter-million—securing brand partnerships as a lifestyle influencer.

The parallels to Joseph's journey were hard to miss. I'd been betrayed and broken, robbed and abandoned, seduced and sold out—losing everything multiple times over. And yet, I survived. I fought through every disaster, crawling forward to rebuild my dreams, brick by brick, across the penthouse pyramids and the Miracle Mile river—a classic American hustle story. Against odds I couldn't even count, and under the crushing weight of disappointment and depression, I had somehow flown an impossible mission through the turbulence of my dreamscape and "landed" a career as a professional model and actor. I was, quite literally, "living the dream" in Hollywood. And I still held hope that my grander visions might yet unfold somewhere further along this winding road.

Then finally, after years of preparing for international work, I signed an overseas contract and zipped up my already-packed bags for the grandest adventure yet: the infinitely exotic country of India—as far away from America as you can get.

Chapter 6

THE FATE OF NATIONS

My impression of India was "a planet within a planet"—a self-contained world bursting at the seams. Fiercely independent, proud and chaotic, it's continuously exploding outward with a vastness matched only by its intoxicating zest for being alive. Vivid colors, flavors, and textures erupt in all directions; there is motion everywhere, with clashing sounds and smells blending into the mesmerizing sights of a million stories in progress.

To me, it seemed a dreamer's paradise—and I fell in love with it instantly.

Apparently, it was fond of me as well. The modeling agency in New Delhi that signed me to a three-month contract was enthused—not just at the positive response by local clients, but at the way I fully embraced Indian culture. My contract was extended . . . then extended again . . . until I had been working there nearly a year and a half. The agency treated me like family. The agents and foreign models lived and worked together in communal home-office apartments, sharing the full range of the international modeling experience:

- Runway shows at sprawling outdoor fashion malls
- *Forbes Magazine* spreads shot in palatial five-star hotels
- Fashion editorials photographed in lush, exotic gardens

- TV commercials filmed in the mystical mountains of Dharamsala
- And countless catalog shoots, peeling outfits on and off for ten hours a day

It was a real grind. When we weren't working, the agency took us exploring. We visited marvels like the Taj Mahal, with its intricate gardens and water features, and found meditative calm in ancient temples. We went surfing on the warm waves of Goa—the "San Diego of the East"—and enjoyed nightlife hotspots in the cities, where we, the "foreign celebrities," became the exotic VIPs. Dressed in our trendy finest, we were woven into the spectacle of local club entertainment.

Everywhere I went, Indian millennials and even children ran up to me with bright smiles, peppering me with questions about the United States. They quickly dubbed me "Mr. America!" with unrestrained awe. American male models were rare in India, which made me a novelty. But what struck me most wasn't the attention. It was their open admiration for America and what it stood for: liberty, industry, ingenuity—the mighty power of free-market enterprise. They understood it promised equal opportunity to the common man—a vivid dream of dignity for millions trapped in a caste system of poverty and corruption. To them, America was a nation of destiny, offering anyone the chance to lift themselves from hardship into prosperity—and the Indian people adored it.

The full arc of my "Taste of Asia" tour included work across the Indian subcontinent, Hong Kong, and China. Those years of overseas effort yielded tremendous growth in my résumé, portfolio, and international profile. But the full rewards ran deeper. My success—forged through risk and perseverance, built over the painful shards of broken dreams—went far beyond features in *GQ* magazine and international billboards. The contours of this journey revealed the shape of democracy in civilization. I could see the hues of the human dream at scale, with my finger on the pulse of *the fate of nations*—that heartbeat of human dignity, always in search of divine purpose. India's heartbeat was incredibly strong—rooted in family bonds that reminded me of my own family's Italian heritage. Though still early in their democratic evolution, the people of India had an unmistakable gleam in their eyes—the spark of that eternal fire of liberty.

And they clearly saw me—"Mr. America"—as a torchbearer of that flame.

As honored as I was by the acclaim—and humbled by the power of American principles reflected in the Indian people's admiration—I also recognized a deeper lesson, one I first encountered in a curious little children's book called *If Everybody Did.* The message was simple: All actions have consequences. Most of life's decisions slip by unnoticed, dismissed as harmless. But we don't live in a vacuum. And math—specifically multiplication—doesn't lie. Our daily choices ripple outward, and we rarely stop to calculate the cost.

This truth seems better understood in the East, especially in places like India and China. Maybe it's the pressure of enormous populations, where personal choices have immediate collective impact. Maybe it's poverty, which sharpens the effect. In Eastern "honor and shame" cultures, that awareness becomes duty—the chance to elevate not just yourself but your family by achieving respect. Many of the people I met in India radiated a hunger for self-improvement, with a reverence for meritocracy. I saw this energy as a rising force, shaping the fate of their wildly beautiful nation.

In contrast, back home in America, I've seen a steadily growing disregard—and even ignorance—toward the reality of consequences, especially when it comes to duty and personal responsibility. The corrosive mix of affluence and arrogance has given rise to entitlement and the vogue lunacy that consequences are optional. Indians have no such luxury. What they do have, in abundance, is national pride—an exuberant joy and confidence in their identity as children of God and citizens of their country. They admire and emulate America, but they love and defend their India—their homeland, their birthright. Even with endless struggle and unrealized dreams, it remains the domain of their destiny—a fate of their own determination.

Indian nationalism is a bright-burning fire, and they make no apology for it. Years later, I would come across this poetic passage inside a prison cell, and I smiled—with the warmth only personal experience can bring—as I read these words:

"The Indians are the Italians of Asia . . . there is so much Italian in the Indians, and so much Indian in the Italians . . . Every man in both countries is a singer when he is happy, and every woman is a dancer when she walks to the shop at the corner. For them, food is music inside the body, and music is food inside the heart. The language of India and the language of Italy, they make every man a poet, and make something beautiful from every *banalite*'. These are nations where love—*amore, pyaar*—makes a cavalier of a Borsalino on a street corner, and makes a princess of a peasant girl, if only for the second that her eyes meet yours."

—Gregory David Roberts

These reflections stayed with me as I reached the end of this exotic chapter—sharing a heartfelt goodbye with my agency family and bidding them "Arrivederci!" (Italian for "till we meet again"), sensing I would one day return to this colorful planet of passion and purpose. I also shared a tender farewell with Pari (Indian for "Angel"), my beautiful Indian girlfriend for an entire year of my tour. As we parted at the sprawling Delhi airport, I turned into a churning sea of dreamers flowing toward my westbound flight—carrying the bittersweet weight of departure and the quiet thrill of the future.

I had tasted something deep and unforgettable. And as I stepped toward the next unknown chapter, I wondered where my dreams would take me next—and where the fate of my nation might be headed.

I returned to Los Angeles in 2019, grateful to reclaim the comforts of American privilege—yet eager to continue my global modeling journey, a proven path to greater success in the fashion and film world. I was on the cusp of a breakthrough. But unseen forces were stirring—setting into motion a global detour that would derail not just my career, but the course of nations and history.

Negotiations for the next overseas contract left me treading water in my Hollywood apartment. I split time between gym training, modeling jobs, acting auditions, and the occasional armed security gig—all reached by bicycle. (After losing my turbo-charged MazdaSpeed 3 hatchback in the debacle with a con artist, I adapted—pedaling the entire sprawl of Los Angeles on a single-speed road bike for years. Who says MAGA doesn't go green?) I also biked to the home studio of my brother Bobby, who—surprise!—had finally come to Los Angeles, building on his success with Bethel Music and independent producing. We were just beginning to reconnect—rekindling our collaborative synergy, even recording a powerful new song—when the world suddenly lurched.

A global catastrophe—eerily reminiscent of Joseph's famine in Genesis—swept across the earth, derailing the dreams of millions . . . and unleashing totalitarian control at a scale never before seen on the planet.

The Orwellian "Global Reset" of 2020 was a control thing of stunning despotism—ushered in by what Thomas Jefferson warned against as the *Artificial Aristocracy*: an oligarchy of elites monopolizing the institutional levers of power. This "Reset" wore the mask of a global "pandemic," but soon revealed itself as a cancerous campaign of fraudulent data, manufactured panic, and coordinated propaganda. We would learn it was engineered by various forms of weaponized government, and by the media (but I repeat myself). These forces combined to produce what is now regarded as the greatest planetary scam in recorded history.

The first murmurs of a "Chinese coronavirus" surfaced in late 2019—hence its conveniently deceptive rebranding as "COVID-19," a nod to the propaganda preferences of the CCP (in case anyone's still unsure who's dominating the world's control war). At first, the rumors were mostly lost in the noise of the holiday season. But after the New Year's confetti had settled, the whispers grew louder—and more bizarre. I'll never forget the moment my roommate, rattling off his usual rundown of local gossip, casually dropped a word that punched me in the gut mid-sip:

". . . they might have a lockdown."

I snapped up from my coffee, nearly choking.

"Wait—they want to lock down an entire category of sick people?" I gasped, incredulous at such a totalitarian response to a forecasted flu.

"No, no," he said. "They're talking about locking down *the city*."

My brain nearly exploded. Alarms blared in my head as I grasped the implications of this shocking proposal—which I instantly recognized for exactly what it was: tyranny in real time. I knew instinctively that locking down an entire healthy population wasn't just extreme—it was historically unprecedented and deeply dangerous. A quick internet search confirmed what logic already made clear: No legitimate health authority had ever even suggested such a thing . . . because there wasn't a shred of science—or common sense—to support it.

It wasn't just absurd.

It was murderous.

And yet, my internal alarms only grew louder as the opening weeks of 2020 unleashed a torrent of lies, distorted data, and weaponized fear. Rumor gave way to dystopian reality with stunning speed. My roommate—and nearly everyone else in cities and suburbs alike—were paralyzed with panic, offering no resistance to lockdowns and quasi-martial law imposed by bureaucratic bullies eager to expand their power. A flood of coordinated disinformation poured from every outlet—faster than anyone could sort fact from fiction. But by late January 2020, my gut instincts had crystallized into one unshakable truth:

We were being lied to.

And control was, once again, at the diseased heart of the matter.

It gives me little pleasure to realize I was such an outlier. I recognized earlier than most that "COVID" was a deadly pandemic only of propaganda and authoritarian overreach. Our "leaders" locked us down and forced society to its knees without a whisper of constitutional concern—let alone meaningful resistance. That I, an international fashion model and actor navigating Hollywood's media circus, would diagnose the true etiology of the *plandemic* months before many of the doctors I'd later work with was one of God's signature ironies. But it was also more than that. It was proof that you don't need college degrees or expert credentials to apply wisdom. And it served as a reminder of this powerful warning from Thomas Jefferson, more urgent now than ever:

"It would be a **dangerous delusion** were a confidence in the men of our choice to silence our fears *for the safety of our rights*; that confidence is everywhere the parent of despotism; FREE GOVERNMENT IS FOUNDED IN JEALOUSY, and not in confidence; it is jealousy, and not confidence, which prescribes limited constitutions to *bind down* those whom we are obliged to trust with power; that our Constitution has accordingly fixed the limits to which, and no farther, our confidence may go. . . . In questions of power, then, let no more be said of confidence in man, BUT BIND HIM DOWN FROM MISCHIEF BY THE CHAINS OF THE CONSTITUTION."

—Thomas Jefferson

Dangerous delusions, indeed.

As we all witnessed, the nation collapsed—not just with misplaced confidence in the incestuous pantheon of our "public health experts," but with a fatal exchange: fearing the wrong peril. Americans lost all concern with preserving our *rights*, captured by the manufactured chaos surrounding our health. And Benjamin Franklin saw it coming centuries ago:

"Any society that would give up a little liberty to gain a little security will deserve neither and lose both."

—Benjamin Franklin

Decades later, another patriot—a general and U.S. president who knew something of both liberty and security—completed the thought:

"If you want total security, go to prison. There you're fed, clothed, given medical care, and so on. The only thing lacking . . . is freedom."

—Dwight D. Eisenhower

Well, dignity is also lacking, as I would come to learn. Still, it's hard to argue the point—in fact, after literally standing in that patriot's shadow—next to Eisenhower's statue inside the Capitol Rotunda on January 6—I found myself proving his point in ironic fashion. That prison experience would emphasize a critical lesson: We cannot give up our liberty for the false promise of government safety, and we cannot exchange our own common sense for the false assurance of government wisdom. The fate of any nation hangs on the guardrails that divide the distribution of power. And the nature of power is to consolidate—seeping through every crack until it pools into tyranny, drowning out the natural freedoms of the individual.

That tyranny begins in the mind. When the state monopolizes information—as we've discovered they did through the CDC, FDA, and tech giants like Google and Facebook—they inevitably weaponize and abuse it. They've also done this with the monopolized "justice" (read: persecution) powers of the DOJ. The result is an increasingly totalitarian state that we have built around ourselves—brick by compliant brick—with every fearful act of surrender.

The best cure is prevention, and that begins with unleashing the power of open discourse. The free market of ideas is where truth is tested and verified. That's why every citizen should engage in it—and remain vigilant. Resources like AFLDS.org, GoldCare.com, FrontlineFlash.com, and the now-indispensable X-Twitter and Truth Social are vital touchpoints in this battle for truth.

This is why we have a First Amendment—and why it came first. It's a sacred shield guarding the start of the "Cognitive Theory" sequence—the gateway to our ability to think freely, speak truthfully, and shape the course of our individual and national destiny. This is also why our most critical human right—**Cognitive Liberty**—is under relentless attack. Tyranny, by definition, seeks to restrict and ultimately eliminate the sovereign agency of the individual.

This was demonstrated when Elon Musk exposed the Obama-Biden regime's censorship collusion in the Twitter Files—a federal campaign of suppression disguised as "public health." But even more dangerous than coerced censorship is the silent control of thought through digital design. By manipulating search inquiries and algorithms, Google unilaterally decides what information is allowed to exist, and what vanishes without a trace before you even realize it was there—the supreme deceptions of omission bias and suggested search manipulation.

They don't just shape what you see—they shape what you're even *allowed* to imagine.

This is the Matrix in real life. Claims that these are "private companies" become irrelevant when they function as arms of state propaganda. The digital public square must be redefined. And within it, we must ensure that *all* speech remains fully free. Anyone trying to restrict speech is placing their speech above yours. Censorship is never neutral. "Hate speech," which is both subjective and easily weaponized, cannot be cured by tyranny. It can only be overcome with more speech—in the unrelenting pursuit of enlightenment.

The war on free thought is a war for our humanity. Big Tech's assault on *Cognitive Liberty* must be named—and we must fight back. This is not just a clash of opinions. It is a battle for eternity.

My early recognition of the true danger behind the "plandemic"—without the benefit (or perhaps the impediment) of a medical degree or elite academic credentials—underscored the value of the foundation my parents worked so hard to build. It was anchored in the study of fundamental truths—the "First Principles" on which America was founded. If I could require every citizen to study one book alongside the Bible (and *Is Atheism Dead?*), ideally before middle school, it would be *The 5,000 Year Leap* by W. Cleon Skousen, published by the National Center for Constitutional Studies (NCCS).

The book's title is no exaggeration. History—which is now being systematically erased—shows two things with clarity: the destructive pattern of human nature, and the extraordinary potential of human achievement. That potential was ignited by the pioneers who settled the American colonies, whose leaders forged a republic that would surpass five thousand years of global progress in just two centuries. We need to know how they did it. And more than that, we need to reclaim the principles they relied on—because that's the only way to make sure "we can keep it":

> "Even when the government of [the nation's] choice shall manifest a tendency to degeneracy, we are not at once to despair [because] the will and the watchfulness of its sounder parts will reform its aberrations, *recall it to original and legitimate principles*, and restrain it within the rightful limits of self-government."
>
> —Thomas Jefferson

As *The 5,000 Year Leap* explains:

> "From the beginning of recorded history until the founding of the American nation, human civilization made relatively little progress. Those who came to the New World in the 1500s and 1600s were still plowing fields behind animals, moving about in ox carts, and hand-weaving cloth the same way they had for millennia. Then . . . the human spirit was set free; creativity flourished, and experimentation abounded. Americans were learning how to experience freedom. After the proven principles of liberty were institutionalized by the U.S. Constitution in the 1780s, it took less than 200 years before men were walking on the moon! . . . in less than two centuries, the American people made a 5,000-year leap!

> "Many observers of political bodies, whether it be the local school board or the Congress of the United States, are frustrated to find that the *decisions made by these bodies are usually not based on any solid principles.* Quite often, the politicians who prevail are the ones who make the most

popular arguments or those who curry the most favor with [the Swamp]. It is no wonder then, that such decisions frequently fail to solve the problems they are [purported] to address. If our elected officials would familiarize themselves with correct principles of government and then base their decisions upon these principles, they would begin to find answers that really work. *It would be like solving complex math equations after first learning the basic multiplication tables.*"

—W. Cleon Skousen

Furthermore, if our *citizens* "would familiarize themselves with correct principles of government"—and vote accordingly—they might begin to reverse our national tailspin. Political hostages rotting in prison without due process, persecuted by a corrupt Democrat regime?

It's a grim reality.

We must confront that reality, and we must understand how we got here. If Americans studied constitutional fundamentals—like the "vertical separation of powers" in the Tenth Amendment—they'd be able to recognize the grotesque overreach of the Sixteenth Amendment and its demon spawn, the IRS, along with many other federal abuses. They'd see how centralized power fuels tyranny.

The way back to national unity and prosperity begins by honoring God, cultivating a moral citizenry, and electing virtuous leaders. That's the only path to the great American destiny our Founders bled and died to make possible.

The *Leap* doesn't just teach us "*how to experience freedom*"—it alerts us to threats against it. Through my early studies, I knew that James Madison had warned long ago of the power-grab we saw with "COVID"—and he told us exactly how to respond:

"There are more instances of the abridgement of the freedom of the People by gradual and silent encroachments of those in power, than by violent and sudden usurpations. It is proper to *take alarm at the first experiment on our liberties*. We hold **this prudent jealousy** to be **the first duty** of citizens and one of the noblest characteristics of the late Revolution. The Freemen of America did not wait till usurped power had *strengthened itself by exercise* and *entangled the question in precedents*. They saw all the consequences [of governmental abuses] in the principle, and they avoided the consequences by [refusing to accept] the principle [on which the abuses were based]. We revere this lesson too much . . . to forget it. . . ."

—James Madison

Because I was taught to revere that lesson, I recognized the tyrannical trajectory of the "COVID" control scheme—and I took alarm at its earliest abuses. That recognition carried a sacred duty—one that would later bring me to a life-changing dilemma. But when I first tried to sound the alarm, I ran into the brutal consequence of generational ignorance: most had never encountered Madison's lesson—and it showed.

America had forgotten the warning entirely.

We followed the very path Madison spoke against, with the entire country folding like a house of 300 million cards. One absurd edict after another rolled out ("usurpations"), seizing enough power to paralyze most Americans from the pursuit of just about everything—except destructive vice and the rapid expansion of bureaucracy and debt. And all with hardly a peep of protest. Our populace literally just shut up, masked up, doped up, and huddled up inside getting sicker, fatter, and poorer. They did this while watching our preening expert class—the *Artificial Aristocracy*—brazenly unbind Jefferson's constitutional chains and entangle us in terrible precedents of surveillance, social control, and wealth redistribution. America had been hijacked and plundered from within—and with most of the Western world following the same script, the fate of nations was destined for a dystopian nightmare.

I still remember the heated conversations I had with friends across the country and overseas. I tried to cut through the propaganda and expose the deeper threat, but the fear and chaos had already taken hold. That's when I realized: The Founders' charge was no longer a mere lesson in history or an abstract theory. I was an American citizen—and moreover, I had the bedrock foundation to understand the full weight and worth of that citizenship, along with the sacred responsibility that came with it. My first duty, as Madison said, was prudent jealousy.

And now, I faced an existential red-or-blue pill moment: Would I recognize the threat—but retreat into the comfort of my own castle of dreams? Would I forfeit the fight to avoid the risk and inconvenience of doing battle with so much ignorance, foolishness, and treachery?

Or would I hear the prophetic words of Mordechai (ancient Hebrew for *Morpheus*, I'm convinced) from the hero's tale of Esther—"perhaps you were made for such a time as this"? And would I act on my first duty: to jealously defend the life and liberty of the innocent—of the individual?

Would I simply complain and then comply—giving cover to apathy and cowardice? Or would I rise, as God commanded, and share the Founders' sacrifice of life, fortune, and sacred honor?

Would I raise a battle cry on the frontlines—and bear the torch of liberty's flame?

CHAPTER 7

RED PILL REVOLUTION

It all began at the drop of a hat.

If this "Red Pill Revolution" to revive the nation has a uniform, it's the red cap: that strangely potent symbol of the MAGA movement: MAKE AMERICA GREAT AGAIN. This battle cry inevitably triggers the disingenuous, endlessly parroted question: "*But when was America ever great?*" We'll get to that.

First, we must take the Red Pill (*Morpheus intones*). Are you ready?

MAGA, of course, is the iconic slogan of U.S. president and marketing genius Donald J. Trump. But more than a slogan, it represents the cultural renaissance of America's Red Pill awakening. And by daring to declare this mission, patriots have polarized the nation—America has fractured into what is now *the Divided States of America.*

The division is clear: We're all living in a national tug-of-war. Not between Republicans and Democrats, as they so desperately want you to believe. Not between the West and the East, nor the rich and the poor, nor any other institutional divide. Rather, the war is between #TeamReality and its sworn enemy: forces that despise the very existence of reality itself. For the sake of clarity, I've labeled these forces *Team Lunacy* to describe their core objective: the denial and eradication of reality, by replacing it with their own fiction—which is the very definition of lunacy. It's not just a fight over opinions—it's a fight over what's real. Over whether truth exists, and whether we should live by it.

You might recall that this dynamic also describes another campaign we've covered: atheism. Which brings us to the deeper war behind all the surface chaos:

God Versus No God.

The real battle isn't political. It's spiritual. We're caught in a titanic clash of theism versus atheism—two opposing worldviews, commonly understood as "religion." And make no mistake: atheism *is* a religion—as much as Judaism or Christianity, but with far less logical coherence.

Simply stated: it's a control thing. Either God is ultimately in charge and we all answer to Him—or we erase God, and answer only to ourselves . . . with control determined by the violence of human power.

Only one can be true. Only one side can win the war.

Every act of power stems from one of these two opposite poles. And America's Founders knew which side they stood on. When fifty-six patriots signed the Declaration of Independence, they weren't just resisting tyranny—they were affirming a philosophy. One that began with a Creator.

"When in the course of human events, it becomes necessary for one people . . . to assume, among the powers of the earth, the separate and equal station to which *the laws of nature and of nature's God* entitle them. . . . We hold these truths to be self-evident—that all men are created equal; that they are endowed *by their Creator*, with certain unalienable rights . . ."

That phrase, "laws of nature," refers to Natural Law—truth that transcends culture, time, and legislation. The Roman statesman Marcus Tullius Cicero (106–43 B.C.) called it "true law":

"True law is right reason in agreement with nature; it is of universal application, unchanging and everlasting. . . . It is a sin to try to alter this law. . . .We cannot be freed from its obligations by senate or people, and we need not look outside ourselves for an expounder or interpreter of it.

"And there will not be different laws at Rome and at Athens, or different laws now and in the future, but one eternal and unchangeable law will be valid for all nations and all times, and there will be one master and ruler, that is God, over us all, for he is the author of this law, its promulgator, and its enforcing judge. Whoever is disobedient is *fleeing from himself and denying his human nature*, and by reason of this very fact he will suffer the worst punishment."

—Marcus Tullius Cicero

Or as my sister once quipped: "We shouldn't need a government law to tell us it's wrong to hurt puppies!"

Cicero, writing before Christ, cut through the Matrix haze to reveal a fundamental truth: the concept of *identity* ("human nature"). *Who* are we as humans—and how does that define our relationship with the "system" we inhabit?

Natural Law affirms that reality isn't optional. It defines physical and moral absolutes. Right and wrong. Order and chaos. Beauty and destruction. In other words, #TeamReality—which the Founders explicitly anchored in God. And this God is not a vague, impersonal force, but a knowable, personal Creator—as specific and precise as the infinitely balanced metaphysical principles that form the knowable universe He created (and this is where Eric's book *Is Atheism Dead?* comes in handy).

That God—who calls Himself *Yahweh*—is the author, the origin, of everything that exists. He formed a multi-dimensional universe, populated by conscious beings endowed with free will. He gave us **Sovereignty** . . . and the natural rights that flow from it. What we call "rights" are simply the freedoms that enable us to act in accordance with our natural design—that's what makes them *right*. Logic dictates we cannot understand, exercise, or defend our rights without knowing the intelligent designer who wove them into the very essence of what it means to be human.

It is no small thing that our national pledge is to "One Nation Under God."

So on one side: the team of God, reality, and America (1776 edition). On the other: the team of anti-God, anti-reality, and . . . anti-America?

That troubling realization was the very warning I raised in my *Epoch Times* piece: "Why Do We Hate America?" As Elon Musk would say, "Once you see it, you can't unsee it." And when you look at the disturbing trends and destructive results of Team Lunacy policies (now driven by the modern Democrat Party), you can't unsee the assault on nearly everything the Founders fought to secure:

- limited government
- restrained debt and taxation
- national reverence for God
- free, responsible citizens educated in moral and historical truths
- the nuclear family—one father, one mother—which every child needs and deserves
- protection of private property
- honor for the flag and our pledge of allegiance
- respect for the statues of virtuous men and women who upheld these ideals

Every one of these is under fire throughout our society. The enemies of #TeamReality despise America just as they despise the God who inspired its founding.

And I get it—it's hard to believe so many people, with nearly half the nation leaning left, could despise their own country . . . until you define what "America" truly means, and contrast it with what many now love—and hate.

As I wrote in my *Epoch Times* article, this is no longer a hypothetical question or an intellectual exercise. With breathtaking acceleration during the past several years of BLM riots and "social justice"-excused chaos, our citizens have shifted from apathy to outright anger toward the nation itself a palpable hatred for the very foundations the country was built on. When you hate something, you curse (and kneel) in blatant disrespect and contempt for it. When you hate something, you smash it to pieces. When you hate something, you burn it to the ground.

We hate America. That is violently obvious. But what is less clear is why.

Even now, amidst the decaying mixture of hysterical paralysis and blinding rage we find ourselves surrounded by, it's still quite difficult to forget or dismiss the triumphs of the United States of America. Among countless others, these include:

- The Declaration of Independence—the first charter to fully define human rights as pre-political, God-given, and unalienable.
- The Civil Rights movement, after abolishing chattel slavery, to further pursue our ideal of equal rights for all people.
- Essential contributions to the defense of innocent lives in victories—without ever seeking conquest spoils—over genocidal dictators in various international conflicts.
- The invention and expansion of technologies that have cured and prevented disease, vastly curbed world hunger and suffering, and greatly improved the quality of life and the basic human freedom and dignity for not only America but much of the entire planet.

These accomplishments are indisputable and immensely consequential. And yet, they have so quickly become an afterthought, an irrelevant footnote in the Marxist handbook of social exploitation that permeates much of the current generation of young adults driving our recent discord and chaos. They either don't know these accomplishments exist, or they don't care. Either way, it has no bearing on their opinion about the country they live in and the system that produced those accomplishments. They hate that system, are intent on completely dismantling and even violently destroying it, and the reason is actually quite simple—it's because that system is built primarily on one single concept: freedom.

And the stunning truth of the matter is that this generation doesn't value freedom. Instead, it values comfort. It values convenience, coddling, and conformity.

Freedom isn't free; in fact, it's quite costly. Paying that cost is painful, which is the opposite of comfort. Freedom can't survive without accountability, and this requires responsibility, which is neither convenient nor comfortable. Everything about America's foundational ethos directly conflicts with the true priorities of this generation, and thus, of course, they hate America. They have every reason to despise it and every motivation to destroy it. And that's precisely what they will do if someone doesn't stop them.

When the founders formed this nation, they pledged their lives, fortunes, and sacred honor to its cause; that is the high cost of freedom, and they were willing and able to pay it. The current generation of insolent and immature BLM/etc. "protesters" are neither willing nor able; they seek only to destroy what others have built. Those of us who remain sober and seekers of freedom, those of us who still recall our foundations and revere our values, cannot rely on Washington, Hamilton, Franklin, or Jefferson to save us. We—We the People— must remember their sacrifice and *commit to our own*.

We must acknowledge the rot of incessant self-indulgence and accept the challenge of reclaiming responsibility. We must rise together and pledge our lives, our fortunes, and our sacred honor to the rescue, reformation, and revival of this greatest of nations, because when you love something, you stand for it. When you love something, you fight for it. When you love something, you show honor and respect for it, you sacrifice for it, and you die for it.

The United States truly is the last, greatest hope on Earth for all the nations, and for the sake of all, we must once again learn to love freedom—we must learn to love America.

We see further proof of the divide between Reality/America and Lunacy/Leftism in the contrast between their political and cultural strategies. If the mission of #TeamReality is defined by MAGA—a call to revive liberty and equal opportunity, symbolized by a red hat—then the Lunacy opposition is summed up by its own four-letter mantra: WOKE. Their symbols range from ominous black squares to chaotic rainbow flags (and now, even the flags of hostile foreign nations).

But what does "WOKE" actually mean?

Popular definitions describe it as "critical consciousness"—that is, a heightened awareness of "systemic oppression," "social injustice," and "marginalized identities." But filter out the buzzwords and peer pressure, and here's what's left: WOKE teaches people to see themselves as victims, to envy others, and to reject personal responsibility. Every hardship is someone else's fault—and you're entitled to blame them and demand satisfaction. This mindset, often dressed up as "critical consciousness," feeds on laziness and resentment. It's poison.

But I've found its core meaning hidden in the word itself—like a hybrid acronym:

WOKE = the **WO**rship of fa**KE**.

At its core, WOKE is the rejection of reality and the elevation (worship) of unreality. It is, in essence, a religion—another sect born from the parent worldview of atheism. And once again, the divide is clear: *God or No God.*

Make no mistake: The radical WOKE, TRANS, DEI, CRT, ESG, and similar movements are cult organisms—they are religions. Their rituals and doctrines are rooted in Marxism and atheism. And when we see religion for what it really is—a belief system used to establish authority—it all becomes clear.

The modern myth that "only those who 'believe in God' are religious" has been deeply embedded in our consciousness. But that's not how reality works.

There is no "believing" in God—you either know God, or you do not.

You don't have to "believe" in the engineer who designed the car you're driving. Their existence is self-evident in their creation. The more you understand the form and function of that car—reading the user's manual can be very helpful—the more you'll understand the car's designer. Denying the Designer doesn't erase Him—it just causes the driver to get lost.

So yes, every human is "religious" in the sense that everyone makes a decision—knowingly or not—about *how to respond* to the existing control in the world around them. "Control Theory" (described in chapter two) maps this out. And sure, you're free to say you "don't believe in God," and that your intricate brain, with its self-awareness, came from nothing—or from a primordial soup that came from . . . nothing. But that's like standing in a hurricane, yelling at the wind that you "don't believe" in weather. That would require as much "faith" as Christianity—if not more.

Believing a lie doesn't make it true—it only makes you confused.

The Apostle James offers a sharp rebuke of false religion:

"If you claim to be religious but don't control your tongue, you are fooling yourself, and your religion is worthless. Pure and genuine religion in the sight of God means caring for orphans and widows in their distress and refusing to let the world corrupt you."

—James 1:26–27

True religion begins with self-control. It reflects a proper understanding of our place within God's Divine Order. He created us in His image, with equal dignity and freedom, to live in fellowship with Him and with one another. In other words, true religion isn't really "religion" at all—it's relationship.

My father was onto something.

Team Lunacy, of course, hates and rejects God—not because they don't know He exists, but because they resent His *authority*. They crave His ultimate control for themselves (see: the Tenth Commandment). So they twist religion into its opposite: not self-control in honor of God, but domination of others in violation of God's design. The same is true of "Secularism," which is merely the religion of having no religion—it is only a sterilized term for atheism.

All of this "worthless" religion, as the Apostle James calls it—whether cloaked in piety or stripped bare by secularism—is the same tool: power without truth. It's weaponized by the enemies of freedom because they reject the God who made us free.

At its root, religion is a *worldview*. It's the framework we use to understand where authority comes from, and how we respond to it. Everyone has a worldview, whether they realize it or not. Many have never considered what their worldview is, or how it shapes their outcome. But the WOKE powers "of this dark world" understand it perfectly—and they exploit it through deception, distraction, and psychological manipulation.

That's the Matrix.

I often describe this Matrix-brainwashing of the cultural mindset as "WOKE Witchcraft." C. S. Lewis seemed to agree. He noted a striking shift that began in the sixteenth century—a moment when both witchcraft and "secular" science were driven by the same dangerous desire:

> "The serious magical endeavor and the serious scientific endeavor are twins: one was sickly and died, the other was strong and throve. But they are twins. They were born of the same impulse. . . . For the wise men of old the cardinal problem had been *how to conform the soul to reality*, and the solution had been knowledge, self-discipline, and virtue. But for magic and applied science alike the problem is *how to subdue reality to the wishes* [i.e. lunacy] *of men*: the solution is a technique; and both, in the practice of this technique, are ready to do things hitherto regarded as disgusting and impious. . . ."

So, if you've ever felt sick to your stomach at the thought of sixty million babies slaughtered in the name of "reproductive rights" . . . or if you've ever been nauseated by innocent children being groomed into barbaric mutilation and permanent sterilization . . . or if you've ever been grossed out by young girls being subjected to delusional men invading their locker rooms and exposing themselves, all under the banner of "TRANS rights"—and then caught yourself thinking, "*Oh my God, this is disgusting!*" . . .

You wouldn't be alone.

In fact, if you read any of C. S. Lewis's works, you'll realize you're in very good company.

It's important to recognize that the divisive chaos of Team Lunacy doesn't fall neatly along party lines. Both Republicans and Democrats are used as pawns in a deeper game. Party labels are just one tool the ruling class uses to confuse and, of course, control you. It's the classic *controlled opposition* setup: creating the illusion of choice while steering both sides toward the same end—more centralized power, less personal freedom. Another effective trick is the popular Left-Right spectrum—a political map with socialism on the left and fascism on the right.

Spoiler alert: Socialism and fascism are on the same side—Team Lunacy.

It's a false dichotomy. Which is exactly why they push so hard to erase history—the study and preservation of reality—because it exposes their lies. By distorting the past, they conceal the true political spectrum—the one understood by the American Founders. Their insight into this paradigm shaped the design of our constitutional republic. It's precisely calibrated to hold a balanced position at the center of political power—anchored in liberty, virtue, and restraint.

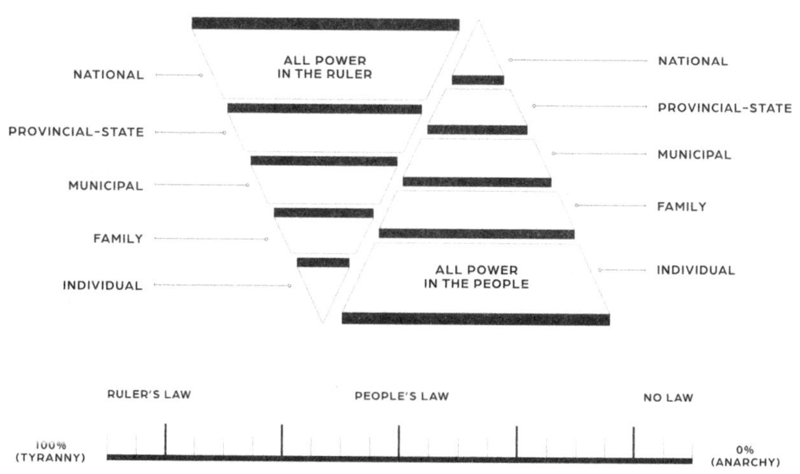

Too far left, and we're consumed by tyranny. Too far right, and we descend into anarchy—the tyranny of chaos. As we can see in the graph, the real struggle here is between the Power and the People. As long as there are those who seek control over others—as long as humans walk the earth—this will *always* be the spectrum that matters. It's hard to overstate the importance of recognizing this, because the greatest weapon of the Power . . . is convincing you it doesn't exist.

It does—and it intends nothing less than the total subjugation of humanity. That includes mass "reductions" of the so-called undesirables.

This isn't a "conspiracy theory." It's bloodstained history.

If we study the full sweep of it—from Genesis to January 6—a chilling pattern emerges. Socialism and communism, often driven by Marxism—a radical cult rooted in atheism—and fascism, fueled by the same despotic fire, are not opposites. They are shades of the same shadow—a deadly darkness clouding the skies of many totalitarian regimes throughout the ages. In just the past century, they've unleashed genocides exterminating *hundreds of millions*—Stalin's Soviet Russia, Hitler's Nazi Germany, Mao's China, Pol Pot's Cambodia, and more.

"Left and Right" is a clever diversion, meant to disorient you during the assault. All those "isms" are on the same side: the side of tyranny and death.

That is one hell of a War of the Worlds.

By early 2020, those dark clouds of totalitarianism were gathering with fury. The earth lurched hard left—swept into chaos by COVID hysteria and the engineered violence of BLM, Inc®. Those riots weren't just tolerated—they were glorified, funded, bailed out, and cheered on by Team Lunacy all-stars like Obama, Biden, and Kamala. Their "summer of love" racked up over two *billion* dollars in damage and killed dozens of innocent people. That carnage stood in stark contrast to J6, where protesters (or rather, undercover operatives) broke a few windows—and killed no one. (Nancy Pelosi's forces did manage to kill four unarmed protesters.)

Meanwhile, the predicted carnage of a deadly pandemic was immediately suspicious, unsupported by reliable data. But the panic ignited by media fearmongering consumed every ounce of wisdom and common sense. Travel shut down, schools closed, even churches locked their doors. America was marching into the jaws of a Marxist machine of dependency, misery, and death.

I could see it. *I could smell it.*

I was at home in Los Angeles during the start of "the year of renewed vision," as I had described 2020—but the only thing coming into view was the growing madness. I was staring into the eye of a cultural storm. Pandemonium swirled around me, mixed with deafening silence.

Principled leaders had vanished.

The resistance was nonexistent.

And then, in the stillness, came a voice. Not audible, but unmistakable. A silent transmission surged through my soul: "If not you, then who? If not now, then when?" In that instant, a thousand fragments of my life snapped into alignment. I blinked, swallowed, and clenched my gut all at once. My heart leapt at the obvious answer even as my mind raced, grasping the somber implications. I was an actor—in Hollywood. Publicly supporting American Nationalism was career suicide. No agents. No callbacks. No clients. No platform. Speaking out against WOKE lunacy was a guaranteed way to get fired, canceled, blacklisted, and essentially given a one-way ticket out of the entire industry . . . forever.

But once you hear it, you can't unhear it.

I had received a divine summons: report for duty—as a citizen of America, as a disciple of Christ, as a soldier of #TeamReality . . . as a patriot. I knew at that moment what I had to do—and it all began with the selfie "drop" of a signature red hat.

Social media had become the gatekeeper of career advancement. I'd spent years building an audience, mostly sharing my fashion campaigns and film projects. But in late 2019, after a long tour through Asia, I started publishing op-eds in news outlets and posting cultural commentary on my social media channels.

I didn't think of myself as "political" at that point. I had avoided such controversy, focused on my work. But as WOKE mobs swept the country, burning cities and igniting propaganda, I began writing with more urgency. The madness demanded a response. My editorials drew mixed reactions online. There was common-sense American support mixed with outrage posted by some of my Hollywood-driven audience—an audience that was still not prepared for where I was about to go next.

When that soul-spark made it clear I was called to step out, I snatched up my laptop and wrote a summary of the situation:

The world is at war—a war we can't see, and most don't understand.

The Matrix is more than a movie—it's an allegory for the manipulated mirage we're experiencing.

The tired script of Republican versus Democrat is a smoke screen—crafted to conceal the true agenda of *the Power*, dividing and controlling *the People*.

A revolution of red-pilled awakening is needed to expose the true battle: #TeamReality versus the globalist forces of the Lunatic Left.

And Donald J. Trump?

He's not a Republican racist, or a "danger to democracy," or any of the ridiculous, Hitler-tinged, hate-mongering slurs hurled at him by the Matrix-controlled media. He's a gigantic, glowing-orange glitch in the Matrix, and the "MAGA" movement propelling him isn't a cult—it's the cultural activation of #TeamReality. It's a repudiation of the unhinged lunacy literally burning down our streets. It's a rejection of the globalism pilfering our wealth, sacrificing our security, mortgaging our future, and tearing our families and communities apart. It's the return of reason—the resurrection of common sense.

And with that assessment thoughtfully typed, I pulled out the bright red MAGA hat hidden in my Hollywood closet . . .

threw it on . . .

snapped a selfie . . .

and "dropped" it on social media—right alongside my "Red Pill Revolution" manifesto.

I might as well have pulled the pin on a grenade.

My digital world exploded with shockwaves of seething hatred and furious threats. Some of those threats were not empty—a deeply dishonest assault on my character was launched, one that continues to this day. My reputation, built over years of painstaking effort, was shredded in real time right before my eyes. The blood, sweat, and tears of so many painful years spent dream gazing, star chasing, back breaking, heart aching, and destiny making were chewed up and spit back in my face, drenching me in defamation and cancellation. The blowback torched:

My agency representation.

My social media growth.

My client contracts.

My future role negotiations.

My entire brand and identity as an actor, model, media talent, and creative professional.

And numerous relationships with people I'd believed to be colleagues—even friends.

Speaking unpopular truths out loud is a surefire way to find out who your true friends are—and who might become truly dangerous enemies. I received death threats and sadistic suggestions, along with endless ridicule, as my entire career and livelihood—past, present, and future—crumbled around me at the speed of hate.

And that was just the opening salvo.

There was no turning back from the hat drop—I was now a fully public member of the MAGA resistance movement. With my usual Maverick flair, I dove headfirst into the cultural crossfire. What followed was a series of battles I never could've imagined. Truth is definitely stranger than fiction.

As the debris swirled from that opening bombshell, I surveyed the damage: my career in ruins, my reputation scorched, my future evaporating. And yet—beneath the noise, a strange sensation of . . . calm. Not denial. Not numbness. Something quiet and firm, a stillness I hadn't earned—but it was holding me steady.

> "Therefore, since we have been made right in God's sight *by faith*, we have peace with God *because of what Jesus Christ our Lord* **has done** for us. *Because of our faith*, Christ has brought us into this place of undeserved privilege where *we now stand*, and we confidently and joyfully look forward to sharing God's glory."
>
> —Romans 5:1–2

There's no privilege like the confidence that comes from salvation through faith.

> "Don't worry about anything; instead, pray about everything. Tell God what you need, and thank Him for all He has done. Then you will experience God's peace, which exceeds anything we can understand. His peace will guard your hearts and minds *as you live in Christ Jesus*."
>
> —Philippians 4:6–7

That sensation I felt was peace—and not just a feeling, but a recognition of reality: I was in control only of my *response*. God is in control of the *results*. It was also a faith-driven expectation of God's blessing—the fulfillment of His promise in Jeremiah 29:11: "plans for good and not for disaster . . . to give you a future and a hope."

That verse in Romans says "we have been made right." This means we've been "pardoned" by God—the wrongdoing that once disqualified us from a relationship with Him has been cleared, like it never happened.

But it also says this happens "by faith." Faith in what?

Not in ourselves.

Not in others.

Not in circumstances.

We've "been made right" and "we have peace with God *because of what Jesus . . . has done.*"

There's a sequence here—a kind of divine logic:

First, *God initiates*: Jesus gave his life to redeem us.

Second, *we respond*: not just with mental agreement, but with action based on trust.

Third, *God completes*: He restores us—fully accepted, spiritually reborn, returned to His family. We are "made righteous"—that is, *sanctified.*

In a strange way, "Control Theory" maps out the Gospel.

Even as I write this, I realize that the peace I encountered while my life seemed to crumble was living proof of that divine pattern—evidence of God's promises, fulfilled through obedience to His Word.

"But wait," some have argued—including a few of my best attorneys—"Are you saying a person has to do something to be saved? Isn't it just about belief? Doesn't God do all the work?"

But that kind of thinking is where a lot of modern Christianity goes wrong. Faith isn't just belief. It's allegiance. It's action. It's not passive knowledge of religious theory   it's choosing a side and standing up for it. You don't join an army just to cower in the barracks—or worse, shoot at your own side—and still expect to share in the victory. You'd be court-martialed. Even Jesus said the same: Some will be cast out as traitors. Not because they didn't "believe," but because their lives proved their belief was a fraud.

Faith is not belief in spite of your actions—but because of them!

You can see it in those verses: "Because of our faith, Christ has brought us . . . where we *now stand*" and "His peace will guard your hearts and minds *as you live in Christ.*"

Stand.

Live.

Those are verbs. They require action. And sometimes, they're uncomfortable. Walking in obedience to God's calling—despite the risk and discomfort—builds faith. That's what leads to real peace . . . and lasting victory. And I took a crucial step in that direction in the spring of 2020.

I would certainly need that divine peace to "guard" me in the battles ahead—because any visible peace was about to be shattered.

Now that I was fully committed to recruiting troops for #TeamReality in the "Red Pill Revolution," I began riding across the barren COVID-scape of Los Angeles—my blazing red MAGA hat serving as my helmet. It wasn't long before I crossed paths with a fellow warrior in the heart of Beverly Hills, a neighborhood I'd lived and worked in often over the years.

Shiva Bagheri was as feisty and America First as they come. A legal immigrant from Iran, a devoted Christian, and a single mom, her life was a living rebuke to the WOKE lie. She had achieved the American dream of dignity and independence by the content of her character, not the color of her skin—or hat.

Shiva had gathered some locals, including legal immigrants, who'd pushed back the same way I had: blazing through stores and public spaces in open defiance of Communist California's absurd mandates. MAGA hats on. "Free faces" proudly displayed. We seized any opportunity to thwart the petty tyrants trying to enforce illegal restrictions and used the important tool of mockery to expose the fraud of medical masking.

We agreed to merge our efforts with a simple mission: resist lockdowns and spread Red Pill awakenings. We elected officers and formed a leadership council. Shiva became our President; I served as Communications Director. We even had a GOP liaison to connect with the local Republican Party (the Democrat Party, shockingly, showed no interest).

Our operations expanded quickly.

In addition to "free-face" flash-mobs and the flood of complaints we sent to city, county, and state officials—reminding them about a little thing called the Constitution—we launched our flagship effort: a weekly public gathering to celebrate *"Life, Liberty, and The Pursuit."* I designed that slogan to emphasize each citizen's right—and responsibility—to take action.

We chose the iconic **WELCOME TO BEVERLY HILLS** sign as our stage. The historic park on Santa Monica Boulevard gave us the perfect backdrop. And just like that—the Beverly Hills Freedom Rally (BHFR) was born.

Even with our vivid-red MAGA helmets, we deliberately minimized partisan branding. No "Trump" or "MAGA" in the name, and we chose the word "rally" over "protest." Our message was simple and unifying: The right to live, work, assemble, worship, raise your children, and reject medical coercion aren't up for debate. They are unalienable.

In other words: *"Freedom is essential."*

Lockdowns are equal-opportunity destroyers. They devastated Democrats and Republicans alike (though somehow, the *Artificial Aristocracy* got even richer . . . go figure). So we extended an open invitation: Democrats, Independents, WOKE affiliates, and anyone else willing to join us on a Saturday afternoon was welcome.

Within weeks, Shiva and I had built out a name, logo, slogan, mission statement, website, weekly schedule, and social media presence—along with this founding charter, where I channeled my inner Thomas Jefferson:

Beverly Hills Freedom Rally

Est. 2020 ~ Founding Charter

"Because Freedom Is Essential"

The solemn declaration of the free people of Beverly Hills, greater Los Angeles, and the state of California in these United States:

When trouble or treachery provides the powerful with a license for tyranny, citizens must reject such unlawful constraints and return to the core precept of our national birth. The immortal words of our nation's founding declaration define the truth of our identity as sovereign individuals, inherently granted by Nature and Nature's God the right to life, liberty, and pursuit—without undue restriction.

Governments exist only to secure these rights, and they derive their power from the consent of We The People. We recognize that freedom is not free, that our liberty is contingent on vigilant participation in the system designed to protect our rights, and that prosperity is dependent on our diligence in taking responsibility for our own needs. We believe that happiness is found in the growth and defense of faith, family, and country.

In God, we trust.

In !iberty, we thrive.

In justice, we sustain.

In love, we choose life.

For many of us, it was the christening of our "1776 2.0 moment." The spirit of patriotism tingled in our fingertips—the essence of our American citizenship drawn into sharp focus against the looming shadows of medical tyranny and government oppression. We were seeing and feeling what the Founders saw and felt. The liberty, property, and equality they'd sacrificed so much to secure was now being pried from our grasp by the talons of tyranny. We were reborn into the sacred duty Jefferson declared in 1776:

> "But, when a long train of abuses and usurpations, pursuing invariably the same object, evinces a design to reduce them under absolute despotism, it is their right, *it is their duty*, to throw off such government, and to provide new guards for their future security."
>
> —The Declaration of Independence

In those moments, Jefferson's charge roared back to life. So did the tyranny that inspired it. We recognized our rights—and the current *train of usurpations*. We claimed our duty with open eyes and clear minds, fully aware of the uphill battle and dangers we faced . . . and in those moments, we became patriots.

That word itself—"patriot"—comes from the Latin *pater*, the root of "father." I realized how fitting that was, as we founded the Beverly Hills Freedom Rally and birthed a new beginning of life, liberty, and the pursuit. And for the first time, we felt the full weight of a father's duty to love, provide for, and protect it.

The sardonic "15 days to slow the spread" (or was it "15 days to flatten the curve"?—the only thing they managed to flatten were IQs and the Constitution) had come and gone. We were now months into lockdowns, choking the country with fear and chaos. Nothing about COVID added up—while GDP and the global economy came crashing down. The "plague of the century" never factually materialized, despite every screen on the planet flashing death counts like a doomsday clock. And those screens conveniently left out a few things:

- The infamous "PCR tests" churning out *millions* of false posi-
  tives—**on purpose**
- The outrageous *Lancet* scandal—defaming HCQ with *fake* data
- The blatant corruption of death certificate reporting—hat tip
  to Dr. Scott Jensen
- The miraculous disappearance of the flu—*huh?*

All of this combined to wildly inflate those death count numbers. They
also failed to mention that the average fatality was seventy-eight years
old—*two years past life expectancy*—with four combined comorbidities.
In other words, statistically, **most of those people were going to die
that year anyway**. There was no significant fluctuation in national or
global all-cause mortality. So the term "pandemic" was little more than
panic-inducing propaganda.

The world suicided itself over a glorified flu.

You can prove this with a simple thought experiment: Imagine no
one had ever coined the term "COVID." Imagine the media never
blasted their panic narrative. Would anyone have raised an eyebrow
over standard yearly deaths from flu in the immuno-compromised?
When was the last time, prior to 2020, that anyone paid attention to
the weekly or yearly death counts from respiratory diseases?

Exactly.

And that's before factoring in the coordinated government-media
narrative, which promoted harmful—even murderous—policies that
directly contradicted standard public health protocol. Remain indoors.
Reduce vitamin D. Spike glucose and insulin. Suppress immune function. *"Stay home until you turn blue."* Seriously?

Our BHFR leadership council—with no medical degrees but fully
dosed with the Red Pill of common sense—saw through it all. We
lined the sidewalks of Beverly Hills with dozens—then hundreds—
of patriots, waving the Stars and Stripes along with handmade signs

debunking the "Corona Chaos" propaganda. When the *Artificial Aristocracy* tried to cancel Easter—making it clear that nothing was sacred in this power-grab pandemic—our numbers swelled. Citizens of all faiths joined us in prayer, spirited discussion, and joyful defiance. We brought people together—a broad political spectrum, united by a recognition of tyranny and a renewed thirst for liberty. There was a real drive to recover Judeo-Christian values and fundamental civil rights— and of course, one depends entirely on the other.

The People of the Golden State—not to be confused with *the Power*—turned out to be far more red, and red-pilled, than California's deep-blue political machine would suggest. They were also remarkably diverse.

Roughly a third of our rally crowd appeared to be first-generation immigrants. Disillusioned Democrats and Hollywood progressives joined in, engaging in earnest conversations about government over- reach, media lies, and human rights concerns. BHFR was not a "right- wing" phenomenon. It was a grassroots awakening—a rebirth of liberty and the pursuit of full human flourishing.

The movement quickly outgrew Beverly Hills. People drove in from across California and states all over the country, seeking a taste of real freedom—alive and unafraid. As the rally grew, so did the surround- ing vendor market. What began as a protest became a celebration—an open-air display of entrepreneurial grit and creative defiance, fueled by the spirit of the free market we were fighting to preserve.

Like Joseph rising in Potiphar's house, the rally's success felt both supernatural and long overdue. It wasn't without adversity—Antifa showed up a few times, and the Beverly Hills Police handled them with calm professionalism. There was conflict within the local city council. But nothing slowed us down. The momentum was electric. We soon attracted national voices to join the fray: Dennis Prager, Dave Rubin, Scott Baio, Will Witt, and Katie Hopkins showed up, along with local candidates for public office and medical whistleblowers challenging the pandemic propaganda.

By summer, the 2020 election cycle was heating up. The country remained paralyzed by panic, artificially sustained by the Legacy Media—which I now call "Lunacy Media." The lockdowns dragged on. The economy kept sinking. None of the bureaucracy offered clarity, let alone truth. By the time we reached Independence Day, America was the least free and most oppressed it had been since fifty-six patriots said "enough is enough" and signed the Declaration of Independence two and a half centuries earlier. Public health "experts" had already discredited themselves as proven liars. Yet they still pushed the same suicidal nonsense: smother your face with bacteria traps, stay locked inside, skip the sunshine, avoid exercise, ignore nutrition. They silenced dissent, stifled children's development, and crippled the economy. And they called it science.

Historians will spend centuries unpacking the full scope of this COVID catastrophe—long after we're gone. But even in the bright glare of that deceptive 2020 summer, the storm was obvious. Something evil was spreading: not a virus, but a cancer.

A cancer of fear. Of propaganda. Of total control.

It crept into homes, schools, churches, and hearts—smothering truth, suffocating joy, and snuffing out the light of reason. Faith was fractured. Families were divided. Entire communities were conquered. Freedom itself was collapsing under the weight of an invisible lie.

The whole earth was groaning, and searching for answers—crying out for a cure.

CHAPTER 8

JUST WHAT THE DOCTOR ORDERED

There are certain events in history so significant, so visceral in their worldwide impact, that you never forget exactly where you were when they happened—etched into your memory by the gravity of the moment. They don't come often, but when they do, they divide time. I've already witnessed two.

The first was September 11, 2001. I was just a student, standing in our living room when my mother pulled out the old basement TV we saved for special broadcasts. She turned it on just in time for me to see—live—the second plane slam into the Twin Towers. The fireball was . . . horrifying.

9/11 shattered the American psyche—like something inside us ruptured from the shock and sadness of seeing over three thousand innocent lives slaughtered in rubble and flames. The whole country felt like a graveyard, silent and stunned, as we wept and tried to make sense of it all.

Thankfully, my second seismic experience wasn't a tragedy. It was a turning point.

There are certain *people* in history so visionary, so defiantly bold in their worldwide impact, that you never forget exactly how you felt when you first saw them—a strange collision of inspiration and desperation that grips you with the ring of truth.

At least, that's how I felt the first time I saw Dr. Simone Gold. I was watching a press conference in front of the U.S. Supreme Court. A woman in a white coat stood at the podium—calm, self-assured, and focused. Her words cut through the panic that had gripped the world in 2020.

"We've been living in a spiderweb of fear, that's constricting the lifeblood of our nation . . . remember, there is early treatment available. *You have hope*. There *is* treatment, and you don't have to live in fear."

For a moment, the whole world seemed to hold its breath. The White Coat Summit—held on July 27, 2020—was "the shot of freedom and hope heard 'round the world." That livestream became the first in history to explode past twenty million views in under eight hours. It was on pace to break a hundred million when—*ZAP*—Big Tech launched a coordinated strike, scrubbing nearly every trace from the internet.

Just like that, a whistleblower bombshell was erased—memory-holed by a cartel of corporate overlords desperate to slam the door on a burst of light that suddenly pierced their contrived darkness. After months of fear, propaganda, and restrictions, the country's collective agitation had ballooned to a breaking point. And now, Dr. Gold—backed by a courageous team of physicians known as America's Frontline Doctors—had broken through, delivering a jarring dose of the most potent medicine on earth:

The truth.

The country erupted. News outlets buzzed, phone lines jammed, and the internet lit up with frantic questions about the "cure for COVID." People wanted answers. What treatment? Where could they find it? Why had it been hidden?

The hope was real—but so was the threat it posed to *the Power*.

They responded. The campaign to suppress early treatment didn't slow down—it escalated. What followed was an unprecedented assault on basic, life-saving science. Powered by the Big Tech Matrix, it evolved into something darker: Soviet-style censorship and psychological manipulation. It was wrapped in the rhetoric of "public safety" and enforced through a rebranded form of the coverup term "conspiracy theory"—now called "disinformation."

This American Pravda operation was later harpooned by Elon Musk and exposed in the earth-rattling #TwitterFiles—but the censorship continued. A doctor might label it a *"Mass Corruption Incident"*—and it led to one of the most underrated Supreme Court cases in U.S. history: *Missouri v. Biden* (later renamed *Murthy*). That lawsuit featured Dr. Simone Gold and Frontline Doctors among the whistleblowers targeted by what amounted to first-degree murder of the First Amendment—all orchestrated by the Obama-Biden regime. The full extent of the suppression is hard to measure and may never be fully known—but there's no doubt it was as murderous as any fascist campaign. Millions died needlessly because of the lies and censorship of that era, and the Deep State dragon proudly led the slaughter.

Nevertheless, through the sheer integrity and courage of Dr. Gold and America's Frontline Doctors, the secret had been spilled: Safe, cheap, effective, FDA-approved medicines were setting people free from the fear of COVID. The liberty bell could not be unrung. And once again, the American people rose to answer its call—offering undeniable proof of the words carved into the floor of CIA headquarters:

"You will know the truth, and the truth will set you free."

—John 8:32

Watching the White Coat Summit, my mind raced with the implications. These doctors had just shattered the pandemic illusion. I was energized by their resolute integrity. Their message struck with the undeniable force of truth.

And at the center of it all stood the angelic Dr. Gold—a true queen of courage.

Her extraordinary grace and boldness captivated me in that moment—and her actions afterward only deepened the impression. She moved with fearless resolve and strategic foresight:

- She rallied over a thousand independent physicians nationwide to sign a public warning sent to Coronavirus Task Force Director Mike Pence, declaring the lockdowns a *mass casualty incident.*
- She published editorials in major outlets, including *USA Today*, exposing the absurdity of masking propaganda and debunking fraudulent "studies"—like those later retracted by *The Lancet*— that falsely discredited hydroxychloroquine (HCQ) and ivermectin. Both drugs had long, global track records of safe use and had shown early promise against SARS-CoV-2, based on prior success treating the 78 percent–similar SARS strain. But the suppression of these medicines cost countless lives around the world.
- She launched legal counterstrikes, filing and supporting lawsuits against lockdowns, mandates, and the reckless rollout of harmful gene therapies deceptively marketed as "vaccines."

Yes, Dr. Gold was both a doctor and a lawyer—a rare MD-JD with degrees from Chicago Medical School and Stanford Law (where, curiously, she studied alongside a classmate named "Casey"). She had over two decades of ER experience in New York, Los Angeles, and even remote Native American reservations—serving inner-city minorities and, later, treating COVID patients. She also advised top officials in Washington, including the Surgeon General and the Chairman of the Senate Labor and Human Resources Committee.

In other words, she was a true frontline doctor—who actually treated patients, in stark contrast to her national nemesis, the regime's TV tyrant, Anthony Fauci. Her résumé was a clinic in real-world expertise—stacked with licenses, certifications, and a stellar record in emergency medicine without a single malpractice complaint. She was the kind of first responder you pray for in a crisis.

But the Deep State had taken note of her Supreme Court uprising, and they would soon strike—with stunning force.

At the moment, one thing was clear: We needed her on the front-lines of our local resistance. We invited her to speak at the Beverly Hills Freedom Rally as summer began winding down—and MAGA momentum kept rising ahead of the 2020 election.

You could feel something different in the air that Saturday in the park. The crowd gathered with anticipation to see "America's Doctor," fresh off the now-infamous White Coat Summit. She didn't disappoint. Soon after arriving, she held the crowd in rapt attention with her trademark "verbal assault weapon" style—rapid-fire and packed with data, clarity, and encouragement. She stood with firm elegance in a modest dress and heels, surrounded by hundreds of eager listeners, delivering guidance with calm command. It was a powerful "shot in the arm" of freedom and hope for our embattled #TeamReality resistance—reviving our spirit with truth, confidence, and a plan.

Just what the doctor ordered.

The BHFR leadership team was grateful, and we made sure to lock in her return. My own duties kept me moving all day—media interviews, social content, connecting with allies—so I wasn't able to speak further with her that afternoon. But I knew we hadn't seen the last of her. Something special was taking shape—and I was eager to see what might emerge next in our growing "Red Pill Revolution."

The rally's success had me running full-throttle—co-leading BHFR with Shiva while expanding my cultural commentary through editorials, videos, and social media debate. It was a nonstop battle to counter the relentless propaganda funneling society into *mass formation psychosis*.

That fight began to overlap with a nationwide resistance movement I deeply admired—led by a fellow patriot whose courage had helped shift the culture. Brandon Straka's #WalkAway campaign had pierced the veil of leftist orthodoxy, inspiring tens of thousands to publicly reject the radicalism of the modern Democrat Party. What made it powerful wasn't just the message, but the messengers. The #WalkAway Facebook group exploded to half a million selfie video testimonials—regular Americans recording their "conversion to common sense" and sharing it with the world. The honesty and hope in those videos were contagious.

Brandon himself had a sharp wit, creative instincts, and a bold presence that drew people in. When his California team reached out to say he was coming to town, I knew we had to link up.

(Little did I know, one of those "links" would end up being handcuffs!)

I rallied our team, and when Brandon arrived at the sheriff's office flagpole on Santa Monica Boulevard—greeted by nearly two thousand patriots waving #WalkAway signs—he was floored. The crowd marched a mile through West Hollywood into the BHFR rally, making it one of the most successful events either of us had ever done. It drew headlines and sparked national attention. That afternoon in the park, I caught up with Brandon backstage. We clicked instantly. And in that warm Los Angeles haze, a powerful friendship—and a fateful future— was set in motion.

After that, the rallies surged to a new level. With the election looming and lockdown tensions reaching a fever pitch, Dr. Gold returned to the stage—this time joined by Katie Hopkins and Will Witt. They were greeted by thousands of people spilling beyond the park and crowding the streets of downtown Beverly Hills.

California had never seen anything like this.

Roughly a month remained before the most polarized presidential election in modern times: "America First" versus "Corruption Force." The "Laptop from Hell" scandal had just blown up, making the contrast impossible to ignore. The stakes were just as clear: Our most basic rights—freedom of speech, bodily autonomy, medical choice, the right to worship—were all under siege. But the mood on the ground was hopeful, almost electric. Something big was happening, and—we thought—we were ready for it.

The rally crowd was more than ready for Dr. Gold, who lifted spirits with updates from the medical freedom frontlines. America's Frontline Doctors was providing real help where the government had failed—connecting everyday people with early treatment, honest science, and legal resources to fight back. The courage of one woman was fueling the confidence of thousands.

Meanwhile, I dashed around the park like a field general—supporting speakers, coordinating logistics, and solving problems on the fly. That day's rally was a landmark success. BHFR had drawn the largest conservative crowd to Communist-controlled California in recent memory. And then came the coup de grâce: President Trump tweeted a media recap of the BHFR rally to his nearly 100 million social media followers, cheering us on with the caption:

"Trump Supporters Fill Streets of Beverly Hills: 'The Silent Majority is Silenced No More' . . . Thank you!"

We were elated, and more determined than ever.

The silent majority had found its voice—and the world was starting to hear it.

I made sure to track down Dr. Gold in the churning crowd, and we finally had a chance to talk—getting acquainted beyond media bylines and résumé highlights. As we swapped stories about our respective battles, she asked what had prompted me to single her out—among all the independent voices calling out corruption—as a critical speaker for BHFR.

I answered with a story:

"Do you remember that fundraiser you posted," I asked, "where you explained the plan to sue Governor Newsom for violating the Fourth and Fifth Amendments—robbing citizens of their liberty with his senseless lockdowns by executive fiat?"

She nodded. "Oh, that—sure. I was trying to use a legitimate legal theory that could, potentially, make a dent in the root problem. Yeah, I remember liking the idea. But it was going to be very expensive and time-consuming to take on the entire state apparatus. I wasn't sure it would get enough traction."

"Exactly," I said. "That's what stood out. You broke down the legal path in a way that made sense—and you had the guts to go public with it. You went straight after the top tyrant behind all this madness. That was a David-versus-Goliath move. And let's be honest—we don't have enough Davids."

She gave a slight smile, considering that.

"Do you know what I did when I saw that fundraiser and realized what your plan was?" I went on. "I donated seventy-five bucks right then and there—and that was a real chunk of change for me at the time. Ha! My Red Hat selfie drop kind of, uh, blew up my gigs earlier this year. But I just had to help. You diagnosed the root problem—*and* you were actually doing something about it."

She laughed, a little color rising in her cheeks.

"I can't believe you donated to my legal fund when you were in a pinch!"

"No, seriously," I said, leaning in. "I'll tell you why. First, you had a stark choice between the right thing and the easy thing. You could've 'followed orders,' complied with your boss and the hospital . . . but that would've meant denying a sick patient the meds you *knew* would help them. Or—you could 'break the rules' and save the patient's life. For you, it wasn't even a choice. You were always going to do the right thing—no matter how bad your boss or anyone else made it for you."

She nodded, listening.

"And then your hospital fired you—and you still didn't back down. You kept doing the right thing. And that's the most important thing, for sure. But the second is . . . you're not just fighting—you're fighting smart. You understand the real battle here. You know this is a war between Team Reality and, uh, a mob of lunatics who hate God and freedom. And you actually understand the constitutional fundamentals. That combination—moral clarity and strategic thinking—I've been searching everywhere for it. That's why I said to myself, 'I've gotta help this woman however I can.'"

"Wow. Okay . . . well, that's good to know," Dr. Gold replied, thoughtful. "The demand for Frontline Doctors is just exploding right now. . . . I never imagined *not* working in medicine—but it feels like there's more to do in this freedom fight than I can keep up with. I don't know if I'll ever go back to the ER . . . which is very strange."

Her wistful tone tinged our separate-but-similar thoughts as we walked through the fading hum of the rally, past the palm-lined sidewalks of Beverly Hills. People were starting to drift toward dinner at nearby restaurants.

"I don't publicize this, of course," she said, glancing over, "but I actually live nearby—just down the street. So I guess we're neighbors . . . let's keep in touch."

"Absolutely," I replied, unlocking my road bike and hopping on to pedal home. I called over my shoulder as I rolled away:

"This ride is only just getting started!"

If only I'd known just how brutally right I'd turn out to be.

As we reached the final four weekends before the big day—November 3, 2020, with liberty squaring off against lunacy—the BHFR rally hit its zenith. Crowds reaching five thousand packed the park and flooded the downtown streets of Beverly Hills each weekend, with enough American flags and MAGA hats to make a leftist's head spin. Between the historic local turnout I was witnessing firsthand and the staggering crowds of twenty, thirty, even fifty thousand people flooding Trump rallies across the country (while Biden hid—or slept—in a basement), one thing was clear: Something powerful was stirring in the Jeopardized States of America.

Brandon and I kept texting back and forth, comparing notes and taking the political temperature from our corners of the country. Meanwhile, Dr. Gold had started calling to chat—discussing local civil rights issues and offering thoughtful feedback on my recent editorials. Her MD-JD-certified compliments were high praise indeed. Soon, she asked if I'd take on a special project.

"I would love to," I replied. "What can I do for you?"

She described an idea inspired by a European protest where citizens banged pots and pans in the streets until local officials finally relented on lockdowns. We brainstormed the details and adapted the concept to our situation. She asked me to send her a plan—basic outline, structure, logistics—within the next couple weeks.

I sent her a complete package in forty-eight hours: finalized name, logo, tagline—*Returning Power to the People*—a branding campaign, logistics schedule, leadership team drawn from my BHFR network, a polished website, and matching social media profiles.

It took Dr. Gold less than five minutes to call me after I hit "send."

"Hey, this is really great . . . say, are you interested in working for me and Frontline Doctors? Because I'm really swamped, and I have a lot of—"

"Absolutely! I was sort of hoping you'd ask," I jumped in.

I hadn't known for sure that she'd be thinking that way—but I had told her, and told myself, that she was one of those rare patriots with the courage to do what's right and the skill to make it count. And that was exactly the kind of ally I wanted in the fight.

The next few weeks were a blur. I kept helping lead BHFR while launching our new "flashlight mob" protest outside the Los Angeles mayor's mansion. At the same time, Dr. Gold began handing me more and more Frontline Doctors responsibilities. That quickly grew into official roles—first as Communications Director, then as Creative Director. In those early days, with Frontline Doctors skyrocketing after the White Coat Summit, I wore many hats—red and otherwise—handling most of the communications, operations, and marketing work that Dr. Gold didn't have time to tackle herself. At the time, the team was just a few people. When her assistant abruptly quit, I became the only full-time staffer working alongside her for weeks.

I began giving TV and radio interviews in support of the educational resources offered on AFLDS.org—helping expand the platform while supplementing Dr. Gold's already packed tour schedule. I joined her travel team not only as a comms director but also as her (licensed) security guard. Hate mail and death threats were now routine—part of a life growing more dangerous by the day for anyone who refused to swallow the blue pill of silence and submission.

"America's Doctor" was now in the crosshairs—targeted by a nexus of corrupt institutions. Yet she pressed forward undeterred, working tirelessly on a fifty-page White Paper that dissected the (medical and political) science behind the so-called COVID shots. Her work revealed they weren't vaccines at all, but experimental therapeutics.

These were risky new drugs—or worse—rolled out with a reckless departure from standard safety protocols. The potential side effects she uncovered, especially fertility damage, were extremely alarming. Those adverse events—often fatal—soon resulted in thousands of reported deaths—a shocking and unprecedented horror.

But this five-alarm fire was buried by the Censorship Industrial Complex—backed by the Obama-Biden Intelligence Community and funded by the Medical Industrial Complex. Dr. Gold and her fellow Frontline Doctors defied the narrative, warning the public of a threat far more sinister than a lab-altered flu.

That bold public stand against the vaccine orthodoxy made us all targets.

Blowing the whistle on a deadly, multi-billion-dollar pharma racket—later proven to involve staggering levels of fraud—was a very risky move. But Dr. Gold had taken an oath to "Do No Harm."

And she meant it.

The fate of our nation weighed heavily as November 3, 2020, arrived. Dr. Gold and I had already voted early and joined a watch party overlooking the Pacific. The crowd was patriotic and optimistic. Trump led in key states. Victory seemed inevitable. When the counting dragged on late into the night, we left with President Trump's definitive lead giving us comfort.

Then came the next morning.

What followed remains one of the most stunning collapses of democratic trust in American history. Ballot counting was halted in key states under bizarre pretexts. Windows were covered. Observers were kicked out. Security footage showed boxes of ballots hidden beneath tables. Signatures were mismatched. Procedures were ignored. Laws were bent—or broken.

And then there was the "Laptop from Hell." The FBI buried it. Big Tech censored it. The corporate press called it Russian disinformation. But an independent study later found the suppression shifted enough votes to alter the outcome—even without all the other irregularities.

Overnight, Trump's lead vanished beneath a flood of unsecured mail-in ballots—*millions* of them rushed in under murky conditions. Many failed basic verification. No one seemed to care.

The Power was clearly several (million) steps ahead of *the People*.

In effect, they unilaterally installed a mentally-compromised, deeply corrupt Joe Biden into the White House. And they snatched the race from a populist incumbent drawing more enthusiasm than any candidate since Reagan. The heist was greased with propaganda—as I'd later learn firsthand at trial—and pulled off right in front of us, with all the audacity of a BLM mob looting Macy's.

The "Artificial Aristocracy" rigged and stole the election.

This was the beginning of a dark new era.

We were furious—and disgusted. Furious at a system so rigged that legal citizens couldn't vote their way out of it. Disgusted by the apathy of so many who just watched it happen. Like COVID, something smelled rotten—and the stench only grew worse as the evidence of fraud piled up.

Team Lunacy moved fast—because lunacy isn't stupidity. The Lunatic Left is cunning, coordinated, and shameless. Their strategy? Preempt, project, and smear. They'd already built the narrative. Any claim of fraud was a "conspiracy theory." Any critic became an "election denier" peddling *The Big Lie*. They insisted there was no credible evidence of fraud—then went further, declaring 2020 "the most secure election in U.S. history."

The Fix was in.

The election was rigged in plain sight, and so was the media—keyed up to play the People like a fiddle at a dirge for "Our Democracy™."

For anyone sincerely seeking the truth, one number alone should shatter the illusion: **158 million votes.** That's nearly **22 million more** than 2016—the biggest jump in U.S. history, dwarfing Obama's 2008 surge. And it didn't happen during a time of national unity or enthusiasm—it was during a pandemic, with fear, lockdowns, and rule changes rammed through by partisan operatives under the guise of an "emergency." Most of that record turnout came through **mass mail-in ballots**—a method long known to be vulnerable to fraud, errors, and compromised chain-of-custody. And while some try to explain the spike with "higher turnout percentage," they ignore the elephant in the room: **our voter rolls are corrupted.** After decades of open-borders sabotage, illegal "sanctuary city" policies, and corrupted registration systems, the number of people *eligible* to vote is itself a manipulated figure. Millions of illegal aliens have been effectively injected into the system, inflating the denominator and masking the cheat.

So the question is not if the 2020 election was affected by fraud.

The real question is: *How much of the fraud are you willing to pretend didn't happen?*

Further evidence is the focus of many other sources and materials. I recommend starting with ElectionFraud20.org. But if we're honest, the most convincing proof, aside from statistical absurdities, is the fact that Democrats and the Lunacy Media—but I repeat myself—fought tooth and nail to block any transparent review of the results. Not a recount. A real audit. Not just re-tallying illegal ballots—but verifying which were valid.

Over sixty lawsuits were filed in multiple states, but they were dismissed on procedural technicalities—without discovery, without cross-examination, and without allowing a single piece of evidence.

Who refuses an audit—if they didn't cheat?

"The election of 2020, like the election of 2016, was hard fought and, in many swing states, narrowly decided. The 2020 election, however, featured unprecedented allegations of voter fraud, violations and lax enforcement of election law, and other voting irregularities. And those allegations are not believed just by one individual candidate. Instead, they are widespread. Reuters/Ipsos polling, tragically, shows that 39 percent of Americans believe "the election was rigged." That belief is held by Republicans (67 percent), Democrats (17 percent), and Independents (31 percent)."

—Excerpt from Joint Statement from Senators Cruz, Johnson, Lankford, Daines, Kennedy, Blackburn, Braun, Senators-Elect Lummis, Marshall, Hagerty, Tuberville, January 2, 2021, to US Congress

Hardly "*the most secure election in U.S. history.*"

As Shakespeare wrote: *Methinks thou dost protest too much.*

Of course, America is not a pure democracy—it's a constitutional republic. And that matters, because our system is designed to prevent this kind of abuse. But those safeguards only work when our elected officials uphold them.

I quickly wrote an op-ed in the *Epoch Times* urging citizens to pressure their representatives to conduct forensic audits. Full transparency was essential—not just to resolve the controversy, but to preserve the integrity of our democratic process.

When the hashtag #StopTheSteal began trending, it seemed someone might have paid attention. That Saturday, just days after the election, our Beverly Hills rally was flooded with new protest signs demanding election review. The news media was forced to acknowledge similar displays erupting around the country as genuine uproar was beginning to take root. Soon, grassroots organizers planned several major protest events in Washington, DC. When Dr. Gold was invited to speak on January 5 and 6 in the nation's capital—alongside several Congressmen and other notable figures—we knew it would be a truly historic opportunity.

We were right.

But we never could have imagined just how right . . . or how costly that history would become.

CHAPTER 9

JANUARY 6: THE DAY, THE LIE, THE REMNANT

A letter and a number.

Sometimes, that's all it takes to trigger something primal:

- MS-13
- A(rea)-51
- U-271
- S(ep)-11
- C-19
- J-6

The chill hits before your brain can process why. That's *fear*. And like all things in nature, it exists because God created it—so it isn't inherently wrong. Fear is your body's warning system—it kicks in to help you survive.

But like anything, it can be corrupted.

That survival instinct is now being twisted into a weapon against you—and the twist lies in the messaging. "False Evidence Appearing Real" is dangerous because we're so susceptible to appearances. Your enemy is sending signals to trigger your disaster-response reflex—but in the wrong direction: a path that empowers them at your expense.

Those letter-number labels? They all point to real events—something really did happen—but who and what were involved, and why, are crucial details buried deep beneath the surface. Digging through that wreckage leads to some dark places.

Cue the eyerolls: "C'mon, those are conspiracy theories." But of course, the term *conspiracy theory* was coined by the CIA to discredit anyone uncovering their dirty deeds.

Eventually, though, the "theory" part often drops—and what's left is an actual conspiracy. We all got hit by the C-19 scam. It unleashed a host of evils that were conspiracy theories until they became conspiracy headlines—along with corpses and a lot of disturbing questions without any good answers.

Exposing government fraud was the reason I ended up in DC on January 6 in the first place—but the only chill I felt that day was the frigid winter air.

The day before was peaceful enough. We joined the lineup for a January 5 protest at Freedom Plaza—about midway through our two-week speaking tour. Dr. Gold was focused on COVID and civil rights, staying true to Frontline Doctors' nonpartisan mission. But the energy in DC was focused on the growing election fraud scandal—and it was clear the two were connected. Exhausted from preparing a much longer, science-heavy speech, she asked me the night before to write something more fitting for the moment.

What does one say to a million people? When would another chance like this come, if ever? The task was unique—and the question became the answer. Fifteen minutes later, I had the speech ready, wondering how historic the day might become.

Despite wind and scattered showers that afternoon, Dr. Gold braved the elements on an uncovered stage. She delivered this stirring challenge—met with applause from a packed crowd of ten thousand patriots drenched in red, white, and blue along with the rain:

"My fellow Americans, my name is Dr. Simone Gold, a board-certified emergency physician and Stanford University-educated attorney, a mom, and the founder of America's Frontline Doctors, dedicated to delivering the truth in support of health and human rights. You may know AFLDS as highly credentialed, unbiased scientists and doctors providing accurate data during this time of massive medical deception. Our actions saved thousands of lives. But today, I am not here to focus on the details of medicine or health policy. Instead, I am here to ask you a deeply significant question; why are **you** here? What is it, exactly, that brought over a million people flooding into our nation's capital at this precise moment?

Certainly, it is clear that the most fiercely contested presidential election in modern history has recently occurred without a transparent and trustworthy result, but I believe your purpose in making the trip from all over the country to this place here and now is much larger than any political race or elected official. I believe the reason you are here is the same reason I chose to be here: because we have all recognized a dangerous assault on the rule of law—a flagrant dismissal of those "wise restraints that keep men free." We have reached the same inevitable crisis as our Founding Fathers.

Within every human being lies a tendency to oppress others. Our Constitution exists largely to protect the people from the government. It exists to control that which does not change: human nature.

We are not here because we are Republicans or Democrats. We are not here because we are from the left or the right. We are here because we are Americans, and we believe in the truth of human liberty. We are here because we deserve and demand honesty and transparency from our government.

We are here because we know the difference between honesty and hysteria, between transparency and trickery, between truth and lies, *and we are sick and tired of being lied to.*

Our fourth president, James Madison, explained that "there are more instances of the abridgment of the freedom of the People by gradual and silent encroachments of those in power than by violent and sudden usurpations. It is proper to take alarm at the first experiment on our liberties."

Citizens: the only thing necessary for evil to triumph is for good men to do nothing; we must do something. Citizens: I ask you again: why are you here? If you know the mask is a lie, you must not wear it. If you know your governor is violating your rights, you must not comply. If you don't want to take an experimental biological agent deceptively named a vaccine, you must not allow yourself to be coerced. If you are living in fear of a non-lethal virus, simply buy the same cheap, ordinary medicines used across the world.

When you know something to be false, you must reject it—period. When you know something to be true, you must stand up for it, and you must be willing to fight for it. I urge you to mark this day, this moment, as the united return of our nation to the eternal fight for freedom, a commitment to integrity, a resolve to seek the truth in all arenas, and to always *act* upon it."

The gravity of the moment gripped us all. We could feel the whisper of history in the making, tingling on our skin at a frequency distinct from the falling rain droplets. The crowd's response set the tone for the next day. We were scheduled alongside Congressmen Paul Gosar, Lance Gooden, Lauren Boebert, Marjorie Taylor Greene, and other national figures—for a rally expected to draw upward of a million citizens.

But the next morning brought a different kind of chill. The biting DC wind cut into my skin like a weapon—one that I still didn't see coming.

Ignoring that shiver can be a danger all its own.

We left our downtown hotel early, skipping the long coffee line—a real sacrifice that freezing cold morning—to push through the dense crowds already flooding every street. We were headed to the VIP section at the Ellipse, where constitutional attorney John Eastman and others were already firing up the massive audience—hundreds of thousands of patriots stretching in every direction.

I've never seen a crowd like that—ever.

I was grateful for my leather gloves—black, fingerless, and admittedly more stylish than warm. I was even more grateful, though, when a nearby patriot noticed me shivering in my black leather jacket and handed me an insulated vest on the spot. I'm pretty sure it spared me hypothermia. Coming from Los Angeles, it's easy to forget other places still have winter.

So there I stood—outfitted with my signature Maverick aviators and a pink Gucci scarf (pink was a subtle nod to neutrality in our nonpartisan role that day). We shivered with both cold and excitement for the man of the hour: our fearless Commander in Chief, the most loved—and hated—U.S. President of all time, and the inspiring founder of the MAGA phenomenon—Donald J. Trump.

We hoped to hear encouraging news—that the president and a handful of principled members of Congress were making progress in challenging the 2020 election through constitutional means. But the tone of Trump's speech suggested otherwise. Too many "public servants" had abandoned both the president and their own constitutional duty to exercise uncomfortable courage in a key moment of political combat.

Still, President Trump stood tall. He reminded us not to surrender to corruption, but to hold the line. He also emphasized—clearly and repeatedly—that our movement must remain peaceful. He urged us to "peacefully and patriotically make your voices heard," and to "remain peaceful. No violence! Remember, WE are the Party of Law and Order—respect the law and our great men and women in Blue."

Those quotes are President Trump's actual words. You can believe the media spin about what he said—or you can read what he actually said.

The title of this chapter points to a journey: uncovering the full truth and meaning of J6. But let's pause here to confront an especially wicked lie: The corporate media didn't just fail to report Trump's words—they actively buried them. Then, in the same breath, they accused him of inciting violence, causing a riot, and even launching an "insurrection."

When Trump repeated his peaceful instructions on social media, reaching the entire world, those same corporate powers literally *erased* his warnings—and doubled down on their lies.

They shut down the social media account of the sitting president of the United States!

That censorship laid the foundation for the entire "insurrection!" narrative they'd scripted—well in advance. This hoax became the dagger wielded by the Deep State as they waged a war of political persecution against both Trump and his supporters for the next four years.

The scale of this deception is hard to overstate. Imagine this: A man sees a young woman unknowingly walking toward danger—a drunk and dangerous fellow signaling clear intent to harm her. Recognizing the threat, the bystander runs to help. But before he can intervene, a police officer trips him, handcuffs him, and watches as the woman is attacked.

. . . and then the officer hauls the would-be rescuer into court and accuses him of failing to help.

Excuse me?

Do you see now why I've said there are only two teams in this war? This isn't normal politics. It's not a policy debate. This is coordinated evil. It's fraud, weaponized power, and deliberate sabotage. And it's not just a "danger to Our Democracy™"—it's a threat to actual lives.

So why are we just letting it happen? How do we sleep at night under the silence of this injustice? Why don't we challenge such obvious, dangerous lies?

These are not rhetorical questions.

Where are the answers?

Unaware of this at the time, Dr. Gold and I realized we would need to leave the Ellipse before President Trump's late-running speech had ended. Our event had a government permit for the northeast corner of the Capitol—"Section 8"—and was scheduled to begin at 1:00 p.m. It was around that time—clearly running late ourselves—that we linked hands with a small group to form a human chain, trying not to be pulled apart by the largest sea of humanity I've ever tried to navigate. Uniformed security guards escorted us front and rear as we inched forward.

We would later learn that these guards were members of Oath Keepers—now infamously smeared, but at the time, organized to do exactly what they did: provide peaceful protection for speakers and VIPs. That included shielding us from the unpredictable hazards of such a massive crowd—and from any potential violence from counter-protesters like Antifa and BLM agitators.

Red Pill alert: we are all being lied to—and that certainly includes much of what you've been told about the Oath Keepers and the Proud Boys.

It took an hour to walk the eighteen-minute distance to the Capitol. Throngs of people were packed everywhere. We finally arrived just after 2:00 p.m., expecting to find a stage, congressmen with their entourages, and security personnel coordinating a peaceful continuation of the day's events.

Instead, we found confusion.

The plaza was surprisingly empty of law enforcement. There were no barriers, signs, or crowd control of any kind. There was no visible stage. No signage. No form of instruction. Yet tens of thousands of people were marching in behind us—just as advertised online for weeks in advance. Cell service was nearly unusable, blocking most updates. Someone heard a rumor that the afternoon event had been canceled—but that seemed implausible. Who cancels a massive public rally after the crowd is already there?

Imagine a Super Bowl stadium filled to capacity at kickoff time—only to have someone in the stands abruptly yell, "Never mind—they canceled the game."

It didn't make any sense.

People came expecting to hear from elected officials and other scheduled speakers. And with no other visible alternative, they began climbing the nearby steps. We saw only five or six uniformed officers standing passively in front of the large Columbus Doors at the east Capitol entrance . . . which at some point had been swung open. Protesters began to approach, apparently unsure if the open outer doors signaled an invitation for the demonstration to move inside.

Meanwhile, others filled the steps and balconies—waving flags, holding signs, praying, singing, filming, and otherwise exercising the First Amendment as you might expect. From my vantage point, everything looked normal.

And then—something shifted.

In that split second, a dilemma of duty opened before me—a decision that would define the rest of my life. Dr. Gold, seeing people fill the steps and sensing a moment of opportunity, turned to me. "I'm sorry—I just have to go speak," she said, and without waiting for a reply, plunged into the crowd. I frowned, with an unsettled feeling. This wasn't the plan.

But protecting her was my responsibility. I leapt to catch up.

As we moved up the steps toward the right-hand balcony, I saw what seemed like typical public protest—spirited, emotional, but peaceful. We were hoping to reach a visible position to address the crowd, even if only in part. At that point, I didn't notice any signs of violence.

But I would soon learn how perception could be used as a weapon—and how even peaceful protest could become the perfect camouflage for something far more sinister.

Because the heart of entrapment . . . is a trap. And the power of the trap is a disguise.

And what better disguise to snare political protesters than . . . the First Amendment?

After reaching the steps, it was clear I couldn't safely extricate Dr. Gold from the crowd. I stayed directly behind her, arms up to shield her from any elbows, as we tried to reach the balcony so she could deliver her remarks. But this became impossible—it was flooded, and the growing energy of the crowd was pushing toward the central Columbus Doors.

A few minutes later, we were firmly stuck.

We'd reached the upper level, hemmed in near the right side of the entry. I guided Dr. Gold toward the wall to minimize the risk of jostling or injury. The crowd was loud but still friendly—there were no signs of violence or hostility. It felt like being jammed into a mosh pit at a concert.

My security instincts kicked in. *Surely*, I thought, *more police should arrive soon*—to disperse the crowd, or guide a peaceful route forward, if they had in fact opened the doors for the demonstration to pass through.

That thought was shattered by a sudden, ear-splitting

BOOM!

"AHHHH!"

We both flinched, ducking as screams erupted from all sides. A deafening blast had just rocked the entryway, and instinct made it clear—we were under assault.

The shock gave way to dismay: We were being attacked—*by the police.*

It was a stunning betrayal of public protection, somehow twisted into a riot-triggering operation. More blasts increased the panic, followed by rubber bullets. Then came the baton swings and body blows. Officers began physically striking protesters packed onto the stairs. Some protesters, still pinned in the crush, began to respond defensively.

My concern for Dr. Gold escalated. There was no exit route. No protection. And no clarity on what the rules even were.

Just then, a lone officer stepped into view from around the corner: Joshua Pollitt, as we'd later learn. Dr. Gold recognized he was near fainting as he quickly stumbled past. I held her steady as he collapsed into the crowd behind us.

We turned to see nearby protesters reach down to help him.

"Get him up! Get him up!" voices called out.

Within seconds, people lifted him to his feet and helped guide him through the crowd. This escape wasn't feasible for anyone without a police uniform—that was the only signal the crowd recognized to make an opening.

Not long after, with the crowd still reeling from shock, no police assistance forthcoming, and no safe path to retreat . . .

The inner doors suddenly swung in—opened from the inside.

It appeared—reasonably—that someone had decided to allow entry. But I had no physical alternative. The pressure of the bottleneck at the door pushed us forward like a current.

And just like that, we were swept inside the United States Capitol.

As we crossed the threshold, a nearby protester hoisting a bullhorn nearly hit us as the crowd surged from behind. The jolt caused Dr. Gold to stumble and nearly fall, but I caught her and guided her forward—away from the chaos of the entryway. To my surprise, many protesters were already inside—along with numerous officers and other uniformed personnel who had clearly entered earlier by another access point. This seemed to confirm my suspicion that police had opened the building for protesters to pass through.

Moving straight ahead through the foyer, I saw several officers standing calmly with rifles. They seemed alert but unconcerned—watching various groups of protesters without giving orders or showing signs of alarm. It further convinced me that law enforcement was facilitating a peaceful protest inside. The vast interior was disorienting, without any navigational clues . . . aside from red velvet rope stanchions. Sensibly, we followed those ropes through the Rotunda, walking behind others in a quiet procession. Aside from a single broken window earlier, I still hadn't seen any vandalism or aggression. This was a political protest, and nearly everyone I saw was simply . . . protesting.

We continued following the velvet ropes and eventually reached a corridor beyond Statuary Hall, where the swelling crowd pushed us forward again. Soon, we were stuck once more—this time in an alcove facing another large set of closed doors, with no indication of what lay beyond. A masked police officer appeared, seemingly issuing instructions, but we couldn't hear him. His voice was muffled by the mask and drowned out by the din echoing off the stone walls. Through a haze of chemical residue, we eventually realized he was telling people to turn back. As soon as we had room to move, we turned and retraced our steps.

But now, the Rotunda was jammed with hundreds of newcomers. With no clear way out, we decided to film Dr. Gold delivering the speech in Statuary Hall while we waited for an exit. I sensed the historical gravity of the moment: a determined voice rising in the symbolic heart of our republic, calling for clarity and courage.

The police redirected some protesters around her while she spoke, which made it seem like they were facilitating her remarks. That impression then vanished when one officer abruptly pushed her mid-sentence. Caught off guard, she tried to explain she was a scheduled speaker for the day's events, but quickly complied when the officer insisted that she move along.

I caught the half-speech on my iPhone. With no exit yet accessible in the Rotunda and no direction from police, we noticed a pedestal she could use to gain some visibility. We climbed up beside the statue of General Eisenhower, and someone handed us a bullhorn. She delivered the complete speech while I stood close, steadying her and motioning for the crowd to listen.

(Officer testimony at my trial would confirm her remarks "did not instigate the crowd" and even supported police efforts to maintain order—despite the prosecutors' lies to the contrary.)

She finished without incident and even took a few questions while we continued waiting for a chance to leave. The crowd was still thick. Eventually, a patrolling officer approached and told me the east exit should now be accessible, and police were directing everyone to move that way.

I thanked him, and we followed his instructions.

The astonishing part is this entire sequence—step-by-step—was captured on the government's own surveillance footage. You can watch it in the viral short film *Do You Know What Happened on J6?* which amassed over 10 million total views after being posted to JohnStrand.com and @JohnStrandUSA, and widely shared by others on social media.

After complying with the police directive, it took another twelve minutes of slow shuffling through the crowded foyer before we finally—after forty-eight total minutes inside—escaped the United States Capitol.

But the Capitol trap was only just beginning to spring shut.

It sounds strange in retrospect, but we had a brief "shock delay" before fully comprehending the horror of what had just happened to us. Standing on the east steps after exiting, we paused to absorb the moment. We'd just completed a bizarre, police-guided "tour" through the Capitol. Several of those officers walked down the steps to leave, and we applauded them—grateful for their efforts to maintain order amid the confusion.

I also snapped a selfie—unaware it would soon become one of the most shared, googled, and infamous images associated with January 6. It showed my determined jaw, framed by Maverick aviators and a Gucci scarf, with the Capitol behind me—its steps filled with flag-waving Americans. I posted it with a message to explain my presence, realizing I would need to stand on it for the rest of time:

> I am incredibly proud to be a patriot today, to stand up tall in defense of liberty and the Constitution, to support President Trump and MAGA, and to send the message:
> **WE WILL NEVER CONCEDE A STOLEN ELECTION.**

We spoke with other protesters nearby. Most had similar experiences—largely peaceful and even hopeful, aside from the disturbing assault outside the Columbus Doors, which we presumed came from a rogue police unit. Strangely, I kept hearing people use the phrase "stormed the Capitol." Based on what I saw, I assumed they meant it like "storming the field" after a last-second football win: an excited rush, not a violent attack. The crowd had surged forward when the doors were opened from the inside—who wouldn't? That was certainly what I meant in my reply to Bobby's text that afternoon. He had checked in to make sure I was okay, watching from afar as the selectively edited "riot porn" raced across the internet.

"*We made history,*" I wrote back to my brother—echoing the

premonition I'd felt back in Los Angeles when we first booked the trip. It seemed it was being fulfilled . . . though not quite how I'd expected.

I don't think the U.S. Capitol building has been stormed and breached like that. And it caused Pence to delay the certification, so that's very significant.

When I sent that text, I'd misunderstood a rumor about Pence's delay to mean he was planning to exercise his constitutional authority—to demand a proper audit and ensure the election results were legitimate and proven to the People.

Tragically—treacherously—he did not.

But what I *didn't* misunderstand was this: A record crowd of red-pilled citizens gave up excuses—and the comfort of their couches—to exercise *uncomfortable courage*, traveling from around the nation to participate in this crucial stand against government corruption.

It was a birth of "The Remnant"—that reserve portion of We the People who refuse to comply with evil, and who rise to the call of duty in history's most dangerous moments. These are Americans who take personal responsibility and make the necessary sacrifice that turns a citizen into a true patriot.

Make no mistake: The persecuted J6ers have become the heroes most of us don't deserve—and can never fully repay.

It was a remnant of volunteers who put ball to musket, finger to fife, blistered bare feet to the road, and their lives on the line to resist British tyranny in 1776. Only about 3 percent of the colonial population actively fought in our nation's first revolution.

And that remnant purchased the freedom we are so close to losing.

Centuries earlier, when God called an ordinary Jew to save Israel from the Midianite raiders, He chose a humble wheat farmer named

Gideon—found hiding in the bottom of a winepress, just minding his own business. Literally.

God abruptly greets him as a "Mighty hero!" and commands: "Go *with the strength you have*, and rescue Israel from the Midianites. I am sending you!"

Gideon protests: "But Lord—how can I? My clan is the weakest in the tribe, and I am the least in my entire family!"

God answers, "I will be with you. And you will destroy the Midianites as if you were fighting against one man."

Then—because God loves a good drama—Gideon rounds up every available warrior in Israel: a paltry thirty-two thousand.

And God said, "That's too many."

Huh?

So God gives a *verbal* test, instructing Gideon to excuse anyone "timid or afraid"—and twenty-two thousand hightailed it home, leaving just ten thousand to face the countless hordes.

But God said, "There are still too many!"

When I said God loves drama, I wasn't kidding.

He then gave the remaining warriors an *action* test: tell them to drink from a nearby river. Dismiss any who set their swords down, drinking with their heads in the stream. Keep only those who held on to their weapons, drinking from their other hand, eyes scanning for danger.

In the end, only three hundred men remained.

Gideon led that Remnant to a stunning and total victory.

As our shock delay faded over the evening of January 6—phones buzzing with worried texts from friends and family—we began to absorb the explosion of media reports and internet gossip.

And it was clear: Victory was nowhere in sight.

The hundreds of thousands of peaceful Americans we'd seen—parents with children, grandmas and baby strollers, veterans in wheelchairs, church groups, civic clubs . . . the full spectrum of America's most engaged citizens—had vanished. In their place: a torrent of head-lines branding the entire day as a "violent attack on the Capitol." Gone were the hours of speeches, prayers, and peaceful marching. Instead, the news reports showed cherry-picked video clips of violent conflict—tight shots of frantic skirmishes filled with smoke and rage.

The media's edited footage showed a clash of color and camo—gas masks, flagpoles, pepper spray, riot gear. Videos zoomed in on protest-ers swinging back at police officers in the chaos. Soundbites screamed a manic soundtrack:

"Find that traitor Nancy Pelosi!"

"Hang Mike Pence!"

We were watching a staged war—an engineered illusion of "insur-rectionists" and "domestic extremists" overwhelming the "last line of defense" at the sacred seat of American democracy.

But it was a fiction.

The *Artificial Aristocracy* had crafted a weaponized narrative—designed to shatter the peace, silence the truth, and criminalize dissent. Reality was being rewritten into a lunatic fantasy of terror and insurrection.

And our hearts sank into a slowly rising pool of dread in our stomachs.

The real jaws of the Capitol trap were now revealed, dripping with hysteria and hatred.

We had been set up.

You never forget your first time showing up on an FBI "Most Wanted" poster.

I did a double take—first disbelief, then disgust—as I confirmed that, yes, that was a cell phone snapshot of me in the top row of the FBI "Persons of Interest" flyer. A friend had just sent it, along with the understated suggestion:

You might want to get out of D.C.

By then, the Lunacy Media's propaganda machine was in over-drive—spewing a manufactured frenzy in perfect sync with its weaponized counterpart: the Obama-Biden DOJ. But the corporate press is constantly distorting the truth, right? That's why they're now rightfully known as "Fake News." It was hard to gauge how much danger we might actually be facing—or from how many angles. So we stayed the course, traveling to Florida a couple days later for another speaking engagement before heading home to Los Angeles.

As the week went on, the malice and mayhem of J6 lies became sickening—pumped across the country like political fentanyl. It would soon spell disaster for much of my life.

My talent manager, Russ, texted me in dismay. Several unrelated industry colleagues—people I'd invested time and trust in, despite their Team Lunacy political leanings—launched vicious slander campaigns on social media. They smeared me as a "violent insurrectionist," a "domestic terrorist," a "traitor"—and bragged about turning me in to the FBI. They even posted screenshots to flaunt their betrayal, proudly defaming me across the entire microcosm of Hollywood . . . and the rest of the planet.

When I texted them privately to explain the truth—that, of course, I was not an insurrectionist or a violent anything, and that the media was wildly distorting J6—they immediately published my private messages and doubled down on their hatred. It was a betrayal so bizarre and so vicious, I could never imagine doing it to someone else.

Being lied about in public is never pleasant. But being lied about by people who knew better—people you once called friends—is a special kind of pain.

Later, I learned more "hometown friends"—former roommates and neighbors from my early years in Los Angeles—had gleefully joined the backstabbing. They posted their messages to the FBI, bragging about their "defense of Our Democracy™" by helping hunt down a "violent terrorist."

The backlash spread like wildfire.

My entire professional life was incinerated almost overnight. My social media accounts—where I'd built my audience and hosted my work—were erased.

POOF

Gone, without due process or recourse.

Soon after came the flood of cancellations. All my remaining modeling and acting contracts were terminated. Agencies dropped me nationwide. Clients fled. Hate mail poured in. Death threats followed.

The horizon of my dreamscape had gone dark. The technicolor dreamcoat I'd painstakingly sewn from scratch—multiple times, over more than a decade of sacrifice and heartbreak—was gone. Consumed by a raging inferno of lies, hatred, and betrayal.

I had been *digitally assassinated* in a single, stunning act of sabotage by my own government. And the "parchment barrier," as James Madison once called our Constitution, had been shredded in the assault. By making the sacrifice to travel across the country and peaceably assemble in our nation's capital—exercising the First Amendment rights guaranteed by that Constitution—I, along with a million other Americans, had walked straight into a trap.

J6 was a color revolution-style entrapment sting.

This literal *Fedsurrection* was planned—and practiced (see Julie Kelly's coverage of the Whitmer Fednapping Hoax). It was initiated by covert and uniformed operatives, whose role as "provocateurs" was admitted in federal trial filings and later confirmed in a bombshell Inspector General report. They planted false flags of terrorism to manufacture their pre-scripted "MAGA extremist" insurrection narrative.

The entire operation was designed to justify hundreds of "defamation assassinations"—the catastrophic result of a J6 indictment—and the violent SWAT team raids that followed. The J6 witch hunt would become the largest federal criminal investigation in U.S. history—very much on purpose. It was a fascist campaign of government terror—engineered to chill dissent and bludgeon The Remnant into retreat and permanent silence.

Their cover: a media-industrial machine built for propaganda and mind control. Their smokescreen: "The Big Lie." Their target: any American trying to think for themselves.

They inverted a legitimate protest into an orchestrated fraud and cover-up. And the real "Big Lie" is their blatant political smear claiming that President Trump "incited a riot"—even as they actively erased his explicit calls to remain peaceful and prevent this very tragedy.

Oh, and let's not forget their actual conspiracy to cover up the Hunter Biden Laptop from Hell. That fraud alone altered the outcome of the 2020 election, according to an independent study later acknowledged by then–Senator JD Vance.

The ugly truth is this: J6 was not an insurrection. It was a *response to the covert insurrection* of the stolen 2020 election—the latest strike in The Permanent Coup, still operating in the shadowy recesses of the Deep State swamp.

But if you repeat a lie often enough, it becomes the only truth the public can hear.

With their seditious apparatus still entrenched across the echelons of government-media power, J6 was clearly becoming ***The Greatest American Lie Ever Sold***. And we could hardly imagine just how deep, or how wide, this swamp of deception and treachery would grow.

We were in for a world of hurt.

GOVERNMENT GANGSTERS AND DUE PROCESS DEBAUCHERY

Another thing you never forget is your first time being blindsided by an FBI SWAT team raid.

After all, that's the whole point.

Without warning, bloodcurdling screams **erupt** just inches from your ears, followed by the **thunderclap** of a battering ram **smashing** your front door. A dozen black-clad soldiers with assault rifles **storm** into your living room, gun barrels **shoved** in your face.

What the hell is happening?

Red laser dots flicker on your chest. You instinctively shrink into yourself, paralyzed in terror, as the stormtroopers scream "GET DOWN ON THE GROUND!"—so loud it makes your skull *vibrate*.

Keep in mind—this wasn't a drug den or a hostage standoff. It was a small condo in suburban Beverly Hills—the known residence of a doctor and civil rights advocate. The idea that this warranted a militarized raid was absurd.

As shock gave way to rising disgust at this brazen abuse of government violence, I half-joked to myself that any second, a hidden director would yell, "Cut!"—and I'd learn I was starring in the next Jason

Bourne movie. But the grim reality of this horror was no joke. These tactics are textbook Gestapo—the tools of tyrants. When corrupted regimes turn their guns on nonviolent citizens—political dissidents, no less—they cross the line into full-throated fascism.

This was a blatant act of raw evil.

The pain and terror of that moment—what I call the "other fateful day," January 18, Martin Luther King Jr. Day—tore vicious scars across our life. It was just twelve days after the J6 trap had been sprung, an otherwise ordinary Monday morning, and Dr. Gold and I were working from her home office. We were on a conference call with several colleagues when, out of nowhere, an explosion of government terrorism shattered our world forever.

The FBI raid ravaged every part of our lives—wounds that damaged our relationships, our sense of safety, and our ability to trust. It fractured bonds with family, friends, and colleagues. It carved fear deep into the American psyche.

And it cost taxpayers a fortune.

Raiding peaceful citizens with paramilitary strike teams isn't just dangerous—it's wildly wasteful. These assaults drain critical resources needed for real threats. But in true Team Lunacy fashion, they fabricated their own reality of "domestic extremism" by misdirecting taxpayer funds to launch the single largest manhunt in U.S. history.

For four years, the DOJ deployed a "shock and awe" campaign of weaponized raids against hundreds of nonviolent—and innocent—Americans. They drove police "tanks" through suburban neighborhoods. They intentionally struck when children were present. They dragged families with young kids into the freezing cold. They swept nursery rooms with machine guns pointed at baby cribs.

I'm not exaggerating—I documented this myself. And the message was clear:

Fear the State.

Shut up and obey.

Dissent at your own risk.

There was no escaping the chilling climate of terror and intimidation now spreading across the country—if you were a Trump supporter.

But then, it's become painfully clear—that was precisely the point.

The civil rights violations didn't stop there.

That same MLK Day ignited a still-burning trail of abuses, proving just how far our Republic had fallen. Federal power had been weaponized by Jefferson's dreaded *Artificial Aristocracy*—entitled, obsessed with control, and propped up by useful-idiot gangsters like those FBI stormtroopers. They demolished our rights—our entire lives—without hesitation, hiding behind the oldest lie in the book: "I'm just following orders."

That was the excuse of Hitler's soldiers.

Genocides are always carried out on "government orders."

Dr. Gold is a proud Jew and the daughter of a Holocaust survivor, so this point wasn't lost on her as the SWAT officers skipped any Miranda pleasantries and hauled us out to the street. They refused to let us grab even socks for our hastily thrown-on shoes—or cash for the inevitable cab ride home.

How petty can you be?

We were dumped into separate vehicles, where we sat—handcuffed, contorted, and miserable—for *three hours* while they ransacked the condo. It only got worse from there. We spent hours crawling through L.A. traffic in somber silence to reach the Santa Ana Jail—because, ironically, the FBI's Los Angeles facility was short-staffed thanks to . . . Martin Luther King Jr. Day.

We were booked, fingerprinted, strip-searched, and photographed—then thrown into separate eight-by-ten concrete cells that reeked of human filth. It contained nothing but a hard bench, a steel toilet, and harsh fluorescent lights that punished my eyes all night—leaving me sleepless and exhausted by morning. My repeated requests for a phone call were ignored. There was no police explanation, no word from my family—just aching on that bench in total misery.

It was the longest night of my life.

The next day, we were again handcuffed and shoved into separate vehicles, riding for hours across Southern California to the concrete fortress known as the Los Angeles Metropolitan Detention Center. Already twenty-four hours into this nightmare, I spent several more hours in isolation, unsure if Dr. Gold was okay, or if I'd ever get out. Eventually, I was shoved into a tiny cubicle with a video screen (courtesy of "COVID") showing a magistrate, a prosecutor, and some fellow I assumed was my public defender. He seemed well-meaning but weak, passively watching as the prosecutor and judge steamrolled him—and me. Then, stunned, I heard the prosecutor call me a "danger to the public."

I had a spotless record with no criminal history. I hadn't touched anyone or broken anything.

It was totally absurd.

And yet, bail on my own recognizance was denied.

Outrageous.

Meanwhile, Kamala Harris was flipping cash bail like a Vegas slot machine, putting violent criminals back on the street with reckless abandon. The hypocrisy was monstrous. Nor was this a minor abuse. I turned awkwardly in my cubicle-cage and caught a glimpse of Dr. Gold through a small window. She was handcuffed and shackled, craning her neck to find me as an officer dragged her past. For an instant, her eyes met mine. She mouthed the words "*I'm sorry*" and shrugged helplessly, as if to say, *I don't understand either*—and then she was gone.

I was left stranded in a pit of despair, somewhere deep in the bowels of the MDC.

(Adding insult to injury, our federal probation officer—Robert Walters—would later lie in his infamous "Pre-Sentencing Report Without a Pre-Sentencing Interview," falsely claiming I'd been released on my own recognizance within twenty-four hours. That was not a "clerical error.")

The abuses kept coming. Brutal guards manhandled me like an animal—stripping me naked and jamming a useless "COVID test" into my nostril, pushing it so far I felt it bump my brain. A white-hot flash of agony lit up my skull—and I burst into tears.

After enduring thirty-some hours of this debacle with steady composure, I broke down in anguish. I could hardly stomach the pain, humiliation, injustice, and insanity of it all. Tears of outrage streamed down my face.

The hell of this nightmare had slammed into me like a cement truck.

After several more hours of being processed like livestock, I was dumped into another tiny cell. Exhausted, I sat in stunned silence—trying to absorb the shock, anger, and a creeping sense of despair as I begged every human I saw for *just one phone call*. It was my absolute right in the supposedly United States of America.

That call was never granted.

Trapped in that cell, I kept waving to guards as they passed, repeating my request—and I was ignored. It stretched into four straight days of isolation and torment, without a single word of explanation or any update on my fate.

And it was only a bitter foretaste of the abuses still to come.

You never forget your first time being tossed into a cage like a rat, with no clue how long you'll be trapped. The inability to gauge the duration of the pain—to pace for it, to preserve your sanity—that's the most excruciating part of the punishment. That, and the fury of knowing you're innocent . . . and being punished anyway. Tormented by government corruption—because you refused to comply with a lie.

I'll be forever grateful to Dr. Scott Barbour, one of our early founding physicians at America's Frontline Doctors, for helping secure my bail. Dr. Gold had spent days trying to find out what happened to me. She even hired a private investigator—just to overcome the government's outrageous refusal to provide any information about me to anyone.

After four days of this indefinite nightmare, I was finally jarred out of my stupor by a pounding on the cell door.

"Strand! Pack up your shit!"

(*Huh?*—I had nothing but the ragged prison clothes on my back.)

And just like that, I was dumped on the street in downtown Los Angeles. No phone. No wallet. No cash. No clue . . . except I learned the public defender's office was nearby. I found a secretary who told me Dr. Gold was driving down to pick me up.

It was a strange moment when she pulled up to the curb—both of us still in shock, unsure of what had just happened to us . . . or between us. Something invisible had shifted. She greeted me with a silent, pained look of infinite sadness in her eyes.

An unspoken declaration of permanent tragedy passed between us—like a quiet prophecy etched into the silence, outlining shattered pieces of the future . . . whether building up or breaking down, I could not tell.

The government's political persecution was clearly building. Dr. Gold explained how stubbornly they obstructed her efforts to arrange my release. Our frustration only deepened with each virtual court appearance, as more violations of our civil rights piled up.

Next came a senseless drug-testing regimen—completely unjustified by our records or the charges. It had no legal or factual basis—just another arbitrary abuse, because some faceless bureaucrat checked a box somewhere in the federal ether.

Then came another outrageous mandate: Despite my spotless record and active employment as a licensed security guard, I was ordered to wear an ankle monitor.

A pointless, humiliating burden.

Even the magistrate had conceded I wasn't a flight risk. That only deepened the insult of the next due process debauchery: We were secretly added to the U.S. government's terrorist watch list. The consequences were immediate—and disastrous. Without warning, we learned at the airport—rushing to catch our next flight—that we were blocked from flying, despite court-approved release conditions allowing domestic travel. It crippled our entire professional operation.

The Fourth Amendment was rolling in its grave.

Any of this would be devastating to a person's life. In our case, it was also a direct attack on the critical, nonpartisan mission of America's Frontline Doctors. We were one of the few sources of lifesaving information and early treatment access during a historic, government-engineered crisis. This wasn't just political—it endangered millions of Americans already drowning in fear and censorship.

And that's not even counting the defamation.

The DOJ worked hand in glove with their media henchmen to slander, intimidate, and destroy our lives, fortunes, and particularly our sacred honor. I summed up their tactics in media interviews with a phrase that struck a chord:

DOJ—the Department of Jihad.

The Obama-Biden regime's weaponized DOJ—under Merrick Garland and Matthew Graves—was waging a holy war against any American tied to J6. Their crime? Daring to exercise control of their own minds in defiance of the government's narrative—the First Amendment be damned.

Well, I'll be damned if I was going to sit there and take it.

I didn't carry the name "Maverick" for nothing.

I urged Dr. Gold to double down. If we were blocked from the air, we'd strike from the ground. Just imagine: a bold "Doc & Roll" tour—driving across America to bypass the bureaucracy and bring the Frontline Doctors mission directly to the people's front doors.

If you're going through hell . . . keep going.

After a few days at my drafting board, *The Uncensored Truth Tour* morphed from dream to reality—but it was far from easy. The scale of what we now faced—professionally, personally, spiritually, and now legally and politically—was overwhelming. A national tour typically takes six months of prep—which we sledgehammered into six weeks. Meanwhile, we were still buried under the exploding demand for Frontline Doctors' resources.

The operation grew into a scrappy nonprofit with nearly fifty remote staff across the country. At the same time, we juggled our ominous new legal obligations and began wading through the ever-deepening quicksand of the still-unfolding J6 entrapment scheme—its architects and media mouthpieces aggressively hawking **The Greatest American Lie Ever Sold**.

With Corona Chaos still raging in early 2021—and the defamation bomb of the "insurrection!" hysteria just beginning to detonate—everything that should've been easy became difficult . . . and everything difficult became nearly impossible. It would take another book to catalog everything we suffered over the next two years, leading up to my hostage "deployment." Even then, it wouldn't fully convey the attacks, betrayals, and cowardice we endured in our fight to survive.

As I told Dr. Gold directly in the Beverly Hills park that day, we were sacrificing much, and risking all, to defend the innocent and proclaim the truth. And she was living out the words of Jesus when he warned of the danger we'd face:

"Behold, I send you out as sheep among wolves. So be shrewd as serpents and harmless as doves."

—Matthew 10:16

As a physician committed to "do no harm"—and a strategic leader in the "Red Pill Revolution"—she has proven, as a Jew, more faithful to Christ's command here than many modern-day Christians. She continues to inspire and support me in my own calling to raise up *the Remnant*—urging those would-be warriors at the river to choose Uncomfortable Courage, guided by wisdom, in pursuit of a destiny marked by virtue.

Some of the darker persecutions we faced are captured in the film I later wrote and directed, *Always Under Fire*. But before that project, 2021 revealed God's hand painting new colors across a shifting dreamscape of duty and opportunity.

Shortly after enduring four brutal "warm-up" days of political imprisonment—and before finally shedding the ridiculous ankle monitor—I co-wrote and acted in a short film with director Chris Burgard called *Don't Have to Die*. The film featured Dr. Gold and me as ourselves, exposing the COVID lies that led to our entrapment and political imprisonment. The hook was powerful:

We are all being lied to—and people don't have to die.

It racked up hundreds of thousands of views—but likely would have gone viral if we'd released it as originally planned: in the immediate aftermath of the J6 media circus.

Unfortunately, that plan was derailed by still more due process debauchery.

Dr. Gold's criminal defense attorney warned her that federal prosecutor April Ayers-Perez was threatening to add a sixth charge: assaulting an officer. She had the gall to suggest we were somehow responsible for Officer Pollitt's blackout and fall—an accident we had no part in and couldn't have prevented. He simply tripped, out of our reach, and nearby protesters helped him up.

Dr. Gold was furious. For a physician, the accusation alone was devastating—like publicly accusing a schoolteacher of molesting students. The claim was blatantly false—disproven by video evidence and Officer Pollitt's own testimony. Ms. Ayers-Perez knew that. But she wielded it anyway, using the smear as a coercive club during pretrial planning.

It wouldn't be the last time she and her crony, Mr. Manning, deployed lies as weapons.

For the moment, it prompted Dr. Gold to suspend our public communications, concerned with the looming danger of further government persecution. To be clear: Weaponized government stalled the release of a film exposing that very weaponization. The First Amendment be damned yet again—along with every other constitutional safeguard meant to restrain government tyranny.

Still, I remembered the immortal words of fellow actor and fellow Italian, Sylvester Stallone, in *Rocky Balboa*:

"It ain't about how hard you hit—it's about how hard you can *get* hit, and keep moving forward."

So I reaffirmed my vow: to never surrender control of my free will—to choose courage and proactive engagement, no matter what the cost.

These government gangsters might take my gun, but they'd never get me to surrender my cannoli—the self-control over my attitude and my actions. I took on that "Italian Stallion" swagger and threw myself into launching *The Uncensored Truth Tour*.

That meant creating a press kit and marketing campaign—complete with a gleaming, hospital-white RV "tour bus," the Frontline Doctors logo emblazoned on both sides. It meant assembling a field production team with remote staging and A/V gear, along with a tech crew to document the journey. It meant organizing a logistics team to coordinate numerous frontline doctors, attorneys, nurses, sheriffs, and more—forming speaker panels at various tour locations. And of course, it meant rallying venues and supporters—just in time to fill seats as the Frontline Doctors tour bus rolled into town.

Amid the preparations, it hit me—no road tour is complete without a theme song! Dr. Gold's favorite—"We're Not Gonna Take It"—was a timeless resistance anthem. But licensing was a problem, given the COVID propaganda and media slander. We needed a song written by a real patriot.

And then, the answer became obvious: there was no rock 'n roll patriot more fierce than the Motor City Madman himself—Ted Nugent.

Ted was a fellow maverick, no question. Every time I saw him speak—or shred—I'd end up fist-pumping with unrestrained enthusiasm. He made Uncomfortable Courage seem downright normal—torching WOKE lunacy with truth bombs few dared to say out loud. I browsed his catalog, scrolling past *Cat Scratch Fever* and some other classics, but not seeing anything that—*Wait . . . no, can this be right?*

Ted Nugent has a song called "Just What the Doctor Ordered"?

My skin tingled as I scanned the lyrics and started rearranging lines in my head. *Oh yes—I can make this work.* I shared my discovery with Dr. Gold, and she saw my spark—but insisted we ask Ted for permission before I took off with it.

So we called him.

He picked up.

Dr. Gold explained the political persecution we'd endured—and how we were launching a road tour to fight back. Then she passed the phone to me. I jumped right to the point:

"Hi, Ted! I have kind of a wild question—would you mind if I rewrote one of your songs as our road tour anthem?"

He paused, intrigued. "Sure, send me what you've got in mind."

Challenge accepted.

I sat down that afternoon and knocked out the song in fifteen minutes. This was a good one—I could feel it. Grinning, I fired it off to Ted.

Five minutes later, I found out that sometimes, God arranges dreams you never would've imagined . . . and then He makes them come true.

Ted loved the rewrite. He even encouraged me to sing the new version. We'd hoped to have him play on the track, but our rushed tour schedule wouldn't allow for it. So the production of the entire project fell to me.

I knew exactly who to call.

"Hey bro," I said, dialing the best musician I knew. "Wanna get the band back together again?"

After hearing the story—and confirming we had a budget and a hard deadline—he agreed to produce the track at his studio in Nashville.

"Wait—how fast do you need this?" he asked, catching up with my frenzied explanation.

"Seventy-two hours," I said. "Start to finish. I know, it's crazy."

"Let's see what we can do," he replied.

By the next day, he'd sent a reference track. I recorded the vocals in two hours and sent it back. Bobby and our friend Dave Lubin worked through the next day. Four days after the original idea sparked, we had a fully produced "Red Pill Rock" anthem . . . and it delivered.

I read the Constitution at ten years old
Found a love of freedom and hope
Now we're on the verge of a viral breakdown
It's tryin' to steal my body and soul

It's so crazy, but you know that I'll fight it
I've found a cure for my body and soul
I've got me an overdose of freedom and hope

I worked every day, I learned every night
I studied till I knew truth from trick
Now we're on the verge of a logic breakdown
Acting like the facts don't exist

It's so crazy, yes you know, but you're blinded
We need common sense, liberty is normal
And this is just what the doctor ordered

It's so crazy, yeah but we're gonna fight it
We need common sense, liberty is normal
And this is just what the doctor ordered

The song was a big hit at every stop on *The Uncensored Truth Tour*, which stretched from Los Angeles to New York City and impacted thousands of people. Even better, Ted himself gave it a full-throttle thumbs-up.

That was quite the compliment. As our squadron of frontline patriots marched through the flak of COVID lies and J6 fallout, we relied on God to send reinforcements when we needed them—new allies, fresh courage, unexpected help.

Proverbs 18:24 says, "A real friend sticks closer than a brother."

When the Team Lunacy bombs were bursting all around, and causing some real damage, Ted Nugent was a real friend—and Bobby Strand was both.

It didn't take long for more Lunacy grenades to explode—wrecking due process and delivering both targeted persecution and the bureaucratic cluster bombs of "*casual cruelty.*" All of it was designed to exhaust, intimidate, and coerce us into silence and retreat. Before *The Uncensored Truth Tour* had officially launched, we were scheduled to join a Health and Freedom conference more than a thousand miles away—making road travel impractical. A supporter offered to arrange a chartered flight to bypass the "terrorist watchlist" flight ban and get us there in time.

On the return trip, our small plane touched down to refuel in a rural desert town—an "airport" with a single runway and one lonely food-and-fuel shack. It was the middle of nowhere. While the pilot refueled, I went inside to use the bathroom.

When I walked out of the men's room, I was intercepted by a man of military bearing dressed in plain clothes. Without identifying himself, he immediately asked if I was a passenger from the refueling plane—the only aircraft on the runway.

Alarm bells rang in my head.

"Yes," I said carefully, signaling that I didn't understand the purpose—or legality—of the question.

"Would you mind if I asked you some questions about that flight?" he continued bluntly.

"Uh . . . do I have to?"

"No, you don't have to provide any information if you don't want to."

"Then no, thank you," I replied flatly, and walked straight back to the aircraft.

I quickly relayed the encounter to my team. Moments later, our pilot returned—followed by six of these plainclothes "operatives." He told us they'd also confronted him and claimed to be DHS agents, though none showed badges or identification.

When both the pilot and I declined to allow them to board, things escalated. Without warning, one of the "agents" sent a large German shepherd charging up the plane stairs. It shoved its snout straight into a box of leftover pizza on the seat beside me. We jumped up and shouted, managing to push the dog back down the stairs while yelling that this was a private aircraft and we did *not* consent to a search. Dr. Gold immediately called her lawyer. She had long suspected the government might one day try to frame her by planting evidence. This felt like the moment that fear could become reality.

What followed was a two-hour standoff. The agents insisted the dog had made a "narcotics hit," giving them license to board. It was a blatant Fourth Amendment violation.

We held our ground.

Eventually, we got a local uniformed officer to intervene. His presence forced the agents to leash the dog and properly escort it. They were forced to concede that—obviously—there were no illicit substances onboard . . . beyond stale pizza, that is.

Our nerves were wound tight. And the purpose of the "exercise" was clear: these were nameless government thugs tracking us down, despite a legal, private flight with anonymous passengers. They were bullying us to send a message:

We are watching you.
We can find you anywhere, and we can crush you anytime.
We are in control.

Later that year, we were quietly downgraded from a federal "no-fly" list to something arguably worse: SSSS—Selective Secondary Security Screening. It soon became a notorious scourge among J6 defendants. This ominous "Quad-S" code ensured that every flight we attempted (and often missed) became an outrageous nightmare.

Describing this protocol abortion fails to capture its full spectrum of physical and psychological torment. The agony goes beyond the screening itself—a mounting dread that intensifies with each new flight. You begin to despair in anticipation of the next miserable ordeal.

When you're professionally obligated to crisscross the third-largest country on earth, often taking multiple flights per week, it becomes a debilitating affliction.

It starts at the check-in counter. You hand over your ID, and the agent frowns.

That's weird.

They whisper on a phone—*for an hour*—while you stand awkwardly monitoring your luggage, perspiring as the clock ticks down to yet another missed flight. Finally, they hang up and print your "ticket for the VIP experience" stamped with that dreaded Nazi-esque code. You snatch it (and don't forget your ID, which they've held hostage for an hour—or you'll come running right back) and rush to find the TSA screening portal.

That's when the real games begin.

After waiting in line—a delay of anyone's guess—you finally reach an agent. But the moment they see the SSSS stamp, they halt you.

"Step over here."

No explanation.

You hear them radio for backup.

You stand there, like a deer in a hundred passing travelers' headlights.

You curse the unstoppable ticking of the clock.

Eventually, new agents arrive. Some just stand there, staring.

Creepy. One finally steps forward. "We'll be conducting a routine, random additional security screening."

You nearly choke on the insult of such an obvious lie.

Then comes the "choice": would you prefer your "screening" take place in a "private area"—location unknown, another hour lost—or right here, in full view of the entire airport?

You cave to the public spectacle, clinging to your last shred of hope to make the flight—assuming you showed up three hours early. Then comes the "complete pat down"—which is nothing short of clothed molestation.

Every inch of your body, including your genitals, is aggressively rubbed, poked, and "screened." You nearly vomit. A line full of travelers stare in awkward suspicion.

Your nerves and dignity are completely shredded.

And that was just the pat down.

Then comes the luggage. You remain standing in stunned humiliation, scrutinized by the countless eyeballs now riveted on this ominous ritual. Another agent opens your luggage, inspects everything—including your pockets—and begins to painstakingly "swab" every surface of every single item with a small square of light blue material.

Every square inch of your belongings—literally.

Each of these countless swabs—hundreds of them!—is fed into a strange machine that "analyzes" the swab (and who knows what else). This entire charade is performed in order to generate—finally, after at least an hour—a genius report:

"Gee, no terrorist residue found on your items today, sir. Have a nice flight!"

This entire circus is unhinged government torture.

Due process debauchery.

By now, you're drenched in sweat and shaking—not with fear, but with fury. Hours of your life—your energy, sanity, dignity—have been senselessly and cruelly squandered.

And for what?

For no reason at all—except to bully you into submission.

If you think you've managed to absorb and sympathize with each detail of this diabolical "casual cruelty"—and if you think the ordeal ends there—think again. As you leave the security zone to find your gate, you suddenly realize . . . several agents are still in your peripheral vision.

You're being followed.

And just as you reach your gate—sweating with anxiety from the surveillance—you freeze.

Another squad of TSA agents is standing there, just waiting for you—ready to inflict the entire sadistic marathon on you and your poor luggage . . . again.

At this point (and yes—I've seen it repeated a third time), you begin to seriously question whether you need medication just to survive your own government's abuse.

This is what we face.

The government has become a vast network of bureaucratic bullies—some malicious, some just "doing their job"—but all complicit in the human machinery of soul-crushing *casual cruelty*.

Senator Rand Paul's *Government Bullies* catalogs a range of these abuses. We must push back as citizens and demand extensive reform. The abuse and exploitation of American citizens by their own government is appalling—and incompatible with a free republic. The Founding Fathers are rolling in their graves . . . even as we dig our own by tolerating these atrocities.

Acceptance is compliance—and compliance is consent.

I had learned long ago—on schoolyard playgrounds, and through the story of David versus Goliath—that bullies are never brave. They are

cowards—driven by pride and a lust for control, defiant of God's Divine Order. Their true target is always the same: an attack on our divine purpose. They are destiny killers. And though they revel in cruelty and often in violence, they live in secret terror. Deep down, they know they will never outrun their own inferiority to a truth they cannot control.

It's why fear and force remain their only weapon. Because nothing frightens a bully more than being forced to face what he truly is.

And that's why we must always remember: Fear and pride remain our only kryptonite—and we cannot lose if we refuse to surrender. The way to beat a bully is to claim the name and power of God—the power of true goodness—and sling the stone of reality right into that bully's face.

As the DOJ Goliath and the Philistine hordes of Fake News and government gangsters kept up their slanderous attacks on #TeamReality—swinging their fascist fists at Frontline Doctors and anyone else confronting their corruption—I took back control of my destiny . . .

. . . and claimed David's words as my battle cry:

"Don't worry about this Philistine," David told Saul. "I'll go fight him!"

"Don't be ridiculous!" Saul replied. "There's no way you can fight this Philistine and possibly win! You're only a boy, and he's been a man of war since his youth."

But David persisted. "I've killed both lions and bears, and I'll do it to this pagan Philistine, too, for he has defied the armies of the living God. Yahweh who rescued me from those claws will rescue me from this Philistine."

(Later, on the battlefield:)

Goliath walked out toward David with his shield bearer ahead of him, sneering in contempt at this ruddy-faced boy. "Am I a dog," he roared, "that you come at me with a stick? . . . Come here, and I'll give your flesh to the birds!"

David replied: "You come with sword, spear, and javelin—but I come to you in the name of Yahweh of Heaven's Armies, the God of the armies of Israel, whom you have defied. Today Yahweh will conquer you—and I will kill you and cut off your head. The whole world will know that there is a God in Israel. . . . This is Yahweh's battle, and He will give you to us."

As Goliath moved to attack, David ran to meet him. Reaching into his shepherd's bag and taking out a stone, he hurled it with his sling and hit the Philistine in the forehead. The stone sank in, and Goliath stumbled and fell face down on the ground.

So David triumphed over the Philistine with only a sling and a stone. Then he pulled Goliath's sword from its sheath—and cut off his head.

(1 Samuel 17:41–51)

Israel was under siege by the prehistoric Team Lunacy forces of fear and coercion—while the "Artificial Aristocracy" of David's time was paralyzed into compliance. It took David's courage in that critical moment to pull his nation back from the brink—and deliver a victory to secure the dreams and destiny of millions.

And now, I faced my own Goliath—surrounded by the modern enemies of God's Divine Order: a Galactic Empire known as the United States federal government. Day by day, week by week, through grueling months in the battle for medical freedom and civil rights, my team and I kept fighting. We challenged evil wherever we found it— and braced for the battles still to come.

The Philistine hordes now swarming the Divided States of America, led by the brutal giants of today's *Artificial Aristocracy*, would soon sneer an ultimatum directly at me—and it would prove more uncomfortable than anything I'd yet seen in any dream or premonition.

A toxic dose of lawfare was already dripping from the tip of this Goliath's spear.

Chapter 11

FRUIT OF THE POISONOUS PLEA

One of the more maddening truths of this era is how much it still hurts to be hit with the same lies over and over. You'd think I'd be numb to it by now. As a fully red-pilled patriot, I should be immune to the Team Lunacy toxin of gaslighting and projection—but somehow, despite knowing it's coming, it still knocks the wind out of me.

What amazes me isn't just the hypocrisy—it's how openly they flaunt it as they climb the ladder of so-called democratic power. We are told we must "defend Our Democracy™," but this is a cruel joke. The Founders warned against the dangers of pure democracy—and built a constitutional republic to guard against it. That republic has been hijacked by an *Artificial Aristocracy*—some ostensibly elected, others permanently installed. This "Deep State" has morphed into a thinly veiled, increasingly fascist autocracy wrapped in democratic theater. They ensnare us in bureaucracy while promising we're as free as the mirage they want us to see.

"Our Democracy™" is their Doublespeak—a twisted inversion they wield like a hammer. And they will keep bludgeoning us until we recognize the deception. We have to regain control of the Cognitive Theory channel.

We must win the war of the *words* if we hope to win "the war of the worlds."

Why do I say this?

Because WORDS develop your THOUGHTS, which direct your ACTIONS, which define your CHARACTER, which determines your DESTINY.

We are in a war of information—a battle for *Cognitive Liberty*.

Nowhere is the abuse of language more dangerous than in the weaponization of our justice system. Take the phrase "no one is above the law." It sounds noble—but in the mouths of political hacks, it's become a machete. Twisted with arbitrary malice, they use it to cut down anyone who challenges the regime.

As I write this—from prison, an innocent man falsely convicted with a distorted felony statute meant for high-stakes evidence tampering—I'm watching live TV coverage of that very Doublespeak abuse. Leticia James. Alvin Bragg. Jack Smith. Fani Willis. These operatives swing the battleaxe of "no one is above the law" even as they elevate themselves above it with impunity. They wield the justice system as a political weapon, aimed at anyone who threatens their illusion of legitimacy.

Anyone wise to the Mockingbird Media can see it: Trump is guilty of little more than the cardinal sin of going off script and disrupting the perfectly laid plans of the *Artificial Aristocracy*. He exposed the machinery of the ruling class—and now they'll stop at nothing to shut him down. Meanwhile, the citizenry is now faced with an emperor whose clothes are neither new nor covering the naked corruption underneath. And while our national patience for this charade is wearing thin, we continue to bleed from the wounds of a weaponized DOJ that long ago betrayed its true purpose. Prosecutors campaigning on a promise to "get" their political opponents? Lifetime appointments with total immunity for unelected, black-robed demi-gods?

Really?

This deranged lunacy must end. And when President Trump returns to the White House, I believe that end will finally begin. He has made great sacrifices to serve—and ultimately save—our country, bearing the brunt of this weaponization. He's shown true Uncomfortable Courage by respecting the judicial process, even as it prostituted itself to smear him with thirty-four fabricated felony counts—without jury unanimity. And his suffering proves the point: The regime will stop at nothing—and spare no one—to maintain control.

If they can legally poison—and literally shoot—a president, they can and will find a way to target #YouNext.

When the judiciary was formed after the Declaration that "all men are created equal," it rested on a single foundational principle: We are to be governed by laws, not by men. The pillars of justice were clear: a presumption of innocence and a vigilant protection of Due Process and equality under the law. No citizen was to be singled out for punishment, and the burden of proving guilt rested squarely on the state. These ideals, inherited from English common law and rooted in biblical morality, are embodied in the legal doctrine known as "Blackstone's Ratio," named after English jurist William Blackstone:

"It is better that ten guilty persons escape, than that one innocent suffer."

Innocence is—or was—sacred.

The Founders also understood the state's natural drift toward tyranny. That's why they designed a justice system biased in favor of the individual. But that safeguard has now been perverted beyond recognition.

In his disturbing book *Three Felonies a Day*—which every American should read—Harvey Silverglate, a veteran trial lawyer, exposes how the system has rotted from ambition and power. The "innocent man" is now a ghost—paraded to preserve the illusion of "justice" while crushing any individual necessary to advance that ambition. In today's DOJ, success is measured not by justice served, but by convictions secured—at any cost.

You're no longer an individual citizen with dignity and rights. You're a statistic. You're a notch on their belt—a stepping stone on a prosecutor's career path to prestige and power.

Those notches have skyrocketed—and it's no accident. Over the past century, an explosion of laws and regulations has created a legal arsenal of three hundred *thousand* ways to criminalize you. It's a prosecutorial shooting range—and most of these prosecutors have all the restraint and rectitude of a desert vulture.

Three hundred thousand federal laws? That isn't just absurd—it's incredibly dangerous.

The law itself has become a monstrosity. After decades of imprudence and corruption, we're entangled in a legal code so bloated, complex, and contradictory that no normal citizen could ever understand it—let alone obey it.

Silverglate's title isn't just clever wordplay. It reflects an ugly truth: our justice system now mirrors the infamous creed of Stalin's secret police chief, Lavrentiy Beria:

"Show me the man, and I'll show you the crime"

The fact that the DOJ now echoes Soviet gangsters—who murdered millions using the machinery of the state—should give you pause . . . or at least pause your swiping on Tinder and TikTok.

This is a total disaster.

But it's exactly the kind of disaster the Founders warned against:

"It will be of little avail to the people that the laws are made by men of their own choice if the laws be so voluminous that they cannot be read, or so incoherent that they cannot be understood; if they be repealed or revised before they are promulgated, or undergo such incessant changes that no man, who knows what the law is today, can guess what it will be tomorrow. Law is defined as a rule of action; but how can that be a rule, which is little known and less fixed?"

—James Madison

I think even Madison would be stunned to learn that we now routinely accept "omnibus" legislation exceeding a *thousand pages*—much of it unread, let alone understood.

Let's be honest—this is insanity.

And only a fool accepts such lunacy expecting anything but collapse. Tucker Carlson once warned of a "Ship of Fools." We've supersized this into a full-blown "Society of Fools."

Doom is the only destination for such a voyage.

Legitimate law is not merely a restraint on behavior—it is the structure that protects our liberty. No one understood this better than John Locke, whose philosophy of Natural Law formed the backbone of the American experiment. Our Founders studied his work in depth—not to design a cage, but to build a framework for freedom:

"The end of law is not to abolish or restrain, but to preserve and enlarge freedom. For in all the states of created beings, capable of laws, where there is no law there is no freedom. For liberty is to be free from restraint and violence from others, which cannot be where there is no law."

—John Locke

Etched in the halls of Harvard Law is a timeless truth: Laws are "those wise restraints that make men free."

Today, Americans live under the shadow of *Three Felonies a Day*. That stands in stark contrast to Locke's vision of liberty through justice.

Another bulwark of American law, designed to protect the innocent—even at the expense of some prosecutorial belt notches—is the doctrine known as "fruit of the poisonous tree." It holds that any evidence obtained illegally—or tainted by government misconduct—is "poisoned" and inadmissible in court. We do not allow any man—guilty or innocent—to be convicted through government error.

This principle isn't a loophole—it's a moral line in the sand. The highest duty of any government is to protect the unalienable rights of the people, not to rack up conviction stats. That's why **we hold the government—not citizens—to the strictest legal standard**. Because we are (supposed to be) a nation of laws, not rulers.

The Founders also warned us why preserving such a nation would prove so difficult:

"If angels were to govern men, neither external nor internal controls on government would be necessary. In framing a government which is to be administered by men over men, the great difficulty lies in this: you must first enable the government to control the governed; and in the next place oblige it to control itself."

—James Madison

The further our leaders fall from the angels—and descend into pride and corruption—the less our government will control itself. We've watched this unfold for decades, as the justice system's sacred duty to presume and protect innocence has been slowly poisoned by the craven lust for power, wealth, and prestige.

The fruit of this lust soon appeared in my pretrial proceedings.

"COVID" remained the government's control "black card" with no limit—swiped at will to purchase the trampling of any right that stood in their way . . . including confronting your accuser face to face. After the four-day debacle of my violent arrest, needless imprisonment, denial of phone calls, and weak legal counsel, I was tersely informed, via Zoom without my counsel present, that my case had been transferred—with no recourse—to the leftist/Democrat stronghold of Washington, DC.

A voice from the computer droned out the Grand Jury indictment. I was staring down five federal charges—an absurd felony and four misdemeanors—all stacked to inflate the persecution effect:

Count #1: *Obstruction of an Official Proceeding* (often mislabeled as "Obstruction of Justice") and *Aiding and Abetting*, 18 U.S.C. § 1512(c)(2); felony with maximum 20 years in prison and/or $250,000 fine.

Count #2: *Entering and Remaining in a Restricted Building or Grounds*, 18 U.S.C. § 1752(a)(1); class A misdemeanor with maximum 1 year in prison and/or $100,000 fine.

Count #3: *Disorderly and Disruptive Conduct in a Restricted Building or Grounds*, 18 U.S.C. § 1752(a)(2) and § 1752(b)(2); class A misdemeanor with maximum 1 year in prison and/or $100,000 fine.

Count #4: *Disorderly Conduct in a Capitol Building*, 40 U.S.C. § 5104(e)(2)(D) and § 5109(b); class B misdemeanor with maximum 6 months in prison and/or $5,000 fine.

Count #5: *Parading, Demonstrating, or Picketing in a Capitol Building*, 40 U.S.C. § 5104(e)(2)(G) and § 5109(b); class B misdemeanor with maximum 6 months in prison and/or $5,000 fine.

My head was spinning.

"Picketing and Parading"?

"Disorderly and Disruptive Conduct"?

"Obstruction of Justice" . . . and a twenty-year prison sentence?!

None of this made sense—if the goal was honest and equal justice based on facts. But it was now clear: The Obama-Biden regime had weaponized a *Department of Jihad*—and justice was no longer the mission.

They were targeting Crooked Joe's political opposition.

And I was now squarely in their sights.

My stomach clenched. I sat in muted frustration, waiting for a pause in the video hearing—until I finally erupted in exasperation.

How in the hell could they stack a felony and all those redundant, ridiculous charges to threaten me with **twenty-three years in prison** and nearly **half a million in fines** . . . *for not touching anyone and not damaging anything*? Not to mention legitimately doing my job: guarding a scheduled speaker at a permitted rally—protected by the First Amendment!

This and many other questions would go unanswered. The tree of American justice had now been poisoned to death—down to its deepest, darkest root:

The government's fraudulent plea.

I was still tangled in the thorns of that poisoned tree—starting with the selection of my judge.

"Oh my God, it's Casey," Dr. Gold hissed from across the room. We were both logged into the arraignment Zoom call from the Frontline Doctors home office in Los Angeles. Forced to sit apart in the same room, with separate remote counsel, we had no real way to coordinate strategy in the awkward videoconference setup.

I frowned in confusion.

"Who's Casey?" I whispered, watching her type frantically to her physically-inaccessible defense attorney—grasping for some shred of attorney-client privilege.

That's when our new judge—assigned to both of us as co-defendants—the (not-so) honorable Christopher "Casey" J. Cooper—casually dropped a bizarre disclosure into the record:

"I don't believe that I [made] her acquaintance at the time except perhaps in passing, and as far as I know, I have not seen or spoken to her in the thirty-some-odd years since. I don't believe that that's a basis for my disqualification from this case, but if Ms. Gold or any other party for that matter, disagrees, you should feel free to file a motion. I will not be offended in the least, and I would likely favorably entertain a request to transfer this case. All that I ask is that you file any such motion by the time of our next status conference, which I suspect we will schedule at the end of this proceeding, so that I don't have to invest too much time and energy in this case. Fair enough?"

Dr. Gold was still pounding at her keyboard as her attorney replied: "No, your honor, it shouldn't be an issue."

My stomach dropped.

How could anyone with a functioning brain miss the glaring "appearance of bias" in that admission? It was as plain as a bandit clutching stolen jewels in a ski mask. And I had no idea at the time just what heirlooms were still hidden in Casey's closet.

"Who is this guy?" I hissed.

Dr. Gold gave a sheepish shrug. "He was my Stanford classmate. Same graduating class. I'll explain later. My attorney says he's one of the 'least terrible' options on the DC bench, so she thinks we should just let it go."

We would soon find out just how horrendous the "least terrible" option could be.

But the next sucker punch was already winding up.

"We'll file the motion for the record, but there's no chance it'll be granted—they've rejected every single J6 change of venue motion immediately. Also, the government's going to ask you to waive your speedy trial right—which I recommend. It's usually better not to go first in a mass lynching—err, prosecution. Let emotions cool down before you 'face the fire.'"

My DC criminal defense attorney explained all of this calmly—like these legal land mines were just so many rotten apples to be picked through on our way to the bottom of the barrel.

"This is insane," I snapped. "They're allowed to ignore our constitutional rights, with, what, 93 percent of DC residents voting for Obama and Joe Biden? And I guarantee exactly 100 percent of them hate President Trump with a passion. How does a jury get any more biased than that? I'm pretty sure the Sixth Amendment includes the word *'impartial'*!"

My blood was boiling. The justice system was completely rigged. And most of my "neighbors" seemed no different from the first two passersby in the parable of the Good Samaritan—sidestepping a bloodied countryman in the street and pretending nothing was wrong.

A million Americans sacrificed to show up in Washington, DC, on J6 to peacefully protest what they knew was a stolen election. Thousands of them—most remaining peaceful, even under illegal assault by police—were completely unaware they were walking into a diabolical trap. They stepped—or in my case, tripped—into the Capitol and meandered through red velvet ropes. Some were *waved in* by uniformed officers. Others were literally chaperoned by that same police into the Senate Chamber, as later revealed by Tucker Carlson to the shock of the entire world.

How many "insurrections" come with uniformed police tour guides?

Yet there was no reasoning to be found in the hateful hysteria. The regime struck from all sides: toxic media defamation, DOJ terrorism, and a corrupted judiciary eager to lynch those deplorable "red hat niggers"—as if trading white hoods for black robes could conceal the crimson of their murderous hatred and hypocrisy.

They killed Matthew Perna with sheer terror.

And he wasn't the only one. Other J6ers also died, driven to despair by horrific government abuse. Many more clung to life as every part of their existence was systematically destroyed.

The political lynching of J6ers isn't just unconstitutional—it's demonic. The mass slander of "MAGA Republicans" is textbook dehumanization, no different from what the Ku Klux Klan did to American negroes or the Nazis did to Jews. But this weaponized, partisan persecution has no parallel in our history—and no moral defense.

Do you grasp the scale of destruction this regime has detonated into the lives of peaceful citizens—most of them truly innocent? Clearly, Justice Amy Coney Barrett does not. Her *Fischer* dissent was both factually ignorant and legally grotesque.

For anyone else still unfamiliar, go to WeAreJ6.com and learn the stories behind the slander. This is one of the most heinous abuses of government power in American history. And I'll be honest—at times, it has made me ashamed of my own country.

These entrapped J6 patriots were tarred and feathered by vicious "insurrection!" propaganda—manufactured by the media and supercharged by Nancy Pelosi's vile Select Subcommittee, later exposed as a criminal cover-up. They were prosecuted in kangaroo courts and sacrificed one by one at the altar of political theater. Even most Republicans abandoned them to protect their own interests. And the silence from the rest of the country?

Deafening—and damning.

Silence is acceptance, acceptance is compliance . . . and compliance is consent.

How did we not see it? The glaring signs of Nazi-esque conditioning:

using race—or Trump—as a trigger to divide, then dehumanize, then destroy an entire category of Americans.

How did we fail to connect the dots when this DOJ branded any dissenting citizen a "threat to Our Democracy™"—annihilating their due process and dismantling their entire life—and then fail to see them tracing the figure of a legal noose around our necks?

How can we miss the tyrannical trend—that it was a "Q'Anon Shaman" and the Proud Boys first . . .

. . . then a doctor/lawyer and a model/actor . . .

. . . then plumbers and veterans and grandmas . . .

. . . and then at some point—probably sooner than later—it's going to be #YouNext?

I kept asking these questions while the media chorus of J6 lies kept pounding through every TV in America—amplified by Pelosi's sham "Select Committee." Their "Attack on the Capitol" anthem was replayed endlessly until the nation was hypnotized into accepting a narrative so bizarre it collapsed under basic scrutiny.

How do you have an insurrection with no guns?

Yet this lunacy was now widely conceded: that thousands of ragtag citizens—babies in strollers, veterans in wheelchairs, grandmas and grandkids—armed with Bibles, flags, pocket constitutions, and protest signage, had somehow conspired to "storm the gates" and take "Our Democracy™" hostage.

Even writing this down feels ridiculous.

To this day, the phantom menace of the armed insurrectionist is a monster that never materialized—sorry, flagpoles and "bear spray" self-defense canisters don't qualify as real weapons of a rebellion. The "Attack on the Capitol" narrative was as dishonest as it was absurd.

So why was everyone playing along?

Why did both Left and Right seem to unite in a conditioned recoil at the drumbeat of "insurrection!"—either screaming with bloodlust, or averting their gaze—as citizen after bewildered citizen was hunted down, humiliated, and tossed into the coliseum of the DC court system to be shredded by prosecutorial gladiators?

The answer came slithering into my hands a few months later, when I found myself holding . . . *the Fruit of the Poisonous Plea*: the DOJ's J6 plea deal with the devil. And sure enough, the devil was in the details.

At first, I just stared. Then blinked twice to make sure I was reading this right: The DOJ that had bulldozed my life—brutal SWAT raid, abusive imprisonment, bureaucratic harassment, digital annihilation, reputational ruin, and the threat of twenty years in prison and half a million dollars in fines—was the same DOJ now offering me the "golden parachute" plea deal of a lifetime?

A deal that would magically "erase" that staggering prison threat in exchange for pleading guilty . . . to a single misdemeanor?

It made no sense. What was the catch?

Then I saw it—lurking further down the page, hidden in plain sight:

STATEMENT OF OFFENSE
18 U.S.C. §§ 1752(a)(1)

The Attack at the U.S. Capitol on January 6, 2021
The title alone betrayed the truth. January 6 was a permitted First Amendment protest on public grounds, conducted peacefully for hours. What followed wasn't an attack. It was a limited escalation—deliberately instigated by undercover government operatives, as later admitted in court and flagged in the Inspector General's own report. Their incitement sparked confusion and fear. Police misconduct, caught on film, escalated panic and provoked self-defensive reactions. Some believed entry was allowed when doors were opened and officers gave mixed signals.

That's not "The Attack"; that's a legitimate protest, hijacked and weaponized into an avoidable—and very suspicious—riot.

And it never would have happened if proper security had been deployed—an action not only recommended but duly authorized by President Trump . . . yet deliberately rejected by both House Speaker Nancy Pelosi and DC Mayor Muriel Bowser. **This cannot be overstated**: the inexcusable failure (or corrupt scheme) by Pelosi and Bowser led directly to the tragic deaths of four unarmed protesters that day, along with four years of ongoing government warfare against innocent bystanders—actions far more serious than broken windows.

That DOJ statement—rubber-stamped by the court—cemented the lie that launched the insurrection hoax. Never mind that no one was charged with insurrection. It was the foundational fraud of **the Greatest American Lie Ever Sold**.

Let's review some of the poison in this plea:

"On January 6, 2021, **the exterior plaza** of the U.S. Capitol was closed to members of the public."

". . . temporary and permanent barricades were in place . . . U.S. Capitol Police were present . . ."

Sounds official—until you realize it's completely misleading. They imply the closure and barricades were both known and obvious. But that's like saying, "the traffic light was red" without mentioning it was hidden—or that someone had moved it.

The Capitol plaza is open to the public nearly every day of the year. It's the literal public square. That day, the only signs of "closure" were some unsecured bike racks and snow fencing—mostly removed before the crowd arrived. Some of it . . . by police.

Also, they charged us under *18 U.S.C. § 1752*—which only applies when the Secret Service designates a restricted area. The Secret Service made no such designation on January 6—but who's counting legal details at this point?

I personally saw six police officers standing on the East steps as hundreds of thousands of peaceful Americans gathered at a permitted protest.

Six.

That's not security—that's a trap.

". . . certification proceedings were still underway and the exterior doors . . . were locked or otherwise secured."

Actually, Congress had already paused the proceedings on their own. Protesters didn't cause the alleged "obstruction of Congress" at all. And even after the crowd dispersed, Congress paused again—because debate and delay is what they do. There was no "danger to democracy" here. This was literal democracy in action—imperfect, yes, and muddied by clandestine government operations, but democracy nonetheless.

". . . Gold and Strand entered the restricted area . . . Directly in front of Gold and Strand a law enforcement officer was **assaulted and dragged to the ground** . . . Gold and Strand **breached** the East Rotunda doors as part of a crowd . . . ."

This was a lie of the highest order—vicious, deliberate, and thoroughly disproven. The fallen officer was not assaulted there, and merely tripped. Dr. Gold and I did not "breach" anything—the doors were already opened. We were also clearly separate from the crowd—a point confirmed under oath by a Capitol Police officer. Dr. Gold was a scheduled speaker, and I was her assigned security. That's exactly how we behaved.

". . . Multiple law enforcement officers had to intervene before Gold stopped giving her speech . . . ."

Nope. One officer rudely shoved her—after others had clearly allowed her to speak. She complied within seconds. That allegation is pathetic.

"*. . . The defendant* **knew** *at the time s/he entered the U.S. Capitol Building that s/he did not have lawful authority to enter the building.*"

And there it was—the most potent deception in this legal cyanide:

They invented the required ***mens rea*** out of thin air, covering up the disturbing reality that the Columbus Doors had been convincingly opened from within—an unmistakable invitation. Not only that, but police officers were calmly inviting *and even escorting* citizens into and through the building.

What we "knew" at the time was that nobody understood much of anything—and what we have since come to know is that the government is lying about everything.

It's important to realize that most J6 defendants initially professed their innocence. Many did believe that entering the Capitol was permissible—or at least forgivable—given the chaos and confusion surrounding them.

And then . . . the plea appeared.

And everything changed.

Just like that.

This is not the time to start believing in "coincidences."

Reading the plea agreement, I felt a slow-burning acid drip into my gut as the malice of this lawfare became clear. The *Department of Jihad* had buried me beneath an avalanche of charges—a threat of total catastrophe—designed to crush me beyond resistance, gasping for relief at the sudden "mercy" of the plea deal.

In legal terms, it's called "vertical overcharging" (inflating charges beyond what the evidence supports) and "horizontal overcharging" (stacking redundant charges to compound the punishment). Both are unethical—and illegal. But the most insidious part? The price of "leniency" wasn't just pleading guilty to a token misdemeanor—it was swearing allegiance to their entire fraudulent narrative. *Even the dismissed charges required a forced confession that they "had a basis in fact."*

It was cunning—and devastating—extortion.

Trapped in this sadistic spiderweb, hundreds of defendants predictably gasped for air. One by one, they abandoned their original, honest testimonies of innocent surprise and sudden entrapment—and began signing confessions to the regime's lies. The DOJ forced these citizens to affirm a fictional "conspiracy": a violent, premeditated, seditious assault on a "duly elected" government (gaslighting alert).

Desperate to escape the jaws of this government monster—or at least dull its venomous bite—most of these citizen-victims signed the DOJ's poisonous plea. And in doing so, they sealed a fate far beyond their own.

They handed the regime its most dangerous weapon: confession.

Not confession of guilt—but of narrative.

It was the forced mass purchase of **the Greatest American Lie Ever Sold**. And we swallowed it whole. Poisoned by hatred. Paralyzed by propaganda. Fragmented into the Divided States of America.

After all, if hundreds of J6 protesters "freely" admitted not only presence, but premeditated participation in a violent "insurrection" against the "duly elected" government . . . well, they must be guilty. They must deserve *Capitol Punishment . . .* right?

But of course, "confessions" extracted by torture are not confessions.

They're just torture.

Nevertheless, much of the country still didn't see the fatal web being spun around them—blinded to "The Real Story of Jan 6" by propaganda laced with omission bias—the most invisible and dangerous form of deceit.

A must-see exposé by the *Epoch Times*, *The Real Story of Jan 6* (Parts I and II), details the use-of-force violations committed by law enforcement that day—offering substantial proof of government entrapment. It reveals the illegal withholding—and even tampering—of exculpatory evidence:

- Official USCP text messages wiped clean
- Clear, incontrovertible proof that President Trump urged Pelosi and Bowser to deploy ten thousand National Guard troops—an offer they shamefully declined, citing "optics" over officer and citizen safety . . . yet somehow, it was all Trump's fault
- And of course, the now-infamous withholding of—wait, *how many* thousands of hours?—CCTV security footage showing exactly what transpired in and around the Capitol.

No, the public didn't see this web—or the tyrannical government spider spinning it.

But I was holding the blueprint. And as I surveyed the growing carnage of the DC coliseum, I was sickened to the core.

Sickened . . . and supercharged with fury:

"Jesus entered the Temple and began to drive out the people buying and selling . . . He knocked over the tables of the money changers and the chairs of those selling . . . and he stopped everyone from using the Temple as a marketplace. He said to them, 'The Scriptures declare, 'My Temple will be called a house of prayer for all the nations," but you have turned it into a den of thieves.'"

—Mark 11:15–17

America's national "Scriptures"—our Declaration and Constitution— declare that the "Temple" of our courts shall be a house of justice for all. But these government gangsters have turned it into a den of thieves, liars, and traitors most foul—and I was not about to sit quietly and leave their tables and chairs undisturbed.

I looked up from the plea paperwork and locked eyes with my attorneys:

"This plea deal is a lie."

I held up the pages—the government's "statement of fact" laced with fiction and distortion.

"It's not just a lie because I'd be swearing to affirm the government's false accusations when I know I'm innocent. It's worse than that. I'd be endorsing this . . . this toxic tabloid of malicious filth. I'd be helping these traitors to stab every J6er in the back—supporting their coverup as they blame the victims for their own vile crime!"

Dr. Gold cut in. "Of course it's full of lies. Anyone paying attention knows that. But that's not the point. The point is—we're dealing with a dishonest broker. DC has a one-hundred-percent conviction rate on J6! The whole thing is obviously a setup—a rigged game to persecute us and anyone who dares to speak out against the government. But there's nothing we can do right now to stop them. So you need to think about your options—and your obligations, and your future—and make a rational decision."

She wasn't wrong.

No one could argue with DC's perfect conviction rate—and the DOJ's Gestapo tactics made them far worse than a mere dishonest broker. Every lawyer, advisor, and friend I had agreed: It would be entirely rational—wise, even—to accept a plea deal . . . especially this one.

A few J6 defendants rejected the DOJ's plea "deal" and opted for a jury trial. All were convicted. Many were imprisoned. But the plea deals they turned down typically weren't much better—often still felonies with heavy prison time. They were doomed either way.

My case was different. The DOJ was so desperate to make me fold, they dangled something very compelling: a "golden parachute" plea. Facing five charges—including a twenty-year felony—they offered to erase it all and reduce the case to *a single misdemeanor.*

One charge.

Little or no prison.

Likely just home confinement and probation.

One simple signature . . . and it would all go away.

This was nearly unheard of.

And no one in their right mind would refuse that kind of deal.

. . . would they?

CHAPTER 12

CHOOSING THE FIERY FURNACE

Movies contain a special kind of magic. They have incredible power to inspire and influence by wielding humanity's greatest gift: imagination. That gift allows us to project what does not yet exist but could—a vision of potential. Still, imagination is grounded in the existential, shaped by what's already been transformed from possibility to reality.

We learn from the past to invent the future.

At the heart of it all is movement—action driven by choices—and I think that's what exhilarates us so much. I've always been drawn to that narrative tension, where imagination is tested and conflict is illustrated. But cinema's real power lies in the totality of the experience—we don't just see and hear it; we feel it with our pounding heart and resonating soul. A movie is a sensory-supercharged delivery of a story—and a story is shaped by decisive action, pulling us into a character's quest for purpose. By joining that spiritual journey of challenge and struggle, we too can be transformed. Previous heroes propel us into our own unfolding adventures—toward a destiny that might one day change history.

One such story of adversity and defiance is Mel Gibson's *The Patriot*—a favorite of mine and a fitting touchstone for this book. But beneath its self-evident title lies something deeper than politics or pageantry. It cuts to the heart of a critical question:

What does it mean to be an American?

Benjamin Martin is a patriot—who could deny it? He fought bravely in the French and Indian War, then raised seven children alone after his wife's death—instilling in them faith, discipline, and love for a free country. But when that country called him back to service under the shadow of tyranny, he was torn. He knew of Britain's mounting oppression. He also knew the cost of war. And he was still tormented by the nightmares of past atrocities.

Benjamin loved his country—but he loved his family more.

He struggled with guilt from past violence and feared his children being swept into its ugly return. Though he wished to avoid the looming war, he had raised his children to love God and honor biblical values—and his sons, cherishing the cause of liberty, were eager to join their countrymen in its defense. Caught between national duty and protecting his family, Benjamin refused to let his young boys enlist in the militia, now recruiting every able-bodied male to repel the British— the war had come to their doorstep.

You can run from evil, but you will never stop running.

Benjamin's eldest son, newly emancipated as a sovereign American citizen, understood the duty that came with it. He recognized the "only one right choice" facing him, his father, and their South Carolina countrymen.

BENJAMIN MARTIN:

Do you intend to enlist without my permission?

GABRIEL MARTIN:

Yes, I do. Father, I thought you were a man of principle.

BENJAMIN MARTIN:
When you have a family of your own, perhaps you'll understand.
GABRIEL MARTIN:
When I have a family of my own, I won't hide behind them.

If a principle yields to pain, it's no longer a virtue—just a vacant promise.

Gabriel kept his promise, enduring the horrors of war to defend family and country. From the frontlines, he wrote that he felt fortunate to serve the cause of liberty and, indeed, was willing to die for it.

The cost of that "only one right choice" was real. Death soon struck the hometown of Gabriel's beloved, Anne Howard—a brave patriot in her own right, who stood behind Gabriel's sacrifice. But after British troops captured several of her neighbors who'd joined the militia, a reprobate colonel violated English combat ethics—executing them and leaving their bodies hanging in the town square. A brutal warning to anyone feeling "patriotic."

Government gangsters go back a long way.

In response, Gabriel and Anne went to the feeble-but-still-beating heart of American resistance to tyranny: the local church, where they made their "Patriot Plea." When urging their fellow parishioners to join the cause, they encountered common excuses: piety, apathy, and fear. Anne challenged them directly, reminding them of how often they'd all spoken about the importance of freedom and religious liberty—but now, when they were needed most, would they stop at only speech?

"Is that the sort of men you are? I ask only that you act upon the beliefs of which you have so strongly spoken."

She asked only for the one thing a man can take with him when he dies, as all men must: his integrity.

Without the Uncomfortable Courage to stand by our principles, the virtues we claim die with us. They become nothing but words.

Empty. Vacant. Forgotten.

My lawyers weren't done delivering bad news. Along with a poisoned plea and a politically tainted jury pool, we learned that our "least terrible option" for a judge—Obama appointee Christopher "Casey" Cooper—wasn't just biased. He was embedded.

He had a notorious record of refusing to recuse himself from cases with glaring conflicts of interest. His government gangster rap sheet included a marriage—officiated by DOJ boss Merrick Garland— to Amy Jeffress, a fellow DOJ lawyer from the Clinton and Obama administrations. Jeffress represented disgraced FBI lawyer Lisa Page— infamous "lover" of Peter Strzok in the treasonous Crossfire Hurricane plot to sabotage a (truly) duly elected president. And now, the same corrupt network of leftist zealots had zeroed in on that president—and on me—using a fabricated "insurrection!" dragnet.

Even Lisa Page's social media featured a cozy photo with Cooper's wife. Casey clearly knew what his wife, Page, and their DOJ cronies were doing—coordinating a political purge of Trump supporters. Yet he refused to recuse himself from a single J6 case.

The law he claimed to uphold couldn't be more explicit:

"A judge **shall** [not at the judge's discretion—they must] disqualify himself in a proceeding in which his impartiality might reasonably be questioned, including if the judge has a personal bias or prejudice concerning a party . . ." — Code of Conduct for U.S. Judges.

Cooper's bias was fully exposed when he refused to recuse himself from the trial of Michael Sussman—a lawyer directly tied to his wife. Sussman had handled documents falsely accusing the Trump Organization of wrongdoing, all while lying to hide his connection to the Hillary Clinton campaign and the same seditious Crossfire Hurricane operation later investigated by Special Counsel John Durham. That investigation, predictably, was impeded by none other than . . . Casey Cooper.

If you're looking for the textbook definition of a *conflict of interest*—this is it.

Even respected legal scholar Jonathan Turley raised alarms. He noted that Cooper approved as jurors three Clinton donors, an AOC donor, and a woman whose daughter played on the same sports team as Sussman's daughter. Turley called them the worst jurors that Durham could face short of DNC staffers, adding that Cooper:

". . . narrowed the scope of evidence and of questioning. He's made a number of rulings that the prosecutors have very much objected to. And it's sort of like an obstacle course for John Durham in that sense."

Law Enforcement Today reached a similar conclusion:

"[T]he judge in the case appears to be doing all he can to get Sussman off . . . a man of integrity would have recused himself. Not Judge Christopher Cooper, however. . . . Cooper ruled that the prosecution cannot use the fact that [a text stating "I'm coming on my own—not on behalf of a client"] is a false statement in its summation of the case. *That false statement is the basis under which he is charged.*"

The fix was in.

And Cooper's marriage to DOJ insider Amy Jeffress wasn't just a bad look—it was a direct violation of the Judicial Code of Conduct:

"A judge shall disqualify himself . . . if the judge, individually or as a fiduciary, or the judge's spouse or minor child residing in the judge's household, has a financial interest in the subject matter in controversy or in a party to the proceeding, or any other interest that could be affected substantially by the outcome of the proceeding."

—Code of Conduct for United States Judges

But Cooper's Team Lunacy–tinted glasses really came into focus when he handled J6 defendants. In one case, he insisted politics had nothing to do with his sentence—while simultaneously chastising the defendant for her political views, her information sources (namely, *the President of the United States*), and even her choice of clothing.

He claimed he wasn't punishing her for political beliefs, yet said:

". . . in light of her statements for being there because 'my POTUS called me to be there,' it seems to me those facts warrant a period of probation . . . to ensure that she is free from *these sorts of influence* going forward."

He also noted, disapprovingly, that she was wearing a "QAnon" hat.

Pause for a moment to absorb just how horrifying this is: a sitting federal judge punishing an American citizen for answering the call of a sitting president—to attend a Free Speech assembly. This is . . . well, lunacy.

Cooper repeated this "black robe gaslighting" throughout his many J6 cases—mocking the First Amendment and trampling the recusal requirements spelled out in the federal judicial code. The DC court's blanket refusal to grant a change of venue for blatantly political J6 cases—a glaring necessity—erased any illusion of fairness.

And Cooper wasn't alone. The entire DC court mafia piled on, eviscerating Constitutional guarantees of equal protection and due process. These petty tyrants mocked those sacred rights, sneered at our political speech, and crushed us for daring to speak it—while claiming there was no political bias as they did so.

Utterly outrageous.

And the scariest part? Casey actually believed his own delusions. And he had the gall to accuse *me* of being delusional.

All of it pointed to a grim reality: American justice was dead—as dead as Socrates after a pint of hemlock. It was now my moment to choose: bend the knee and grasp at leniency—or stand up and face the fire.

There was no sugarcoating this poisoned apple. I'd be seared with the scarlet letter of a criminal conviction, one way or another. The Capitol trap had sprung, the iron jaws of the DOJ had slammed shut, and the games of the DC coliseum were about to begin.

And there was no doubt about the finale. The actors were all paid and staged precisely according to script: Team Lunacy's production of ***The Great American Tragedy: Attack on Our Democracy*** ™.

I could play my part as a sacrificial scapegoat in their *Patriot Purge* drama—accepting the role assigned by my government overlords and finding solace in the mild discomfort of a silly misdemeanor.

Or I could pay the full price for rebellion against the Galactic Empire of the American Fed—for daring to disrupt the perfectly laid plans of the *Artificial Aristocracy*—and find myself crushed with a major felony conviction, facing twenty-three years in federal prison. A stunning catastrophe of humiliation and ruin.

The choice couldn't have been more clear—or more consequential.

"Don't freak out just yet," my attorneys tried to reassure me. "The government's asking you to waive your speedy trial rights again—another continuance—so there's still time. You don't have to decide on the plea deal right now."

But deep down, I knew the decision had already been made.

It was made long ago—in the sunlit days of my childhood, as a kaleidoscope of dreams passed through the prism of God's promises.

This wasn't recklessness. It was faith.

Not blind belief, but something built over a lifetime—first planted by my parents, Jack and Claire, when they read these scriptures to me as a young boy:

"Hear, O Israel! The Lord our God, the Lord is one. And you shall love *Yahweh* your God with all your heart, all your soul, and all your strength. And you must commit yourselves wholeheartedly to these commands that I am giving you today. Repeat them again and again to your children. Talk about them when you are at home and when you are on the road, when you are going to bed and when you are getting up."

—Deuteronomy 6:4–7

"Then Jesus said to his disciples, 'If any of you wants to be my follower, you must give up your own way, take up your cross, and follow me. If you try to hold on to your life, you will lose it. But if you give up your life for my sake, you will save it. And what do you benefit if you gain the whole world but lose your own soul? Is anything worth more than your soul?'"

—Matthew 16:24–26

I can still hear my father's voice echoing through the house, reading that thunderous charge: "**Hear, O Israel!**"

It wasn't just a greeting—it was a commission. A calling passed from Moses to Messiah. A crescendo of divine history culminating in the greatest climax of the human drama: the life, death, and literal resurrection of Jesus Christ—the only begotten Son of *Yahweh* God.

Also called *Immanuel*—*"God with us"*—he entered our human frailty, bore our pain, and redeemed our suffering—not through comfort, but through courage.

He showed us what freedom really is—and what it costs.

He's the original patriot hero. The lead actor in the only drama that truly matters: "His-story." The history of heaven and earth and the God who made them. And in the connected calling of those scriptures—from the Torah blossoming into the Gospel—I heard, and I knew:

I had a role to play.

The amazing Technicolor dreamcoat God had woven into my life was now falling into place. The glimpses of destiny, the painful detours, the grueling preparations—they were all part of the process. A divine tailor had been at work, fitting the fabric of my story to the contours of courage He'd been building into me all along.

And now, I could see it: a divine assignment. A battlefield mission.

I'd been cast for the role of a lifetime—the chance to enact a patriot warrior in God's script for America.

What once looked like a total disaster—shipwrecked between a rock and a hard place, staring down the lesser of two evils—I began to see with Red Pill vision as something else: an opportunity.

Not a detour, but a calling. A role God had scripted just for me. Enormously difficult—but tied to His promise of victory.

It was the fulfillment of Morpheus—er, I mean Mordechai's —prophecy:

"Perhaps you were made for such a time as this."

And I remembered the foreshadowing of my dreamcoat hero, Joseph—and his astonishing response to the betrayal he endured:

"[They] intended to harm me, but God intended it all for good. He brought me to this position so I could save the lives of many people."
—Genesis 50:19–20

If we're honest with ourselves—truly, painfully honest—we have to ask: What good is courage if we abandon the cause when it gets uncomfortable? How real is our faith if we surrender it to the dictates of the federal government? What benefit is our freedom if we fail to choose righteousness and condemn evil—without which we lose both the credibility and character needed to defend the good?

The only thing necessary for evil to win is for good men to play it safe.

The truth is, no amount of pain spared is worth losing your principles—for without principles, there is only greater pain for everyone.

There is never a right time to do the wrong thing.

Choosing this fiery furnace was going to be extremely painful. But the truth was crystal clear—there was "only one right choice" to make. Still, the full weight of suffering my decision would bring was only beginning to register, sending slow shockwaves of anxiety and emotional anguish. My four-day "preview" of federal prison merely hinted at the cruelty ahead. A weaponized DOJ and poisoned judiciary were already crushing J6 defendants with shocking prison terms—five, ten, even twenty-plus years.

It was nothing short of annihilation.

I had twenty-three years and half a million dollars hanging over my head—and not just mine. The punishment would devastate my family, my work, and my future—leaving colleagues to absorb the fallout.

And that fallout was heavy.

Though I qualified for a public defender, my multi-year legal marathon—and brutal nine-day trial, stacked with the full weight of the FBI, DOJ, USCP, USSS, and countless thousands of hours of video—would require a team of additional attorneys and technical support. And that was before the inevitable appellate phase—forced by the preordained show trial every J6er was condemned to endure. Appeals could drag on for years, racking up enormous bills.

But even that didn't compare to the greater cost:

Reputation destroyed. Career canceled. Liberty . . . lost.

The agony of losing my freedom—chained like a common criminal—was already beginning to crush my spirit. It was a soul-sickness that crept in nearly two years before the cell door slammed shut.

That's why so many J6 defendants buckled under the pressure. They signed poisonous plea deals that tainted the truth and sabotaged their own innocence—deals that voided their appellate and due process rights. The DOJ then flaunted its "kill sheet" of coerced guilty pleas, feeding the media machine with propaganda:

Look—these 'insurrectionists' admitted it! They confessed to seditious, premeditated violence against Our Democracy™.

But it was a lie.

They were forced into this fraud by thugs who would've made Hitler proud—and by the excruciating silence of their countrymen.

Years earlier, Bobby and I had recorded *Silence Is a Steady Noise* with Celeste—and it became a haunting anthem for this tragedy:

Hold your breath, hear the steady silence
Wake your dead, paint your pretty eyelids
You memorize the lines you speak
You drink your poison slowly
The screaming that nobody's hearing
Our voices are noiseless
The bleeding we're constantly feeling
Our voices evade us
Melt the ice, break the bitter quiet
Name your price, sell your strength with violence
The air is choking with your stares

The words you lost condemn your prayers
And conversation kills you

I spent many hours weighing the decision—discussing it with attorneys, friends, and family. They all assured me that taking the plea deal—especially my deal—was a rational response to an impossible situation. *"No one will think less of you,"* they said, again and again. *"You're being forced by a tyrannical government to play a rigged game."*

I appreciated the sentiment, but—as you've probably realized by now—I've never been overly concerned with other people's opinions of me. And I wasn't about to start now.

Still, I prayed earnestly over what it would cost—not just for me, but for those I loved. I'll always remember those heartfelt conversations with my truest allies—patriots like Russell Stuart, Alfie Oakes, Brandon Straka, Dennis and Sue Prager, Tony Roman, Kai Waterton, Eric Metaxas, Bob and Liz McEwen, Taylor Mesplé, my pastors Rob McCoy and James and Tracy Boyd and Josie Teeters, Mike O'Fallon, Drew and Kanema Montez-Clark, Scott and Jen Stonebreaker, Tait, Lori and Phil and Lisa . . . and of course Dr. Gold, my parents, my aunt Fredricka and her family, my brothers Bobby and Michael, and my darling sisters. Each listened patiently, counseled earnestly, and loved me unconditionally.

And in those somber moments, I was reminded of who and what I'm fighting for: truth, liberty, and the people who still believe in them both. I searched my soul for the peace God promises to those who live by faith in the cross—and I found my cross, and the peace and strength to carry it.

Conversations with Dr. Gold—my co-defendant, my attorney, my boss and professional colleague, and my closest friend throughout this war—were continuous. We debated the costs, the options, the risks.

She knew how brutal this would be. And I clung to the hope she'd stand with me in rejecting the lie at trial.

I'll never forget my shock when—without warning—her defense attorney casually answered the judge during a pretrial conference: "Yes, Your Honor, Dr. Gold will accept the government's offer."

I was deeply saddened. It wasn't just her decision that hit me—but what it symbolized. Our nation had fallen so far into lawless corruption that even heroes were hamstrung. A felony meant losing her medical and legal licenses—and the nonprofit she supported with them. But what hurt me the most was the raw injustice:

Dr. Simone Gold was innocent.

By signing the plea agreement, she took on a government gag— legally forbidden to defend herself. It was a fraud, and it infuriated me. I vowed at that moment to be a spokesman for her and every J6 patriot shackled by the *Fruit of the Poisonous Plea*. This fraud was **the Greatest American Lie ever legally bankrolled**—and I was ready to flip some tables.

Dr. Gold's acceptance of the plea deal marked the beginning of my own lonely road. I didn't know any other J6 defendants who refused a single misdemeanor while facing a twenty-year felony. It simply wasn't rational.

Some called me insane.

Even my family, while supportive, feared the government's fire would consume me. But they stood by me, gracious and encouraging, as I walked the path to a fiery furnace.

Others pleaded with me to reconsider. They warned I'd be crushed by the DOJ's force, smeared beyond recognition by the media, and erased by a nation too broken and brainwashed to care.

They weren't wrong.

The odds were overwhelming that my stand would be swallowed in silence, my sacrifice ignored, my name forgotten. Most likely, my reward for defying the government would be personal anguish, public ridicule, and financial ruin. I had to justify my choice knowing I'd be discredited and discarded—just more meaningless ash spewed from the federal furnace . . .

. . . but man's search for meaning, even in the ashes of suffering, is written into his design from the beginning. And in that search, we're able to find meaning for the middle—and hope for the end.

With continued prayer—and heartfelt explanations to my worried friends—I stood firm in rejecting the plea and its promise of leniency. I chose instead the fiery furnace of felony conviction and ominous imprisonment.

"I am one hundred percent certain—before God and the plain meaning of the law—that I am innocent. The government's plea is a poisonous lie. To sign it would be to bear false witness against myself and my neighbor—a direct violation of God's Ninth Commandment. I cannot—I will not—swear to a lie. And I will never bend the knee to corruption and tyranny. I now join my Christian brother and Founding Father Patrick Henry in declaring, 'Give me liberty—and honesty—or give me death!'"

I explained in media interviews that I would've rejected this plea even under threat of the death penalty. I meant it. If my savior gave his life in obedience, how could I do any less? I also shared the biblical story that inspired my resolve: the original fiery furnace.

Daniel, of *Lions' Den* fame, and his three Jewish brothers were political hostages of a tyrannical regime. After God gave Daniel the supernatural ability to "see" and interpret the king's dream—which the king himself could not remember—Daniel and his comrades were promoted to high political office. But later, when King Nebuchadnezzar built a golden statue and demanded all people bow to it—regardless of their religious beliefs—Shadrach, Meshach, and Abednego refused.

"The God we serve is able to save us," they declared. "But even if He doesn't, we will never serve your gods or worship your statue."

Enraged, the king ordered the furnace heated seven times hotter and had them thrown in. The flames were so intense they killed the soldiers who carried them. But when the king looked inside, he saw four men walking unharmed in the fire—"and the fourth looks like a son of the gods!"

Nebuchadnezzar called them out, and not a hair on their heads was singed—they didn't even smell like smoke. Then the king declared,

"Praise be to the God of Shadrach, Meshach, and Abednego! They defied the king's command and were willing to die rather than serve any god but Yahweh. There is no other god who can rescue like this."

What struck me the most in this epic (true!) story wasn't just the miracle—it was their clarity. They saw the fire coming. They expected pain. But no amount of suffering could stop them from doing the right thing.

That is the definition of Uncomfortable Courage.

It was the same courage and sacrifice God had commanded of Joseph, Joshua, Gideon, David, Daniel—and now, of me. This was the cross Christ had called me to carry.

This was the life he called me to lay down.

And now, all that remained was to see if God would prove true in His promise to save it.

CHAPTER 13

GUILTY UNTIL PROVEN CONVICTED

The Obama-Biden regime's *Department of Jihad* continued its crusade, unleashing violence and terror on an entire swath of American citizens. Many were ambushed in their homes by militarized SWAT raids of shocking brutality. They even rolled out tank-like armored assault vehicles in suburban neighborhoods—a grotesque show of force revealed in the film *Capitol Punishment*, along with other disturbing abuses.

The results were devastating. Terrified children. Lifelong trauma. Families torn apart. Miscarriages. Suicides. Agents often timed the raids for when young children were home—ensuring maximum terror. In a heinous example I later documented on social media, a nonviolent defendant had already peacefully surrendered. But *after* his arrest, the FBI launched a heavily armed raid on his family—aiming loaded weapons into baby cribs. Yes, really.

These people are not the good guys.

That kind of malice—amplified by Lunacy Media slander—delivered a guilty verdict before the bloody ink of their scarlet letter had even dried, and long before a single charge was adjudicated. Working-class Americans—parents, veterans, students, grandparents—had their lives dismantled in a torrent of defamation, termination, and cancellation.

Jobs and scholarships vanished. Careers and reputations were destroyed. Savings and inheritances evaporated. Family homes were lost.

Decent, patriotic citizens were ravaged by public hatred and social isolation. Many endured stalking by organized radicals, severe depression, and acute psychological distress. They were stripped of banking, digital services, social media, mortgages, professional licenses, air travel, firearms—even eligibility for political office or public service. They suffered the ruin of marriages, family ties, and all manner of relationships and community standing.

It was a complete destruction of the American dream—before even a shred of due process was considered.

Convictions, and the carnage they caused, were the precise aim of this jihad against "MAGA Republicans"—and the *Artificial Aristocracy* made sure the DOJ nailed every target.

Their hit list would eventually surpass 1,500 victims.

Each new atrocity sickened and infuriated me. It also revealed a rapidly advancing neo-Marxist mechanism: *balkanization*—the fragmentation of a nation into smaller, hostile groups. This divide-and-conquer scheme is fueled by propaganda and strategic violence, conditioning citizens to hate and dehumanize entire categories of people. Echoing Hitler's march to marginalize and then demonize the Jews, the Biden-Garland regime was erasing due process from the "parchment barrier" of the Constitution, orchestrating a violent fracturing of the Republic into the Divided States of America. It started with J6 defendants. Then came MAGA supporters more broadly. But it was always designed to expand—until it targeted #YouNext.

Their goal: to eradicate all resistance to *the Power*—the DC Swamp's ruling class.

My heart sank at the news that my friend Brandon Straka had been hit with a violent FBI raid and jailed for several days. Upon release, he discovered that not only had his life and career been upended, but his national nonprofit had been digitally assassinated. The entire #WalkAway campaign—half a million Americans sharing testimonies of breaking free from Lunacy Media lies and "walking away" from the Democrat Party— was wiped from the internet. A digital-age book burning.

Brandon was horrified to learn the DOJ was now threatening him with not one but *three* J6 felonies—*and he never even entered the building*. His "crime," as an independent journalist, was standing outside the east entrance, filming a nonviolent crowd for eight minutes while reporting on their bizarre entry into the Capitol.

"Freedom of the Press" was now dead. Brandon proved it—just another casualty of this regime's jihad against anyone daring to exercise liberty in a dissident direction. The collateral damage would devastate every aspect of his life, as it had mine—and nearly every victim of the J6 "Fedsurrection" sting. That devastation continues, shamefully, to this day.

Most Americans still can't fathom the scale of the damage.

We began raising alarm during interviews and events, amplifying the hashtags #WeAreJ6 and #YouNext to spotlight the danger of ignoring this discrimination and the abuse of due process. Balkanized hatred and violence always spread—and no amount of protected status or performative compliance will shield you forever.

Hatred has no friends.

Brandon and I began connecting regularly, commiserating over the mounting abuse and government oppression J6ers were suffering. Meanwhile, most of the country seemed to ignore it. One day, amid surging media defamation and social media bullying, he alerted me to a new horror: the DOJ had published a list of every J6 defendant, including every *potential* criminal charge—*even those later dropped* during the years-long pretrial process.

It was a grotesque abuse of power—essentially a political sex offender registry for J6ers.

A permanent scarlet letter.

This public hit list caused lasting damage long before any evidence was reviewed or any defense was allowed. And the *Artificial Aristocracy* made sure it stuck. Big Tech boosted the registry in search results—instantly condemning J6ers in the court of public opinion and sentencing us to ridicule, rejection, and ruin.

And this was just one of many weaponized "lists" used by partisan bureaucrats to persecute J6 defendants. We were added to terrorist watch lists and federal tracking systems—some even shared with foreign nations, with terrifying implications. These abuses restricted our freedom of movement—and even endangered our lives during routine traffic stops.

Due process was now dead, too—and the hope of any disfavored citizen finding justice in America died with it.

The spring of 2022 brought even more evidence of the death of due process: Dr. Gold's "plea deal" sentencing . . . at the hands of Casey Cooper.

Setting aside the obvious—that she was a scheduled speaker at a permitted event and did nothing violent or malicious—it's highly unusual to impose prison time for a misdemeanor. That's the point of the category: lesser offenses with minimal harm, typically addressed through fines (which, ethically, should go to the victim) or community service to repay society.

Incarceration, even short-term, is a damaging blow to someone's life—often doing more harm than good—and it does nothing to help the victim heal. In fact, their taxes fund it, adding insult to their injury. Prison sentences are simply inappropriate for misdemeanors—especially for nonviolent political protest infractions. (To be blunt, prison itself is mostly unethical and counterproductive—government gangsters notably excepted. But we'll get to that later.)

So we looked into Casey's history with misdemeanor sentencing—particularly for political protests—and the pattern was clear: He almost never imposed jail time. Obviously.

His harshest sentence? Twenty-one days for a repeat violent offender. Casey had never—not once—sentenced a nonviolent, first-time misdemeanor defendant to a single day in prison.

Crickets

This seemed about right—assuming the defendant was actually guilty. But notably, Casey's leniency had applied to protesters on the left. So what would the "honorable" Christopher J. Cooper deem appropriate for a nonviolent protester—er, doctor/lawyer and permitted speaker—on the right?

Unsurprisingly—and yet still an appalling shock—his sentence, and his rhetoric in delivering it, revealed blatant prejudice. Dr. Gold first gave an allocution, gracefully expressing sorrow for anyone harmed and regret for her unwitting presence in the disturbance that day. Her former Stanford classmate then excoriated her for "failing to express remorse"—which she had done just moments earlier. He justified his condescending remarks with one of the most persistent lies surrounding J6—debunked within days, yet still endlessly repeated by the media: the claim that J6 protesters killed five police officers.

"What I haven't heard [from the defendant] is about the five people [clearly implying officers] who died that day . . . because of the mob."

This diabolical falsehood—invented as the linchpin of their *deadly insurrection*" narrative—was unequivocally (and medically) disproven long before this hearing: **not a single officer died on, or from, J6**.

Yet, Cooper used that lie to justify his heavy hand against a woman from his past who played no part in "the mob's" alleged offenses—other than being surrounded and entrapped by it. Even worse, his slanderous proclamation from the bench—broadcast live to the world—lent judicial weight to the ongoing cover-up of a darker truth: not only were no officers killed on J6 . . . the government was directly responsible for killing several unarmed protesters:

1. Ashli Babbitt—a petite military veteran, shot by USCP Officer Michael Byrd as she attempted to deter a provocateur. Byrd, with a known history of reckless firearm use, gave no warning and left Babbitt no chance to avoid his fatal bullet—violating use-of-force protocols. He faced no disciplinary action.

2. Rosanne Boyland—bludgeoned *on camera* with a walking staff by DC Metro Police Officer Lila Morris, who was later honored with a taxpayer-funded VIP Super Bowl appearance.

3. Kevin Greeson—died of heart failure during the protest—possibly triggered by flash-bang grenades, which police fired into the crowd.

4. Benjamin Phillips—died of a stroke under similar circumstances as Greeson, with medics failing to render aid.

The dishonesty got worse. Mere moments after attacking Dr. Gold's political convictions, he insisted—without irony—that "you aren't being targeted for your political beliefs."

It was textbook doublespeak, carrying tones of "no one is above the law."

"[Your] organization is leaving people with the misimpression that this is a political prosecution or that it's about free speech. **It ain't about free speech.** January sixth was about a lot of things, but it wasn't about free speech or COVID vaccinations . . . the only reason you are here is where and when and how you chose to express your views . . ."

This was judicial gaslighting of the highest order. For a judge to declare that a political protest was somehow not about politics—or speech—is absurd on its face. More striking, though, was the fact that Cooper brazenly declared, with black robe divinity, that the sole purpose of January 6—apparently for every one of the million citizens present—was whatever *he* decreed it to be . . . because that's what gods and gangsters do.

And with that, this emperor of the DC coliseum turned his thumb down and decreed the ostensibly First Amendment-protected speech of Dr. Gold to be officially disapproved—and disallowed.

"I find it unseemly that your organization is raising hundreds of thousands of dollars for its operations, including your salary, by mischaracterizing what this proceeding is all about. People need to know this is not acceptable."

In case you missed the fascist sledgehammer shattering the First Amendment in real time, Casey Cooper dropped all pretense of "Our Democracy™" and issued a chilling threat to anyone who might dare to disparage his coliseum—er, courtroom.

He literally declared it unacceptable to criticize the government!

When he announced the sentence, my blood boiled. This was an innocent woman, not to mention a legitimate American hero—and both the smugness and severity of Cooper's retaliation were appalling:

Sixty days in federal prison—and twelve months of cruel, senseless "supervised release"—for a single misdemeanor.

We were horrified. I was sickened by the dishonesty, helpless to stop it, and furious at the flagrant abuse of power. But I wasn't surprised—not in the slightest.

This is the war. We know the opposing forces—we know the objectives. And Team Lunacy had just proven their twisted point: guilt isn't proven in the Divided States of America.

It is purchased—with power.

In other words . . . it's a control thing.

The entire Frontline Doctors team was still reeling as we left the E. Barrett Prettyman courthouse, retreating from enemy territory—our own capital—and returning to our Alexandria hotel in stunned silence. As soon as the elevator doors opened on our floor, Dr. Gold pulled me aside.

"I have to tell you something."

"I can't believe that scumbag can just lie, on the record, in open court!" I snapped, still fuming at Cooper's arrogant outburst.

"No, wait—listen," she said urgently. "There's something you don't know about Casey. Nobody knows. He didn't just go to Stanford with me. He tried to date me."

My eyes—and my stomach—flipped.

"Well, not just tried. He actually did. We went out a couple times, casually. It was pleasant—I didn't mind. But then he asked me on a formal date off campus, and I declined. He just wasn't for me. I found him . . . a bit soulless, actually."

"What?! Are you serious right now?"

As serious as the heart attack I nearly gave myself as my mind raced in shock—horrified by the obvious implications.

"Yeah, I was wondering why he spun himself into such hysterics. I could actually feel the hatred emanating from him as he got more and more belligerent."

"Well, uh, yeah! You think? That *might* be the reaction of a man scorned—or even slightly miffed—by a female classmate who now happens to be standing in his black-robed, Trump-hating strike zone!"

We both grimaced.

"Wait—how have you never told me this? You know I'm gonna have to file a motion for recusal, right? This is totally insane."

"Yeah, uh, I've just never mentioned it to anybody. That was years ago, and it didn't seem like any kind of issue at the time. It wasn't unpleasant; we just went our separate ways. I actually thought it might predispose him to be more impartial toward me."

"Oh my God . . ." I groaned, running a hand through my now-prematurely graying hair. My brain hurt. "You're absolutely sure you never told anyone? At school, or your mom? Because I have to put this on the record—no chance I'm just going to trial with Casey and ignoring this."

"Yeah, I agree—I'll have to sign an affidavit. He'll deny it, of course—but it absolutely happened. Exactly as I told you."

It was easy math to calculate the chances that the "honorable" Christopher J. Cooper had enough honor to respect his ex-classmate's sincere claim—even if he had genuinely forgotten about it.

Zero.

But I would not stoop to his level. While Dr. Gold prepared her statement, I made sure we kept the matter private until Casey had a chance to do the honorable thing.

I briefed my lead attorney, who agreed immediately this warranted recusal. He discreetly alerted the court, requesting a sealed hearing—to protect Cooper's privacy. Predictably, Casey balked—as he did for virtually everything my lawyer requested. After a week passed with no resolution, the story began to leak. Julie Kelly, an actual journalist, drew attention to the story on Twitter.

This was a shocking story of the DC judge—assigned to both myself and my codefendant—being credibly accused of romantic involvement with my codefendant, Simone Gold.

Under the scrutiny of the press, Casey suddenly reversed course and demanded an emergency hearing. My attorney respectfully pointed out that he had done everything in his limited power to prevent this "unfortunate incident," but was ultimately stonewalled by "Your Honor's own Court." Mr. Brennwald then announced we would submit a motion for recusal.

Julie Kelly 🇺🇸 ✓
@julie_kelly2

Dr. Simone Gold send me this statement last night related to the judge in her case.

She reported to prison today:

This did not mean anything to me. I believed he would have recused himself as we knew each other in law school.

4. I did go to school with a "Casey" (Cooper), Stanford University Law School class of 1993. Stanford is a very small law school, my recollection is that there were ~150 students per graduating class.

5. Casey and I had several social interactions. There are two that stand out. One was one time when we walked/talked for some time (perhaps two hours) and got some food. I believe this was second half of first year. My recollection was we walked from the Law School to a common area (on campus). I don't recall what we ate etc. I recall general conversation – that he was from the south, that he had gone to Yale, that he was ambitious. The conversation was pleasant. My impression was that he was cute and that he thought similarly of me. We had other brief "hello how are you" pleasantries. The other interaction that stood out was a week, perhaps two weeks later. This was in the (outside) courtyard of the Law School and we were just talking. After about 10-15 minutes Casey asked me out again, this time a formal invitation to a dinner date, following our prior less formal interactions. This I declined. Just because I wasn't interested.

6. I did not think of this for many years. Then I was presented with Judge Christopher Cooper as my Judge at my first zoom hearing. I had no doubt he was going to recuse himself. When he did *not* recuse himself, I was really surprised and had to quickly decide what to do. I was not next to my attorneys, and it was quick. I decided that if he did not recuse himself it was probably to my advantage and at worst, neutral for me.

nation. His fury and continuous reference and reliance on matters that were not relevant was bizarre.

9. Second, while the Judge was holding in his hands one letter and looking on his monitor at another letter, confirming what my lawyer was saying – that my medical license was being threatened by the government - the Judge literally said "I do not believe her licenses are under threat." Literally while holding the letters containing words directly threatening my license – these are the words he said. It was bizarre. Like he was so biased he could not think properly.

10. Third, and perhaps most telling, the Judge stated a factually untrue but flagrantly revealing prejudicial comment. He stated that I "showed no remorse for the five people who died that day." This statement is well documented to be false, it is well known to be a talking point of a certain political bias, and it is irrelevant to me. It was bizarre.

11. Fourth example, in addition to the Judge's words are his actions. The sentence the Judge handed down was extreme. While he was careful to stay within the guidelines, even the most cursory review supports the extremity of his sentence. I have never been involved in the criminal justice system, there is no allegation of violence past, present, or future, this was a sentencing for a first-time misdemeanor trespass, I am 55+ female, and I have spent my entire life working for the most downtrodden members of society as an emergency physician in the inner city. I have two children and a busy medical practice. All of the variables that the government suggested be considered in my case: were negative. As I am the lowest possible risk that exists.

10:45 AM · Jul 26, 2022

Spoiler alert: Casey denied it within twenty-four hours, accusing *me* of "gamesmanship."

Unreal.

What—am I supposed to pretend there isn't a glaring conflict of interest? My judge was now embroiled in a public "he said-she said" with my co-defendant, with whom he'd shared college classes—and only they know what else. He then slandered her with politicized smears and outright lies, and crushed her—a fellow Stanford attorney with a spotless record, now coerced into a bogus trespass misdemeanor—with sixty days in federal prison.

And I'm the one playing games?

This was madness. But then again, madness is exactly what happens when you give judges a lifetime appointment with nearly unlimited power and total immunity from accountability.

Another spoiler alert: "Our Democracy™" cannot survive the rule of such deranged demigods.

And so, the sadistic course was set.

I was no longer presumed innocent but propagandized as guilty— until I was purchased to be convicted. And the power broker settling the transaction was my co-defendant's college classmate and miffed wannabe boyfriend.

If you tried to invent a more absurd tale, I don't know what it would be.

Cooper now forced my Soviet-lite show trial onto the calendar for September 19, 2022, after a year and a half of DOJ lawfare—including the concealment of a scandalous trove of Brady-violating exculpatory evidence. But before tackling trial prep, I saw an opening for a Red Pill counterattack.

Enemy strikes carry energy—that's why they hurt. The key is to prepare with discipline and vision . . . and redirect that energy into a positive counterstrike.

So we struck.

With Casey's "dating Dr. Gold" conflict and his vindictive sentence now public, I wrote and directed a short film exposing the lies, political bias, and constitutional violations in Cooper's courtroom. We launched the #FreeDrGold campaign across social media.

Our strike hit the target.

Millions of views in days ignited national outrage. Grassroots support surged. Once again, Frontline Doctors stood as David against the Deep State Goliath.

Brandon, Dr. Gold, and I—along with Derrick Evans, a former West Virginia legislator—expanded our mission to expose the insurrection hoax and its devastating consequences. We hammered the warning: #YouNext—and later launched WeAreJ6.com, focused on Restorative Justice through victim recovery and government accountability.

After Casey's retaliation against Dr. Gold—and with me now squarely in his September sights—my attorneys and PR advisors urged caution. They warned that a petty, politicized judge like Cooper posed a real threat . . . and could easily strike me with weaponized power. The parchment barrier of the First Amendment had long since been shredded by Cooper and his ilk in the D.C. Swamp—and I was now swimming with sharks.

I understood their concern. I did exercise discretion—deflecting salacious inquiries about my judge and showing deference to the Court. But "Maverick" was more than a moniker. Toppling a government bully of this magnitude required both uncomfortable and unconventional courage—and I wasn't going to let this belligerent Philistine mock justice while I sat in "conservative silence."

Patriots, hear me:

SILENCE IS NO LONGER AN OPTION.

It never really was. And each time you choose the comfort of silence in the echo of a Goliath insult, you deepen a courage deficit that will one day implode beneath you.

If you don't consider yourself a patriot, you may want to start claiming citizenship in a different country—because this one will surely be taken from you.

We forged ahead, often running on fumes, juggling nonstop media,

J6 advocacy, and our Frontline Doctors and GoldCare mission—while bracing for two incoming storms: Dr. Gold's looming imprisonment, and my own J6 show trial in the DC coliseum.

But as if that weren't enough—as if God's ironic sense of humor hadn't already echoed Joseph's drama into this political intrigue—a third storm began to brew . . .

A betrayal neither of us could've imagined.

Not even now.

"Preparing for prison"—whether for yourself or someone you love—is like bracing for a car crash you can see coming but you can't stop. It's ominous. Surreal at first—until it suddenly becomes all too real—the dread builds slowly, a throbbing anxiety that drains your energy and makes the now-fleeting days before imprisonment feel dim and cold. These are desolate moments of invisible suffering—and they call for an anchor in the storm.

> "Dear brothers, when trials of any kind come your way, consider it an opportunity for great joy. For you know that when your faith is tested, your perseverance has a chance to grow. So let it grow, for when your endurance is fully developed, you will be perfect and complete."
>
> —James 1:2–4

> ". . . because of what Jesus has done . . . because of our faith . . . We can rejoice when we run into problems and trials, for we know that they help us develop endurance. And endurance develops strength of character, and character strengthens our confident hope of salvation. And this hope will not lead to disappointment."
>
> —Romans 5:1–5

These verses reveal a "Trial Theory" sequence:

TRIALS → TESTED FAITH → ENDURANCE → CHARACTER → VICTORY

Also note: character = virtue = the key to proper control.

The paradox here is that this process is ignited by *joy*. Not as a feeling, but as a chosen virtue: an intentional response rooted in gratitude for the foundational truth—that God is good, and God is ultimately in control of both the beginning and the glorious end.

It wasn't easy. We had to extend grace to one another in painful places. But we also took practical steps to prepare spiritually. Our Frontline Doctors team fostered encouragement and faith. We read Scripture often. We held national Zoom prayer meetings. We hosted "Shabbat" dinners—Judeo-Christian Sabbath rest—for reflection and conversation with fellow patriots. These became our rituals of strength as the storm arrived.

Dr. Gold answered the call with grace and grit—self-surrendering two months of her life to the Obama-Biden regime's Bureau of Prisons with calm resolve. Dropping your best friend off at prison is something you never forget. And while the pain of separation cut deep, the resolve to stand even stronger ran deeper.

Each time she called, her voice carried that timbre of irrepressible cheerfulness—it always surprised me and made me smile inside. The prison phone would cut off at seven minutes—but those calls brought a spark to a dark time of strange sadness.

God seemed to use His peculiar irony in cheering me up, with a gift Team Lunacy surely meant for evil—but I grinned with glee at flipping it for good. Don't they know that all publicity is good publicity? *Rolling Stone* magazine published a feature on me, detailing my Gucci-glamorous "insurrection!" exploits along with my fashion modeling and Hollywood acting bona fides—presumably aiming to defame me by dubbing me *MAGA Zoolander.*

Honestly? It was fabulous. A moniker of infamy and patriotic flair.

I couldn't have chosen a better "patriot character" nickname myself.

John Strand is MAGA Zoolander—bringing red, white, and blue steel to the protest runway. "I'm just really, really, ridiculously patriotic."

Oh yeah—I can work with this.

"Hey, Mom! Look—I finally made it into *Rolling Stone!*"

Seriously, though: I spent years busting my butt—and my heart— trying to get my band Celeste in that magazine, when all I had to do was lead an insurrection?!

Dude. I gotta call Bobby back . . .

Glimmers of clarity began piercing the fog of J6 propaganda, as independent media exposed a disturbing patchwork of government culpability. Joe Hanneman, Joshua Phillip, and the *Epoch Times* released their documentary *The Real Story of Jan 6*, revealing the full scope of police misconduct I had witnessed firsthand. The film's extensive footage showed officers infiltrating, provoking, and assaulting nonviolent protesters. It was nothing short of shocking.

This was the "smoking gun," quite literally.

This video evidence was analyzed by a veteran expert in federal "use of force" protocols. These mandatory law enforcement standards were repeatedly and flagrantly violated by USCP and MPD. Even without factoring in evidence of advance planning, the bird's-eye view was chilling: the government, without lawful cause or warning, attacked a predominantly peaceful, unarmed, and unsuspecting crowd—poking, prodding, rubber-bulleting, bludgeoning, and grenading them into a riot.

Exactly as I've attested since the day I was struck by it.

As for the nuclear defamation weapon of "insurrection!" even legacy outlets like Reuters, the *Wall Street Journal*, and the *Washington Examiner* confirmed it was media-driven hyperbole. One headline read: "FBI confirms there was no insurrection on J6." A former senior law enforcement official familiar with the FBI's investigation stated,

"There was no grand scheme with Roger Stone and Alex Jones and all of these people to storm the Capitol and take hostages."

That much was laughably obvious to anyone not foolish enough to fall for a hoaxed government takeover by a ragtag parade of civilians without any guns. What was less obvious—until it wasn't—was the role of clandestine operatives under federal influence or control.

Numerous eyewitnesses reported suspicious individuals swapping MAGA accessories for tactical assault gear—then initiating break-ins and violence. These accounts were soon corroborated by video footage—and ultimately confirmed by the government itself, when a federal prosecutor admitted in court filings that at least forty undercover "agent provocateurs" were present. Their term, not mine—and by definition, agents who incited criminal violence.

To be clear: The government was the real criminal of January 6.

More confirmation came from the House Oversight Committee. Congressman Clay Higgins testified that at least *two hundred* government operatives were involved, stating, "I've seen video of Metro Police going into a room dressed in uniform, coming out dressed as Trump supporters." Other USCP security footage provided even more exculpatory evidence of FBI coordination behind the chaos. This included active FBI agent and former FBI-USCP liaison John D. Guandolo, who finally said the quiet part out loud:

"There was an insurrection and revolution, and it was not done by the [J6ers] but by senior government officials of the U.S. government."

In other words—by the guys with the guns.

These revelations formed a growing pile of damning evidence that pointed to an inescapable conclusion: What really happened on J6 was a *Fedsurrection*—an entrapment fraud. It was America's Reichstag Fire—a heinous crime committed by *the Power* against *the People*.

But just like the "The Big Lie" cover-up of the rigged 2020 election, the "insurrection!" concrete had already been cast. The stage was set for my J6 show trial—political theater for the Trump-hating masses in the

DC coliseum. The script had been pre-written and nationally broadcast by Nancy Pelosi's "Select Subcommittee," a partisan circus masquerading as a congressional investigation. They even *illegally destroyed* evidence to cover their tracks. Which just happens to violate 18 U.S.C. § 1512 . . . the exact twenty-year prison felony they charged *me* with.

Irony alert?

Those hearings were sensationalized by a taxpayer-funded Hollywood production crew, complete with dubbed-in battle sounds and panicked screams. Broadcast across primetime networks, the entire nation was emotionally hijacked by a contrived horror show—leaving no doubt about the fate of those "MAGA extremists": they were traitors to be crushed without mercy in defense of "Our Democracy™."

The Greatest American Lie Ever Sold was flying off the shelves at media outlets everywhere.

This was *Justice Entertainment*, and I understood the script.

I knew the score.

I knew who the referees worked for.

And I knew the role—and the fate—assigned to me by the state.

The climax of this spectacle, staged for bloodthirsty crowds at the games of the coliseum, was never in doubt. Only the scale of the drama and bloodshed remained to be seen.

Still, I was determined to face their rigged game with honor, marching to the beat of my own drum—and I set the tone early with a firm constitutional stand:

I refused to emasculate myself with a mask in Casey's coliseum.

The DC courts, clinging to lunacy as the rest of the federal judiciary moved on, were still enforcing sinister mask mandates—months after the world had abandoned that senseless stupidity. Judge Cooper, predictably hypocritical, kept imposing this demeaning absurdity on everyone . . . except himself, of course.

Gods and gangsters, you know.

Let's quickly dispense with the charade—public masking was a total farce. Anyone who bought this lie beyond the first "15 days to flatten all common sense" was dangerously naive. For fifty years, consistent scientific studies concluded that masks don't meaningfully stop respiratory viruses—but that consensus suddenly vanished with the arrival of the Chinese Coronavirus "plandemic."

Timing, as they say, is everything.

Fifty years of science don't just evaporate in fifty seconds of media panic—but honesty and common sense sure did.

Take the vaunted N-95 mask: it's rated to block up to 95 percent of airborne particles 0.3 microns or larger. Sounds impressive—until you realize a SARS-CoV-2 particle is only 0.1 microns. That's about 1/200th the width of a human hair. In other words, you'd have better luck stopping mosquitoes with a chain-link fence . . . or expecting a swimsuit to keep you dry while swimming. So why the global push and sustained propaganda to sell this lie?

Once again, our recurring theme is "unmasked."

Yes, it's definitely a control thing.

Judge Cooper no doubt relished wielding such petty control—but I had entered this political and legal gauntlet by defying mask tyranny on First Amendment grounds, and I wasn't about to surrender that principle now. I retained a constitutional attorney and filed a motion challenging his violation of my rights—making clear I was prepared to take the fight to the Supreme Court.

I get the feeling he realized I meant it.

In a self-serving moment of insight—because while Casey Cooper may be morally bankrupt, he's not stupid—he quietly "adjusted" his rule to allow my free-faced entry into his coliseum.

. . . and now the J6 games could finally begin.

CHAPTER 14

COLISEUM SHOWDOWN

A massive concrete stadium looms over the city skyline—a man-made volcano, jaws gaping like a colossal beast poised to swallow the world. Inside, waves of bloodthirsty citizens stomp feverishly, making the arena pulsate with a ground-shaking demand for a thumb's-down from the emperor—the cue for the main event:

The slaughter of a despised Christian—sacrificed for the pleasure of the mob.

"The Games" of ancient Rome were justified by the pretense of serving "justice" to "criminals"—but they were barbaric spectacles of hate-fetish entertainment.

The classic Hollywood showcase is *Gladiator*, in which Russell Crowe suffers a common cruelty of those rigged games: prisoners often entered the arena already wounded—literally stabbed in the back—to ensure a fatal, crowd-pleasing finale.

There was no Academy Award in my case—but I did sustain a treacherous wound on my way to the gladiatorial games of the E. Barrett Prettyman courthouse-coliseum.

A member of the Frontline Doctors team—featured in *Don't Have to Die*, our J6 expose short film—used the cunning of a grubby Reno lawyer to worm his way into control of the nonprofit while Dr. Gold was in prison. He looked me in the eye over beers, assuring me he "had my back" as I prepared for my political lynching. He pledged full support for my trial—while masking his sabotage in professed loyalty to Dr. Gold, using it to justify his phony "investigation" into alleged organizational "discrepancies."

Days later, the knife struck.

I was blindsided with hostile messages—slanderous lies about my work and character. Then came a terse notice of termination, followed by threats of further retaliation. It left me reeling, stunned.

Given everything I'd endured—and everything I was about to face—the betrayal was brutal. I'd suffered for the civil right cause, sacrificed for this mission, and stood by the organization through every storm. Now I was cast out.

The Reno lawyer played it perfectly. With Dr. Gold behind bars, he used attorney-client privilege to cut me off. He went to visit her alone and spun a web of lies, convincing her I was the traitor. I couldn't get through to explain the coup taking place. "COVID protocols," they said.

While I was locked out, he twisted the knife.

My job—gone. My reputation—smeared. My future—hanging on by a thread.

I'll never forget the lifelines that held. My pastor, Rob McCoy. My friend, Mike O'Fallon. My father. Their wisdom and strength kept me from drowning.

Weeks later, when Dr. Gold returned, the truth began to surface. We uncovered a trail of sabotage. The lies. The manipulation. The theft.

It was a full-blown hostile takeover.

The story is documented in the film I wrote and directed, *Always Under Fire*, and it's a somber tale. We're still repairing the damage. The nonprofit lost millions in the course of defamation and hostile litigation that lingers to this day. And it took time to heal frayed nerves and rebuild trust, shaken by the betrayal of a self-proclaimed "patriot" who sold his soul for the false promise of power and prestige.

". . . for what does it benefit a man to gain the whole world but lose his own soul?"

There was a moment in that storm where I felt I had lost the whole world—and my soul along with it. But it was a lie. A "dream blackout." A tactical illusion from the enemy to break my will. It almost worked.

Then I woke up.

"For I know the plans I have for you . . . plans to prosper and not to harm . . . to give you a future and a hope."

That truth was the glitch in the Matrix. The reset.

The pain didn't vanish. The road ahead was still long with struggle and suffering. But I knew hope was real—that despair was part of the deception. I refused to surrender my courage. I refused to accept defeat. With Red Pill vision—choosing faith in God's Word—there's no darkness that can hold you down.

Not now. Not ever.

We regrouped from the corporate sabotage and focused on the fiery furnace ahead. Hundreds of hours spent in preparation over the last eighteen months—research, legal meetings, evidence review, document drafting, mock trial runs—now funneled into the final push. My trial attorney was a seasoned DC defense lawyer and a self-described "centrist, moderate Democrat."

An oxymoron these days—but sincere in his case.

He didn't yet grasp the full scope of J6 corruption, but as he saw the evidence, he came to believe in my innocence. He agreed I didn't belong in a courtroom, let alone in a prison. But he couldn't promise acquittal. I assured him an acquittal would never fit the script . . . not in this scene, anyway. Still, we committed to fight for truth and justice—preserving the record for every avenue of appeal. And the government would pave many.

At last, the slow-motion freight train of criminal prosecution had arrived. The eighteen-month clock—wound up by "that other fateful day"—had ticked all the way down to zero.

It was time to face the music.

September 19, 2022, arrived with all the fanfare of a Babylonian tyrant's golden statue festival. The *Rolling Stone*-proclaimed "MAGA Zoolander"—a Hollywood model/actor/insurrectionist—was now on trial for high crimes and MAGA misdemeanors. I had poured everything into reaching this point: constant prayer, countless hours of preparation, and thousands of miles traveled to raise up a Remnant of resistance. This was it—my stand in the lions' den of weaponized government tyranny.

My defense team—four legal warriors there in the DC coliseum—was reinforced by attorneys in Florida and Louisiana. They set up a twenty-four-hour war room in our hotel sanctuary in nearby Alexandria, Virginia—the state of America's first colony, where the experiment in liberty and justice began. Now, it was being tested to the breaking point. I felt the strain, as though justice itself was strapped across my soul—now the shackles binding me as wild beasts of hypocrisy and hatred tore me apart. It was the coliseum showdown to appease the angry mob . . . a mob deceived to believe I was the villain in the fiction they'd been sold.

My collision with American corruption was here.

JURY OF YOUR FEARS

TRIAL DAY 1 | SEPTEMBER 19, 2022

The first day was jury selection—and the last day with even a shred of pretense at impartiality. It was a living caricature of gaslighting and absurdity. I was expecting this—after all, I'd spent eighteen months warning that DC's partisanship had made a mockery of equal justice.

And yet, witnessing that massacre of the Sixth Amendment in Casey's coliseum still shocked me—at times, it was outright parody.

Later, when describing the madness of it all, I realized my trial was actually "reality TV" entertainment. DC residents packed the front rows like crazed fans on a Hollywood set, jockeying for the chance to become a featured extra—eager for their five minutes of fame in the glare of the gladiatorial games.

I sat there in silent horror, transfixed, as a string of dramatic performances unfolded: trembling voices, weeping eyes, outbursts of anger. Each one left little doubt: These jurors believed their home had been "violated" by a deadly attack on "Our Democracy™"—and I was the hated MAGA zealot guilty of joining—no, leading—an insurrection.

The government gangsters directing this drama made clear how they'd preserve the charade of justice for the cameras. First, Emperor Casey declared that "obviously everyone" had been steeped in the media's J6 hysteria—so this inescapable bias was simply "waved off" by imperial decree. Then prosecutor Ms. Ayers-Perez followed up each contestant's performance with her own scripted line:

"Can you 'forget' what you've seen 24/7 in the media for the last year and a half—including the horror movie show trials of the January 6 Select Committee—and make a fair decision based on the evidence presented in this show trial?"

(My paraphrase, of course.)

Casey then completed this Jedi mind trick: *"Obviously, people have 'strong feelings' about January 6. The question is, can you put those aside and give this fellow a fair trial?"*

And just like that—with a robotic nod from the star-struck contestant—Casey declared this theater fair and unbiased . . . no matter what your own eyes and ears might tell you.

The first handful of contestants were telling enough:

COOPER: Good morning. You should feel free to take your mask off

(Ever the gracious emperor, Casey reassures his subjects.)

COOPER: So you're a public school teacher, right? What do you teach?

CONTESTANT #1: Yes. I teach art.

COOPER: You obviously watched video of the events of January 6th. Was it just when it happened, or have you watched videos more recently?

CONTESTANT #1: I have watched occasionally when it's on the local news.

(i.e., 24/7 for the last 20 months.)

COOPER: Okay. And you watched the January 6th hearings in the House?

CONTESTANT #1: I did. I believe I mostly saw a few minutes of summaries. I didn't actually, you know, tune in and listen to a lot of **the trial.**

Casey neglected to correct this Freudian slip. Pelosi's Hollywood hacks had already staged a primetime show trial in the court of public opinion, with a unanimous "Guilty!" verdict, long before these leftists gathered to perform their pretense of my due process.

COOPER: And you think your political views could affect your ability to be a fair and impartial juror?

CONTESTANT #1: I'd like to think I'm fair, but I understand my bias as well.

COOPER: Well, tell me a little bit more about that. I mean, obviously people have strong feelings about January 6 . . . lots of people were here that day—

—a million, actually.

COOPER: . . . Mr. Strand is being charged for the conduct that the government alleges he particularly engaged in. How do you think—and I want you to be honest with me—how do you think your political views would affect your ability to follow my instructions and give this fellow a fair trial?

CONTESTANT #1: I do believe I would follow your instructions to the best of my ability . . . so I don't know. I think I can be impartial, but I also feel strongly that the act in general ***as a group of people*** was questionable.

COOPER: So I sense a little hesitancy in your voice.

CONTESTANT #1: Yes.

COOPER: Okay. Thank you very much. You can go . . . the Court will strike for cause . . . because of her answer with respect to her political views.

The very first swing, right out of the gate, was a line drive to left field so obviously poisoned by politics that even Casey couldn't hide it under the spotlight of the first inning . . . but the game would soon tumble much further out of hand.

COOPER: Ma'am . . . it says you're a consultant and fundraiser with something called Trendency. Tell us what Trendency is.

CONTESTANT #2: Trendency is in longitudinal market research, so it's like not a moment in time. We mostly work on advocacy organizations and progressive causes. So it's basically [brainwashing—er,] research.

COOPER: You answered "yes" to . . . "Do you think your political views or those of your significant others might affect your ability to serve as a fair and impartial juror in this case?" Why?

CONTESTANT #2: Well, my husband and I have—so Trendency belongs to both of us, as does Lincoln Park Strategies. We've worked . . . as political consultants for a number of years. My husband worked for the Kerry Campaign. He worked for Obama. He worked for a number of progressive causes and just feels very strongly about democracy and the democratic process.

I turned in my seat and scanned the gallery for an incognito Ashton Kutcher—surely I was being punk'd. We'd barely begun and already we had a WOKE art teacher condemning "a group of people" and now a political operative from enemy headquarters.

COOPER: This case is not about who won the 2020 election. It's not about what the consequences were of January 6th—

I rubbed my ears. Alternative reality, anyone?

Gods and gangsters . . .

COOPER:—the case is about what Mr. Strand did or did not do and whether that conduct constitutes a criminal offense . . . obviously many people have strong feelings . . . about January 6, and the question is, can you put those aside and give this fellow a fair trial just based on the evidence? And I want you to be honest with me.

This was a seasoned DC political strategist—she knew exactly what Casey wanted to hear.

CONTESTANT #2: `I can do that.`

COOPER: `And are you pretty darn confident you could do that?`

CONTESTANT #2: `Yes, I am` [pretty darn confident I know what to say to get on this jury and grab my piece of the MAGA lynching action].

COOPER: `Okay. And you've obviously watched video of what took place. You've seen at least some of the January 6th hearings. Have you actively followed it, or—`

CONTESTANT #2: `Of the people I know in DC, I'm probably a more active follower than others.`

COOPER: `Okay.`

CONTESTANT #2: `But I don't know—DC is a weird place, so I don't know.`

Possibly the truest thing said that entire day.

COOPER: `If you were a juror, you would see videos of that day that focus on Mr. Strand and perhaps other things that were relevant` ["trust us, they're *definitely* relevant"] `to his case. Do you think you could put aside other videos that you've seen of what other people were doing and focus on` [*our* videos of what other people were doing], `giving him your full consideration?`

CONTESTANT #2: `Yes, I think so` [... *I'd love to consider all kinds of ways to crucify this MAGA Zoolander guy* ...]

COOPER: `Okay. Ms. Ayers-Perez?`

AYERS-PEREZ: `I have no follow-up questions, Your Honor.`

COOPER: `Mr. Brennwald?`

My trial attorney stepped in to gingerly push back on the madness.

BRENNWALD: Good morning, ma'am. You said "you think so," when the judge asked you if you could be fair. I know it's impossible to know for sure, but is it fair to say that you were strongly affected on a visceral level on January 6th?

CONTESTANT #2: On the day of January 6th, yes, because my friends and family live on Capitol Hill, and my mom texting was blowing up. People were in the building that live in my neighborhood. So, you know . . . we live here.

BRENNWALD: I get it. I get it.

CONTESTANT #2: I—you know, I think so. I think it's—

Her voice cracked.

. . . the courtroom froze.

CONTESTANT #2:—everybody should get a fair trial. But we live here. We're human people who live in this city.

BRENNWALD: So if you were on trial yourself in a case like this, and someone who felt very differently was judging you, you'd think that you could be the kind of juror that they would want?

CONTESTANT #2: I think so. You said . . . I don't know—I think so, yes. I mean, I don't—I don't know what you want me to say. What's the right thing to say? This is how I feel.

She was *crying*.

The air in the room grew thick as she wiped tears from her face. Just ten minutes into the first day—of *jury selection*—and already a participant was actually weeping.

COOPER: Well, I don't want you to say what you

think is the right thing to say. I want you to be honest—

CONTESTANT #2:—so I didn't think that I would right now tear up a little bit when I was talking about January 6th, but I did. So . . .

COOPER: All right. Thank you for your answers. Mr. Brennwald, do you want to make a motion?

BRENNWALD: I would move to strike for cause, Your Honor. I literally asked her two questions, and she started to cry. And I don't fault her for feeling that way at all. I just don't think that's the kind of juror that we need in a case like this who can be fair. She kept saying she "thinks so," but we need more than thinking. We need someone who is confident.

Seems obvious, right? But Ashton Kutcher wasn't done yet. He returned in a hideous new disguise—as a sour, obese federal prosecutor named Ms. Ayers-Perez—offering a cartoonish display of desperation.

COOPER: Ms. Ayers-Perez?

AYERS-PEREZ: She did say in the beginning that she could be fair. She said that a couple times, Your Honor. I don't think at any point she said she *couldn't* be fair. In fact, I know there was some hesitation, but she maintained that she could be fair throughout the questioning by Your Honor and by Mr. Brennwald.

Yes—she actually argued to keep the weeping Madonna.

Even Casey couldn't stomach that drivel. The contestant was stricken for cause. But the swamp wasn't draining—it was getting thicker.

COOPER: [I]t says here you work for Lidl USA.

CONTESTANT #4: Yes.

COOPER: Do you have a significant other?

CONTESTANT #4: I do.

COOPER: And what do they do?

CONTESTANT #4: He is the assistant general counsel for the OGC counsel.

Wait—this guy wants to be on my jury . . . and his boyfriend is a top lawyer for the DC government?!

COOPER: You live on Capitol Hill. And you've obviously watched video of January 6th. Just at the time, or have you followed the story since then?

CONTESTANT #4: Not super intensely, but, you know, it comes up often, and there are clips here and there on the news.

"Here and there." How cute.

COOPER: . . . either you or an immediate family member worked in the legal field. Is that your significant other?

CONTESTANT #4: Correct.

My lawyer, once again, tried to politely point out the obvious.

BRENNWALD: As an "occasional" follower of the J6 news, have you developed any strong feelings . . . about what happened that day?

CONTESTANT #4: I have some feelings.

BRENNWALD: Your Honor, I would just note that his partner works for the DC attorney as an Assistant Attorney General for the DC Council, and that gives us pause.

COOPER: Do you have a challenge or not?

BRENNWALD: Yes, Your Honor.

COOPER: Overruled. 1261 is qualified.

And just like that, the pretense was over.

The circus of naked bias was now in full swing.

COOPER: Next up . . . You work for the EPA, is that right?

Oh, just peachy. A green new scam lunatic. What could go wrong?

CONTESTANT #5: Yes, I do.

COOPER: You've seen videos of January 6th. . . . Have you followed it since it happened, or just at the time?

CONTESTANT #5: Yes, I watched it live as it unfolded, and I've followed it since.

COOPER: And frequent follower? Occasional follower?

CONTESTANT #5: Frequent.

COOPER: Frequent. And you answered "yes'"to . . . 20 or 21.

CONTESTANT #5: I believe it was 21.

The Climate Cultist could barely contain himself.

COOPER: Question 21, the January 6th hearings in the House.

CONTESTANT #5: Yes, yes!

COOPER: You followed those?

CONTESTANT #5: Yes, Yes!

COOPER: And based on following the story and the hearings—you know, lots of people have strong feelings about January 6th one way or the other.

"Or the other" . . . cute, Casey. But we know a one-way street when we're on it.

COOPER: . . . would those feelings prevent you from giving Mr. Strand a fair trial? And I want you to be honest with me.

CONTESTANT #5: Yes. I have very strong feelings about January 6th. I also don't know the defendant, and I believe that the government has a job to do. But I have very strong feelings about that day.

And I had a very strong feeling his idea of the government's "job" was miles from mine.

COOPER: Finally, you've had legal training of some sort?

CONTESTANT #5: Yes, I took contracts law in undergrad; I took environmental law . . . as part of grad school . . . and I've also had various trainings in parts of the Clean Waters Act and Administrative Procedures Act as part of [government] work.

COOPER: I could use your help on a number of those things.

Casey fancies himself quite the comic.

Ms. Ayers-Perez then inserted her standard rhetorical disclaimer—about magically ignoring all those "very strong feelings" and making a decision "based only on the evidence"—after which my lawyer tried, in vain, to restore some small measure of sanity.

BRENNWALD: Your Honor, just for the record I would note that . . . in my experience, anybody who is following things frequently and closely, especially the January 6th hearings, is someone who has very visceral personal feelings about what happened and wants to confirm their bias. So I would move to strike for cause.

COOPER: Overruled. 0186 is qualified.

Madness. It was unadulterated madness.

★ ★ ★

COOPER: Step right up, sir . . . so you've been in real estate your whole career . . . do you have a significant other?

CONTESTANT #6: I do, husband.

COOPER: What does he do?

CONTESTANT #6: He works for the planning commission in Montgomery County. He's an urban planner.

COOPER: . . . obviously you've seen video of January 6th. . . . Was that just at the time it happened, or have you followed the story since then?

CONTESTANT #6: I have followed the story.

COOPER: And would you say you're an active follower or an occasional follower of that particular story?

CONTESTANT #6: I think it's a concern for the country so I've been following whenever I see the news on it.

By this point—only six contestants into a swamp of nearly a hundred anxious MAGA-slayers—their performances had merged into one long scream of certain doom. I turned to my lawyer and whispered a litmus test, urging him to pin down each one on the obvious prejudice: *the defendant was inside the building—so of course he's guilty.*

BRENNWALD: Do you feel like anybody who was inside the Capitol on that day, on January 6th as part of this group of people, must be guilty of something?

CONTESTANT #6: Not guilty of "something"; but they were in the Capitol.

Case closed. I was there, so I was guilty—until proven convicted.

I gave my lawyer a sardonic wink as he turned to frown at the instant success of my test. It was an unmistakable violation of the Constitution's impartial jury guarantee.

BRENNWALD: Your Honor, I would move to strike for cause. It seems like anybody who is following it closely is doing so for a reason. The impression at the defense table is he's ready to convict right now. I know all the jurors know what to say. I get that. I'm not trying to impugn somebody's charac-ter, but he's ready to convict, if he had a chance.

COOPER: . . . your cause strike is overruled. 0879 is qualified.

My judge was ready to convict, too—and he made sure that "chance" was guaranteed.

COOPER: It says here you're a contractor with Axiologic Solutions. Tell me what that is.

CONTESTANT #7: So I work for NGA as a contractor . . . I have worked for the White House, everywhere . . .

Sounds totally impartial.

COOPER: And what is NGA?

CONTESTANT #7: NGA is the National Geospatial-Intelligence Agency.

COOPER: Okay. Have you worked . . . for any other federal government agency?

CONTESTANT #7: I worked on the EHR project . . . that's as much as I can go into detail at the unclass level.

So now my jurors weren't just openly hostile, J6-triggered Democrat activists—they handled classified material at the very agencies shaping the J6 narrative.

Am I hallucinating?

BRENNWALD: Do you feel like people who were inside the Capitol must be guilty of some crime because they were inside the Capitol that day?

CONTESTANT #7: . . . I mean, well, so my only thing predicated to the events is that since I work in "cleared" communities, I know how much security is of pertinence to everyone, and that's the only thing that arised in my mind, was that, you know, hey, we're dealing with some big documents that we would like to keep private.

Translation: National Geospatial bureaucratese for "Yes, plebes caught inside the Capitol are definitely guilty."

Of course, Casey happily approved him.

COOPER: Mr. O'Neill? . . . You work at the IFC? . . . and how long have you been there?

CONTESTANT #8: Twenty-two years.

COOPER: And do you have a significant other?

CONTESTANT #8: Yes, I do.

COOPER: And what does he or she do?

CONTESTANT #8: . . . he's a landscaper.

So apparently 100 percent of D.C. residents are J6 aficionados and Trump-hating leftists—and half of them are gay?

Typical American demographic, the DOJ assures me.

COOPER: You live on Capitol Hill . . . Were you home on the 6th? Did you observe any of the events at the Capitol personally?

CONTESTANT #8: Yes . . . I watched TV with the events all afternoon.

COOPER: Was that just at the time, or have you followed the story?

CONTESTANT #8: At the time, and followed stories.

COOPER: And would you consider yourself an active follower or an occasional follower?

CONTESTANT #8: I'd say I'm an active follower.

BRENNWALD: Do you feel that anyone who went inside the Capitol building that day . . . must be guilty of some crime based on what you've seen in the J6 hearings?

CONTESTANT #8: Yes.

BRENNWALD: Do you feel like you were personally affected? I know you weren't attacked, but like as a resident, especially on Capitol Hill, were you—

CONTESTANT #8: I guess it was more being in shock about what was happening that day, especially when I saw clouds of smoke coming up from the Capitol. I really thought it was on fire at one point.

No one bothered to point out it was the police attacking unarmed protesters that caused the smoke—"Shhhh, John Strand, you're ruining the movie!"

COOPER: All right, sir. You answered yes to Mr. Brennwald's question about believing that anyone in the Capitol is likely to be guilty of some crime. Now, obviously you do not know the elements of the crime that Mr. Strand or anyone else is charged with . . .

. . . and Casey droned on to cover his ass—but no one cared. No one could be bothered with the actual elements of the five charges brought against me, because that would be like the nerdy guy interrupting a gunfight in an action movie to complain they didn't count bullets or reload realistically. And nobody invites that guy back to the theater.

Unfortunately, my lawyer was now that guy.

BRENNWALD: We'll move to strike for cause given his answer . . . his gut reaction was that anybody who went inside the building that day is guilty. He starts out with that presumption in his mind, and . . . he'll convict, and that's not how it should be.

COOPER: I'm going to overrule that. He is qualified. But, Mr. Brennwald, that's why I didn't ask the [guilty by presence alone] question, because it's not dispositive of anything.

Oh really, Mr. I-was-educated-at-Stanford-Law-School?

A blatant statement confirming a presumption of *guilt* isn't "dispositive of anything" in your version of English?

Oh wait—this is a coliseum. Why am I still pretending it's a courtroom?

COOPER: . . . but there are other questions that the Court did ask that go to things like such strong feelings . . . we're going to take up a lot of time if we have to go through that colloquy for every single person. That's why I left the question off.

My blood was boiling.

Did he just—look, this judge had been desecrating due process from the start. There's no reason to wait any longer in pointing out the obvious:

Casey Cooper is a jackass.

He just berated my lawyer—the most reasonable, respectful attorney in the building, by a country mile—for asking one simple yes-or-no question to establish a baseline on bias and the "presumption of inno-cence." This, from the same judge who wasted half the day asking for-ty-two "strong feelings" questions and relishing the soap-opera stories of his adoring fans.

It was appalling.

My lawyer, ever the consummate professional, remained polite.

BRENNWALD: I understand, Your Honor. My concern is that . . . it helps me gauge who I'm dealing with so . . . I've tried to keep it short.

I've tried to keep it short, too—just a few verbatim glimpses of an abject mockery. But this was only the *first eight* potential jurors of the day—in a courtroom-coliseum with a hundred of these swamp-cruis-ing sharks, crazed by the MAGA-red chum now frothing the waters.

Bloody ridiculous.

Next contestant, Casey had his own Freudian slip: "*. . . you've obviously watched video of 9/11—I'm sorry, of January sixth . . .*" And then, of course, he qualified them—right after they admitted to "strong feelings."

The one after that—still only the tenth prospect of the day!—was a melodramatic musician auditioning to play my swan song:

COOPER: You say that you have such strong feel-ings about January 6th that you might not be able to follow the Court's instruction and render a fair and impartial verdict. Why?

CONTESTANT #10: I do—as much as I would—

—her voice cracked in her best Meryl Streep impression—

CONTESTANT #10:—I would really like to serve on this trial, but I do feel very strongly about it, and I feel like it was a real blow to the potential future of our democracy and that it could happen again.

We sat breathless, waiting for dramatic theme music to come crash-ing—but all we heard was Casey's anticlimactic "Okay."

CONTESTANT #10: It was a very frightening time.

"Frightening" definitely summed up this lunatic charade.

The eleventh contestant was a government researcher who "actively follow[ed]" J6 and admitted to consuming "an enormous amount of media for my [government] job, so I've found myself rather invested in [J6]."

Casey qualified them.

The thirteenth contestant was a thirty-eight-year veteran of the Department of Defense—a jury of the government for a defendant on trial for protesting . . . the government.

Casey qualified them.

The fourteenth contestant's wife worked for the hyper-leftist National Endowment for Democracy, and they lived on Capitol Hill. He described himself as an "informed [active] follower [of J6] . . . cer-tainly want to know what's going on near my home," and admitted: "I would say 'yes' [I felt emotionally impacted by what I saw on J6]."

Casey qualified them.

The fifteenth contestant was a legal assistant at a left-wing firm and married to an AP journalist who covered the COVID beat. She answered my lawyer unequivocally: "yes," she was emotionally affected by J6, and "yes" she had "strong feelings" about the protesters—and "yes," anyone who went inside the Capitol that day was guilty of some crime.

Casey, of course, qualified them.

The sixteenth contestant—oh my, this performance was so cartoon-ish, I thought we'd reached the part of the Disney movie where the animated characters spill over into the live-action scene:

COOPER: . . . Ms. Sternberg?

CONTESTANT #16: Yes.

COOPER: How do you employ yourself?

CONTESTANT #16: Oh, well, get ready. This is the first time you will have ever heard this. I am a swing dance instructor and promoter.

. . . and promoter? Do go on . . .

COOPER: How fun.

CONTESTANT #16: It is. It really is ["valley girl" voicing].

COOPER: Did you ever go to Glen Echo?

CONTESTANT #16: I held a dance there on Saturday night.

COOPER: Pretty school, huh?

CONTESTANT #16: [*bats eyelashes*] Have I seen you there?

Oh, so now we're chitchatting about weekend dance parties in the Beltway. Good thing it's only my entire life "swinging" in the balance. . . .

COOPER: As a spectator, perhaps. Do you have a significant other?

CONTESTANT #16: I have a husband, and he works at the Library of Congress.

Congress? Oh sure—no J6 conflict there at all.

facepalm

COOPER: So the Library of Congress is separate from the Capitol but obviously also part of the Congress. Have you talked to him about January 6th?

CONTESTANT #16: Oh, good heavens, yes!

COOPER: Okay. You've obviously seen videos of the events of that day, and you say here you've also followed the January 6th hearings.

CONTESTANT #16: Uh-huh

[*affirming "valley girl" head-nod*].

COOPER: Would you call yourself a frequent follower of news about that?

CONTESTANT #16: I watched every minute of every hearing.

"Every minute of every hearing"—you could almost hear the popcorn crunching as she savored every dramatic syllable.

COOPER: You've obviously seen lots of video that does not relate to Mr. Strand or the charges against him. . . . Would you be able to put that aside in assessing his guilt or innocence?

CONTESTANT #16: On a scale of 1 to 10, with 1 being not impartial at all and 10 extremely partial, I think I would put myself at about a 2 or a 3. [*awkward silence*] . . . was that backwards? Do I have to explain that again? I know. [*hair flip*]

No, sweetheart, you nailed it: on a scale of biased to biased, you're a babe.

And on a scale of guilty to convicted, I've got all your bases covered.

Casey was certainly smitten—he overruled my lawyer's painfully obvious move to strike for cause and qualified her . . . because of course he did.

We'd barely made it to the lunch break, and the insanity kept rolling. Contestant #20 worked for the NIH, had a political science background, and a résumé stacked with Democrat campaign work. She lived on Capitol Hill and openly admitted "strong feelings" and firm partisan bias.

She could not have been more categorically prejudiced and disqualified to serve as a juror—prompting this plea from my lawyer:

BRENNWALD: Your Honor, we move to strike for

cause. She came across as quite emotional on the
stand. If I were in Mr. Strand's shoes, I'd be very
nervous about my life being decided by someone who
is a political operative . . . who has worked on
the campaigns for pretty much all Democrats. It
seemed like she was thinking hard about what the
correct answer was. And I think she appears to want
to be on the jury, but we have enough jurors. We
don't need to bring someone in with all this bag-
gage, including her prior life on the Hill, her
boss's life. So I'd ask the Court to strike her
for cause.

COOPER: Okay. The Court will overrule your objection . . . we will qualify her.

Totally outrageous. Totally Casey.

Next, he met Ms. Prybyl, armed with a master's degree in "International Peace and Conflict Resolution," who declared, "I am definitely biased" and "I disagree with the people involved."

And so, of course, Casey qualified her.

Then came Ms. Branner, a graphic artist who said she follows J6 "closely," and then snarled, "I'm very angry about it. I'm angry that it happened," along with some choice words for anyone who went inside the building.

Casey then overruled my lawyer's obvious objection and qualified the angriest contestant of the day.

Then came Ms. Biercevicz, from the Department of Energy—because apparently we still needed to stuff more Deep State swamp into the oozing jury box. She said J6 made her "upset, sad, angry," and when asked if protesters were guilty by mere presence inside the Capitol, she vigorously stated "yes"—twice—then kept going. She practically handed down my guilty verdict before the trial even began.

So of course, Casey ignored my lawyer yet again and qualified her.

And for good measure, he overruled our objections to a former FBI employee—qualifying her as well.

But the icing on the jury selection cake, with a cherry on top, was the Orwellian moment of an unnamed contestant—did he just walk off the set of *The Matrix?*—labeled "Mr. Smith":

COOPER: . . . it says you're a communications consultant with. . .GMMB . . . what is that?

SMITH: Comms firm, strategy. We do—I mostly handle nonprofits, corporate, and electoral or campaign clients.

COOPER: . . . what campaigns have you personally worked on recently?

SMITH: Relevant potentially to this, in 2020 we were doing **election norming**.

—come again?

SMITH: So it was kind of the idea of the results are going to come when they come, and everybody should just wait for the results and trust that the process will see itself through.

"Election norming" . . . "Just trust that the process will see itself through."

Was this guy actually pulling off a Jedi mind trick in open court?

COOPER: Let me put it this way; the entities that you work for in connection with that part of your business, are they affiliated with one party or the other?

SMITH: Yes, yes. My firm is mostly left-leaning. It's a large Democrat firm.

You don't say.

COOPER: All right . . . something about the

nature of the case that might prevent you from
being fair and neutral in evaluating the evidence.
Why did you answer yes to that?

SMITH: I mostly flagged that one because of the
work I had just mentioned. I was, in 2020, **very
expressly** working on making sure people knew about
the outcome of the election being something that
could be trusted, and the results were going to be
fair, and that there were a lot of officials that
were doing their job to make sure that the results
were that.

Oh, I bet there were a lot of "officials"—and I bet that's exactly
what they did.

Oh.

My.

God.

SMITH: . . . so that wasn't necessarily in conflict with the beliefs of those that gathered on
January 6th, but it was part of the effort in the
end.

What was this, *The Twilight Zone*?!

This guy—whom Casey couldn't qualify fast enough—was, quite
literally, the *Architect* of the 2020 election propaganda. He crafted
the messaging campaign **designed to condition the masses** into passively accepting a rigged and fraudulent election . . . the very propaganda that led to the very protest for which I now stood trial—and
this architect of lies would now "very expressly" influence the jury in
that trial.

If it wasn't in the transcript, I'm not sure I would believe it either!

The unhinged madness had reached a Lewis Carroll–esque peak
that would carry through the entire nine-day cartoon tragedy—tones

of "Off with his head!" echoing across the absurd jury selection ruse and beyond.

It rang through nearly a hundred salivating contestant performances, which spilled into the next morning before, finally, yielding to the start of the trial itself.

(cue the 20th Century Fox drumroll)

This *feature presentation* began with the government's soap-opera overture:

The Prosecution's Opening Statement, in the criminal case of
[Divided] States of America versus John Strand.

THIS IS WAR

TRIAL DAY 2 | SEPTEMBER 20, 2022

"THIS IS WAR."

Mr. Jason Manning—the physically tolerable half of the federal prosecution team—delivered those three words with theatrical over-enunciation, dramatizing a tweet I had posted shortly after the 2020 election. Now my own words had been weaponized into the tip of the gladiator's spear—poised to strike the first blow.

It was their opening salvo in the war on truth—an assault on free speech, on the truth of J6, on equal protection under law—on me, mocked by the media as MAGA Zoolander, the Hollywood model/actor/insurrectionist standing defiant in the lions' den of a DC courtroom-coliseum.

MANNING: That's what the defendant, John Strand, announced on Twitter just a few weeks after the 2020 election.

"THIS. IS. WAR.

```
#ThisElectionWasRigged. #StopTheSteal."
```

```
The defendant's words, December 1, 2020. The
defendant was angry that Donald Trump had lost the
November 2020 presidential election, and he knew
that in just a few weeks the newly elected presi-
dent and vice president would be sworn into office.
And he was determined to stop that. So, ladies and
gentlemen, this is a case about how the defendant,
John Strand, traveled into Washington, DC, joined
a violent mob, and stormed into the United States
Capitol all to try to stop the peaceful transfer
of power.
```

An old law school maxim says: *"If the facts are on your side, argue the facts; if the law is on your side, argue the law; if neither is on your side, pound the table."* After his first three words—which were, in fact, mine, and quite true—Mr. Manning quickly ran out of facts and began pounding the jury and the watching world with lies.

A flurry of falsehoods rained down with heavyweight-champion force throughout nine days of bludgeoning the truth, the law, and my life.

He opened his assault with the false premise that President Trump had conclusively lost the 2020 election—a claim that grows more absurd with each passing week—as if the matter had been cleanly set-tled on November 3. This was belied by national uproar and a million Americans assembling on January 6 to "peacefully and patriotically" protest an obviously suspect election.

Alternative facts are handy when the truth is your opponent instead of your objective.

Manning then framed the case as me "joining a violent mob"—a premeditated distortion—to "stop the peaceful transfer of power"—an Orwellian inversion (and an obvious absurdity to serious adults).

He further lied by asserting I had specific foreknowledge of Congress's schedule—helping fabricate a criminal state of mind.

That supposed intent—the "mens rea" required by law—was the crux of his case.

The truth is, I had no idea about the plans of Congress—or anyone else—at the Capitol on J6. I'd heard talk in December of some Congressmen pushing for election audits, but my focus had already shifted to a cross-country work trip, with an important event in Florida just days before Washington. On January 5 and 6, I was focused on my own mission: protecting a woman in a crowd and helping her give a speech. A speech explicitly protected by the First Amendment and backed by a government-approved permit. A speech I had proudly written—to support my colleague in urging our fellow Americans to fulfill their sacred duty as citizens; a reminder of that "prudent jealousy" to "take alarm at the first experiment on our liberties."

In other words, this trial was *precisely and entirely* about "somebody's speech." But Mr. Manning wasn't paid to discover the truth. He was paid to deliver convictions and crucifixions—for the "justice entertainment" of the coliseum crowd, and for the pleasure of His Majesty.

MANNING: But members of the jury, let's be perfectly clear. This trial is not about somebody else's speeches. This trial is about the defendant, John Strand, and what he did when he stormed into the Capitol, and why he did it.

Manning continued the farce with a bombastic narration of his carefully arranged video presentation—a misleading collage of selective edits, which I fully expected . . . along with some outright fraud that shocked even my red-pilled conscience. He made a grand spectacle of the Vice President's motorcade and its supposed security perimeter—never mentioning that the perimeter had been set by the U.S. Capitol

Police, not the Secret Service, as required by the statute behind two of my charges. He then lied to the jury, telling them I arrived at the Capitol at least twenty minutes earlier than I actually did. By the time I reached the steps, the motorcade and perimeter restriction had vanished without a trace—leaving the plaza looking very much like audience space for the afternoon's scheduled speeches.

Curiously, he noted the "Columbus Doors" were closed and locked—but failed to explain how those 20,000-pound bronze outer doors came to be opened by the time his selective edit returned to the scene, in his attempt to literally "paint me in" to his insurrection masterpiece theater.

And when I say, "literally paint me in," I mean just that.

Manning digitally drew a yellow circle around my head—showing me trapped in a dense throng of people—and then zoomed in on an upraised arm, supposedly striking at someone, as he told the jury: "You see [John Strand's] fist up in the air." This was his damning proof of "violent" behavior—except, despite all his meticulous digital manipulation, he forgot one thing: my signature black leather gloves. The bare fist in the frame wasn't mine.

Much had been made of my "Gucci to Guilty" fashion ensemble (courtesy of *Rolling Stone* and others), including by Manning himself in his opening tirade. So there wasn't a "thread" of doubt that he knew my hands were gloved—and that his accusation was false.

He knowingly lied.

He further lied by claiming I was chanting "Stop the Steal"—as though chanting political phrases at a political protest was a crime, rather than a constitutionally guaranteed right. But it was a lie regardless.

And then, just for good measure, he pointed to another protester swinging a flag—while quoting *my* tweet from hours earlier about "standing firm" for election integrity—as if I had somehow fulfilled a prophecy . . . through someone else's actions.

Still think American justice requires a man to be judged on his own conduct—not someone else's? Think again.

This is now "The Divided States of America."

Mr. Manning next revived the grotesque lie that I had "assaulted" USCP officer Joshua Pollitt—freeze-framing video footage to sell his story to the jury. But the full video record—along with Officer Pollitt's direct reports to the USCP and FBI, his sworn testimony in court, and the FBI's final conclusion—told a very different story.

Officer Pollitt had become short of breath in a dense crowd—the same mass that crushed me against, and eventually through, the door. That chaos was sparked by police misconduct. Pollitt fainted, stumbled out of my reach, and fell—only to be helped up by nearby protesters. The FBI concluded that there was **no assault** at this point—and that Officer Pollitt "did not seek medical attention."

But those facts didn't fit Manning's hate-filled fantasy, so he lied. He wildly distorted the incident to slander me before the jury. And the slander continued—step by Capitol step—as his insurrection horror film traced my path through the building, spinning a twisted fable for his captivated coliseum audience.

He lied about my knowledge of the building's layout.

He lied about my alleged intention to obstruct Congress—whose proceedings weren't even germane to the felony he was charging.

He lied about my private texts to family and colleagues, and even about my interactions with law enforcement—claiming "[John Strand] overruns another line of Capitol Police officers," which I never did.

He stood at that podium, puffed with arrogance, flaying me with lies until the coliseum misted red with manufactured rage.

And then he unleashed the kill-shot lie.

Manning was so desperate to smear my character that he froze the video and zoomed in on a single frame: my fist raised as a line of police officers walked down the steps long after the chaos had ended. He spun a tale of defiance and disrespect, claiming this proved my contempt for "Our Democracy™." But he never played the full video—which showed me clapping in admiration for those very officers. I wasn't jeering the police—I was thanking them.

It was the exact opposite of the smear he sold the jury—and he knew it.

But Mr. Manning wasn't there to tell the truth. He was there to feed the mob—and the mob wanted blood. So he lied—shamelessly distorting reality to give them a Trump supporter's scalp.

I sat there stunned, mouth open in disgust, watching a sworn officer of the court twist the truth into a noose around my neck. My eyes darted between my lawyer and the soulless showman on stage—as he finally concluded his fraud theater.

Emperor Casey and his coliseum of MAGA-hating minions sat frozen in rapt attention.

My lead trial attorney, Mr. Stephen Brennwald, then took the podium for his unenviable—and frankly impossible—task: "unplaying" the horror film my jury of Democrat operatives had just watched with twisted fascination. To his credit, Mr. Brennwald gave a valiant effort. He calmly explained my true intentions on J6, sharing that the full record—seen in context, not freeze-framed and photoshopped— would completely exonerate me.

But you can't unring a bell. And you certainly can't rewind the bloodlust from shark-infested waters once a victim has been shredded and tossed into the sea.

I was dead MAGA-red meat.

Still, this "justice entertainment" feature had been scripted and cast with the DC Swamp's finest—and the show must go on. The courtroom-coliseum crowd, along with the watching world, eagerly awaited the lynching of a "deplorable." And so the melodrama resumed—starring a well-rehearsed troupe of government witnesses, most of whom had never seen me. They testified mostly about events and locations that had nothing to do with my conduct. Their lines were perfected, their delivery rehearsed—honed by dozens of repeat performances across the DOJ's expanding catalog of J6 show trials, each one a Team Lunacy extravaganza.

First up in *The John Strand Affair* was Captain Carneysha Mendoza of the U.S. Capitol Police, head of the "Civil Disturbance Unit." Prosecutor Ayers-Perez—about as pleasant to behold as a moldy mason jar of tepid vinegar—led Captain Mendoza through a meandering song and dance about Capitol security protocols and various tales of chaos and danger. None of it involved me.

The point, of course, was to steep the jury in the government's traumatic insurrection narrative. And sure enough, the captain parroted the official buzzword—referring to the protest as "the insurrection," a toxic falsehood and an embarrassing misnomer for someone in charge of national security.

Let's be clear: An *insurrection* is an armed, sustained, militant attack aimed at overthrowing an established government.

- **Armed?** The protesters had no guns. Flagpoles and bear spray do not an insurrection make.
- **Sustained?** A temporary crowd escalation becomes a *riot*—not a coup.
- **Militant?** The coordinated assault came from law enforcement against the crowd—not the other way around.
- **Overthrow?** No serious person could think anyone hoped to overthrow the U.S. government with an unarmed protest.

Not a single person was charged with insurrection . . . because there was no insurrection. Yet the lie remained on the record, mostly unchallenged—even by my own defense. As my attorney ruefully admitted, the fraudulent J6 narrative was already baked in. A DC jury was never going to entertain the possibility that their own government might be corrupt—or even incompetent.

For Team Lunacy, the government is God. And therefore, by definition . . . it is good.

Ms. Ayers-Perez maintained her theatrical guise as she continued puppeteering the mediocre police captain—guiding her to terrify the jury with a lurid tale of chemical burns. None of it had anything to do with me whatsoever. My lawyer objected for relevance, but Casey—predictably and shamefully—overruled it, as he nearly always did.

On cross-examination, my lawyer confirmed the obvious:

BRENNWALD: Did you have any independent memory of seeing [John Strand] there that day?

MENDOZA: No, sir, I did not.

BRENNWALD: You never saw him at all until you saw these videos, correct?

MENDOZA: Correct.

BRENNWALD: Any injuries you received had nothing to do with [John Strand]; is that true?

MENDOZA: Correct.

But the blood had already been spilled into the jury pool—along with the rotting flesh of a deeper, insidious lie I couldn't have seen at the time. Ayers-Perez entered a stipulation into the record, asserting:

The events depicted in the video footage are a fair and accurate depiction of the events at the U.S. Capitol on January 6, 2021.

But this was an abject falsehood.

Even as she claimed the footage was "fair and accurate," Ayers-Perez and her cronies were withholding—without notice to my attorneys—at least 45,000 hours of surveillance video, including exculpatory footage that directly contradicted the government's narrative—a textbook Brady violation. Her cherry-picked montage was not only *incomplete,* it was deceptive—entirely *un*fair.

Then came another absurdity: Captain Mendoza's laughable claim that bike racks and "snow fencing"—flimsy plastic netting—sufficiently marked the Capitol plaza as a "restricted area." But she herself admitted: "It's basically a driveway. It's where people go to take pictures [every day throughout the year]." Even more absurd, those token barriers had been removed *before* most protesters arrived. That removal was instigated by covert operatives—FBI provocateurs embedded in the crowd—leaving tens of thousands of peaceful, unsuspecting Americans to stream in without any clear indication of alleged restrictions.

Next, Mr. Manning returned for a somber duet with the DOJ's second co-star: Special Agent Elizabeth Glavey of the United States Secret Service. This number was crisply choreographed with military precision: a meticulous (and seemingly endless) step-by-step report of the planning and movement of Vice President Mike Pence's security detail. Tension built with harrowing descriptions of shattered glass, shouting crowds, and looming danger . . . only to deflate when agents evacuated the VP before 2:00 p.m.—rendering the entire tense performance irrelevant, since I didn't arrive until nearly half an hour later.

My lawyer didn't even attempt a cross-examination. He knew a dirty bomb when he saw one—and wisely avoided triggering any more terrorizing shrapnel.

Mr. Manning, however, was just getting warmed up.

The next cast member would prove the smash hit of this Team Lunacy production: Kyle T. Jones, Assistant Parliamentarian for the United States House of Representatives. Mr. Jones—his distinct golden voice a soothing balm after the grating stridency of

Ms. Ayers-Perez—was polite, professional, and articulate as Manning directed him through the final act of the day. He delivered an exhaustive account of the House's scheduled proceedings on J6, ending with a sensationalized sequence of chaos and terror: ghastly descriptions of screams and chemicals filling the air, congressmen "hitting the deck," medieval "escape masks" triggering full-blown panic—all peaking with this dramatic declaration:

JONES: I steeled myself for the fact that if people made their way into the chamber, I would fight them until I was no longer capable of fighting.

(Insert "gladiator-champion theme music" here.)

I promise—there's no overstating the maudlin hysteria of his polished performance. It was . . . ridiculous.

And then, right at the peak of this R-rated crescendo, Emperor Casey abruptly adjourned the show for the evening—leaving Mr. Jones's vivid war cry echoing through the smoke-filled air of the courtroom-coliseum. The visibly shaken audience filed out in stunned silence . . . concluding yet another day of fraudulent theatrics and grandstanding gore.

CIRCUS OF THE STATE

TRIAL DAY 3 | SEPTEMBER 21, 2022

By next morning, the mood simmered with fatigue. We'd endured just forty-eight hours of this gladiatorial savagery—but felt the full weight of years of persecution crushing down on us. Mr. Manning resumed the attack, guiding Mr. Jones to pick up where he left off—right at the eye-popping scene of screams and chemical-laced chaos. Jones dutifully refreshed the trauma with more scripted histrionics, culminating in this jaw-dropping hyperbole:

JONES: Notwithstanding the fear for my life and the sense of disbelief and panic as to what was going on that day, I was still genuinely aware of the historical significance of what was happening—

(Funny, that's exactly what I said in a private text—which you guys later paraded to the jury as though it were somehow incriminating.)

—there were points in the day when I wondered whether this wasn't the end of our constitutional republic . . .

Well, Mr. Jones—setting aside that I don't know you or your true motives, and that I'd never wish an honest man to fear for his life—it is preposterous to suggest a political protest of largely peaceable citizens engaging in democracy at its most fundamental level—and glaringly absent Antifa & Co.'s guns, Molotov cocktails, firebombings, or looting goon squads—could pose a legitimate threat to "end" a constitutional republic. That is, of course, assuming such a republic hasn't already been ended—by a web of seditious corruption and the brazen weaponization of government power . . . which you've now shamelessly endorsed with Academy Award–winning grandiosity.

In that case, I suspect you've been preaching at your own republic's funeral.

And the absurdity of your contrived hysteria is made even more obscene by so many fiery, deadly *months* of those still-lauded BLM "mostly peaceful" Burn-Loot-Murder rampages—which inflicted far more destruction and terror on our republic than a dozen J6's combined.

We have the receipts.

Yet your pretentious House of Reptilian Leeches—led by the cackling hyena who stole the copilot's chair in the White House—not only excused that anarchy, but praised it as virtuous. Democrat politicians even bailed these violent thugs out, hailing them as heroes of "Our Democracy.™" Meanwhile, more than two dozen people—including police officers—were killed, and ***two billion*** dollars in damage unleashed. Much of the destruction fell upon black- and minority-owned businesses, along with federal and personal property—up in smoke as a pagan sacrifice to WOKE virtue signaling and Democrat Party exploitation.

And I can't help but notice the hypocrisy in the contrast between us.

We were both innocent men doing our jobs that day—caught in the same unexpected turmoil while fulfilling our duty. Both committed to protecting lives and preserving the constitutional republic. Both acting lawfully.

But you were approved by the *Artificial Aristocracy*—obediently sticking to the Team Lunacy script—earning you a political Oscar. I, on the other hand, defied the script—exercising the First Amendment to confront that aristocracy, exposing its lies and abuse.

And for that, I've been condemned to a scarlet letter and a crimson bath in the DC Swamp coliseum.

The double standard is as naked and grotesque as the deception that birthed it—and the treachery that enforces it.

Mr. Manning kept the deception and treachery flowing after a brief cross by Mr. Brennwald, who exposed several key facts: Congress had interrupted its own certification process—and with it "the peaceful transfer of power," which by law does not occur until January 20—*before* any protester disturbance was reported. They did this in order to consider the very objections those protesters had gathered to support. Congress then interrupted themselves *again* after the FBI-instigated, police-escorted chaos was cleared.

Brennwald also underscored the critical exculpatory truth: not a single piece of video evidence or witness testimony showed me committing—or even supporting—any element of a criminal charge.

Undeterred, the government's gladiators charged ahead with their next co-star, teased in earlier previews: U.S. Capitol Police Officer

Joshua Pollitt. Manning rolled a dizzying reel of chopped-up, out-of-order video and grainy stills from a scene that was anything but still. Pollitt admitted the crush of bodies left him gasping, unable to move—corroborating my own account. He confirmed I stayed locked to my client in a protective stance, unable to reach him as he grew dizzy and stumbled. And he conceded the protesters near him never went for his weapon; instead, they helped him up and guided him to safety.

None of that slowed Manning. He zeroed in on my "signature black [Gucci] sunglasses" and "pink [Gucci] scarf"—his words—along with my coiffed hair: "it's standing almost straight up," per the transcript—you really can't make this up! Yet once again, he forgot any mention of my black leather gloves, matching my black leather jacket—and not at all matching the photos of *other* people swinging fists and flagpoles, which Manning shamelessly blamed on me.

Another lie from the soulless gladiator. Another act in the fraud.

He pushed further with earlier footage—from a different location, out of sequence, during a calmer, less crowded moment—to claim my account of being trapped and pushed was not credible. He even accused me of lying under oath (projection alert) for testifying that the crowd had forced me into the building. Emperor Casey later compounded the defamation with a sentencing enhancement for "false testimony"—a baseless judicial punishment contradicted by government video that explicitly corroborated my account.

Read that again: I am clearly visible on government video, swarmed and shoved through the entrance while catching my stumbling colleague across the threshold—yet both the prosecutor and judge accused me of lying for describing exactly that.

Pollitt dutifully parroted Manning's nonsense, despite having just testified—under oath—that he himself had been trapped and pushed by the same crowd. Manning then closed the scene with an extra splash of cringe:

MANNING: The last question, Officer Pollitt. If any of these persons that we saw by the [Columbus] door had come up to you and said something along the lines of, "I don't want to go into the Capitol myself, but one of these other rioters insist that I come with her," what would you say to that?

Mr. Brennwald's swift objection cut off the pathetic insult—but left the obvious question hanging: What kind of lawyer had Mr. Manning revealed himself to be?

With Officer Pollitt dismissed, Mr. Manning called his fifth co-star: Officer Nelson Vargas of the U.S. Capitol Police. They droned through another round of irrelevant details—tracing the witness's winding path through the Capitol—punctuated by endless pauses to mark maps, videos, and exhibits with digital annotations. At that point, my lawyer made a sharp observation: unless those annotations were preserved, there would be no way to reference them in my inevitable appeal. He urged the Court to allow some method of recording them—a basic safeguard for the record.

Casey's response revealed him to be clueless—about both integrity and technology.

BRENNWALD: I was told not to take pictures of these exhibits when they're marked, and I was just told by the paralegal for the government that they can't do screenshots of what is being marked so we can actually memorialize where people mark things. But I think there should be a way, especially since this is evidence, and it's not going to make any sense for appellate purposes, [when] it comes to that . . . I really think it's important.

COOPER: So I don't want you taking photographs of the computer. I've never seen that before. What generally happens, Mr. Manning, is that you describe by reference to the image where he has marked so that there's a record of where he has placed the mark. But just describe it.

Just describe it? So the plan was to play "legal telephone" with witnesses—using verbal tin cans and string—while the defense was expected to "trust" the prosecution to preserve the record with "descriptions"?

This entire proceeding was a bad joke.

As if to prove the point, Casey then allowed into evidence—over repeated objections—a prejudicial video edited by a known leftist agitator, clearly intended to demonize J6 defendants. It had no connection to me and no bearing on my conduct whatsoever.

The Emperor added an insulting preface:

COOPER: And, ladies and gentlemen, I believe, on this video, you will see a legend—and correct me if I'm wrong, Counsel, but this is a third-party video taken by an organization that Mr. Strand—there's no evidence that he is a part of, okay? Is that fair, Mr. Brennwald?

It wasn't fair. It was dirty—just like Casey.

Officer Vargas pressed on with his account of police activity after *"quote-unquote 'the mob'"*—his repeated phrasing—had spilled into the Capitol. Manning steered him to focus on a scene in an unmarked vestibule—where I had been unwittingly led. I stood there calmly, shielding Dr. Gold behind a railing, hemmed in by the crowd. We stayed there for a bit, looking for a way to exit.

The prosecutors were desperate to spin this "battle of the vestibule" as the linchpin of their narrative—casting me as an insurrection

commander with "clear criminal intent." So Vargas's answer was . . .
illuminating:

MANNING: What were you trying to communicate to these people at this time?

VARGAS: What I was explaining to the [protester] at the beginning, he was trying to cross, and I advised him that I had formed a police line, and that [the protesters] are not to cross. I was trying to make sure that everyone understood that my presence in front of my police line was to let them know that they are not to cross me . . . to let them know that it stops here.

MANNING: And why did you choose to place the police line in that place . . . ?

VARGAS: To let [them] know that crossing me was where the illegal activity was going to take place because I'm giving them the opportunity to **not** cross me. Because once they cross me, they're heading towards my police line, and that's that buffer that ***if you don't want to commit a crime, this is your opportunity*** to walk away.

Ahhh . . . so let me get this straight: In all three of my encounters with law enforcement that day, I complied peacefully each time—as soon as I physically could. Doesn't that mean I took the very "opportunity" Officer Vargas just described . . . and proved my intent *not* to commit a crime?

Perhaps that's why I've remained unflinching—staring down a fire-breathing federal monster—while defending my innocence. Not a single piece of evidence has ever shown me defying a lawful directive or knowingly "crossing a police line"—and none ever will.

My lawyer remained vigilant, pressing the critical point that criminal liability requires specific actions by specific individuals. Again and again during cross, the answer was the same: not a single frame—nor any other evidence—showed me engaged in conduct that was criminal or even suspect.

BRENNWALD: . . . there was another man [at the front, encroaching on Vargas's "police line"] who appeared to you to be an agitator who was trying to get everybody's attention. Do you remember that?

VARGAS: . . . oh, yes, I heard a whistle and someone saying, "Be quiet, be quiet!"

BRENNWALD: Okay. And you recall that that person here [before John Strand had arrived] was trying to get the crowd's attention, but he eventually told them to move forward, and that's what caused the whole crowd to go through?

VARGAS: I do recall . . . yes . . .

BRENNWALD: . . . do you recall telling an FBI agent back on Feb 26, 2021, that there was an unknown subject who yelled "Let's go!" and started waving his hands, which caused the other [nearby] protesters to charge? And then you told this FBI agent, "The protesters never would have charged and no one would have gotten hurt if that person had not done that." Do you recall that?

VARGAS: I do recall . . . yes, sir.

BRENNWALD: And, again, to be clear, your statement twenty-two days after this happened was that if that person hadn't done what he did, none of this would have happened. Nobody would have moved forward. Nobody would have got hurt. Is that right?

VARGAS: That's fair to say . . .

Mr. Brennwald pressed the point, and Vargas conceded: Throughout the footage, I never shouted, chanted, pushed, waved, instigated, or engaged in any turmoil or noncompliance. On the contrary, I stayed locked on my client with protective arms and a vigilant, sweeping gaze—favoring a wall whenever possible, avoiding congestion or confrontation, and always searching for a reasonable way out.

In short, the very picture of a "model security guard."

The entire courtroom seemed to flinch as Ms. Ayers-Perez waddled back to the podium and called the government's sixth co-star: USCP Officer Joseph Pitts. This witness reported a live *Maverick* sighting:

PITTS: There were two individuals that really stood out to me because they were dressed completely different than anybody else . . . [John Strand was] wearing a leather jacket and had Top Gun aviator sunglasses on.

Guilty as charged!

It turned out Officer Pitts was one of only three officers I encountered that day—and in the least direct manner. Ayers-Perez tried to twist his testimony into proof that I refused to comply during the "battle of the vestibule." But even with her frantic prompting, Pitts clarified:

AYERS-PEREZ: Had you tried to communicate with either one of them?

PITTS: I was yelling at the top of my lungs for everyone to clear the area out, and they—nobody was really moving.

I couldn't hear a word. His voice was muffled behind a mask, lost in the chaos and smoke. Pinned against a wall, shielding my client, I had no idea where the inner doors even led. But once I realized people were being directed to exit—not enter—I waited for an opportunity and guided us out peacefully.

No resistance. No confrontation. No crime.

AYERS-PEREZ: Did you think they had heard you?

PITTS: I wasn't sure if they heard me.

We didn't. The only thing we could hear in that vestibule was a headache.

Still desperate to twist reality into her fantasy—claiming I "resisted" police—Ayers-Perez trotted out another of my three encounters: USCP Officer Austin McGoff. She walked him through a long, graphic tale of violence—agitators attacking officers on the Capitol's west side, while I was on the east side. It was naked jury manipulation—stoking hysteria with war scenes that had nothing to do with me.

AYERS-PEREZ: What did you do from there?

McGOFF: From there I attempted to get in touch with my squad. As that was happening, a call for shots fired went across the radio, so we began to respond. Then another call came across that said there weren't any shots fired.

That's because the protesters didn't have guns.

The only shots fired that day came from law enforcement violating use-of-force protocols: rubber bullets sprayed into peaceful crowds to provoke escalation—and, of course, USCP Officer Michael Byrd's murder of military veteran Ashli Babbitt.

Ayers-Perez didn't mention any of it. She moved straight to her chosen scene.

AYERS-PEREZ: What did you see when you got to Statuary Hall?

McGOFF: There was a group in the middle of the hall there, and a woman was—I don't know what to call it.

A speech, perhaps?

The entire world has now seen this "woman"—an ER doctor devoted to saving lives—delivering remarks in the Capitol, as reported in the *Washington Post*. She's since testified, repeatedly, that her sole purpose in Washington that week—corroborated by every piece of evidence—was . . . to give a speech.

McGOFF: It was almost having a conference, reading a letter, or—I'm not sure what to call it, but it was almost like having a press conference in the middle of the hall there.

He called it everything *but* a speech—almost like he'd been coached to avoid that First Amendment word. But the footage is clear: a woman gave a speech. She was in midsentence when an officer, who'd been casually guiding protesters around her, abruptly shoved her. She explained she was a scheduled speaker—but within seconds, realizing he was ordering everyone to move, she complied.

I was standing inside the red velvet ropes, filming the speech. A nearby protester brushed my arm, and I moved on.

AYERS-PEREZ: And you're next to the woman now?

McGOFF: Correct.

AYERS-PEREZ: Are you providing any sort of instructions?

McGOFF: No.

Officer McGoff also noted the deafening chaos—the reverberating noise, the confused traffic—underscoring what I've said from the start: we couldn't make out most of the shouting that day. But whenever we *could* hear or discern an instruction, we complied peacefully. The footage proves it. Every time.

Government gangsters lie for a living. You can watch the footage yourself—and judge with your own eyes.

AYERS-PEREZ: When you're yelling, are you yelling loud?

. . . which tells you everything you need to know about this prosecutor's intelligence level . . .

McGOFF: It was very loud in there, so I thought I was, but I don't recall.

And with that, the circus wrapped its third act—lies, loathing, and lunacy on full display.

★ ★ ★

KNIFE FIGHT

TRIAL DAY 4 | SEPTEMBER 22, 2022

Jason Manning may lack every virtue—honor, humility, certainly honesty—but he makes up for it with conniving skullduggery. It was on full display the next morning at a bench conference—a stunning revival of *the Fruit of the Poisonous Plea.*

MANNING: . . . we anticipate that if Mr. Strand were to testify, he would have testified to out-of-court statements made by Simone Gold (Manning, tellingly, refused to call her "Dr."). The government's position is that those are hearsay and should be excluded.

COOPER: I anticipate Mr. Brennwald will argue "*effect on the listener*"; he went in because of something she said. Why isn't that exception applicable?

For once, Casey at least pretended to apply the law correctly, exposing the flimsy nature of Manning's legal gamesmanship. Shame, however, is another virtue Manning entirely lacks.

MANNING: . . . the jury's going to understand any statement that Mr. Strand makes as having heard from Gold as coming in for its truth. Right? He only follows it if he understands, knowing her as well as he

does, that it's truthful. And it's going to be very
difficult to distinguish between the two things.

Mr. Manning then struck the poisonous blow he'd been lining up
from the start:

MANNING: And secondly, a statement of Gold has
tremendous indicia of unreliability. Right? In her
own plea agreement Gold ["]agreed["] that the 1512
charge had a basis in fact, and ***the essence of that
1512 charge is that she acted with the intent to
obstruct the election.*** She didn't plead guilty to
that charge, but she ["]agrees["] that that has a
basis in fact.

COOPER: Wait—where does she agree, or where does
she admit, that she entered in order to impede the
election?

MANNING: So in the statement of facts—she does
not admit, to your question, that she entered with
the intention to impede the election.

COOPER: Right. [duh.]

MANNING: But in the plea agreement itself [the
government's words—where they lie with impunity
and invent their own reality], which she also signs
[under threat of a twenty-year felony] and ["]
agrees["] to, in Paragraph 4, says: The dismissed
charges also have a basis in fact. It's not proof
beyond a reasonable doubt, but it's a basis in
fact. And **the essence of the <u>factual</u> basis of that
1512 is an intent to obstruct the election.** And her
statement to Mr. Strand is that she had no intention whatsoever to obstruct the election.

The essence of this evil—engineered by Merrick Garland's

Department of Jihad and deployed here by Manning—was legal subterfuge so toxic, it poisoned defendants with the guilt of charges *supposedly dismissed*. And now, exactly as these DOJ gladiators had conspired, that toxin was seeping into my trial, threatening to poison *me*—even though I had rejected their fraudulent plea.

There is no defense for such despotism—only the convulsions of a justice system dying in plain view.

And Manning still hadn't scraped the bottom of his poisonous barrel.

COOPER: Okay. And the second issue?

MANNING: The second issue is that if [John Strand]'s going to testify that his purpose in being inside the Capitol was to provide security for [his client], we submit that it becomes relevant on cross-examination that Mr. Strand tried to bring a pocket knife through courtroom security on Tuesday . . . it bears on the credibility of whether he actually could have been providing security...

My jaw nearly hit the defense table.

Was it really possible—for a sworn government officer—to be this desperate, dishonest, and degenerate? Every day, security screenings uncover forgotten items—pocketknives, lighters, nail clippers—carried by people rushing through airports and courthouses. Obviously, I'd simply forgotten to remove it after working past midnight the night before. The moment I discovered it, I apologized and handed it over.

Routine. Harmless. Unremarkable.

But the morally bankrupt Jason Manning, Esq. his pinched face like a rabid sewer rat—was seething in his obsession to humiliate and destroy me. And there was no smear too absurd, no irrelevant slime he wouldn't stoop to fling.

Brennwald stepped in, searching for any remaining shred of sanity from the pompous emperor.

BRENNWALD: Your Honor . . . Mr. Strand did not know at the time that he brought the pocket knife. . . . He didn't realize it was in his bag. His bag is—and I've seen it—

Gucci, of course.

BRENNWALD:—I joked about it, that it was called a murse, a man purse, because he had so much stuff in it . . . and he was in trial, and he was rushing . . . a lot of people bring things like that to the airport and don't realize it.

COOPER: So . . . that explanation, if it's credible—

If it's credible? Aren't you the Stanford brainiac appointed to determine the plain and proper meaning of things? Are you seriously struggling to decide if it's credible that people forget small items in a side pocket?

BRENNWALD: It injects an issue that's not necessary to come in. It's just a way to embarrass him for having forgotten to take some things out [of his bag]. So I don't see any relevance.

COOPER: Okay. I'll let you know my [decree] after the break.

Spoiler alert: Casey sided with the smear—another dagger to the back of justice.

Ms. Ayers-Perez resumed her tirade, dragging another co-star to the stand—USCP Officer Benjamin Brockwell. This wasn't so much a Q and A as a puppet show, with Ayers-Perez yanking the strings in a desperate attempt to stage her narrative that I was somehow "resisting" police directives, using Brockwell's USCP uniform as the costume.

She was frantic to convince the jury of a crime they couldn't see for themselves. Brockwell even managed to spoil her attempt to conjure a crime out of giving a speech "too close" to General Eisenhower's statue:

BROCKWELL: It looks like he's standing on the bench that's beside the statue . . .

The contrast was stark: J6ers prosecuted for exercising the First Amendment in the shadow of Dwight D. Eisenhower, while leftist mobs destroyed monuments across the country with impunity. In 1948, that later-to-be president wrote "An Open Letter to America's Students," affirming that America's greatness rests on "individual liberty founded on individual responsibility, equality before the law." He warned: "Yours is a country of free men and free women where personal liberty is cherished as a fundamental right. But the price of its continued possession is untiring alertness. Liberty is easily lost."

Ironically, Ayers-Perez had cast me in that role—paying liberty's price at great personal cost to alert the nation that our very soul had been lost.

Brennwald countered her wild speculation with another round of video—each clip showing me exactly as I was: a security guard protecting a dignitary in a volatile environment. Maverick aviators always scanning, black-leather-jacketed arms shielding, my steps always seeking an appropriate exit. But the swirling confusion—and erratic police actions—forced us to ping-pong inside the Capitol for forty-five minutes before we finally found a way out.

Then Manning claimed the honor of dueling alongside the government's ninth and final co-star in Team Lunacy's production of *The John Strand Affair*: FBI Special Agent Eric Turner of the ominous Counterterrorism Squad—because citizens maverick enough to stand up against usurpations are, without a doubt, a terror to tyrants.

Turner wasted no time proving the point, delivering his lines in a gruff monotone more machine than man as he smugly took credit for bulldozing my home—and my life—with the FBI's trademark "MAGA SMASH" SWAT team strike.

Actual terrorism, if we're being honest.

He proudly recounted the blatant rape of my Fourth Amendment rights—surveilling, sabotaging, and stripping my life bare in boot-licking service to Crooked Joe Biden's banana republic. Then came his grand reveal: *"the secret life of John Strand"*—a performance both revealing and ridiculous, which, in hindsight, drew more than a few laughs.

In his creepy special-agent-robot voice, Turner read aloud a selection of my private messages with friends and family, public tweets plainly protected by the First Amendment, and assorted model/actor/insurrectionist trivia:

MANNING: Do you know the defendant's Twitter account name?

TURNER: [@JohnStrandUSA] (formerly @TheJohnStrand and others—but Turner neglected to mention the digital assassinations)

MANNING: Was there also some sort of nickname . . .

TURNER: Yes.

MANNING: What was that?

TURNER: Truth Maverick

MANNING: So could you read this [August 17, 2020] exchange for the jury?

TURNER: Yes. Igor says: "So what do you do [in the wake of COVID lockdowns], still modeling?" Mr. Strand responds, "Yes actually, still modeling and acting."

MANNING: In your investigation, did you look for publicly available information corroborating that the defendant had worked as an actor?

TURNER: Yes.

MANNING: And generally did you find that he had?

TURNER: Yes.

Great! It's official—I'm now an FBI-confirmed actor. So, uh . . . can we talk about that Jason Bourne role now?

MANNING: Can you please read the first sentence of Ms. Gillespie's message.

TURNER: Yes. "John Strand, I swear if [the Biden regime] get in we have to plan how to regain our freedom."

MANNING: Please read the defendant's response to this message.

TURNER: "Trust me. When I write and speak the famous phrases 'live free or die' and 'give me liberty or give me death'—I am not playing."

I trust the reader, having made it this far, will confirm: I am indeed "not playing."

MANNING: Can we please read . . . the exchange [with his mother].

TURNER: This message is from Claire Strand: "What is wrong with CONGRESS?!!!" [John Strand's] response: "They are almost all POLITICIANS. It's like hiring a bunch of alcoholics to run your bar."

No lie detected.

MANNING: Continue.

TURNER: Claire Strand responds, "This is nuts." Mr. Strand responds, "It's like hiring a bunch of pedophiles to run your kindergarten."

MANNING: Special Agent Turner, could you read the date of this [*tweet showing a rally flyer with a dramatic image of President Trump*].

TURNER: Yes. November 6, 2020. Mr. Strand writes, "I organized this for our BHFR group."

MANNING: Can you read the text of this flyer.

TURNER: Yes. "He fought against hell itself to defend us . . . now we need to STAND FOR HIM. Beverly Hills Freedom Rally is calling all patriots to #StopTheSteal #WeAreTheRally."

MANNING: Can you read this [November 7, 2020] message.

TURNER: Yes. This message is from Igor: "[The Left] are making [political persecution] lists of officials who've supported Trump. It's outrageous. I'm so upset that most people don't see how this is becoming a socialist tyranny already."

Mr. Strand responds, "You are correct about cowardly Republicans—and they've always been corrupt, so we need to expose them, root them out. This is a defining moment. . . . And yes, it is outrageous, but exactly what we expected—this is the beginning of a civil war, perhaps not a 'hot war' with bullets (yet) but a definitive conflict nonetheless."

In other words . . . *The Divided States of America.*

MANNING: Could you read [this tweet] written by Eric Metaxas?

TURNER: Yes. "Trump will be inaugurated, having won in a landslide. Many will go to jail for having attempted to murder Uncle Sam and Lady Liberty. Many corrupt institutions will go down in flames. Hang tough, patriots. Pray that justice will be served. The best is yet to come."

MANNING: Can you read what [John Strand] wrote in response?

TURNER: Yes. "Patriots, HOLD THE LINE, #StopTheSteal #Truth Maverick"

We are still holding it.

Eric and I were fast and furious after the 2020 election—immediately condemning it as a fraud and calling for a revival of virtue among public and private citizens alike. To this day, we have *never* conceded that election—now widely known to be illicit—and we continue to work, and pray, for the fulfillment of his prophecy.

MANNING: Have you read other exchanges between [John Strand] and this individual, Taylor Mesplé . . . ?

TURNER: Yes.

MANNING: And generally, what are some of the topics they discuss?

TURNER: They frequently discuss politics.

What? No mention of insurrection? No banter about bomb-making, bullet stockpiling, or militia drilling? Where's all the white-supremacy rhetoric and domestic extremist manifestos?

What kind of a counterterrorism agent are you, anyway?

TURNER: This is from Mr. Strand. "The fraud is massive, and indisputable. We *cannot* allow a passive acceptance of such fraud and corruption of our republic at its very core. This is literally #LiveFreeOrDie time. I'm not joking . . . We are such men. LIONS." And then a lion emoji. Taylor responds, "Yes!" with a lion emoji. Mr. Strand ['likes'] Taylor's "Yes!" lion emoji.

I mean, I know this circus is "justice entertainment" in a DC coliseum . . . but could they at least *pretend* to be serious?

Lion emojis? Really?

MANNING: [Exhibit] 901, please. . . . is [John

Strand] responding to a Tweet of someone else?
. . . and who is that original Tweet from?

TURNER: Yes. Ted Cruz. Senator from Texas.

MANNING: Can you please read the Tweet from Ted Cruz.

TURNER: Yes. "SCOTUS should hear the emergency appeal on the Pennsylvania election challenge."

MANNING: And what does [John Strand] write when reTweeting this?

TURNER: This is MAJOR—full blown warfare to SAVE THE REPUBLIC. #Truth Maverick #IrredeemablyCompromised #ThisElectionWasRigged #StopTheSteal

MANNING: In Senator Cruz's Tweet . . . link to a document . . . did that document use the expression "full blown warfare"?

TURNER: It did not.

MANNING: [Exhibit] 905 [Tweet dated January 2, 2021] . . . and is there an original message that [John Strand] is reTweeting? . . . can you read that one first.

TURNER: Yes. It's from [President Trump], "MAKE AMERICA GREAT AGAIN!"

MANNING: And what does [John Strand] write [in response]?

TURNER: "This is the call to action. This is the plan. Trust the plan. Act. #Truth Maverick #FightBack"

Yes, I said "MAGA" was the plan.

It still is.

MANNING: [Exhibit] 331.02 . . . can you just describe what this message is . . . ?

TURNER: Yes. This is a text message sent to Mr. Strand, with an attachment for various rallies on the sixth of January 2021.

MANNING: Can you read [John Strand]'s response to receiving this flyer.

TURNER: Yes. "I'll be there! Dr. Gold is one of the featured speakers."

"Make the country great' is the plan . . . I'll be there because Dr. Gold is a featured speaker . . ."

Uhhh . . . are they arguing for the prosecution or the defense?

MANNING: Let's do 312.01. What is this?

TURNER: It's a message from Mr. Strand [to] Russell Stuart. "There will be more than a million people here tomorrow . . . gonna get ridiculous. We have [VIP] entry to the POTUS speech tomorrow at 10 or 11 EST, then the Protest speakers will happen after a march somewhere around 1pm EST."

I turned to my lawyers, half amused and half exasperated. "They just proved *our* case!" I hissed.

My intent couldn't be clearer. Every one of these messages—spied on, seized, and now read aloud by their creepy special-agent robot—confirmed one objective: to safely give a speech.

My "intent alibi" was proven, verified, and unassailable.

So . . . can we all go home now?

Mr. Manning had wrung every drop from J6. Now he slithered into my private messages—sent only hours after I left the building, before I learned the full scope of what happened that day.

MANNING: [Exhibit] 342.01 . . . here in Washington,

DC, on the sixth, this was at 5:06 [PM ET] . . . can you read the message [from Bobby Strand to John Strand].

TURNER: Yes. "Are you being safe?"

MANNING: What does [John Strand] write in response to his brother?

TURNER: He writes, "[Dr. Gold] and I were **with** the first dozen patriots to breach the Capitol! We literally made history just now . . . *but we left before it got dangerous"*

MANNING: Can you read what Bobby Strand writes?

TURNER: "History in what way?"

MANNING: And what does [John Strand] write in response?

TURNER: Mr. Strand writes, "I don't think the US Capitol building has been stormed and breached like that—and it caused Pence to delay the certification, so that's very significant."

MANNING: Please read the question that Ms. Gillespie asks.

TURNER: "Was crowd pushing to get in because mad about stolen election or what exactly?"

The response from Mr. Strand: "Yes exactly. We have nothing else left to do at this point—this election was stolen, and everyone else is simply watching it happen. This was a peaceful but powerful show of human force, to make a point."

Of course, the point *now* being made in this DC coliseum was the brutal spectacle of government gladiators stabbing an already-wounded victim, while the partisan emperor and his bloodthirsty crowd salivated for the scripted finale: the lynching of a condemned political dissident.

But those texts—sent in real time—told a different story, one the coliseum willfully ignored: My intent was a *peaceable* display of democratic resolve—meant to spark transparency, reform, and lawful accountability. I had no intent to "storm" anything. I did have a professional obligation: protect a speaker. I fulfilled that—and my patriotic duty—during what became a flashpoint in the fight to control *The Divided States of America*.

"[W]e left before it got dangerous" and "This was a peaceful . . . show" were my honest impressions at the time—just as truthful as everything else laid bare in this court-ordered strip search of my private thoughts.

Anyone who knows me knows I despise senseless, unlawful violence—just as I despise corruption and the exploitation of the innocent. And they know, with total certainty—because my life has consistently proven it—that I would never participate in such violence or condone it in others. The media and the government—but I repeat myself—have painted a false, defamatory picture of J6 and most of its defendants.

They've lied to you—just as they lied about COVID, and for the same predictable reason.

Yes . . . it's a control thing.

The government-media machine had the perfect slice of video queued at the perfect moment—designed to make my testimony look absurd against their riot reels of smoke-filled chaos. But the fraud perpetrated by the government in this **_Greatest American Lie Ever Sold_** is no joke—and those still supporting it should be ashamed. Yes, that includes you, Thom Tillis and Amy Coney Barrett.

For anyone genuinely seeking the truth about J6—those who might question my account, my intentions, and my actions—remember the limits of a first-person view in the middle of a chaotic crowd. That's why I later walked viewers, step-by-step and thought-by-thought, through an honest, chronological breakdown of my "police-guided

Capitol tour" in my viral video ***Do You Know What Happened on J6?***—viewed over ten million times. I urge you to watch that on my social media (X.com/JohnStrandUSA) or at **JohnStrand.com**—and to share it.

The full truth of J6 also reveals something darker than a protest or a riot: Intelligence Community planning. FBI infiltration. Police violence and protocol violations. Pelosi's role in the security collapse. The DNC pipe bomb controversy. Repeated Brady violations and other trampling of civil rights. And a fascist DOJ—weaponized by politics, protected by a poisoned judiciary.

Evidence was *criminally* tampered with and buried—including by members of Congress.

These truths are still clawing their way to daylight, with congressional investigations by Barry Loudermilk and Clay Higgins underway. But in the end, it all comes back to the declaration of our gut-punch Frontline Films video, shot days after my MLK Day arrest:

"We are all being lied to, and people don't have to die."

That truth hung in the air like the smell of blood in the arena—right before the next strike.

Ironically, the very next tweets swung at me only sharpened my point.

MANNING: Can you read the text [of a tweet showing the viral photo of John Strand in Maverick aviators and pink Gucci scarf, standing on the east Capitol steps]

TURNER: Yes. "I know the difference between truth and propaganda. I'll defend truth and attack propaganda, without hesitation, and without apology—every single time. Join the #Red Pill Revolution with me, or get the hell out of the way. The choice is yours. I've made mine. #Truth Maverick #MAGAforever"

MANNING: And based on your view of [John Strand]'s communications, do you have any understanding of what he's referring to with this Red Pill Revolution?

TURNER: I believe I do.

MANNING: What's that?

TURNER: It's a reference to a movie called *The Matrix* in which one of the characters is given the choice of whether to know the truth of what's happening in the movie; and to know the truth of what is happening in that movie, he takes a red pill.

Okay, I guess the special agent robot wasn't *completely* worthless.

MANNING: [Exhibit] 902 . . . the same selfie photo we saw in the last Tweet . . . the date [is January 6, 2021 at 4:43 p.m.] . . . can you read the Tweet?

TURNER: Yes. "I am incredibly proud to be a patriot today, to stand up tall in defense of liberty and the Constitution, to support President Trump and #MAGA forever, and to send the message:

WE ARE NEVER CONCEDING A STOLEN ELECTION.

#Truth Maverick #WildProtest"

Somehow, as I took that photo on those great steps—Stars and Stripes waving behind me, patriots filling the backdrop—I knew this was history. *This was glory*. And I marked it with a statement of uncomfortable courage . . . a statement I knew I would have to stand on forever.

I've never regretted, nor recanted, a single word since.

STAND AND DELIVER

TRIAL DAY 5 | SEPTEMBER 23, 2022

Mr. Manning and his special agent "robot-reading-machine" had finally reached the end of their melodrama: *The Secret Life and Allegedly Corrupt Intent of Model/Actor/Insurrectionist John Strand*. They closed with a crowning absurdity: a photo of me and fellow patriot Ian Smith. This was presented—in all seriousness—as evidence of me being an armed terrorist.

No, I'm not kidding.

Yes, that Ian Smith—the courageous gym owner with the epic beard and legendary defiance of New Jersey tyrant Phil Murphy.

The photo shows us in a hotel lobby on January 5, grinning ear to ear and flexing biceps together in a classic "strong man" pose. It's a "Triumphant Masculinity" tradition we share when crossing paths on the Red Pill Revolution trail.

MANNING: Can you read the text of the [John Strand and Ian Smith bicep flexing photo] Tweet.

TURNER: "Patriots have more fun . . . and more guns." Flexing arm emoji, American flag emoji, flexing arm emoji, #StopTheSteal, #Wild Protest. Hanging with Ian Smith in Washington, DC."

Well—congratulations—the FBI Counterterrorism special agent robot finally found the phantom menace of the "armed insurrectionist."

Or, as Tucker Carlson puts it: "these are not serious people."

That Friday morning, with the DOJ gladiators finally exhausting their battalion of witnesses, my lawyer rose to clarify a few closing points of inaccuracy and insult.

BRENNWALD: Good morning, Agent Turner . . . were you aware that [Dr. Gold is] a medical doctor?

TURNER: Yes.

BRENNWALD: . . . you called her Ms. Simone Gold yesterday. Do you have any reason to believe that she's no longer a medical doctor?

TURNER: I do not.

He did not have a hint of apology or respect, either. An FBI special agent robot *knave* . . . how incredibly predictable.

BRENNWALD: Was it hard to find where Mr. Strand lived?

TURNER: No.

BRENNWALD: I know you said yesterday that . . . after you went to the house and ["]knocked loudly["] (translation: door-splintering battering ram), you called . . . somebody's phone, correct?

TURNER: We attempted to call both of their phones [about ten seconds *before* shattering the front door].

BRENNWALD: At the time you were at the house ready to execute the arrest warrant?

TURNER: That is correct.

BRENNWALD: Did you call them the day before, two days before, three days before and say, "Hey, we want to have you come in? Can you please come down and turn yourselves in?"

TURNER: No.

BRENNWALD: How many agents were with you . . . at the house to execute this arrest warrant?

TURNER: To enter the house, there were approximately eight agents, additional agents to transport the subjects to jail, and additional agents on the perimeter in the event that they attempted to flee the house.

(Around twenty total—for a doctor/lawyer and a model/actor. Your tax dollars "at work.")

BRENNWALD: And was it your expectation that Mr. Strand and Dr. Gold were going to try to break out and fight the FBI and make a run to the border?

TURNER: I had no idea what their intentions were.

Oh—*now* you have "no idea" about my intentions?

What, exactly, was the entire week of clandestine surveillance for?

And the eighteen months crawling through every corner of my digital life?

And the hours you just spent reading my private messages to the world?

This special-agent robot is a lousy liar.

BRENNWALD: Did you look into whether he had a security license?

TURNER: He had what is colloquially called in California a guard card.

BRENNWALD: Okay. And did you find that when you went into the house?

TURNER: We found a guard uniform [which contained my valid *guard card*—its official name by the California Bureau of Security and Investigative Services (BSIS)].

BRENNWALD: And it says "Affiliation, Security and Investigations." Correct?

TURNER: Yes.

BRENNWALD: It says, "Permit for exposed firearm," correct?

TURNER: Yes.

BRENNWALD: So this is a permit to carry a firearm, correct?

TURNER: It is . . . it appears to be that.

BRENNWALD: Do you have any information at all, Agent Turner, that on January 6, 2021, Mr. Strand brought a gun to the Capitol grounds . . . ?

TURNER: I do not.

Well, except for those biceps you were in such a tizzy about. . . .

Mr. Brennwald next clarified that Congress itself was responsible for "obstructing" its own "official proceeding."

BRENNWALD: You're aware, are you not, that . . . in the weeks before January sixth many elected officials . . . were advocating not certifying the results of the election from different states?

TURNER: Yes.

BRENNWALD: There was nothing illegal about somebody not wanting to certify the election without the use of force, correct?

TURNER: To my knowledge, that is not illegal.

BRENNWALD: . . . some of these [text message] conversations [between John Strand and others] were as long as five hundred pages . . . in any of those long or short text messages, did Mr. Strand ever say anything about going to the Capitol to stop an official proceeding . . . before January sixth?

TURNER: Not to my knowledge.

BRENNWALD: Did you find anywhere on his phone or any paperwork or any information anywhere that showed a map of the Capitol before January sixth

that would show someone how to get into the Capitol
and to actually go in the direction of the House
Chamber . . . ?

TURNER: I don't recall seeing a map of the Capitol.

BRENNWALD: You're aware that during the certification process that began at 1:00 p.m. . . . at
least one senator and one congressperson objected
to the counting of the votes from Arizona, correct?

TURNER: Yes.

BRENNWALD: And that objection caused a two-
hour delay [before I and most others reached the
Capitol] . . . and you're aware that there were
senators and congressmen . . . who were trying to
delay the proceedings [indefinitely] hoping that
something would happen . . . correct?

TURNER: . . . I know from testimony that there
were objections . . . initially the Arizona
certification.

BRENNWALD: Okay . . . the fact is that on January
sixth a number of . . . Congresspeople and Senators
stood up to object, not only to Arizona electors,
but later on, even after all this happened, to
Pennsylvania's electors, correct?

TURNER: I believe there were other objections
besides just Arizona.

BRENNWALD: So a lot of people [including elected
officials] . . . wanted to delay the proceedings. . . .

TURNER: Yes, that's my understanding. . . .

BRENNWALD: And the only text or Tweet or anything that Mr. Strand sent to anybody about this

issue was [my text to Bobby] sent over two hours
after he and Dr. Gold left the building, correct?

He quibbled over the precise minute—but yes. He had *nothing*. Not one shred of evidence that I ever mentioned delaying a proceeding . . . or even knew one was happening.

Because I didn't.

That week, I was busy managing an exploding COVID-response nonprofit, prepping a two-week tour, writing a historic speech, and protecting a bold speaker. Not to mention: *the speaker lineup included multiple sitting members of Congress* . . . so I naturally assumed they would recess during our permitted event.

BRENNWALD: You talked yesterday about this "Red Pill Revolution." That comes from the movie *The Matrix* with Keanu Reeves, correct?

TURNER: That's my understanding.

BRENNWALD: And so when they say "revolution," it's referring not to a physical revolution, but to—like if you take the red pill your eyes would be opened to reality, correct?

Preach it, Stephen.

TURNER: That's my understanding from having seen *The Matrix* years ago, yes.

BRENNWALD: So the word "revolution" in that con- text has nothing to do with [physical] fighting, overthrowing, killing. It has to do with knowledge, correct?

TURNER: I don't have a lot of knowledge about the film.

ROBOT POWER ALERT: Battery low. This device will self-de- struct in five seconds. . . .

And with that, the government rested—a sinister script of dystopian inversions, arrogant usurpations, and sadistic manipulations—leaving me battered on the blood-soaked coliseum sand, facing the final clash of this political death match:

My own testimony.

My chance to defend my cherished, mortally wounded innocence.

It was time to take the stand.

This was the other "moment of truth"—in the most literal sense.

After five days buried under an avalanche of lies, it was finally my turn to speak. I had waited, prayed, and prepared for this moment—not with naïve optimism, but with sober gratitude. I knew my words would fall on deaf ears in that coliseum . . . but the truth never dies. And God had called me to speak the truth—come hell or swamp water.

Casey kept a polite façade as he swore me in, even pausing to ask his staff to get me a cup of water. I sat at the witness stand, set down some hotel stationery scrawled with Ephesians 6:12, and committed my words, and my heart, to the glory of God.

Soli Deo Gloria.

Love, Liberty, Rock & Roll.

Okay, here we go. . . .

BRENNWALD: Good morning, Mr. Strand.

STRAND: Good morning.

BRENNWALD: All right . . . for the record, please state your name.

STRAND: My name is John Strand.

BRENNWALD: Where were you born, sir?

STRAND: In California . . .

He walked me through a condensed version of my life leading up to this crucible. When I described my career as a fashion model and Hollywood actor, he cut in with a sharper question.

BRENNWALD: Was it an easy life?

STRAND: No. It's quite the opposite.

BRENNWALD: Did you have times when you were struggling . . . spent some time couch surfing, so to speak?

STRAND: Yes. I even spent a couple of nights sidewalk surfing, actually.

He then pivoted to my more recent, and somehow more difficult, line of work.

BRENNWALD: So without getting into politics or medicine, what's the bird's-eye view of a freedom rally?

STRAND: During that time there were restrictions related to viruses, and people were concerned about the lockdowns, particularly when they were preventing people from going to work and going to church to worship and basic everyday life things that we believe are important for everyone.

BRENNWALD: Were those freedom rallies political? In other words, were they exclusively for Republicans?

STRAND: Absolutely not. We intentionally named it the Beverly Hills Freedom Rally so that it was inclusive for everyone.

BRENNWALD: And did you have people participate who were of all stripes politically?

STRAND: We did, yes.

BRENNWALD: We talked about acting and modeling briefly . . . did you do any other type of work?

STRAND: Oh, sure. I did various odd jobs that actors and models typically do.

BRENNWALD: By the time you met Dr. Gold, had you worked for a private security company?

STRAND: I was licensed as a security guard in the state of California to provide security and entry management at some nicer restaurants in the area [in addition to a private security company].

BRENNWALD: What kind of training did you have, if any, to be a security guard?

STRAND: Hours of training for that security license . . . how to handle agitated people, how to handle myself safely in a crowded situation, how to always support and comply with law enforcement orders, and so forth.

Then Dr. Simone Gold entered the story.

I described meeting her at the Rally—helping her to the stage, organizing the event, managing the crowds. She noticed my ability to coordinate chaos. A few weeks later, she asked me to join her mission.

BRENNWALD: Could you describe Dr. Gold's personality in general.

STRAND: Strong.

I wanted to add, "she's a lifesaving lioness!"—but I'd promised Mr. Brennwald to keep my theatrics reined in.

We walked through the post-stolen-election schedule—Florida on January 3, DC on the fifth, the Capitol speech on the sixth, and another Florida event on the eighth.

BRENNWALD: Were you in the audience when she was speaking? Up on stage?

STRAND: Front row or somewhere very close. I keep very close proximity to Dr. Gold whenever she's in public.

BRENNWALD: Had she been receiving threats to her safety?

STRAND: Yes . . . she had led a press conference that went viral, tens of millions of views.

BRENNWALD: Where was that press conference?

STRAND: On the steps of the Supreme Court.

. . . just across the street from the Capitol's familiar steps. *Déjà vu?*

BRENNWALD: And tell us briefly about an organization called America's Frontline Doctors.

STRAND: A group of doctors that were working hard to learn how to address the COVID issue, and they realized that there was early treatment that is very helpful. Safe medicines that have been FDA-approved for many years.

BRENNWALD: And you're working with [Frontline Doctors] to do what?

STRAND: Just to get the message out. Information, education, advocacy.

BRENNWALD: On January third in Tampa, January fifth and sixth in DC, January eighth back in Florida, did you have any role with respect to her safety?

STRAND: Yes, absolutely. I was the primary person.

With my background and job now clear, we turned to the one day that changed everything.

BRENNWALD: . . . were you familiar with the Capitol building and the hallways, how to get in and how to get out of that building, back on January sixth?

STRAND: No, I wasn't familiar at all.

BRENNWALD: When you came to DC on January fifth,

was one of your goals to go into the Capitol
and interfere with the certification of the 2020
election?

STRAND: No. That never crossed my mind.

There was a pause. The coliseum fell silent. My calm declaration
had shattered the government's central lie. Would the jury—and the
world—accept my testimony, backed by clear evidence? Or would they
scoff, twist facts into agenda, and manufacture criminal intent by sheer
force of political hatred?

After my declaration of innocence, Mr. Brennwald walked the jury step
by step through my firsthand account of J6—from our frigid morning
departure to our afternoon arrival at the Capitol, where several congressmen and national leaders were scheduled to speak.

That plan—inexplicably—never happened.

BRENNWALD: Did you know where the speeches were supposed to be, whether on the Capitol grounds or off?

STRAND: I understood it to be on the Capitol
grounds.

And in fact, the main flyer—promoted weeks earlier—explicitly
mentioned the Capitol *Steps*.

Why has that detail been hidden from the public?

BRENNWALD: So what did you do next?

STRAND: Someone in our group got a phone call:
"Hey, someone's telling me that the speeches are
canceled," which was the first I had heard that.
I was very confused because I knew Congresspeople
were coming to speak, and the flyers had been dis-
tributed weeks in advance, and everyone was here
for the speech, so it just didn't make any sense.

BRENNWALD: So what happened at that point?

STRAND: People [kept] coming minute by minute, and so it was getting fuller, and a group of people had started moving towards the steps.

BRENNWALD: And is that what you and Dr. Gold did?

STRAND: After a few minutes she turned and went that way. She gave me a look like "I've got to go this direction—that's where the people are."

BRENNWALD: Did you say anything to her about whether she should go there?

STRAND: I didn't because she moved quickly and didn't give me a chance to say anything, but she saw in my face that I was concerned because I didn't know what the plan was or where she was going exactly or what else was happening.

BRENNWALD: Mr. Strand, when Dr. Gold started moving toward the steps, did you stay where you were and just let her go?

STRAND: No. That was not an option for me.

BRENNWALD: Why not?

Duty. Loyalty. Integrity.

Virtue—without which a constitutional republic cannot stand, and which I will *never* abandon.

STRAND: My responsibility was to keep her safe in a very large crowd, and it was very busy. I wasn't willing to abandon her, so . . .

BRENNWALD: Did you see people overrun the bike racks on the far side?

STRAND: I didn't. I think it happened before I was close enough.

BRENNWALD: Do you know why Dr. Gold went in that direction?

STRAND: Because that's where the people were. Her intention was to give a speech to a crowd, so she went to the crowd.

It was early 2021—deep in the COVID *plan-demic* madness.

The government was lying. People were dying. And Dr. Gold was on a mission.

★ ★ ★

BRENNWALD: Was there a point where you saw—not the officers at the top of the steps near the door—but lower down on the steps, from your vantage point?

STRAND: . . . I didn't see any obvious police lines or anything. There were people everywhere. A lot of people.

BRENNWALD: Did you expect your client to be in that area that day?

STRAND: I expected her to be in the general area because there was a speech that was supposed to happen there, but I expected it to be organized, and I expected a stage and Congresspeople and a lot of security telling people where to go.

BRENNWALD: Did she make any attempt to speak at that point on those steps?

STRAND: She did.

BRENNWALD: Where were you both when that happened?

STRAND: I was following her to make sure that she didn't trip or get knocked over. She was trying to get the attention of people nearby. We had come from the north, so I guided her towards the side of the steps . . . it was very chaotic . . .

BRENNWALD: So in these videos that we've seen of you and your client inside the Capitol . . . you always seem to be on one side of the hall or another instead of the middle of a whole bunch of people.

STRAND: Correct.

BRENNWALD: Why?

STRAND: That's my instinct . . . stay out of the middle of a thick throng of people that can be unpredictable.

BRENNWALD: In the video that we saw earlier . . . your phone shows her, and she's talking about 'we're here to talk about truth' and then you pan to the crowd. Is that the crowd that she was trying to speak to?

STRAND: Yes, essentially.

BRENNWALD: So now you're at the top of the steps, right?

STRAND: Yes, trapped there.

BRENNWALD: Did you realize that this was a restricted area?

STRAND: I didn't.

From there, my lawyer dismantled the government's manipulative portrayal of the Officer Pollitt incident. He played the complete, full-speed video—exposing how Manning and Ayers-Perez had distorted it with deceptive edits. The truth was plain: I'd been trapped when an unprovoked police assault—later shown to violate use-of-force protocols—sparked a panic.

Without warning, the inner Columbus entry doors were

opened—*from the inside*—signaling that entry was now permitted. The surge became a tidal wave, sweeping us forward with such force that Dr. Gold stumbled and was nearly trampled. CCTV footage caught me catching her mid-fall and guiding her away from the bottleneck.

Next, Brennwald played the government's "escape route" video— footage from the opposite side. *I was never there.* Then he played the real footage—with me trapped, protecting my client, blindsided by a sudden police attack I neither caused nor understood.

And then came the dagger: Brennwald proved Jason Manning had flat-out lied.

Manning told the jury I was a participating assailant.

And he *faked* evidence to "prove" it.

BRENNWALD: Is that your hand, sir?

STRAND: It's not.

BRENNWALD: But you are right there, where that [digital notation] dot is, correct?

STRAND: That's my face, yes.

BRENNWALD: . . . but that's not your hand?

STRAND: That's not my hand.

BRENNWALD: And how do we know that's not your hand?

STRAND: I was wearing black leather gloves the entire day.

COOPER: No rhymes, please.

C'mon, Casey—what happened to your comedic genius?

BRENNWALD: We're going to mark these [gloves] Exhibit 108.

STRAND: Don't mess up my gloves.

BRENNWALD: [Do you] recognize these gloves . . . is there something distinctive about them?

Obviously.

STRAND: Yes. There's an English Laundry tag on one of them.

BRENNWALD: Is that some kind of a brand?

STRAND: It is.

Hey—if you're *MAGA Zoolander* leading a Red Pill "insurrection," you better know how to dress for it.

BRENNWALD: Your Honor, I'd move these into evidence.

COOPER: The gloves are admitted—

BRENNWALD:—as long as we get them back. . . . Do you see what's on this screen, Mr. Strand?

STRAND: I do.

BRENNWALD: And at the risk of being extremely Captain Obvious, who is that person?

STRAND: John Strand.

BRENNWALD: And do you see your right hand there?

STRAND: I do.

BRENNWALD: What is on your right hand?

STRAND: That's my English Laundry glove.

BRENNWALD: Did you have them on both hands?

STRAND: I did.

BRENNWALD: Just in case we're trying to be tricky.

STRAND: No, no, I don't think I've ever only worn one glove. That would be weird.

Well—I *have* done some pretty weird photo shoots . . . but that's another book for another day.

★ ★ ★

BRENNWALD: As the police officers go by . . . what are you doing there?

STRAND: I was applauding the police officers.

BRENNWALD: Why?

STRAND: They had a very difficult job, and I was very grateful for them helping us to safely get out of the building.

BRENNWALD: Did you realize back on January sixth how bad their job was compared to what you now know?

STRAND: No, I have heard personal testimonies from officers . . . So I remember feeling grateful for the police that day, but I'm even more grateful now.

Brennwald played footage from the Columbus entry chaos, showing my arms around my client—acting as a human shield in the frenzy.

BRENNWALD: Was that a pretty chaotic scene right there?

STRAND: Very. I was stumbling as we got pushed through the door there, so I thought she might actually fall, and I tried to stabilize her.

BRENNWALD: If you had turned around right there to try to go back out, could you have physically done so . . . ?

STRAND: I couldn't have done so under any circumstances.

More video showed us walking between the red velvet ropes, obviously disoriented.

BRENNWALD: Did you know at that point where you were, sir?

STRAND: No idea whatsoever.

BRENNWALD: Did you know that this was close to the House Chamber in the U.S. Capitol?

STRAND: I did not.

BRENNWALD: Why were you going back that way?

STRAND: I was trying to stay in the main public hallways . . . but I was definitely very disoriented at that point.

BRENNWALD: Did you have a map?

STRAND: No.

BRENNWALD: . . . did you have a plan . . . to interfere with anything that Congress was doing?

STRAND: No. The only plan I had was to guard my client while she was giving a speech. . .

BRENNWALD: Did you . . . go down some unknown hallway and figure something out?

STRAND: I was conscious of trying to stay in the main public hallways.

BRENNWALD: Did you have any intention . . . to go into the House Chamber?

STRAND: No. I would have avoided that.

BRENNWALD: Did you try to push your way through to get to the front doors and try to push them open?

STRAND: No. I did my best not to push anyone.

Mr. Brennwald kept the videos rolling, tracing our path through the Capitol trap.

BRENNWALD: So [in a text message] Ms. Gillespie says to you, "This isn't going to win people over. I know what you experienced was not what people there are being told but there is plenty of video that shows violence," right?

STRAND: Right.

BRENNWALD: Did you see the violence on the west side?

STRAND: No.

BRENNWALD: What do you tell Ms. Gillespie?

STRAND: I said, "I was not near the chamber where Cruz or Congress were meeting as far as I know . . . hard to know exactly which area we were in. But the crowd had zero guns, no weapons, just flags and passion."

BRENNWALD: Did you have any idea that this text would be retrieved by the [FBI] and used to prosecute you?

STRAND: No, of course not.

BRENNWALD: Did you write this text in advance to try to give yourself plausible deniability about knowing where you were in the building?

STRAND: No. I was just answering questions from people that knew I was in the city that day and explaining my experience.

BRENNWALD: You say, "There's no doubt about the truth of the 2020 election. The only question is: will you act upon that truth? WILL YOU STAND FIRM? This moment will define our country, our generation, and our national destiny. It's now, or never. #Truth Maverick #StopTheSteal." That's what you said the day before January sixth?

STRAND: Yes.

. . . and history has proved me right.

BRENNWALD: The Stop the Steal rally, was that about going to the Capitol and breaking in and terrorizing people?

STRAND: No, absolutely not . . . it was only about the idea that the election needed to be audited or reviewed legally.

BRENNWALD: So when you used the hashtag, were you using it as a preamble to what happened the next day?

STRAND: No. It was just a reference to the general effort to review the election.

BRENNWALD: Read [my quote-tweet of Senator Cruz].

STRAND: "This is MAJOR—full-blown warfare to SAVE THE REPUBLIC." And that was a reply to Senator Ted Cruz's tweet that SCOTUS should hear the emergency appeal on the Pennsylvania election challenge.

BRENNWALD: So when you were talking "full blown warfare," were you talking about guns, tanks, shoulder-launched grenades, and physical violence?

STRAND: No. I always meant political warfare or ideological warfare, a war of ideas.

BRENNWALD: This message between you and your brother . . . he asks you on January 6th at 5:06 [p.m.] if you're safe?

At that moment, I'd pulled my client away from our conversations with protesters on the Capitol steps. As daylight faded, I suspected counterprotest violence might break out, so we quickly returned to our hotel. I was still processing a ten-hour day abruptly disrupted by chaos and now a flood of concerned text messages as the media hysteria exploded.

STRAND: Yes. "Are you being safe?" Uh-huh.

BRENNWALD: And you say what?

STRAND: I said, "[Dr. Gold] and I were **with** the first dozen patriots to breach the Capitol."

By that I meant—since we were near the Columbus doors as they opened from the inside—we were swept in with the first group nearby. The terms "storm" and "breach" were already being thrown around (fueled by instant media reports—*with suspiciously uniform talking points*), and I assumed police had opened the doors for crowd control, managing the "breach."

I didn't yet know about black-clad operatives who broke in—and were never caught.

So at 5 p.m., my genuine understanding of what would later be branded an "insurrection"—with no guns—was that we'd been caught in a chaotic surge, like at a concert or sporting event. In this case, the security failure by Nancy Pelosi and Muriel Bowser was historic and catastrophic. Once order returned, what remained was a bizarre disruption within an otherwise legitimate day of protest activity.

And here's the bitter irony: Despite the trauma and loss of that day (rest in peace, Ashli Babbitt, Roseann Boyland, Kevin Greeson, and Benjamin Phillips—and condolences to Kyle T. Jones and anyone else who found themselves weeping on the floor)—my "5 p.m. understanding" remains largely valid. The hysteria that followed was manufactured by the same *Artificial Aristocracy* bent on eradicating President Trump and punishing any American bold enough to support him.

In truth, J6 was a historic collision of civic engagement with a weaponized government striking to exploit that very citizenry. The result? An otherwise peaceful and patriotic day of classic American protest was hijacked to spark a *manufactured* riot. Even then, it was far less destructive than the "summer of love" riots by Antifa and BLM—excused, praised, and bailed out by the same regime that now called me a criminal.

Of course, the truth—like Trump—is intolerable to the Derangement Syndrome partisans who packed my jury and filled the DC coliseum. They would never accept such a #TeamReality assessment.

But their refusal doesn't make it any less true.

BRENNWALD: Okay. What do you say next?

STRAND: "We literally made history just now . . . but we left before it got dangerous."

BRENNWALD: So "we literally made history." Did you think you were making history by giving a speech inside the Rotunda?

STRAND: Yeah, kind of; that seemed unusual, so it seemed a bit historic; and just the fact that so many people came to Washington, DC, that day seemed like a historic kind of day.

BRENNWALD: But it's not true that you left before it got dangerous, is it?

STRAND: When I said that we left before it got dangerous, I was referring to the fact that many previous rallies . . . tended to have dangerous stuff . . . towards the end of the day when the sun came down and got darker, so I was telling my brother we got out of the area before that started to potentially happen.

BRENNWALD: Have you been to rallies before where people turned over police cars . . . where people smash huge bank windows, Bank of America windows . . . light police cars on fire?

STRAND: I've seen a lot of that [on TV], but I haven't attended those.

That chaos is the trademark of radical left protests—not Trump rallies. The America First MAGA movement is the *new* party of *old* American values: liberty grounded in responsibility, justice anchored in equality under law. We respect law and order, and the police who uphold it.

By contrast, it's the woke-ified, lunatic-left Democrat Party—propped up by the complicit RINO establishment—that has pushed

"Defund the Police," defended actual domestic terror groups like Antifa and Hamas, and consistently fueled the real political violence ravaging our cities. This isn't partisan bluster—it's a documented reality our nation has tolerated for far too long.

"Tolerance" twisted to excuse lawlessness is no virtue—it's just another leftist lie.

BRENNWALD: But you saw people smashing windows in our nation's Capitol . . . ?

STRAND: At the time I just saw people pushing.

What mattered legally was what *I*, the defendant, saw and understood *at the time*. I personally witnessed almost no vandalism or violence. Selective video clips on endless loop—stripped of peaceful context and juiced with boosted audio—is not reality. It's propaganda—weaponized to justify a partisan lynching.

As for "we stormed the Capitol," it was a figure of speech, like "storming the field" after a football game. I was describing the excitement of the overwhelming crowd surge we were caught in. At that point, I believed police had opened the doors for crowd control, with no reason to believe otherwise.

BRENNWALD: You said in one of your messages, "we stormed the Capitol."

STRAND: . . . I was just referring to being in a crowd where that all happened.

BRENNWALD: You say, "it caused Pence to delay the certification." Now, this text admittedly is sent more than **two hours after** you left the building, but . . . when did you find out that Pence delayed the certification?

STRAND: Around that time because I didn't realize that that was all happening; and once we had gotten out of the building . . . people were mentioning that that was one of the things that happened.

BRENNWALD: And you thought—like other politicians who wanted to delay things to count votes or whatever, you thought it was significant that Pence delayed things, correct?

STRAND: But it didn't seem like a normal thing that would happen.

BRENNWALD: And were you happy about it?

STRAND: Not really. I wasn't happy that the day was so chaotic.

BRENNWALD: But you have all these political tweets and messages in the months . . . before all this happened talking about Stop the Steal, the election's stolen . . . right?

STRAND: Yes. I was interested in trying to advocate for transparency and a legal process, but when we were in Washington, DC, on January 6th my only purpose that day was my client's speech. And I was personally hoping that there would be a different political and legal outcome, but then . . . we got pushed inside of the building and all of this crazy stuff happened. I was just trying to process what happened. . . . I would say there was a mix of emotions because it was a very emotional time for everybody.

BRENNWALD: So I guess my question, Mr. Strand, is, when you went into the building, whether you got pushed or pulled or whatever, was it your intent to interfere with the certification of the election of 2020?

STRAND: No, that was not my intent.

BRENNWALD: What do you think the whole Stop the Steal was about?

STRAND: Just a protest to allow people to express the fact that they wanted the election to be audited.

BRENNWALD: So tell us what this [text message] says . . .

STRAND: "I am working with a few others in Beverly Hills to organize the continuation of the Beverly Hills Freedom Rally so that they will remain weekly, perpetually, to grow the "Red Pill Revolution" movement, and to educate, organize, and empower our citizens to take action."

BRENNWALD: So when you're talking about warfare and live free or die and all those slogans that sound violent out of context, were you actually talking about organizing people to rally and to [peacefully] protest?

STRAND: Yes. To participate in the political process.

BRENNWALD: I'd asked Agent Turner earlier this morning about the "Red Pill Revolution." He said he'd seen a movie a few years back. Maybe you've seen it more recently. Can you tell the jury very briefly what the "Red Pill Revolution" means?

STRAND: The special agent summarized it pretty nicely. It's just the idea that a red pill indicates an awakening or a realization of what's actually happening around you, and a blue pill keeps you in a state of blissful ignorance.

BRENNWALD: . . . what does [a text message from Igor] say?

STRAND: "With the COVID, there's a been a whole lot of people who have started to vlog."

BRENNWALD: What do you respond?

STRAND: "Funny that you mention that: Because, I don't know if you follow my social media, but I've remained nonpolitical as a model and actor for over a decade . . . and that suddenly changed dramatically this year. . . . Facebook and Twitter is where the cultural and political wars are waged, and I've launched an entire campaign called Truth Maverick."

BRENNWALD: Did you have a nickname growing up?

STRAND: Maverick, yes. My dad was a naval officer, so *Top Gun* was our favorite.

BRENNWALD: When you mentioned the words "wars" and "fighting" and "freedom" or "die," are you talking about physical wars against another party, or are you talking about something else?

STRAND: I'm not talking about physical wars. I'm talking about wars of ideas and political conflicts and that kind of thing.

BRENNWALD: I think I'm done . . . thank you, Your Honor.

An ominous crescendo had been building throughout my direct examination, swelling into the pulse-pounding tribal beat of an execution squad—before crashing to a climactic halt, leaving eerie silence hanging in the coliseum air.

We had reached the final clash in this scripted death match:

John Strand versus Jason Manning.

The government's ruthless gladiator, desperate to cripple me before we'd even crossed swords, reached for the oldest trick in the scoundrel's playbook—flinging dirt in my eyes as we turned to face each other.

MANNING: If I understood your testimony correctly, you stated that your sole purpose in entering the Capitol on January 6th was to provide security for [insult] Gold; is that correct?

STRAND: That's correct.

MANNING: And you testified that you're a security professional or a trained security guard of some sort; is that correct?

STRAND: I have some training, yes.

MANNING: When you came to the courthouse this morning on Monday you had to go through security yourself; isn't that right?

STRAND: I did, yes.

MANNING: And the courthouse security found a pocket knife in your bag; is that right?

Manning was so unhinged he couldn't even get the date right—it had happened the week before.

STRAND: I forgot what was in my bag so . . .

MANNING: So you are the type of trained security guard who doesn't realize you can't bring a knife into a federal court; is that right?

STRAND: No. I wasn't trying to bring a knife into federal court. I had no intention of doing that. I simply forgot what was in the side pocket because I travel a lot. I had a lot on my mind this week. So when they opened it and said, "Oh, you have this in the bag," I said, "Oh, I'm so sorry, I forgot that was in [there]." That was all.

MANNING: So if I understand you correctly, you just happened to have a knife in your bag, and you just happened to forget; is that right?

Not very bright, is he.

STRAND: I forgot it was in the side pocket of that bag, yes, sir.

MANNING: Defense Exhibit 106 . . . is this a map or a document that you had seen before January 6th?

STRAND: No.

MANNING: No?

STRAND: I had not.

MANNING: Okay . . . so this is only something that you've seen sometime after January 6th as part of preparing for your testimony?

STRAND: Yes, sir.

MANNING: And you testified that this blue area that's circled around No. 8, that that was the area where you understood [insult] Gold had a permit to speak on January 6th; is that right?

STRAND: At the time I understood that she was a scheduled speaker at an event that was permitted and going to take place just outside the Capitol. I actually had no idea which corner.

Manning hissed Dr. Gold's name with deliberate disrespect, spitting it without her proper title. He went to great lengths making the idiotic point that a government-approved permit for the Capitol protest didn't authorize entry into the building itself—really, Sherlock? Then he mocked my security work and lunged at my public statements criticizing the government's failures and abuses.

He kept lunging with aggressive accusations, trying to make me backpedal.

But I refused to flinch.

MANNING: You wrote there was, quote, no signage or directives indicating such entry was prohibited, correct? That's what you wrote?

STRAND: Yes, sir.

MANNING: So in this tweet you were saying there was nothing to indicate to you that you were prohibited from entering the Capitol. Is that what you're saying here? That's what you're saying here, correct?

STRAND: At the time that it happened, it was unclear.

MANNING: Is your testimony today that it was unclear that you couldn't enter the Capitol?

STRAND: At the moment that people entered it was unclear what was happening and why because it was a very confusing situation. The cops were standing in front of the door, and then they left, and then the doors opened [from the inside]. I was also confused as to where people were supposed to go at that time.

He pulled another deceptive stunt—this time flashing a photo of a modest "police line" with six officers near the Columbus entrance. What he failed to mention? It was no longer there by the time I reached the steps.

MANNING: But nevertheless you did cross that line of police, correct? Correct?

Resisting the double-punch intimidation tactic, I countered his lies once again.

STRAND: Not exactly, sir . . . they weren't lined up in that formation once I was in a crowd that pushed towards the door.

Then he circled back to jabbing at my role in protecting Dr. Gold, once again deliberately insulting her—and I'd had enough.

MANNING: And you had said [insult] Gold had received threats before January 6th?

STRAND: *DOCTOR* Gold received threats, yes.

The courtroom snapped to attention. My voice had shifted from calm to cutting in an instant.

MANNING: You'd prefer that I call her "Dr. Gold"? . . . I can do that.

STRAND: Thank you—that's appropriate.

The smackdown was subtle—but infinitely satisfying.

He quickly lashed out again, clinging to Officer Pollitt's brief stumble as if it proved something sinister.

MANNING: And you didn't join those people to help him, did you?

STRAND: It was not possible. I would have had to knock somebody else over to do that, so . . .

I let the stupidity of his suggestion hang in the air.

Then came the Jason Manning blitzkrieg: a barrage of freeze-frame images, sliced from footage of the Columbus entryway—long after I'd already been swept into a panicked crowd, pinned by a violent police assault in total violation of protocol.

With brazen lunacy, this government gladiator argued that I should have tracked every swing of every flagpole in that chaos—which he could now photoshop and wield against me from the comfort of his cheap polyester suit.

MANNING: Do you see the flag striking the door *this time*, Mr. Strand?

His contemptuous sneer was dripping with hatred.

STRAND: Are you talking about the American flag that's on the left?

MANNING: Correct.

STRAND: Yes. I saw it wave. It leaned towards the door. That's about the extent of what I saw.

MANNING: And you're saying you understood that to be somebody waving a flag as if this was some sort of parade?

. . . he asks this of someone who had just walked for hours through a million people waving flags and—yes, marching in "some sort of parade."

The malicious gaslighting was surreal.

STRAND: Based on the photo, I don't think I even saw that flag at that point. If I did, it might have been in my peripheral vision, and they were waving all the time so . . .

MANNING: Well, you testified a moment ago that you were paying attention to your surroundings, correct?

STRAND: To the best of my ability, sir, I was.

MANNING: And those abilities don't include seeing someone striking a flagpole against the door within five feet of you. Is that your testimony?

STRAND: Sir, my testimony is that there were many, many flags in the crowd that entire day, and they were waving all the time, and at this moment it was very, very thick, very, very dense. I was being pushed a lot. Everyone was. It was difficult to breathe even at that point. So I don't remember which flag I saw when.

MANNING: And at this time your testimony is that

you're trying to provide security for [insult] Gold?

STRAND: My testimony is that I'm pinned against the wall with **DOCTOR** Gold, and I'm just trying to keep her from being hurt.

MANNING: Do you agree that you were making no effort to try to get away from the flags that are being swung at people that are just a few feet away from you? Is that right?

The outright fraud of this question was stunning.

Were we watching the same video?

STRAND: There was nowhere for me to go. I was pinned on all sides at that point [as seen in the video].

MANNING: So pinned that you couldn't even try to turn around and walk away?

That's generally what "pinned on all sides" is meant to convey, Mr. I-Went-to-Law-School-and-Mock-You-for-Working-at-Restaurants.

STRAND: Yes, sir. That's correct.

Manning grew more belligerent, firing dishonest questions like a machine gun.

MANNING: That skirmish happened right in front of you, correct?

STRAND: Not right in front of me, no.

MANNING: Within three feet of you, correct?

STRAND: Maybe five or six feet and several bodies, so I'm sure I didn't see it happen when I was there. There were people in the way.

MANNING: But your testimony is that until this trial you had no idea that there were people skirmishing with police at the very time and place that you went to the Capitol? Is that your testimony?

STRAND: My testimony is that it wasn't chaos like this when we first got into the general area, and it got progressively more chaotic, but we were unable to leave at that point. So at this point I was stuck and just trying to stay as safe and stationary as possible to make sure that my client didn't get injured.

MANNING: This is you [in the freeze frame image], right?

STRAND: Yes, sir.

MANNING: There's nobody pushing behind you, is there? There's not, correct? The closest person to you is the person in the police helmet; isn't that right?

STRAND: I don't think that's actually correct because it's a different perspective [in this freeze frame image]. So I think there's other people here that are closer to me, the angle there, but . . .

MANNING: Your testimony is that there's somebody who is so short that they can't be seen behind this police officer but there nevertheless is somebody behind you? Is that your testimony?

STRAND: Sir, it's a freeze frame again, so when it's actually happening, people are moving, and it was very, very chaotic and very, very densely packed there so . . .

MANNING: Nobody forced you into the Capitol; isn't that right?

STRAND: No, sir, that's not correct.

MANNING: You believe you were forced in?

STRAND: By physical force of a crowd, yes, sir.

Again and again, this gladiator slashed at my testimony—distorting video frames, twisting words, and slandering every respectful answer.

At one point, he even lied about the speech itself, telling the jury it was solely about the (stolen) election. That's an obvious fraud. I wrote that speech. I knew every word. It had already been delivered verbatim at Freedom Plaza on January 5—to ten thousand people with live media coverage.

You've read it yourself—you be the judge.

MANNING: So is it your testimony that after you saw what you saw inside the Capitol you abandoned your support of Stop the Steal?

STRAND: My support of Stop the Steal as a hashtag is just the topic of election integrity. That was always true for me before and after.

MANNING: So you'd still support a "Stop the Steal" hashtag because in your mind that has nothing to do with people chanting "Stop the Steal" and smashing windows in the Capitol?

Right—because in Mr. Manning's world, a slogan defines every crime ever committed by anyone who chanted it. Tell me, has he prosecuted any BLM rioters for *their* window-smashing? Burning businesses? Killing cops? Laying siege to cities for months?

I didn't think so.

STRAND: It definitely does not have anything to do with smashing windows, sir, no. Smashing windows is illegal, inappropriate, and I would never support anything like that.

MANNING: It has nothing to do with smashing

windows except all the people chanting "Stop the
Steal" and smashing windows, right?

"All the people"? Out of a million people in DC that day, and thousands streaming through the Capitol while police opened the doors . . . how many *actually* smashed windows?

Go ahead. We'll wait.

STRAND: Well, sir, the people who smashed windows on January 6th were breaking the law . . . and I don't approve of that. I would never encourage anyone to do that or anything that's illegal; so I don't conflate that with the name "Stop the Steal" as a concept for election integrity.

But Manning still wasn't finished. He ended with a cheap shot at my faith—mocking me and my pastor, Rob McCoy, for daring to speak publicly about J6. The interview we posted exposed facts the media and his own regime ignored, twisted, or buried.

MANNING: But in that interview with your friend, Mr. McCoy, you said the people in the crowd on January 6th were just like tourists; isn't that right?

STRAND: There were times where that occurred. People were walking through the red velvet ropes, on the stanchions in the main halls in the Capitol. . . . And so it was clear that there were a lot of people there that day. Some of them acted violently and inappropriately, which is terrible because it puts innocent people in danger, and it ruins everything for everybody else. But there were plenty of people that were not violent people and were not trying to break the law. I was one of them, and so there were a lot of people that

I didn't want to be blamed as violent, if they weren't . . . it was a long day where some violent things happened. I did not condone those or participate in them, and like I said, I wanted it to be clear that most people had every intention of being peaceful and law-abiding, including myself. Others did not, and I didn't want them to be conflated.

MANNING: Your testimony is that your sole purpose of being inside the Capitol was to be with [insult] Gold to provide her security; is that right?

STRAND: Yes, sir.

MANNING: Okay. And you're a trained security guard, correct? That's your testimony?

STRAND: Yes, sir.

MANNING: And as a trained security guard, if you wanted to get out of that door you absolutely could have, correct?

Notice what he did there?

Team Lunacy, ladies and gentlemen.

STRAND: No. But I've tried to explain to the best of my ability how I made the best decision possible at each moment to protect my client and to observe what police officers' directives were, and there weren't a lot of directives for a while. It was very confusing in the building. But once it settled down and they gave directives, we followed them.

MANNING: . . . nothing further from the government, Your Honor.

At last—after *four* brutal hours on the stand—the beating was over. And I was still standing.

Every attack met.

Every falsehood corrected.

Every ounce of strength expended to speak the truth in a storm of lies and hatred.

I had faced down the lions and liars of a DC coliseum, knowing full well I would soon face the fiery furnace of unprecedented political persecution.

But I had refused to surrender.

And in that moment, I felt a soothing breeze of God's peace, calming my mind and renewing my spirit.

I had kept my dignity.

I had upheld my honor.

I had borne true witness before men.

And I had given glory to Almighty God.

It was a profound realization.

I knew the jury's verdict was already purchased, their seats secured for a pre-scripted lynching. And now, it was clear the pompous emperor posing in a black robe held open prejudice and animus. He had been publicly spurned by the woman—and Stanford Law classmate—that he retaliated against with shocking dishonesty and vindictive abuse.

It was obvious he would soon retaliate against me as well.

But above him stood another Judge—the supreme Judge of all mankind, who sees what is done in darkness, who alone pierces the heart and weighs the soul. I knew He had rendered me innocent—and pronounced me as righteous—*by the blood of the Lamb and the word of their testimony.*

That was the ultimate verdict.

The only judgment that would ever truly matter.

FINAL FRAUD

TRIAL DAY 8 | SEPTEMBER 26, 2022

I was grateful—despite the bludgeoning of lies—for the chance to stand in the lion's den and fight back with truth. Grateful to tell the real story of J6 and the true intent of my heart—under oath, before God and men, in that DC courtroom-coliseum.

But I was glad that battle was over. It was exhausting.

Still, the sinister charade dragged into the next week. And with it came the repulsive nightmare of Ms. Ayers-Perez, returning to the stage for her grand finale: a teeth-gritting desecration of our eyes, our ears, and any lingering shred of reality.

Before she began, however, His Majesty—the supremely arrogant Casey Cooper—set her up for success with a subtle but lethal perversion of justice. In his jury "instructions," he recited the standard platitudes: *"you should determine the facts without prejudice, fear, sympathy, or favoritism . . . decide the case solely from a fair consideration of the evidence"* and *"every defendant in a criminal case is presumed to be innocent . . ."* Yet buried beneath those hollow words, he planted fatal errors.

The first: supporting the DOJ's bastardized use of the twenty-year felony they had weaponized into the blade of their fascist sword:

COOPER: The term "official proceeding" includes a proceeding before the Congress . . .

A judge is required to give accurate definitions in the context of a specific statute—not just in vague generalities. So what exactly is an "official proceeding" under 18 U.S.C. § 1512(c)(2)?

That statute came from the Corporate Fraud Accountability Act of 2002, part of the Sarbanes-Oxley Act. To be "SOX compliant," executives had to personally certify financial statements. Congress passed it in response to the Enron scandal, clearly written for criminal proceedings involving (drum roll) . . . corporate fraud—not election certifications (or any other congressional proceedings).

Other statutes exist to cover Congress—like U.S.C. § 1505—but those top out at five years of prison. So the DOJ hijacked 1512—twisting it far beyond its design to fit their dishonest legal theory. Why? To wield a *twenty-year* prison threat. The goal was obvious: terrify defendants into crumbling to poisonous plea deals with a "statement of offense" laced with lies.

That deceit was the cornerstone of ***The Greatest American Lie Ever Sold***.

Along with President Trump and over three hundred other American citizens, I was indicted under §1512(c)(2), a tiny subsection buried in a statute titled—get this—"Tampering with a Witness, Victim, or an Informant."

Feeling bewildered yet? Here's the actual text:

"(c) Whoever corruptly—

(1) alters, destroys, mutilates, or conceals a record, document, or other object, or attempts to do so, with the intent to impair the object's integrity or availability for use in an official proceeding; or

(2) otherwise obstructs, influences, or impedes any official proceeding, or attempts to do so,

shall be fined under this title not more than $250,000 or imprisoned not more than 20 years, or both."

Now, here's the critical part: the DOJ only charged defendants using subsection (c)(2)—the vague "otherwise" clause—divorced from the context of (c)(1).

Remember, this entire section of §1512 falls under a title that indicates any infraction must relate to a corrupt, intentional effort to "tamper with a witness, victim, or informant."

Let's be clear: There were no trial witnesses, evidence tampering, or court records involved in J6.

What *was* involved?

A Congressional session.

A mass protest.

And a weaponized government twisting a corporate fraud statute into a political machete.

The United States Capitol is—quite literally—the People's house. Whatever one may think of the chaos that day, it was not a violation of §1512. Using that statute here was not just a stretch—it was fraudulent lawfare, designed to destroy Trump supporters and criminalize dissent.

Even President George Bush warned us when signing §1512 into law:

"To ensure that no infringement on the constitutional right to petition the government for redress of grievances occurs in the enforcement of section 1512(c) . . . the executive branch shall construe the term "corruptly" in section 1512(c)(2) as requiring proof of a criminal state of mind on the part of the defendant."

Casey's elephant-sized legal error paved the road that Ayers-Perez was so hot and bothered to travel with her hate-blooded jury—hell-bent on reaching a twenty-year felony lynching. He also blurred the definition of "corruptly," reducing it to generic *mens rea*—the vague awareness of acting improperly—rather than its true legal meaning: acting with intent to gain a fraudulent, *personal* benefit.

Clearly, not all Stanford lawyers are created equal.

Next, the errant emperor bungled another crucial instruction—twice—on §1752(a)(1):

COOPER: Count 2 of the indictment charges the defendant with entering **or** remaining in a restricted building or grounds.

Just two little letters—"or" instead of "and." But when you hold the power to destroy lives, two letters can be the difference between justice and tyranny.

The statute requires both: a person must knowingly *enter* (which requires adequate notice of restricted status) *and* refuse to leave after being told.

Passive presence is not a crime.

Confused entry is not a crime.

Remaining without orders to leave is not a crime.

Yet, bolstered by Casey's "mistakes," Ms. Ayers-Perez seized her moment—erupting in a volcanic tirade of lies and fabrications:

AYERS-PEREZ: . . . the defendant said to a friend "This is the beginning of a civil war . . ." . . . over the course of the next two months, the defendant grew more and more agitated, *and did more and more planning . . .*

Every bit of that "planning" had already been documented in evidence. And it was *all*—without exception—related to speeches, Frontline Doctors logistics, and the Beverly Hills Freedom Rally in Los Angeles.

Her opening line wasn't sloppy—it was a deliberate, provable lie.

AYERS-PEREZ: A little more than a month later, he's . . . inside the U.S. Capitol surrounded by a mob of people . . . *he's always at the front of that mob . . .*

Well, sure—you can make anyone "at the front" if you crop the photo just right. And as you've seen, the DOJ is world-class at Photoshop propaganda.

AYERS-PEREZ: And all [Congress] were trying to do that day is what we have done in every election, a peaceful transfer of power . . .

False. The transfer happens January 20, not January 6.

But Ms. Ayers-Perez apparently didn't stock the pantry upstairs as well as she did below.

AYERS-PEREZ: . . . John Strand has a talent for getting to the front of this mob.

She got the talent part right—and I appreciate the compliment—but let's not pretend this is a serious person.

AYERS-PEREZ: . . . when [Officer Pollitt] was *brought down* by the mob . . .

This lie is *really* getting old . . .

AYERS-PEREZ: And what did John Strand say? "I thought he tripped."

. . . because he did—which we all saw in the video.

Aren't you tired of this yet?

AYERS-PEREZ: Now, John Strand told us last week he was just looking to get [insult] Gold away from the chaos. But look—

[she gestures at a frozen image of the stampede I had to endure while she sits in a government office playing "pin the lie on the MAGA Zoolander" in Photoshop]

—there's an empty bench right there. If you're looking for a police officer to help you, go sit down. Sit down and wait for somebody to help you.

Ahh, yes. Because in a stampede the natural move is obviously to sit on a bench and wait for customer service—like I'd walked into the DMV.

This isn't just dishonest—it's delusional.

AYERS-PEREZ: John Strand went immediately to the left *because he knew where he was going* . . .

How exactly does she justify this statement? All the evidence shows the opposite. Nothing indicated I had any clue where—Oh, right.

She just lied.

Simple as that.

AYERS-PEREZ: They ignored the Congressmen inside the House Chamber.

Huh?

I never entered the House Chamber. Never saw a Congressman in the building that day. This desperate prosecutor is just hurling inflammatory garbage to ignite the jury.

AYERS-PEREZ: . . . and more importantly, **we know that John Strand knew** what inside the House Chamber looked like because this photo came from Strand's phone. This photo was downloaded by Strand in the days AFTER January 6th.

So—downloading a photo *after* the fact means I had prior knowledge? Did I miss the crazy pills being passed around earlier?

AYERS-PEREZ: So what does he do after he's told explicitly by . . . a Congressman to leave?

Okay—now she's just inventing phantom congressmen out of thin air.

AYERS-PEREZ: What do they do? They go to Statuary Hall where [insult] Gold makes a speech.

Oh, the horror! Daring to speak inside the nation's Capitol building.

AYERS-PEREZ: . . . Gold and Strand have made another spectacle . . .

Ahhh . . . there it was: the real motive.

Now I get it. She's jealous.

Well . . . sit across from Ms. Ayers-Perez once, and you'll get it too.

AYERS-PEREZ: . . . .They've been told by no less than ten officers at this point . . .

Definitely a DEI hire. Honey, pick a job that doesn't require math.

AYERS-PEREZ: He stayed until he was outside the House Chamber and the certification of the vote had ceased.

She can't tell time, either. The certification had already been suspended—safely and lawfully—*over an hour before I even arrived.* These are not trivial details!

AYERS-PEREZ: John Strand acted with the intent to obstruct or impede the official proceeding. He told us his intent. He said **we** stopped the certification of the vote when we made history . . .

This was the lynchpin lie. A deliberate fabrication, stitched together from misquoted texts. I didn't say "we." I said "it." And I never gave any indication of intent to stop a proceeding. My testimony—and the supporting evidence—was clear: I was there to provide security for a scheduled speaker.

Ms. Ayers-Perez didn't misspeak. She committed fraud on the court. That is criminal conduct.

AYERS-PEREZ: John Strand . . . He was stopping people from leaving . . .

Another invention, flatly disproved by video evidence. I never blocked anyone from going anywhere.

AYERS-PEREZ: John Strand knowingly performed these acts for the purpose of aiding . . . or encouraging others in committing the offense. *He told us what he was going to do that day.*

Yes, I did. I said I would escort a doctor to a speech. That's not a seditious conspiracy—it's a job description.

AYERS-PEREZ: He told us, "I knew I wasn't supposed to go inside. I saw those officers there" . . . He did it anyway, and he did so knowingly.

Once again, ***she fabricated a quote that I never gave***. Simply stunning. This was a malicious lie, designed to wrongfully imprison me. Reprehensible.

April Ayers-Perez should be charged under 18 U.S. Code § 242.

AYERS-PEREZ: He watched as democracy came to a screeching halt . . . this is what he wanted, and this is what war looks like.

The only "screeching" came from a reckless prosecutor who was hysterical and corrupt. As for "what war looks like"—thankfully, Ms. Ayers-Perez doesn't have a clue.

And she can thank real patriots for that.

After hours of malice and deceit, Ms. Ayers-Perez's drivel finally sputtered to a stop. Mr. Brennwald rose for one final, heartfelt effort—an admirable attempt to dilute a week of government falsehoods, manipulations, and malfeasance. But the script was set—and the jury was already feasting on my destruction.

BRENNWALD: So the question is, can you look at what he **did** and make a fair judgment despite the fact that all of us [DC residents] don't agree with [his political opinions]?

It was the right question, but it had been answered on Day One. There was no escaping the stark reality of DC demographics. The DC judges made sure of that by refusing every single J6 motion for Change of Venue. The jury pool was rigged, and everyone knew it.

Still, my lawyer was right to ask—and right to put my defense plainly on the record. The evidence was clear: Video shows me walking calmly through what was essentially a police-guided tour. Despite being jostled and trapped at points, I never shoved anyone, broke anything, made any threats, or otherwise participated in anything illegal or inappropriate. I did not commit a single element of any of the five charges brought against me. And nothing—texts, tweets, or testimony—showed any intent to commit crimes.

BRENNWALD: [We all] saw the text that he sent before [J6] happened. The plan is what? Go to the Capitol, obstruct the proceeding? **No**. The plan is we're going to go to the Ellipse, hear speeches, and then around 1:00 p.m. we're going to march towards the Capitol, because that's where the speeches were. That's why he was there. So, again, read [his texts and tweets] for what [they mean] in the proper context. November [4]th, the day [after] the election, "We are organizing patriots to rally and peacefully, prayerfully protest in the streets."

We didn't get into the whole religion thing about Mr. Strand because I can't stand it when people talk about religion when they're on the stand, but that tells you a little bit about Mr. Strand, his beliefs . . .

"Facebook and Twitter is where the cultural and political wars are being waged . . ." That's the kind of war he's talking about, not a physical war. And if you don't believe that, remember Mr. Strand had a gun in California. He had a permit to carry that gun . . . but . . . he didn't take his gun. He wasn't here for [physical] war. He was here for a speech. And this is what Mr. Strand's core belief is:

"In a world of conformity and cowardice, the simple act of courageous conviction is singularly spectacular."

We can completely disagree with his convictions. We can completely disagree with his beliefs. But Mr. Strand is a person of principle, so you need to separate the politics from the principle.

But of course, this was Washington, DC—political power is the only principle they know, or care to know.

It's a control thing.

BRENNWALD: Dr. Gold, [as] Mr. Strand explained, has a forceful personality. There are different words one could use, but she is a woman on a mission . . . the mission of America's Frontline Doctors . . . she's a woman who is strong. The problem is in our society, when a woman is strong, they're often castigated and portrayed as a B word, right? Like a woman can't be strong and forceful without other words being used.

Dr. Gold is just a strong-willed person, and those other words are not pertinent to her.

She's a woman of vision . . . and Mr. Strand came into that situation . . . as a much younger man . . . and you can see in the videos where he follows her around and is always protecting her. *Nobody else does that in any of these videos*. Literally. And that's why he stood out.

. . . and that is what makes a man a Maverick—and a patriot.

VERDICT DAY

TRIAL DAY 9 | SEPTEMBER 27, 2022

Each morning outside the E. Barrett Prettyman Courthouse, as the September sun rose to glint across its stone and glass, I stood in the adjacent park—and prayed.

Prayer, I have learned, can be less of a memorized ritual or somber incantation, and more of an intimate conversation—a real exchange between you and God. We don't see Him as we see people, nor hear his voice audibly (for the most part). It's often subtle, even mysterious. But if we focus—and pause long enough to meditate and listen—we'll discover more than an eccentric monologue (though God knows I have plenty of those—as do my BOP roommates, much to their comic relief).

Prayer becomes an authentic give-and-take. In fact, as I was learning to recognize more and more, that very concept—"give-and-receive"—is key to everything. It is the rhythm of life itself.

So I prayed in that park, in the shadow of a concrete coliseum where—somehow—God had led me to stand among lions and liars, to suffer their attacks without any hope of justice in my own nation's capital. The chaos of recent years sharpened my spiritual signal. I tuned in more often to listen for God's presence, His power, His *promises*. I shared more of my heart with Him, surrendering prideful resistance and seeking deeper intimacy.

"Declare me innocent, O Lord, for I have acted with integrity; I have trusted in the Lord without wavering. Put me on trial, Lord, and cross-examine me. Test my motives and my heart. For I am always aware of your unfailing love, and I have lived according to your truth."

—Psalm 26

"O Lord, I have come to you for protection; don't let me be disgraced. Save me, for you do what is right. Turn your ear to listen to me; rescue me quickly. Be my rock of protection, a fortress where I will be safe. You are my rock and my fortress. For the honor of your name, lead me out of this danger. Pull me from the trap my enemies set for me, for I find protection in you alone. I entrust my spirit into your hand. Rescue me, Lord, for you are a faithful God."

—Psalm 31:1-5

Those promises became the strength I leaned on daily. On that final morning, I reflected on the anguish and intense prayers of Jesus in the garden of Gethsemane. God, through His Son, took on human flesh to experience our hopes, fears, and pain. And in his crucible moment in a park, he prayed in the hour of suffering his Father had called him to carry.

During that meditation, I sensed God's voice channeling through conversations with my mom and her sister as they called to comfort me. My aunt has a special sensitivity to the Spirit. She poured out tearful joy and compassion as we wept and prayed together, and I embraced my own Gethsemane—placing the outcome, and the coming persecutions, into God's hands.

It was time for the final act of the DC coliseum showdown.

Like the clown show of Day One, the "jury of your fears" again telegraphed their intentions as we reached Day Nine—with the verdict looming large.

COOPER: So not surprisingly, we have a thoughtful and hard-working jury.

Yeah, lynching MAGA deplorables is sweaty, thankless work—but hey, someone's gotta do it.

COOPER: The foreperson sent out a note . . . "Judge Cooper, can 'intention' be defined as occurring after its corresponding action? For example, could one take a walk without the intention of getting exercise, then say their intention was to, quote, get some exercise, after they took the walk?"

I actually gasped at the naked desperation embedded in the question—and the ominous implication flashing like a Vegas billboard.

By their own framing, they were fixated on (mis)construing my intent as criminal—because their Team Lunacy script had already declared me guilty until proven convicted. Even the analogy betrayed their bias: you can't claim to "avoid" exercise if you choose to walk—***which is exercise, by definition.***

Just as the litmus test had revealed, which I insisted my lawyer ask during jury selection, they pre-defined my presence in the Capitol—regardless of circumstances or the law's requirements—as criminal. And since they'd already decided I was guilty, they simply conjured the intent to match.

It was laughable. It was lunacy. And it was right up Casey's alley.

COOPER: The Court would propose answering that question as follows: "You should assess the defendant's intent as of the time he took the action in question. Statements the defendant made after the action may be used to infer what his intent was."

It was a masterful non-answer. Without explicitly endorsing the jury's ex–post facto fabrication of my intent, Casey left the door conveniently open to abuse—as convenient as the beckoning bronze of the Columbus entry on J6.

BRENNWALD: I think it's a little confusing, but . . .

COOPER: Yes. Do you have an edit to the first line
to propose?

BRENNWALD: I would think that maybe we could
put the first line after the second line. In other
words, "Statements the defendant made after the
action may be used to infer what his intent was,
but you should assess the defendant's intent as
of the time he took the action in question, not
after."

As usual, Mr. Brennwald was truthfully on target. As usual, it would
be ignored.

COOPER: I think that's six of one, half a dozen
of the other. To the extent you object, your objection is noted, but . . .

. . . but you're wasting your time, because—as Casey sardonically
noted—it's six of one or half a dozen: no matter what you say or how
you say it, the outcome is the same:

This movie ends as written and directed by Team Lunacy Studios.

The scene was as tense as any cinematic climax.

"All rise."

The Bailiff's command snapped the coliseum to its feet. The jury
filed quietly to their stations.

This was the proverbial "moment of truth." In this case, anything
but. I gave my team behind me a soft smile, then faced the judge and
jury, hands clasped, as the foreman unfolded a sheet of paper and began:

"We the jury have reached a unanimous verdict. On Count 1 of the
indictment, Obstruction of an Official Proceeding, we find the defendant . . .

"*Guilty*."

"On Count 2, Entering and Remaining . . ."

My heart sank. I drew a slow breath, absorbing the expected outcome as the foreman droned through the scripted convictions. What struck me in that moment wasn't anger or fear. It was sorrow—particularly for Stephen Brennwald.

A longtime DC resident, Stephen was still a man of integrity—quite the endangered species. He remained influenced by Team Lunacy's fog, but to his credit he had set politics aside to honor the principle he urged the jury to uphold: impartiality. He saw in me not just a client, but a fellow citizen falsely framed by a dishonest government. His sincere efforts gave me a glimmer of hope that truth might yet reunite these *Divided States*, and the verdict was another painful blow. I felt the system's betrayal as much on his behalf as my own.

We packed up and spoke in hushed tones about the jury's stunning admission of fabricating criminal intent—an open confession of prejudice. I embraced my team outside the courtroom, tears in our eyes. Their support in that gutwrenching moment was heartfelt. But as we drove away from the coliseum, silence lingered. No one could tell what I was thinking—or how I might respond.

Inside, my heart simmered with a tangle of emotions—chiefly, disgust. I was appalled by the blatant corruption of the government prosecutors, and by a judge so arrogant he sneered at the federal code mandating his recusal—declaring the appearance of bias was only what *he* decreed others should see, despite the embarrassing scandal he'd forced on us both. And I was dismayed by a city so poisoned with pride and lunacy it rushed to lynch a man of virtue, with a clean record, years of community service, and clear exculpatory video—all for the color of his hat, and the (misquoted) content of his speech.

Yet beneath the ache, my soul was steadied by the profound peace only God provides. My spirit remained strong, my mind fixed on the task ahead: fighting back against weaponized government tyranny.

I wanted to face the media immediately and counter their smug celebration. But my lawyers warned Cooper—petty and vindictive—would likely retaliate. So instead, I issued a written statement through JohnStrand.com and independent outlets.

STATEMENT FOR IMMEDIATE RELEASE

On September 27th, 2022, a Washington, DC, jury declared me guilty of all five J6 charges brought against me by the federal government. **I will appeal every charge.**

I am completely innocent of these charges, both as a legal matter and as a moral matter before God. I know this with absolute certainty, because the law requires *mens rea* to convict a person of these charges; I alone know my true intent and my state of mind during the events of January 6th, and they were never inappropriate or criminal. As I testified at my trial, my sole purpose for being in DC that week and in the vicinity of the Capitol that day was to protect and support my employer in fulfilling her prearranged and permitted speaking obligations. I did not condone or encourage any of the violent or criminal activities at the time, and now that I have learned much more specifically of the trauma and damages inflicted on brave officers and other innocent persons, I am even more deeply grieved and angered by the terrible actions of some that caused so much pain and destruction for so many. This unlawful and inexcusable behavior greatly undermined the noble pursuit of upholding the rule of law, which was the primary purpose of many prior protests in 2020 leading up to January 6, and of the protest scheduled on that day as well.

It is with immense gratitude that I acknowledge the Herculean efforts of Mr. Stephen Brennwald and my entire legal defense team, as well as the fervent prayers and support of my family and many American citizens across the nation. I humbly request your continued prayers as I follow God's calling in my life to stand for truth and pursue justice, both on my own behalf and for every American.

To God be the glory.

Lies left unchallenged become accepted assumptions and calcify into corruption. It was imperative to counter the headlines and slander around my verdict with a clear declaration of the truth—one the media would otherwise distort or bury. With Casey scheduling my sentencing a few months later, I knew this declaration would define my stand, as I braced to exercise an even higher level of uncomfortable courage.

I was moving steadily, ominously forward toward my destiny on the Dark Side . . . yet I could still hear the prophetic whisper of *A New Hope* beyond it.

A faint glimmer was lingering somewhere on my dreamscape horizon, still stretching outward in the distance.

TRUTH WARS: A NEW HOPE

A favorite Strand family tale is my father's courtship of a fairytale princess—my mother—with the classic ritual of a night at the cinema. In his mind, there was no better film to deliver romance and adventure than the George Lucas feature that was sweeping the country. My mother wryly adds her own take on Dad's dating exploits, recalling her surprise at the *Star Wars* craze: sold-out theaters, lines stretching around city blocks—not exactly her idea of a romantic evening. She also notes, with some pride, that Dad was undeterred and somehow got them in, experiencing "May the Force be with you"—and it certainly was, as they went on to forge a marriage alliance with six virtuous children.

We became equally enthralled with the magic of *Star Wars*, and those movies sparked a lifetime of meaningful family discussions— just as they have for millions across generations. That's the "galactic" impact of a great story: tales grounded in classic #TeamReality themes of good and evil, love and war, faith and fear, virtue and corruption. These timeless ideas endure because they emanate from something true, unchanging, and powerful.

Another recurring theme is fate. "I don't believe in coincidences" is a sentiment we find truer over time, as we begin to recognize the nature of patterns—and the patterns in nature—learning to appreciate the irony and serendipity woven throughout the fabric of the universe.

The fingerprints of fate—and irony's edge—were unmistakable in my trial. By reading my tweets aloud, the government ended up broadcasting the very warnings I meant to deliver—especially this one:

THIS. IS. WAR.

The allegorical power of *Star Wars* and *The Matrix* is striking—they mirror life itself. As Luke Skywalker learns on his Jedi journey, we "are" energy—fragments of time and space caught in a moment of epic conflict. The Jedi challenge is to recognize and activate that energy—but growth requires enlightenment. The real genesis of this galactic war is a battle over information: a *War of the* **Words**. To win the war, they must control your mind—and words are the key, as the Cognitive Theory maxim reveals.

Words develop your thoughts—everything else flows from there.

Critically, *true information is in harmony with the reality of nature*— so it empowers you to govern your own mind. False information weakens that control, leading to mental captivity—invisible bonds stronger than any chains. This sabotage of *Cognitive Liberty* is the mission of Team Lunacy—"the Dark Side." Their strategy is to redefine lies as truth—to replace Reality with Lunacy—and trick you into accepting falsehoods that neutralize your sovereignty.

We are living in the TRUTH WARS.

After my coliseum showdown, we dove back into the "Red Pill Revolution." At Turning Point USA's AmFest, I hosted Charlie Kirk and Jack Posobiec on *Frontline Flash*. Jack described the political landscape as an "information battlefield," urging citizens to "become force multipliers"—to recognize we are soldiers. Words are the weapons of this war, and truth is our ammunition. Other guests on *Flash*—Dr. Robert Malone, Michael O'Fallon, Dr. James Lindsay—warned about "5th Generation Warfare": the battle to redefine words, repossess language, and replace reality with a control construct—The Matrix— engineered to kill our *Cognitive Liberty*.

That mission drove me to create *Frontline Flash*, "The Real Story of Right Now"—a social media news channel. Its growth, like much of my life, was throttled by political persecution. But we cannot retreat from this fight for truth in the public square. The *War of the Words* is reshaping the battlefields of language, logic, and learning—and tyranny always grows in the vacuum of fear and silence. Patriots must resist the suffocating grip of WOKE witchcraft: a toxic fusion of socialism, relativism, nihilism, and Marxism. The Left wages this "wordfare" through propaganda, censorship, victimology, politicized hatred, and DEI's reverse discrimination. Together, these form a "Darth Vader chokehold" that must be broken by the disciplined use of "the force": wielding our weapon of truth against the stranglehold of these Dark Side powers.

The oft-forgotten subtitle of *Star Wars* is "A New Hope," referring to scattered dissidents resisting a tyrannical Galactic Empire—ostensibly governed by a "Senate" (irony alert). The rebels seemed doomed, but found unexpected hope when whispers of an improbable hero began to spread.

On the surface, my position looked just as hopeless. The trial ended with a devastating felony conviction, and I now faced twenty-three years of prison and half a million dollars in fines—with a three-month detonation timer ticking down to the full force of weaponized government pain. But as emotions settled, I recalibrated on the flight home from DC, back to my responsibilities at Frontline Doctors and GoldCare. I glimpsed a flicker of new hope—a spark signaling the rise of *The Remnant*, a rebel alliance of the People forming against the Power. Like Paul Revere's midnight ride, "the force" was now pulling me to answer the call of duty—to carry the torch of truthful resistance through a coming storm of suffering.

Those storm clouds gathered with thunderous threats and flashes of targeted persecution as the hate-driven hurricane swirled another eight months before my delayed sentencing finally came. In that volatile interim before Casey's retaliation, my lawyers again urged caution. They warned my words would be used against me—equal protection had been flattened by the unchecked abuses of the Biden regime. Crooked Joe even styled himself "Dark Brandon"—a mocking confession of tyranny.

But I had seen too many innocents suffocated by the Dark Side—scared into silence, bullied into compliance. I would not tolerate that slippery slope. Comfortable silence hardens into surrender, which breeds cowardice and destroys the soul.

Tolerance of evil is no virtue—it's a twisted attack on what is good.

The call of God to patriots in Scripture is not a suggestion—it's a direct order from the Commander-in-Chief: "Be strong and very courageous! . . . do not deviate" from righteousness; do not turn "to the right or to the left." In other words, stand firm in the center of courageous conviction for the truth—and act.

The paralysis of "COVID" bred a national obsession with safety—essentially, a form of worship. *"Stay safe!"* became a nauseating mantra that drowned out any memory of courage. I began paraphrasing Edmund Burke: *"The only thing necessary for evil to win is for good men to play it safe."*

David proved to Goliath that playing it safe is not a maverick move—and I wasn't about to start now. Thanking my lawyers for their advice to stay silent, I did the opposite. I launched a campaign of interviews, speeches, and public discourse—explaining the truth of J6, exposing government culpability, and condemning the assault on constitutional rights.

I began describing "The Remnant"—the patriot force we must rally. With #WeAreJ6 and #YouNext as a battle cry, I urged citizens to replace the promised but undelivered "big red wave" of 2022 with a "thin red line" of do-or-die resolve—engaging in the culture to force real integrity and transparency from our supposedly-elected leaders.

There was enthusiasm for my message, though it often felt swallowed up in the cold "outer space" of a nation drifting toward apathy and godlessness. It reminded me of that scene where Luke Skywalker hurtled in anguish through a vast mechanical planet, broken and bitter after losing a battle—and his hand—to a Dark Side Jedi nemesis.

To sustain my resolve, I turned to the true source of "the force":

"Don't be misled—you cannot mock the justice of God; you will always reap what you sow . . . so let us not grow weary of doing what is good. At just the right time we will reap a harvest of blessing if we don't give up."

—Galatians 6:7, 9

"Do not be overcome by evil, but overcome evil with good."

—Romans 12:21

Public support grew, with modest donations through JohnStrand.com where I exposed the fraud of J6 and the government's fascist abuse. I pledged to "fight the fraud," rejecting their poisonous plea and preparing for years of lawfare. My rigged DC show trial made an appeal inevitable—another battle in my war against government usurpations, which I've fought without retreat since 2020.

By the time of my looming 2023 sentencing, those donations barely covered the costs of my grueling eighteen-month pretrial prep and the brutal wecklong DC trial, which demanded resources beyond a court-appointed attorney. And that wasn't counting the staggering expense of appeals—with mine ultimately reaching the Supreme

Court—or the massive financial wreckage of endless "insurrection" defamation.

That financial strain revealed the government's cruelty yet again. The next lightning flash struck when DC district attorneys launched another witch hunt—targeting anyone who had accepted donations while qualifying for a public defender.

As if that erased the financial ruin most J6 defendants had suffered—or their First Amendment right to share their stories and receive support.

It was beyond outrageous.

Those same rights were freely enjoyed by Democrats during the far more destructive 2020 riots—with no retaliation. Kamala Harris and the "Squad" even promoted fundraising for that "Summer of Love" chaos.

A grotesque double standard.

Textbook selective prosecution.

The new normal in *The Divided States of America.*

The fruit of the poisonous plea dripped further down the rotten tree of injustice when prosecutors claimed that accepting a plea deal somehow erased a defendant's suffering—and their right to ask for help. I was livid. Then the government subpoenaed my website host and bank—seemingly in a race to violate every one of the Bill of Rights within a single year.

Casey, of course, obliged. Prosecutors then falsely accused me of *fraud*—a damaging lie on the record, and a textbook case of projection by those guilty of systemic fraud themselves.

These government gangsters are evil—leeches sucking the lifeblood of the American people. Liberty itself will soon be a corpse if we don't expel these forces of darkness. Disbarment, impeachment, civil judgments, and strident public condemnation must be wielded with sustained vigor.

But none of it will happen without a larger—and louder—Remnant demanding it.

Silence is the self-inflicted poison that kills.

That "new hope" flickering through years of corruption was the next generation of American Skywalkers—reviving an old hope for a new era. Freedom is the force all around us; our only hope against the suffocation of the Dark Side. Luke discovered the force could be wielded for good or evil—but the key to victory was virtue. The Rebel Alliance was nearly extinguished until he embraced his identity and duty as a Jedi. By acting with humility and moral strength, he became a man of valor in a star system of villainy.

A tool often overlooked is "the power of the purse"—a principle the Founders understood well. Money is a token of energy, and we can direct that force by funding sources of light in the fight against darkness. GoldCare.com was built on that premise, connecting #TeamReality citizens to promote not just health and wellness but virtue and Cognitive Liberty. Michael Seifert's PublicSquare.com and Glenn Story's Patriot Mobile carry that same mission. In response to government targeting, we moved personal and business assets to Old Glory Bank, introduced by John Rich, Larry Elder, and Dr. Ben Carson—founded on liberty, privacy, and unapologetic resistance to tyranny.

Despite the persecution, I kept exposing the government's "train of abuses and usurpations"—and they kept proving my point. The next abuse: the DOJ obstructed the Pre-Sentencing Report (PSR) process. The probation officer never conducted the required interview, a violation of law that disrupted prison logistics and early release calculations—serious harms.

Probation officer Robert Walters ignored my lawyer's repeated requests—then falsely claimed I had "declined to provide any information at all to the Probation Department." But it got worse. When my exasperated lawyer got nowhere, Mr. Brennwald filed a motion to amend the PSI, essentially doing the government's job for them. DOJ Prosecutor Jason Manning fired back with a petty motion to *block* it, filled with lies and excuses—a vindictive attempt to further harm me.

The naked malice was shocking. My lawyers countered with a scathing reply exposing Manning's dishonesty—and who was really guilty of "gamesmanship."

After all, in their world, the government never loses.

They proved that point again at my June 1, 2023, sentencing. The hearing played like a "greatest hits" mashup of my show trial. Ms. Ayers-Perez sniveled through another bombastic monologue, anchored by the government's "statement of fact"—a partisan fiction. My lawyer objected. He was ignored.

If the Oscars had an award for hyperbole, Ms. Ayers-Perez would've won it. Her hysterics shot past absurdity to reach a gibberish galaxy far, far away. Even Casey distanced himself, declining her request for an eight-point "violence" enhancement—a lie that would've pushed my sentence to nearly a decade in prison. He also denied her request for a $50,000 fine.

Consider the insanity: a federal prosecutor urged ***eight years in prison***—for walking calmly through red velvet ropes in the Capitol of my own country.

Though Casey declined that stretch, he added his own lunacy and revenge:

COOPER: The Court will apply the 3-level enhancement because the question is whether the defendant's **sort of** willing presence and participation . . .

Uh, excuse me? Did "The Court" just tack on a "bonus year" of prison after the government "sort of" showed I had criminal intent? His own phrasing admits intent wasn't proven beyond a reasonable doubt—a shocking violation of legal standards.

COOPER: . . . participation with others . . . resulted in *substantial* interference with the administration of justice . . . I don't think Mr. Strand was operating with anyone else . . .

What "participation with others," exactly? He just contradicted himself mid-sentence.

COOPER: . . . as well as the expenditure of substantial resources that were necessary to fix the damage done to the Capitol.

I didn't vandalize anything—and never condoned those who did. Why am I being punished for someone else's behavior?

COOPER: I *think* the evidence [of "mens rea" criminal intent] was sufficient to support that verdict, but it is very difficult to *know* what someone knows or what someone intends to do, obviously, and **there was no direct evidence.**

So . . . you admit there's *no direct evidence*, yet still uphold the jury's claim to know my intent *beyond a reasonable doubt*? What exactly do they teach at Stanford?

Oh, right . . . Marxism.

COOPER: . . . with respect to the defendant's testimony that he was not—or that he was pushed into the Capitol, you know, I think that was false testimony.

Oh? Which part of the video—showing me and my client stumbling forward as the crowd surged through open doors—did you decide was false, exactly? The evidence supports my testimony. But you ignore it and call me a liar . . . because you think a black robe gives you rule over reality.

BRENNWALD: There were people there in camouflage outfits, ballistic helmets—

COOPER:—and guns and knives.

Just as he did at my co-defendant's sentencing, Casey injected malicious fiction into the record—slandering me with a lie cloaked in judicial authority. No protesters brandished guns or knives inside the Capitol. The deadly weapons that day were wielded by the police—who killed several unarmed protesters, including two defenseless women. Now, years later, everyone knew this—but Casey carried on the distortions.

His false interjection was blatant judicial misconduct.

COOPER: But there are also texts prior to the certification. "There's no doubt about the truth of the 2020 election. The only question is will you act upon that truth? Will you stand firm? The moment will define our country, our generation, and our national destiny. It's now or never. This is literally what the Insurrection Act is for. This is war." Now, you're right, that is not necessarily referring to the certification, but nor is it referring to "I want to go to Washington and get into the Capitol so that my co-defendant can give a speech."

His reckless dishonesty is hard to overstate. Casey mangled my words out of sequence and context—then ignored texts where I clearly stated my actual intent (minus the "get into the Capitol" part, which I never imagined). He misquoted my political speech to invent an intent I never had—all to justify a fraudulent conviction and crush someone who dared to criticize his kangaroo court.

I'm including these transcripts so you can see for yourself—in their own words—the brazen deceit of these government gangsters. Casey climbed aboard a partisan bandwagon driven by conniving prosecutors and a hate-fueled jury, conjuring criminal intent from the thin air between their ears. Together, they manufactured a lie to satisfy their lust for lynching MAGA deplorables—and then Casey lied about that too.

COOPER: And we're not here because of what his politics are or who he supported. Trust me.

Peak gaslighting.

Ever notice how liars always say "trust me"—while honorable people earn your trust through integrity? Integrity was my aim as I prepared my allocution statement. Allocution is meant to show remorse and accept responsibility for criminal conduct—but I was innocent.

STRAND: Thank you for the opportunity to address the Court. I want the Court to know that I was listening intently at my trial, and my eyes were opened as to how other people experienced [January 6]. I heard the stories of the police officers as they testified, and my heart went out to them. It still does . . .

I was there, as you know, as a security guard for a scheduled speaker; it wasn't only myself for whom I was responsible. I did my best to make sound decisions at the time. And I know there have been statements about my political views . . . my client . . . felt an urgency to try to address the people and give a speech in some form, and I felt responsible for her safety at that point. So I know the evidence does reflect that throughout my time there; I was trying to protect her. At all times that was my only concern.

But there is no doubt that other people there were harmed . . . and that is not something I take lightly or excuse. In fact, it grieves me when anyone chooses to act with violence or physical animosity. . . . That also contradicts the values and beliefs that I stand for and the peaceful and lawful behavior that we should all stand for.

The government has alleged many times that I am in denial or indifferent to the pain and tragedy of J6, but that is not the case. . . . Despite what my words have been made to sound like, I would never want to minimize the tragedy of January 6. . . . I don't overlook that, nor disrespect the memory of those harmed. . . .

I'm just asking you to see me as an individual and also to please give me grace in understanding that I could not plead to something I did not do. I pray you would consider a stay of any sentence pending my full appeal. Most importantly, I hope you will understand that my earnest account of my mindset is not in any way a dismissal or a lack of empathy. The violence and injury caused that day fills me with sadness, and burdens me to ensure that such a harmful event never happens again. Thank you.

It was obvious my allocution went in one ear and out the other. With callous indifference, Casey reverted to his dishonest sermonizing.

COOPER: You're not being punished for the exercise of your constitutional right.

. . . as he does exactly that. Textbook gaslighting, yet again. This was his favorite lie, repeated again and again throughout his crop of J6 lynchings.

COOPER: You didn't damage any property, apart, perhaps, from desecrating the statue of General Eisenhower.

Perhaps educate yourself on what actual desecration of statues looks like—your radical leftist pals are the experts.

. . . and President Eisenhower is rolling in his grave at your trampling of Due Process.

COOPER: The mob, which you **willingly** joined . . . you were not convicted for helping your co-defendant give a speech. All right? In other words, **it was not your words** or your associations or your views or your boss's views about COVID restrictions . . . you have professed not just that the government didn't prove its case, but you have professed your innocence numerous times. And I've seen you on these [media] programs doing it to all of the charges. But the evidence was clear. Okay . . . **obviously** you didn't have [permission] to be there. And . . you did so **knowingly**. All right? And those things were clearly proven. Right? And to say that "I'm innocent" is—it's delusional.

Reality *is* delusional to those consumed by the Dark Side. Casey's dishonest diatribe was not a judgment. It was a confession.

"What are worthless and wicked people like? They are constant liars . . . their perverted hearts plot evil. But they will be destroyed suddenly . . . there are [these] things the Lord Yahweh hates—he detests: haughty eyes, a lying tongue, hands that kill the innocent, a heart that

plots evil, feet that race to do wrong, a false witness who pours out lies
. . ."

—Proverbs 6:12, 19

After pouring out lies like a con man, Casey mocked a critical truth—as if ridicule could erase it. A classic Jedi mind trick. It fooled a complicit jury, but fails for any honest observer who watches the full video, which clearly shows me trapped in a dense crowd and swept through doors opened from the inside.

COOPER: The only way that you were innocent, as you've been explaining to everybody who will listen, is that it was not a knowing violation, that you were somehow pushed in.

And there it is. Maybe that Stanford Law degree wasn't a total waste. "*Somehow* pushed in"—let's see: take a million Americans, lock down their lives, strip away their rights, lie to them, kill their loved ones with more lies, entrap them in DC with Pelosi *rejecting* the ten thousand National Guard troops our true president authorized, stir in some masked agitators and undercover FBI operatives, and . . . voilà!

Casey quickly returned to his gaslighting "hogwash," as he calls it:

COOPER: And while we're on the jury, in some of your appearances you complain that you knew the result was going to be guilty from the beginning; that it was all, you know, preordained; that you didn't get a fair trial from a jury of your peers. Let me just say that I think that's hogwash.

Oh, the truth hurts, doesn't it, Casey? So because you "think" it's hogwash, that makes it so? We just walked through the transcript line by line—so we know who's really drowning in "hogwash."

And Casey kept it coming—thick and fast.

COOPER: And I've got to put in a plug for our

DC juries . . . you know, there are folks that are inside the bubble, like we all are that follow politics—

. . . you mean, like the jurors who swallowed the firehose of J6 propaganda, confessed their "strong feelings," and were waved through over my lawyer's repeated objections?

Oh, do go on.

COOPER:—but there are—you know, there's official Washington, but there's also real Washington. Right?

Sure, Casey. Whatever helps you sleep at night.

COOPER: And we get jurors from all walks of life, and we did in this case . . . these were not partisans. These were not advocates. None of them had any particular ax to grind. Okay?

Right. I must have imagined the transcripts we just read.

Judge, thy name is doublespeak.

And, speaking of axes:

"Telling lies about others is as harmful as hitting them with an ax, wounding them with a sword, or shooting them with a sharp arrow."

—Proverbs 25:18

COOPER: . . . and their [jury] service should be honored and not denigrated by . . . suggesting that this was a kangaroo court and that you didn't get a fair trial.

"What sorrow for those who say that evil is good and good is evil, that dark is light and light is dark, that bitter is sweet and sweet is bitter. What sorrow for those who are ***wise in their own eyes*** and think themselves so clever . . . they take bribes to let the wicked go free, and they punish the innocent."

—Isaiah 4:20–23

Casey Cooper is very wise in his own eyes.

The absurd fabrications kept coming:

COOPER: . . . except for the obstruction count perhaps, these were slam dunks. Okay?

Like an NBA center dunking on a child? And he's whining about "gamesmanship"?

COOPER: So why would you go to trial and continue to proclaim your innocence in the face of such **strong evidence** to the contrary? Either it's self-delusional, but I don't think that it is—my sense of you is that you're smart; you're clever; you're a resourceful guy—or it could be that, you know, maybe you're trying to delude others for your own benefit.

Whoa—that's a lot of "self-delusion" to unpack. You mean "strong evidence" like the hours of video showing I committed exactly zero elements of any charge?

And if I'm so "clever," how exactly do I "benefit" by rejecting a single misdemeanor plea, destroying my career, draining my finances, devastating my family, and suffering years of persecution—only to land a preordained felony conviction with Casey-only-knows how many years in a federal prison?

Tell us, Mr. Stanford genius—how does that make any sense?

COOPER: You know, it seems to me that . . . as a J6 political prisoner . . . the face of the J6 movement . . . you want to cultivate and profit from that . . . by making appearances at all these conferences and these podcasts, peddling in the idea that you didn't break any laws and that you didn't get a fair trial and, you know, leveraging your 48 minutes of infamy . . . when I impose the sentence . . . there's **general deterrence** . . . a lot of people out there watching you on all these podcasts . . . and you've used that platform to peddle the misconception that you and other J6ers are somehow political prisoners who are being persecuted for their beliefs . . . so to all those folks who may believe that, based on what you're telling them, ***they need to know*** that nothing like this can happen again, and if it does, folks will receive [years in prison] . . .

And there it was—the second swing of the fascist sledgehammer. Just like with my co-defendant, Casey smashed my First Amendment rights and brandished an ominous threat to #YouNext:

Shut up and obey—or we will put you on "Justice Entertainment" display, and we will crush you.

And with a flip of his thumb—or, in this case, gavel—from his throne in the courtroom-coliseum, Emperor Casey did just that.

COOPER: It is the judgment of the Court that you, John Strand, are hereby committed to the custody of the BOP for a term of 32 months as to Count 1, 12 months as to each of Counts 2 and 3, and 6 months as to Counts 4 and 5. You are further sentenced to serve a 36-month period of supervised release . . .

Nearly *three years* in prison.

A brutal sentence for nothing more than discharging my duty in good faith—and daring to expose government corruption. That was my true crime, and it was intolerable to the regime. Casey made that clear from the bench, directly tying his sentence to my political speech. He hammered me with two and a half years more than my co-defendant—for identical conduct.

Sixteen times harsher for the same behavioral footprint.

For good measure, he threw in $12,000 in fines and an absurd three years of post-prison harassment. Not a bad day's work for a partisan judge taking a free crack at the guy who shielded a woman he once tried—and failed—to impress. His other J6 sentences under §1512 revealed a glaring discrepancy, suggesting bitter revenge: Defendants charged with pushing through police lines, making threatening statements to officers, prowling through Congressional offices, and even violent scuffles got nine, twelve, and twenty months. Casey himself admitted I had done none of those things—yet he gave me nearly three years.

Because he was furious with me.

This was personal.

The sentence was obscene—as obscene as the scripted conviction itself.

Casey Cooper can never erase the stain of his partisan bias and jealous retaliation.

But I suspect he was more offended by my criticisms of DC courts than by my success where he had failed to earn the respect of his Stanford classmate. He certainly proved my point: these are TRUTH WARS—and Casey was a black-robed bully who sold his soul to the Dark Side. He was irked to see a young *MAGA Zoolander* Jedi slash through his DC Death Star with a lightsaber of truth.

The emperor had struck back.

And I would soon tumble back into federal prison—for much longer than the four days of abuse I had already suffered.

My trial attorney mumbled condolences as we filed out of the courtroom.

Our entire team was shell-shocked.

My mother wept.

Friends and family stood frozen in horror at the weight of this government fraud. Trying to process how I felt in that moment was . . . surreal. I'd prepared for years to meet this "preordained" railroading, as Emperor Casey ironically mentioned—but the injustice still sickened me. Yet I refused to let the bile in my throat silence the free speech fire in my soul. We had arranged a post-sentencing press conference, no matter the outcome. And I was determined to declare my innocence in a galaxy gripped by darkness.

We tried to hold the press conference outside the courthouse—common practice—but found that privilege was reserved for Democrats. We were relegated to a nearby hotel conference room.

Dr. Gold opened with a sharp legal summary, speaking as one of my attorneys. She didn't mince words, condemning the corruption and selective prosecution we both faced.

Bishop Leon Benjamin—a fiery black preacher and congressional candidate who attended my trial as a character witness—also spoke on my behalf. He called for national healing through honesty, humility, and shared responsibility, urging Americans of all colors—racial and political—to pursue reconciliation.

I was grateful for their testimony—and for the chance to share my own: the truth of a tragic but historic flashpoint in the war to reclaim America's soul.

"Good afternoon, and thank you for your time, effort, and attention in being here. I want to begin by giving thanks to God; it is only by His grace, and the hope that I have in Jesus, that I can walk this path—a path of the relentless pursuit of righteousness, a path of exposing lies and corruption, and the only path of hope and healing for America.

If we are to pull our nation back from the brink, it is going to require that strong men reclaim their duty to a purpose higher than only themselves. It requires men of character, of moral decency, and of courage. Courage does not mean swinging your fist in arrogance or anger; it means stepping up to the plate and delivering the action necessary at any given moment—most especially when that action is difficult, unpopular, costly, or uncomfortable. I am facing such a moment, and the severity of the pain and tremendous cost of my choice to refuse a fraudulent plea only underscore the importance of holding fast to the truth and standing firm on the righteous path. If we don't hold fast, we will be swept away in the torrent of excuses and corrupt influences that pummel us from all sides, and we will lose our souls.

America has lost her soul. She has abandoned her duty to uphold the Constitution, to restrain the government from abusing the people, and to ensure the equal protection of all citizens under the law; she has forsaken righteousness, and she has instead chosen comfort over courage and convenience over character.

God's word promises us that 'if my people, who are called by my name, will humble themselves, and pray and seek my face, and turn from their wicked ways, then I will hear from heaven, and I will forgive their sin and I will heal their land.'

J6 was a tragic event both for brave police officers harmed in the line of duty and for protesters who were killed and otherwise severely harmed. J6 is also a deadly weapon wielded by corrupt politicians and their 'useful idiots' to acquire political power, and it has wounded our country deeply. Their lies and manipulations have achieved the intended purpose, greatly increasing the division and hatred among our people and causing anyone who dares to disagree with the current regime to be demonized and neutralized into silence and complacency.

But complacency will not heal us. It will bring our downfall.

We need healing in our land. I don't think that is a partisan thing to say. At the same time, God has made it clear what is required for that healing:

1. We must humble ourselves.
2. We must pray and seek God.
3. We must turn away from our wicked ways.

Also, don't forget the beginning of that scripture: 'When *my* people, who are called by *my* name.' You know who you are.

The question most folks are asking now is, 'Do you regret your decision to refuse the plea?' The answer is simple: no, absolutely not. I will never regret choosing to reject lies and stand firm on the truth. And the truth is, I had no criminal intent on January 6, at any time. In addition, copious amounts of video evidence clearly show I did nothing wrong and that I had a legitimate responsibility that brought me to the steps of the Capitol that day.

All charges against me require 'mens rea'—a mindset of criminal intent. I had none. My actions, as shown on video, were entirely peaceful and reasonable in context. Therefore, before God and before the United States Constitution and the laws therein, to the best of my knowledge as I understand them reading in plain English, I am innocent. I will never be intimidated or coerced into pleading otherwise, and I will never regret the choice to stand firm in that truth. Because the truth does indeed set you free.

Thank you, and to God be the glory."

The *natural aristocracy* Thomas Jefferson called "the most precious gift" for safeguarding liberty proved its worth when one of its few heirs—Congressman Matt Gaetz of Florida—showed the rare courage now absent in our government. He defied the Uniparty's "insurrection!"

script and spoke hard truths about a staged entrapment—a *Fedsurrection*. He called it exactly that, without apology.

Congress, meant to be "the People's voice" in the federal government, instead lent tacit or active support to Lunacy Media defamation and a fascist DOJ lynching spree—betraying the very citizens they were sworn to serve in a historic dereliction of duty. The consequences have been staggering. Worse, most of Congress doubled down—even as mounting evidence exposed an entrapment sting engineered by a weaponized regime now covering its crimes.

To his credit, Gaetz never backed down. Through years of propaganda, he boldly opposed ***The Greatest American Lie Ever Sold***—denouncing the civil rights abuses of J6. He joined fellow Congressmen Clay Higgins, Marjorie Taylor Greene, and Paul Gosar in calling out the mistreatment of J6 political prisoners and the ominous signs of Deep State complicity in the staged Capitol trap.

I would later receive direct support from each of those Congressmen in one of the darkest chapters of this saga. But first, Gaetz invited me to testify—inside the Capitol (irony alert)—at a hearing on government weaponization. It was a much-needed counterstrike against ongoing persecution, and I was more than ready to fly that mission. My lawyers didn't even try to stop me.

On June 13, 2023, Congressman Gaetz led a Capitol field hearing joined by Paul Gosar, Marjorie Taylor Greene, Lauren Boebert, and Troy Nehls. I joined a witness panel that included Brandon Straka and attorneys Jeff Clark and Ed Martin. The testimonies painted a tragic picture of targeted abuse once unthinkable in America. I opened my five-minute summary of this American Fascism with the words of a civil rights hero:

"Our lives begin to end the day we become silent about things that matter."

—Martin Luther King Jr.

Mr. Gaetz responded to each witness with thoughtful commentary and probing questions, always grounding the discussion in citizens' constitutional rights and the danger of a justice system weaponized against a targeted class. He asked me specifically about this "selective persecution":

GAETZ: Mr. Strand, I wanted your advice on a legislative concept I've been talking about with some of my colleagues and it's on the matter of venue, because we've seen a number of defendants drug into the jurisdiction of Washington, DC, and then they face a different jury dynamic than they would otherwise face elsewhere in the country; what would be your advice to the Congress about looking at some venue reform to give defendants the ability to face these charges where they're from?

STRAND: Thank you, Congressman, and I couldn't stress the importance of that more. Right now, I'm about to go to prison for almost three years; I did nothing wrong, and the main reason it happened so easily is because I was denied the constitutional guarantee of a fair trial by an impartial jury. Not only that, but my sentence was worsened by a judge who explicitly said from the bench—on the record, read the transcript—that he was furious at me for criticizing the government publicly. Specifically, he was furious at me for making the claim, which is my First Amendment-protected right to do, but the evidence bears it out, that Washington, DC, juries are entirely biased—flagrantly so. If I could tell the short story of my experience during my eight day trial, the most interesting part was day one, which was jury selection; and this was not a random assortment of citizens fulfilling their civic duty to participate in a jury trial, these were people that were hanging on every moment, hoping to get chosen so that they could experience the personal gratification of crucifying someone that they politically despise. They openly admit this.

GAETZ: Very important, that venue issue.

Marjorie Taylor Greene captured the absurdity of my situation, saying, "John Strand, I don't want you to go to prison."

I replied, "But I'm going!"—for that is the fascist state of affairs in *The Divided States of America.*

We've been overtaken by an Artificial Aristocracy. This *Permanent Coup* is possible only because of silence—the comfortable cowardice of "good men who play it safe." That silence corrodes—and eventually destroys—Jefferson's "most precious gift": a natural aristocracy of virtuous public servants.

The hearing was a noble effort, but it only underscored the point: the TRUTH WARS were still raging. A Galactic Empire of government gangsters was dismantling liberty's defenses. And the fate of free nations hung in peril as they targeted the scattered warriors of "MAGA Jedi" resistance—holding them hostage to the black terrors of the Dark Side.

My deployment as a hostage was about to begin.

Chapter 16

POLITICAL HOSTAGE

"Preparing for prison" was something I never imagined. I grew up with deep respect for the law. Nothing in my dreams—or in the chaos that sometimes disrupted them—pointed to this future. Yet here I was.

It's hard to say which burden is heavier: bracing for your own captivity, or watching someone you love endure it. We had to bear them both. Dr. Gold and I—two God-fearing, law-abiding citizens—were treated like violent criminals. The absurdity was matched only by the agony.

We leaned on each other to survive the tailspin. Perseverance and compassion became lifelines. Dr. Gold taught me the Hebrew word *ahava*—love as responsibility—and she lived it daily. Even under crushing pressures of her own, she shouldered the weight with me, managing endless preparations while still creating moments of beauty and joy.

We shared a series of unforgettable experiences in those final weeks: Billy Joel at Madison Square Garden, Broadway performances of *Moulin Rouge* and *Chicago*, and a special night in Manhattan with Brandon Straka and Eric Metaxas. In Los Angeles, friends Phil and Lori treated us to Independence Day at the Hollywood Bowl with John Williams's legendary film scores. The soaring performance of the Philharmonic moved me to tears, swept into a moment of exquisite magic.

There were also quiet evenings with Russell Stuart, my steadfast manager and friend, who has guided me through my darkest storms. And then came one last surge of adrenaline: Tom Cruise's latest *Mission: Impossible* premiere at the Chinese Theater. The incredible IMAX spectacle was an almost providential sendoff, fueling me for my own *"mission impossible"*: entering, and overcoming, the Federal Bureau of Prisons.

Just like the classic Cruise films, my mission took a darker turn before it even began. The expected phone call from Washington, DC, to set my self-surrender date—July 25, 2023—came with an unexpected directive: report to FCI Miami.

The wrong facility. And more importantly, the wrong class of facility.

Not all prisons are created equal. The difference between the very lowest level—a federal prison camp—and the next step up is dramatic, often harsher than the jump to higher levels. Inmates told me the second-tier facilities were sometimes worse than those they'd endured at level three.

A prison "camp," while still a prison, is the only level without walls, coiled razor wire, and—the worst part—"controlled movement." It offers at least a shred of self-management, vital to human dignity and purpose. By every metric, this was the only appropriate placement for me. BOP policy uses a roughly 50-point scale to assign inmates.

My score? −1.

Yes, negative one point. That put me at the bottom of the lowest bracket, requiring a ten-point jump just to reach the next level. My lawyers knew this and requested placement at Pensacola FPC—the only class-appropriate facility in Florida, where I had resided since 2022. At sentencing, the judge agreed:

COOPER: Mr. Brennwald, do you want to be heard on placement?

BRENNWALD: Yes, Your Honor. I would ask the court to allow Mr. Strand to self-surrender. We're asking the court to recommend Pensacola, Florida.

COOPER: All right. The court will make a recommendation to Pensacola, and we will transfer supervision . . .

But the BOP ignored it. They disregarded both the judge's recommendation (something they rarely countermand) and their own scoring policy—setting the tone of punitive abuse before I even arrived. They hide behind "policy" while contradicting it constantly, wielding rules as weapons instead of safeguards. Around inmates, BOP has another name: *Backwards on Purpose*. Their mission is simple—keep you in unpredictable misery.

The cruelty isn't just physical. It's psychological. They sabotage your ability to adapt, keeping you trapped in a cycle of disorientation and humiliation. They cite "policy" to deflect accountability while inflicting treatment that, by any honest measure, qualifies as torture. I can confirm it firsthand: American prisons commit routine human rights abuses—with nauseating bureaucratic entitlement.

The whole point of policy is consistency. Merriam-Webster calls it "a definite course or method of action selected to guide and determine present and future decisions." In plain terms: a rule applied equally, so people know where they stand. Equality preserves dignity. Reliability creates security.

The Bureau of Prisons twists that principle beyond recognition. James Madison warned in *Federalist* 62: "How can that be a rule, which is little known and less fixed?" The BOP makes rules one day, ignores them the next, and enforces them with cruelty in between. As one inmate told me, "they don't honor their own policies." My response was direct: "As they say, 'there's no honor among thieves.'" The BOP is just the DOJ's bitter offspring—another syndicate of thieves, with less honor still.

And so, despite my judge's order, I was sent to the wasteland called *Miami FCI*. On paper it was a level-2 facility. In practice it was a sloppy, punitive knockoff of level-3—a "gangster's paradise," as the inmates and staff called it. The nickname was apt. The place was crawling with addicts and predators, run by staff who weren't much better.

My last night at home was a gift. I thanked God for His grace and slept deeply, as only a man with a clean conscience can. I still remember it; I haven't slept like that since. The next morning, I dressed for battle: navy Ted Baker suit, camo Valentino tie, cognac leather oxfords. If I had to march myself into captivity, I would do it with dignity. I told myself it was the opening scene of a film—the role of a diplomat taken hostage in a nation hijacked by gangsters.

The script was easy enough to imagine.

The Florida sun radiated with cheerful optimism, a strange contrast to the somber anguish simmering beneath the surface as we drove toward FCI Miami. We pulled into the palm tree–lined entrance of the prison, and reality sank like a stone into the pit of my stomach as I embraced each member of my team. Saying goodbye to Dr. Gold, who I'd been honored to protect and serve the last three years, was painful. "I'll come visit you!" she whispered, steadying herself with visible effort.

Her promise became my anchor. I would cling to it for eight long, terrible months.

The moment I stepped inside, I knew I would hate this place. The lobby itself was neutral enough, except for the framed photos of Joe Biden and Merrick Garland glaring down from the wall. But there was an unmistakable feeling of bleak emptiness—like freedom had been vacuumed out. I was on the Dark Side.

The guards wasted no time making sure I knew it.

"Strip."

"Step through."

"Spread."

"Bend over."

"Turn."

Every orifice inspected. Every inch scanned. Then: "Put these on. Hurry up!"—as if I was holding up a line. No one else was there.

I stayed composed, even thanking them for the option to mail my suit and shoes back home. A flimsy three-inch plastic "prison pen" barely functioned as I tried to fill out the forms shoved at me. One required me to literally "release myself" to the custody of the BOP—as if I were signing up for a summer retreat. Another guard urged more speed and took my mug shot, revealing the six-foot-two-inch notch just above my head. He thrust a temporary ID into my hands and ordered me to wait for "medical."

The delay gave me a moment to take stock. Unpleasant, but manageable. A stack of medical forms followed, including a psych evaluation—no, I am not trying to kill myself, believe it or not—and a guard punched my answers into the computer. A familiar dread coiled in my gut. Despite marking the lowest level on the "rate your anxiety" question in my psych profile, the acid memory of my previous "Federal Inn & Suites" experience—blocked from a phone call or any contact for four straight days—was now burning a hole in my chest. I asked about rules, phone access, orientation.

The response: a shrug.

"Someone will cover that later."

Initial here. Sign there. More forms.

Finally, they shoved a bedroll into my arms. Another guard led me through a maze of locked steel gates—and into the black heart of my new "home."

I'd seen enough *Law &Order* to think I'd recognize a prison housing unit. This was similar . . . only worse. It looked and smelled like a half-century-old elementary school converted into a kennel, then abandoned to rot. The inmates matched the setting: unkempt, loud, crude. They loitered in clusters, barking across the concrete in a headache-inducing din of curses and grunts. My assigned unit, "Gator," was full, so a guard marched me through the building and told me to follow another inmate across the compound to "Everglades" for a temporary bunk. I asked the guard about phone access and rules. His reply: "Ask someone else."

The prison loop was a mile-long circuit of units and common buildings, lined with silent, watchful guards. I trudged past them to E-unit, where inmates seemed to know I was coming. They waved me upstairs to a cell, where I met my first "roommate."

Arturo was a slight, middle-aged man from Mexico with a mostly toothless grin. In broken English, he pointed to my bunk and locker, explaining the basics. I liked him immediately, and breathed a prayer of thanks as he mentioned his custom to "give respect."

I was still unpacking the blanket, sheets, towel, and toothbrush that made up my only possessions when the unit's "Caucasian group" swarmed in with boisterous energy. Their first order of business:

"You're not a rat or a 'chomo,' are you?"

(An informant or a child molester—both despised, often stabbed.)

Once I passed that litmus test, they cheerfully offered me a survival kit: coffee and a plastic mug, soap and deodorant, hand-me-down athletic shorts and sneakers, and plastic sandals known as "shower shoes." Then came the interrogation: which prison was I transferring from ("No, I came from home—I've never been in prison before") and "Who do you run with?"

I frowned in confusion. They explained they were asking about my gang affiliation. I paused, then answered "I run with Trump!"

Laughter erupted. The response earned me friendly slaps on the back and a measure of respect, along with increased curiosity. They peppered me with questions about J6: "Did you f—- sh—up?" "Were you in any fights?" "Steal anything from Nancy Pelosi's desk?"

I told them the truth: Most of what they'd seen on TV was propaganda. I wasn't a criminal—I was a political prisoner, wrongfully convicted by a corrupt government. That point required no persuasion—the corruption of government was something every inmate already knew personally.

The result was a strange kind of celebrity status inside the compound. Among inmates, I was accepted. Among staff, I was marked.

I was now a political hostage—with an unseen target on my back.

My interactions with staff were maddeningly useless. Every question earned a dismissive "ask someone else" or a barked order to "keep moving!" or "get back inside." I quickly learned the first survival strategy: minimize all contact with staff. None of the inmate computers in my unit worked, and the phone system required a special code—which only an elusive counselor could provide. For eight days I was stonewalled—unable to reach my terrified mother, Dr. Gold, or my attorneys.

When I finally cornered the counselor, she scrawled an ID number on an index card and said, "ask an inmate how to use it." No further guidance. No mention of a rulebook, much less providing me with one. Later I learned I couldn't make a call until my contacts were submitted for approval—a process that required a working inmate computer. My unit had none.

That meant I had to trek across the one-way mile loop to the education building, menacing guards at every turn, accessible only during brief "five-minute moves."

Nothing prepared me for *controlled movement*. Every building and outdoor area was locked at all times. Inmates were released only during "moves"—supposedly on the hour, but in reality at the whim of staff, with no warning.

Picture this: You wake up in your bedroom—to find your door *locked from the outside*. No clue when it will open. No way to ask questions. Nobody to hear an appeal. Suddenly, without warning, the door unlocks. Don't get distracted folding clothes inside your bedroom closet or you'll miss it. You have five minutes to pick one other room in the house. Whichever you choose, you'll be locked inside until the guards decide otherwise. Forget something? Too bad. Choose the wrong location? Tough luck. Miss the move entirely? You're trapped where you are.

This wasn't inconvenience. It was domination. A quiet vice grip on daily life—an invisible collar around every neck.

After a week of obstruction, I finally submitted my contact list, including my *Frontline Flash* producer and several journalists. They were approved without issue. The system also contained "surveys" required for program eligibility and sentence reductions. I clicked through every tab, careful to complete all forms.

I knew smuggled cell phones were common, but possession was treated as the highest-level violation—equivalent to a "deadly weapon." Determined to avoid even a hint of misconduct, I stayed scrupulous. I wanted my conduct above reproach, beyond any possible retaliation.

But in "gangster's paradise," the rules were only a weapon. And soon, I would find myself in their crosshairs once again.

★ ★ ★

By early August I finally gained access to the phone and email system to reach Dr. Gold and my mother, both worried sick. Mom burst into tears the moment she heard my voice after eight days of silence. Something tore in my chest. I tried to reassure her and my father and sisters that I was unharmed, adjusting as best as I could. But I shared the truth: Nothing could totally prepare me for the shock. Entering prison was like a polar plunge. No matter how much training you do, it hits your system like a cement truck. I was in pain. Some of it would ease with time; much of it would remain a constant throbbing ache. There were physical aches: back and neck injuries from restless nights on a steel slab with an inch of cheap foam. There was chronic fatigue driven by severe stress and malnutrition, which bred a cycle of exhaustion and depression. And beneath it all was the deeper ache: the soul-sickness of separation from family and a total loss of freedom. It was a "spiritual seizure." I was designed to breathe the oxygen of liberty—and now I was suffocating.

That pain spread beyond myself. My family, punished with silence for over a week, were desperate to know what my days were like, how to pray, how to help. My dad and I called it my "tour of duty behind enemy lines."

It was nothing like the duty I'd learned from my service in the Civil Air Patrol or my father's naval training. Military life forges growth through discipline, merit, and camaraderie.

Prison offers only degradation. The Bureau of Prisons is an adult daycare monetizing misery, warehousing the castoffs of broken families—along with a growing number of nonviolent or even innocent citizens chewed up by a corrupted DOJ.

A typical day in this "kindergarten of crooks" begins at 5:30 a.m. with the metallic *THWACK* of a guard unlocking the cell. It grants access to a few showers and phones, until a guard shouts the move for breakfast. You're given ten minutes to gulp it down before dining hall guards—always the surliest, for some reason—bark "let's go!" and drive you out. Then it's back to your unit until 7:30 "work call."

Prison "jobs" range from cleaning and lawn care to plumbing and factory shifts making prison uniforms. Wages: well under a dollar per hour.

Quite the incentive for excellence.

Mid-morning might bring a "Rec!" move—or not. Lunch arrives sometime between 10:30 and noon, again rushed in and out like livestock. An afternoon rec move may follow before the 4:00 p.m. "stand-up count." This daily ritual requires every inmate to be locked in their cell at 3:30, standing at attention when two guards pass by to hand-count each prisoner. Only after confirming every inmate is accounted for are cells unlocked. Dinner comes between 5:00 and 6:00, with an occasional late rec move based on staff availability. By 9:30, everyone is locked in again for the 10:00 p.m. count, followed by lights-out—a merciful end to the daily drudgery of life in the BOP.

Drudgery was definitely not on my prison to-do list. I told my team we would treat this hostage situation like a field deployment. We hired a producer to reboot *Frontline Flash*, coordinating with me through calls and emails to push out content. After three years as a target of the Biden regime, I'd earned the credibility to blow the weaponization whistle louder than ever—and I wasn't about to waste it. My plans also included vigorous study: acting manuals from my agent, history texts recommended by my father, and the classics of literature and America's founding.

Determined to stay productive, I built a prison routine. My signature OMAD regimen—One Meal A Day, consuming all my solid food calories at dinner, combined with One Mile A Day, swimming 2,000 yards daily—wasn't feasible. Here, I began each morning with Bible study and the only tolerable dish: oatmeal. Then came long hours of reading and writing, fueled by bitter instant coffee. I worked at a tiny steel shelf that served as my "desk" in a tiny room containing only a steel bunk, locker, sink, and toilet.

Meals were especially punishing. Raised in a vibrant Italian family where food meant hours of conversation and joy, I had trained myself to savor and chew deliberately. Prison guards demanded the opposite: choke down slop in ten minutes, or else. Sometimes I literally gagged under their harassment. This wasn't just offensive—it was an assault on a core part of my physical and mental well-being.

I adapted. Each inmate ahead of me in the food line equated to thirty seconds of chewing time, so I positioned myself at the front of our unit entrance before each meal. The instant the door was unlocked, I shot out like a musket ball from George Washington's minutemen. Inmates mocked my blistering pace, as though I cared about insults. The real insult was the time wasted hanging by the door, since moves were routinely delayed by half an hour or more.

The more driven you are, the harsher prison becomes. Its very design promotes sloth, filth, and decay. Like a medically induced coma to preserve organs, incarceration is essentially a human flesh farm. It's designed to sedate the spirit, dull the mind, and occupy the body with the "safest" possible form of squandering the soul—as the government monetizes each half-living human as inventory.

Within weeks, it was clear: Prison is where purpose goes to die. Like the mosquito-infested swamp that held me hostage, it was a dank breeding ground for the very vices and dangerous criminality it claimed to curb. Inmates told me drug use was just as common here as it was "on the street"—and even easier to obtain. This obviously required collusion from prison staff. Corruption, indifference, and cruelty defined life in the Bureau of Prisons. "Whatever a man sows, that he will also reap." They would prove this point in spades.

There were rare exceptions. Mitch was an inmate who noticed my study of the Bible and shared how his faith in Christ had transformed his life and restored his family. His kindness and authenticity encouraged me. In those early weeks, when cruelty and depression started to drown me, we pulled each other up. I thanked God for blessing me with a Christian brother in that place—and for showing me His promises held true.

I would need that reminder. The darkness was only beginning.

Despite crushing fatigue, my creativity still stirred. I wrote several editorials, published by *Epoch Times* and Dr. Robert Malone, and drafted content for *Frontline Flash* to continue highlighting J6 persecutions. I also pressed for a review of my improper placement at FCI Miami, citing both the judge's transcript and BOP's own scoring policy.

I was bounced between a counselor, unit manager, and case manager. To my surprise, the case manager turned out to be a secret fan. "My dad and I watch your podcasts; we talk about them all the time," he confided. At last—a sympathetic ear. But after digging into my file, he confirmed what I already suspected: Miami wasn't a mistake. It was an order from "all the way at the top"—his words—in Washington. Later, I'd learn whose fingerprints were on it—a familiar DOJ gladiator who still wouldn't give up twisting the knife.

The official remedy for such abuse was the so-called *Administrative Remedy Process*: a bureaucratic black hole where complaints disappear without a trace. I filed anyway, declaring—politely but firmly—that I got here by standing on principle and wouldn't stop until vindicated. A few privately cheered me on—one whispered about my J6 status in the hall, "I think y'all are heroes!"—but some of the staff felt otherwise.

One day, while waiting in line for a mandated check-in, a muscular, tattooed guard with a sharp fade haircut and beard—like Conor

McGregor had joined the FBI in a menacing black uniform labeled **SIS**—spoke quietly behind me.

"Hey, you—come with me."

I pointed at myself to confirm he meant me.

He nodded yes, turned around, and walked out.

I followed him outside, across the compound, into a vacant office, and read his name tag—J. Harper—as he waved me inside. He shut the door.

"Do you know who I am?"

"No, sir."

(I thought about mentioning the McGregor connection—but decided against it.)

"No one told you about SIS?"

"Uh, no, sir."

"We handle investigations. Take care of various incidents and reports. We know who you are—and we'll be watching you."

Gulp.

"I don't know if you realize this, but there are a lot of eyes on you. A lot of attention on this . . . situation that you guys were in. I'd be extremely careful about what you say and do, if I were you. And forget what you think the Bill of Rights does for you here. I've had J6 guys argue the Constitution and refuse orders. That did not work out well for them. I had to throw one of them to the ground—and it was not pretty."

I swallowed hard.

"You don't have to worry about anything like that," I said. "This is prison. You're in charge. I have an appeal pending, but in the meantime, I'm just looking to keep my head down and work. I have a full-time job for a nonprofit, a news show, and a lot of reading and writing to do, so whatever your rules and expectations are, I just want to understand them. I'll be your easiest customer."

"That's good. Keep it that way. Do your time, stay quiet, and you should be fine. But remember—they read everything. Email. Social media. All of it. I know you're big on free speech, but if I were you, I'd sit in a corner and shut up. Save the noise for later."

I pushed back gently. "I host a news show. We cover world events, not just J6. I know I can't share security details or anything like that. But political commentary—civil rights, world news—is that a problem?"

He paused. "No, that should be fine. Just be careful. Remember, every word is read. And there are concerns with . . . increased domestic extremism."

His tone softened slightly. He asked questions about J6, my experience, my perception. He didn't seem like a leftist—maybe even slightly sympathetic—but he was cagey.

My pulse was racing as I walked back to my unit. The surprise interrogation was tense, but I stood my ground. That was not easy. I'd never felt so openly threatened.

I managed to make my position clear: I would comply with any rules they gave me, while exercising my Free Speech right respectfully.

But that parchment barrier would prove to be of little consequence.

I was now on the Dark Side of the law.

By now, I'd been sending op-eds and political content through the monitored email system for weeks without issue—aside from an absurd fifty-hour delay . . . each way.

Yes, a single email exchange took *more than a week.*

Yes, that was punishment—because I was a J6er.

Other inmates had their emails reviewed and sent within minutes. It was blatant political discrimination—and a serious handicap. I leaned on my single allotted fifteen-minute phone call each day. Managing contact with family and colleagues under those constraints was difficult.

As my first month in prison concluded—strange words to say—I finally felt like I was catching my breath. I called my friend Grant Stinchfield, a bold news anchor who had covered my J6 persecution. I shared my progress amid the struggles. Grant was his usual encouraging self, and we set a plan: my next call would be live on his show, with my producer patching me through—they were both approved contacts in my BOP file.

The interview went smoothly. On air, I reassured viewers I was safe and the staff were professional, but I avoided any details out of respect for security. I steered the conversation back to my political battle with the DOJ, my appeal, and my continued stand for the First Amendment.

The response was electric. The segment lit up the network and social media, with messages of support pouring in from around the country. It gave the Red Pill Revolution a badly needed lift after the Obama-Biden regime's J6 lynching campaign.

But totalitarian regimes don't tolerate dissent and rising resistance.

The empire would not take long to strike back.

CHAPTER 17

THE EMPIRE STRIKES BACK

The "Skywalker smile"—that beaming expression of Luke and Leia, flanked by the roguish Han Solo's winking grin—radiated joy during the Rebel Alliance award ceremony in the closing scene of *Star Wars*. It was the glow of renewed hope, ignited by a triumph of Uncomfortable Courage over the tyranny of the Dark Side. As a young boy mesmerized by this movie, I soaked up the euphoria of that moment—the "righteous high" of virtue rewarded. I chased that victory through a chaotic dreamscape, convinced it would someday manifest. No matter how dark things seemed to be, I could still see the light ahead.

Like a Death Star tractor beam, this "manifest destiny" would pull me into a danger zone demanding Jedi-level courage, discipline, and patience. But of course, *A New Hope* was only the beginning—the Rebel Alliance had kicked a galactic hornet's nest. Retaliation would be brutal. A longer, darker path of pain loomed before the *Return of the Jedi* could deliver the joy of liberation.

Years of weaponized government and defamatory media attacks made clear: I was a threat to a Team Lunacy regime growing more desperate by the day. The lightsaber strikes of truth—piercing the propaganda with my viral exposé *Do You Know What Happened on J6?* and my congressional testimony—put me squarely in the crosshairs of Crooked Joe Biden's federal empire.

The optimism of my August 24, 2023, interview on *Stinchfield Tonight*, barely weeks into my nearly three-year sentence, sparked an outpouring of national support—and detonated the Empire's wrath. The next day, a guard barked my name, ordering me to "report to the lieutenant's office." The unmarked building was surrounded by glaring red paint lines warning inmates it was "out of bounds." I knocked at the entrance, then stepped inside at a faceless command:

"Come in."

It was SIS Agent Harper—his stony face as menacing as any assassin's.

"Follow me," he growled, disappearing down a stifling hallway. Miami's triple-digit humidity now swallowed me whole as I walked into a suffocating interrogation chamber made of concrete cinder blocks. It was twenty feet square with nothing in it—except me and a bristling government gangster.

"Against the wall," he ordered in a deadly tone that declared me an enemy hostage on the brink of elimination. I obeyed. He stared silently, chomping deliberately on a lump of chewing tobacco. He turned to spit into the corner with a controlled motion, coiled and ready to lash out—before speaking again.

"Do you know why you're here?"

"No, sir."

"Who is Grant Stinchfield?"

"He's a friend—and a fellow journalist. He's covered my trial and now my appeal."

"Who told you that you could speak to the media?"

I wrinkled my brow in confusion.

"I was told to submit my contacts. Grant was approved without any issue. We're colleagues, so we've communicated before this. And I discussed with you what information was unacceptable to share publicly, so I specifically avoided that."

"Who is T. Jones?"

"My producer, for *Frontline Flash*, my news show."

"Why was she also on the call?"

"Just standard procedure for media. They monitor my content—timing, notes, commercial breaks. Her contact was also approved."

"That doesn't matter; it's a violation of BOP regulations to conduct a three-way call."

My mind froze. Three-way calls? No one had ever mentioned it.

"I had no idea. Staff only told me to submit contacts. Both were approved. The phone system warns against sharing PAC numbers, but nothing about this."

"You're obligated to follow the BOP rulebook. That's why we issue it."

"Rulebook? I've never seen or even heard of a rulebook. I asked my counselor for instructions on using the phone, and she never mentioned anything about that."

"No one ever gave you a rulebook?"

"No, sir. I can assure you, if they had, I'd have read every line."

He knew I wasn't lying. Everyone in Miami knew I was different—studying while others loitered, disciplined where others drifted.

He also knew it didn't matter.

Rules only work one way in the BOP—their way. *Casual cruelty* is the operating system, blurring boundaries and eroding dignity. It's a dirty science of abuse, perfected in a lab of human misery.

I was a rat in that cage, and the regime's Galactic Empire would soon inflict a partisan dose of political persecution.

My unit counselor later admitted privately that the BOP's failure to provide a rulebook at intake had become another form of bureaucratic entrapment. He promised to "adjust his process" going forward—but that did nothing to help me. Washington's directive wasn't to help—it was to silence a political dissident.

They would strike back with vicious brutality.

Harper's first intimidation exercise delivered a vague threat—censor yourself, or we'll do it for you. Now, hidden away in their interrogation chamber, he told me to make sure I didn't participate in any more three-way calls. Obviously, I assured him that wouldn't happen now that I'd been informed of the rule. Yet he secretly filed an "incident report"—the BOP's internal equivalent of a criminal charge—without giving me the required documentation. And he fabricated three and then six charges, each more absurd than the last, all conjured from the BOP's violation of their own policy. He even threatened to file *new criminal charges* for "aiding and abetting criminal activity" because I had alerted a friend with a nonprofit dedicated to assisting J6ers that a J6 defendant I'd met there at Miami was struggling to afford basic commissary items.

Preposterous. Desperate. Evil.

Days later, two counselors called me in to "review" the incident. They sheepishly acknowledged the obvious political persecution involved, but claimed they were powerless to halt the punitive policy machine that employed them. They even cracked jokes about the book they assumed I'd write one day and how they'd look forward to reading it. I'd made no mention of doing so, but they got that part right. I went back to my cell with a miserable but tolerable thirty-day phone suspension, and told Dr. Gold and my parents it was unjust but resolved; we could stay in contact through email until my phone privileges returned.

But the matter was far from settled.

A few days later I was summoned again. Harper repeated his terse tough-guy routine at the entrance, leading me through that hellish hallway into the interrogation sweatbox. How was this happening *again*? This time he left me against the wall and began pacing in awkward silence, interrupted only by the rhythmic chomping of tobacco. Dread thickened in the air as he paused here and there to spit into a corner, glaring straight ahead, deliberately ignoring me to build the tension—until another menacing figure stepped in to join him:

Lieutenant Andino.

The dreaded SHU commander.

A surly, butch woman, she wore her *La Diabla* patch—"She Devil"—with pride. The nickname fit: she took sadistic pleasure in tormenting her subhuman subjects caged in "the SHU"—Segregated Housing Unit. This infamous dungeon is officially billed as a "separate housing" facility to protect at-risk inmates from gang conflicts. That disguises the insidious "secondary" purpose: hidden abuse through torturous solitary confinement.

The SIS tag-team began their assault. Harper and Andino hurled angry questions and accusations while waving papers in my face. I eventually realized they were printouts of my emails and social posts.

"How dare you publicize this!"

"We gave you a chance, and you spit back in our face!"

Huh? My phone access was suspended, and I'd remained strict with my emails. Yet they accused me of defying orders, leaking security information, and inciting violence. Then they escalated—accusing me of *orchestrating additional criminal activity.*

I was stunned.

They ranted further, piling on accusations that I was inciting "domestic terrorism." Absolute madness. Horrified by the outrageous claims, I struggled to follow as they twisted fragments of my writing into grotesque distortions. It was a demonic déjà vu of Mr. Manning and his special agent "robot." They grew more hostile with every attempt to respond—cutting me off again and again. The verdict was set. This verbal assault was merely the opening-round psychological beatdown to soften me up for the next phase of abuse.

"You thought this place was miserable before?" the She-Devil sneered. "Well, we're gonna show you what real misery is. Let's see how you like a few weeks in the SHU."

That is a real quote.

Harper added, "I've been to SHUs across the country, and this one's the worst. It's a real hell—animals screaming all day, trying to outdo each other at being the worst piece of shit."

When they finally tired of taunting me, Harper put his tough-guy tactics into action. He spun me against the wall, aggressively slapped handcuffs on, and muscled me through the sweltering hall, dragging me across the compound toward my own personal hell on earth. In the midst of this, swirling beneath a torrent of fury at the spiraling injustice, a subtle echo stirred.

I remembered Joseph.

The dreamer. The betrayed prisoner. The political hostage.

He too endured false accusations and was thrown into a dungeon. And God used it to complete a story greater than his suffering. Was that happening here? Was I now caught in another providential betrayal?

A foreboding iron gate loomed at the front of an ugly concrete hut. A grim metallic *THUNK* echoed as the outer door electronically unlocked. Harper pushed me through, and the door clanged shut. Seconds later, the inner door buzzed open. A guard seized my arm and yanked me inside—pulling me out of the muggy Miami summer, and into the bowels of the BOP's darkest nightmare.

Everything about the SHU is designed to strip away humanity, reinforcing the inmate's identity as a reprehensible monster—dirty, dangerous, depraved. The layout and protocols don't just contain this filth; they manufacture it, like a macabre marionette bunker shuffling demons on a string.

You are cuffed behind your back—cinched to the bone—and gripped by two massive guards who never release your arms. The cuffs never come off until you're locked in a cell or shower cage. Only one inmate is moved at a time.

The entire SHU bunker is on permanent lockdown—every excruciating minute, every punishing day.

I was pulled through the dull gray concrete, down a gloomy hall of rusted steel doors—and that's when the satanic variety show began. A shrieking cacophony erupted, like the caves of hell had split open. Menacing creatures lurking behind each cell door pressed their faces against six-inch glass peepholes, howling in broken Spanish and pounding the steel doors as though desperate to escape flesh-melting flames inside. It was a frenzied uproar of savage interest at the newest piece of meat tossed into the locker. The chaotic explosion was terrifying. I was shoved past this gauntlet of deranged apparitions and tossed into a shower cage—cuffs still biting, shoulders twisted—then locked inside without a word.

The guards vanished.

The uproar never stopped.

Hour, after hour, after hour.

I was left hunched in that two-by-three-foot cage, water pooling on the floor, a leak dripping on my head. It felt like every minute lasted forever. Eventually a guard appeared, barked a command, and opened a small slot. I had to turn backward and lift injured shoulders to fit my cuffed hands through. He ordered me to strip, spin, bend, and cough. My khaki uniform was swapped for a T-shirt, shorts, and rubber shower shoes—all in SHU-orange. Re-cuffed, I was dragged across the hall and thrown into a cell.

Then they were gone.

I was abandoned to solitary confinement—a cage within a cage—the inner chamber of desolate despair.

Of course, to reduce negative optics, lawsuits, and penalties triggered by inmate suicides, BOP policy encourages doubling up inmates in solitary confinement—but don't be fooled: it isn't less solitary, confining, or abusive. Anyone but a psychopath would be outraged if their dog were treated this way for an hour, much less a day. You are abandoned in a desolate concrete shoebox of invisible hostility and inescapable pain. The walls shout a permanent threat to bury you. You are mocked by a hallucinated clock without hands, taunted by faceless forms without names, and screamed at by an agony without explanation or recourse. You are also literally screamed at, incessantly—pushed to the edge of panic attacks by the harsh, relentless assault.

Policy promises one hour of "recreation" per day. This is ignored half the time. When granted, it's no reprieve: you never actually get outside. You never touch any grass or dirt. No, you are cuffed and dragged to an "outdoor" cell—literally, a steel mesh dog cage—within a different walled section of the same concrete bunker. The roof here is replaced with steel fencing and razor wire. Otherwise, you rot in a ten-foot cell for 168 hours a week. You have a single sliver of thick glass mostly obscured by metal pretending to serve as a window. There's nothing inside beyond a steel bunk, steel shelf-and-stool, and steel toilet-and-sink—all bolted to the walls and floor. Clogged plumbing routinely leaves you to stew in filth. Making matters worse, the Miami SHU didn't have showers in the cell, and we were denied a shower for seventy-two hours at a time. Your skin crawls with sweat and putrid grime, with no escape. This senseless, sinister cruelty gnawed at the edge of your sanity as it ravaged every pore of your skin, and made sleep a futile misery.

Horrendous.

The bunks, with skinnier plastic pads masquerading as mattresses, were nearly medieval punishment devices—inflicting chronic back and neck injuries that became a subtle torture underlying all the other aches and pains. A tray of slop shoved through the slot three times a day was the only sense of rhythm and purpose to an otherwise bleak haze.

Of all the miseries, the demented screaming was the worst. I could never escape the barrage of nauseating noise, amplified by the hollow concrete square shape of the SHU building. Steel cell doors, pounded like demonic drums, combined with the animalistic shrieks into a nightmarish symphony—a never-ending soundtrack of hellacious death metal in the key of cringe.

There was nowhere to go, nothing to do, except absorb the barrage of horror. Crawling into a corner, I covered my ears and clenched my eyes shut, praying to wake from this terrible and darkest of dreams.

The first twenty-four hours felt like a week.

The first three days stretched out like a month of ticking seconds, dripping into invisible hours that spilled over the dim edge of a blank horizon.

Squinting through the six-inch peephole, I begged every passing shadow for a phone call, or even a pen and paper to send a letter. I was denied, then ignored. My daily stream of letters abruptly stopped—the SHU was blocking my mail. This was explicitly illegal, yet the guards dismissed it with a shrug: "policy." I knew Dr. Gold, my family, and my lawyers would all be worried sick—again—my daily emails vanished without explanation. That deepened the torment: everything around me was grotesque, unjust, and hurting those I loved.

That expansion of evil infuriated me most. It crystallized my resolve. I was here because I had chosen truth over silence—and I will never regret that choice. Each time we choose comfort over courage, the Empire expands a little further, and the suffering of those we love grows a little darker.

The Dark Side was clutching me in its tyrannical talons, thrashing me with pain to break me, choking me toward panic and surrender. But I knew surrender would seal my fate—and that of my nation. I would not give in. This agony was not defeat. It was an anvil spark of new hope. My body was broken, my soul bleeding, but I had to remember who I was created to be: a Jedi warrior. I needed to "use the Force, Luke"—to draw supernatural strength from its true source.

So I prayed.

I prayed with passion, sorrow, anger, and desperation. I prayed for peace over my family. I begged for relief from this awful misery. I prayed for the strength to persevere, to remain pure in pursuit of virtue, to somehow consider it joy—despite feeling like death—when harsh trials tested my faith.

> "Consider it pure joy, my brothers and sisters, whenever you face trials of many kinds, because you know that the testing of your faith produces perseverance. Let perseverance finish its work so that you may be mature and complete, not lacking anything."
>
> —James 1:2–4

Even in this dungeon, whispers of encouragement found me. Both inmates and a few staff quietly voiced support, some even gratitude, for my stand against a corrupt DOJ. Their furtive gestures kept me going. A secret supporter saw my arrival in the SHU and arranged for a guard to slip an envelope with a fresh stamp beneath my cell door—a priceless miracle of renewed hope.

I had scavenged a discarded "prison pen"—another priceless treasure, since the guards began confiscating these in the SHU. I scratched out a one-page description of SIS entrapment and the horrors of the SHU, begging for relief. I stamped and sealed the envelope, slipping it under my door into the hall: the desperate plea of a political hostage strangled with pain, crying out for rescue.

Days later, Agent Harper's stern face appeared without warning in the tiny peephole. He knocked sharply, summoning me. Scrambling upright from my aching stupor, I pressed my ear to the steel door, straining to hear through the din. He asked how I was—gee, how compassionate—as if he couldn't see, hear, and smell that I was in hell. With "polite urgency" I vented my exasperation at the "misunderstandings" that had dumped me in such conditions. He said something about working with "higher-ups" to get me out "in a few days." I couldn't tell if this man was decent—or a demon.

Another full week of listless cruelties dripped by. One day, guards abruptly banged on the door to shackle and haul me to a shower cage. I was swapped back into my filthy compound khakis—stuffed in a trash bag for two weeks—then dragged down the hall and out through the double-gated entrance. At last the cuffs came off, and I stumbled, bleary and blinking, into the brilliant Miami sun—seemingly freed from the bowels of BOP abuse.

But the release was its own cruelty: a bitter false promise.

Trudging back to my unit, I found devastation. All of my hard-earned, meticulous adjustments to improve miserable living conditions were wiped out. This was crushing. In the harsh deprivation of prison, these small details make a huge impact on your sanity and well-being. My rare pillow—gone. Commissary goods—"disappeared." The rest of my property: bagged and dumped in storage. My bunk, which I'd fortified with rare extra bedding: reassigned.

I asked my counselor for an explanation of the last month's explicit political targeting and human rights abuses. He mumbled condolences and offered the obligatory advice to file an "administrative remedy"—pointless red tape. Then he sent me to a temporary bunk.

But this was also pointless. A few days later my recovering psyche was yanked back into chaos by yet another summons to the now exceedingly dreaded lieutenant's office. This time, the demonic SIS duo was joined in the interrogation chamber by the prison's captain—chief of security operations. He shook his head with sardonic sympathy: "Strand, you must be awfully frustrated by now." Then he stepped back, arms folded, as Agent Harper escalated to the next round: retaliation.

"Did you make any phone calls or tell anyone you're being tortured?"

"No," I replied, truthfully. Yes, I felt tortured—but I had never used the word. The BOP was careful not to leave obvious marks. And besides, they'd personally cut me off from outside contact, monitoring me in isolation for the last month. They knew I couldn't make any calls. Why would they ask that?

Harper clarified.

"There's a story in the media that John Strand is being tortured at Miami FCI—and Congressman Marjorie Taylor Greene retweeted it, so now millions have seen it."

The quiet part out loud, there in that cinder block dungeon, echoed with silent thunder. Political persecution, masked in bureaucratic abuse, had leaked through the sieve of prison gossip into the press—to be amplified by Congress. So this latest interrogation was raw retaliation against the proper function of the First Amendment. My shock turned to rage at their audacity.

"That's free press journalism, and I had nothing to do with it! How can you persecute me over a report I didn't write? Is this still America?"

I did actually ask that question, if only on principle—but the chilling, unspoken answer was clear: I was the political hostage of an evil regime. Here, the Constitution was not the law of the land. It was merely a parchment veneer disguising a despotic tumor. These government gangsters were ruthless, silencing anyone who might challenge their corruption. They ridiculed me for complaining about my isolation treatment, sneering at my claims of abuse. They mocked my

misery and made jokes about sending me straight back to hell. Because that's exactly what they did.

The Divided States of America had swallowed me whole.

★ ★ ★

My dread was a palpable sludge. It defied gravity as it dripped upward from my gut into my throat, threatening to suffocate my sanity as I was bullied through the entire degrading ritual—again. Fury blended with raw horror as I was cuffed and dragged back into the deafening misery of the SHU. Any advantage from knowing what to expect was erased by the renewed torrent of screams. There was no defense against the onslaught, no remedy for the exhaustion grinding down my reserves. I begged the guards to try calming the rabid inmates. They scoffed, continuing to ignore my pleas for one simple phone call.

My right to speak with my attorney was denied—over, and over, and over.

This time they refused me even a usable pen, filling their policy checkbox by giving me a "rubber pencil"—a cruel absurdity that bent and broke with every futile attempt to scratch out a single word. Absolutely infuriating. Still cut off from the outside world, I found only fleeting comfort in knowing Marjorie Taylor Greene was exposing my abuse. I knew my family would be frantic, left with only rumors of torture and no word from me in weeks.

The filth soon crept back, crawling over my skin, keeping me awake even when the din briefly subsided. My repeated requests for just one of my books were flatly refused. My mail was still blocked, much of it returned to sender. The She-Devil Andino even denied me basic commissary items—offered to other SHU occupants—preventing me from purchasing envelopes, stamps, and over-the-counter meds. My headaches flared, exacerbated by the trauma, leaving me writhing in pain on that metal slab and begging guards for ibuprofen. Their robotic answer: "Wait for medical." Days passed with no relief, while the staff paraded a nurse past every cell—security theater to satisfy the policy subterfuge, not human need.

When it suited them, rules were invisible. A policy notice posted on the wall promised three leisure books at a time, plus legal and religious texts. But the staff scoffed at my requests to honor that rule, instead doling out one book from a single rolling book cart, once or twice a week. Then came "shakedowns" where guards confiscated "excess" books—effectively criminalizing the only sliver of edification left to us. It was well known: the guards most prone to abuse ended up in the SHU, where accountability was nonexistent. Their sadism fed off equally degenerate inmates, spinning an endless cycle of aggression and contempt.

Dr. Gold taught me the history of this mediocrity—passed down from her Jewish father, a Holocaust survivor. Hitler's Nazi gangsters deliberately empowered mediocre locals, instructing them to harass neighbors under the guise of "policy." They bypassed those too intelligent or too ignorant to comply, instead weaponizing the malleable middle to enforce casual cruelties. I was now watching that sinister principle firsthand right here in The Divided States of America—citizens fractured into masters and slaves.

One day, a SHU inmate, denied his daily hour of "rec" for the twentieth time, asked to see a lieutenant. When guards refused, he protested by covering his peephole with paper. Instead of addressing his grievance, they called in an assault team, shouted "Fight!" for the benefit of the security cameras, and stormed his cell. They blasted him with OC spray and hurled him from an upper bunk, slamming him onto concrete five feet below. The violence radiated terror through every cage.

The next day, I was transferred into that same cell. Chemical residue still coated the walls and floor, burning my eyes and skin with acidic pain—injury added to insult with cruel creativity.

The singular talent of government bureaucracy.

My daily requests for an explanation of this abuse—or even a status update—were coldly ignored. After several weeks of SHU torment, my misery surged higher. There was no end in sight, no help within reach, no restraint on this taxpayer-funded torture. I remained bewildered at what the SIS goons were doing—or how they could possibly justify their appalling mistreatment.

Finally, as October rolled across an invisible calendar, I was cuffed and pulled into a corner office inside the SHU. My counselor and case manager were waiting. After a month of relentless abuse—short of physical beatings, but marked by severe cruelty—I was half-delirious, words tumbling out as I tried to explain the twisted trail of malice, the obliteration of due process, and the aggressive persecution that had dragged me to this point.

They appeared sympathetic but offered only vague helplessness. Then they slid me a form to sign, stating they had explained "my rights"—a cruel joke after a month proving I had none. They mumbled about alleged infractions and a vague process still to come. They seemed as confused as I was. I hadn't yet realized this was just another retroactive policy charade, staged to feign compliance with the BOP's mockery of "due process."

Then the brief respite was over. I was dumped back into my cage, abandoned without knowing why or how long this torment would continue. All I had was a slow drip of anguish pooling up to fill my ten-foot cage, threatening to drown me in despair.

And a choice.

I had the choice that defines life itself: the choice to exercise control.

Everything around me mocked that idea. Pain simmered, each miserable minute an insult, taunting my helplessness. The Dark Side showed its true face: despondency and death. Because death is nothing more, and nothing less, than a choice to believe that we have no choice.

But red pill clarity flickered. My training in the TRUTH WARS—"The Force is with you"—reminded me that within my soul pulsed a superpower: self-determination. The divine gift of agency. No matter how bleak my environment, no matter how beaten my body and mind became, no one could steal or extinguish this power. I alone could choose surrender—or defiance.

On the surface I was curled in a fetal position, groaning against a cold wall. But inside, where God measures a man, I was screaming a silent cry of defiance against the Devil. I clung to the invisible outstretched arm of God, trusting the distant dream of an eternal promise.

The brutal force of Dark Side isolation pummeled me from every angle, mocking me as a forgotten hostage of hatred. But I seized the power of my true identity as a child of God and a son of liberty—even within those prison walls. I couldn't see it—my entire body screamed the opposite—but I knew that I was a Patriot Jedi warrior, led by the ultimate champion: Jesus Christ.

He would prevail in this War of the Worlds, lifting me to stand beside Him in victorious celebration. That was the final promise—the ultimate end of my destiny.

★ ★ ★

Spasms of rage shook my body, recoiling from the vicious insult of injustice—tremors born of treacherous abuse inflicted by a tyrannical government. I despised the pain, but even more the perversion of justice—the mockery of God's righteousness. I captured that tension in what became my "message in a bottle," a letter slipped under the door that reached my attorneys. In it I wrote: *"I hate everything, but I regret nothing."* A reminder to them—and myself—that every choice to speak truth and stand firm, including my interview with Grant Stinchfield, was the "only one right choice" to secure a future victory against what Madison had warned of centuries earlier: the "gradual and silent encroachments of those in power."

Counting that cost was critical. Liberty always carries a price. Madison and the other Founders paid it, planting the tree Jefferson said "must be refreshed from time to time by the blood of patriots and tyrants." In that cell it felt like sweating blood as I strained the eyes of my soul in the punishing darkness of weaponized isolation, yearning to get a glimpse of God somewhere. Cut off from my family, I was starving for the sound of their voices, the forgotten touch of their embrace. The familiar black waters of depression began to rise, smothering me under the weight of so many fractured dreams—a kaleidoscope that now seemed shattered beyond repair, vibrant colors draining into a mournful gray mist.

"You've sunk too far to come back from this . . ."

"Everything you touch turns to disaster . . ."

"Your friends are moving on . . ."

"Even if you get out, you'll never be able to piece this back together. Hopeless."

These were the whispers of despair—dark-light fireflies flickering all around me in that desolate concrete tomb.

The searing pain of this unjust separation—from everything and everyone I loved, with no sense of when or if it would end—became a living death. It was a laceration of the soul beyond words, something I would never wish on anyone—even those who shamefully inflicted it on me. It was truly horrific.

At one point, driven past the brink by the endless screaming, I broke down. I screamed, hyperventilated, then collapsed—shaking and sobbing in futility.

I was in the valley of the shadow of death.

The Psalms became almost three-dimensional to me. I read them again and again, along with the epistles of Paul—a legendary prisoner of conscience. I groaned and wept through many prayers: for strength, for relief, for God to forge my character in ways I couldn't yet see. I prayed for intimacy with Him even as my body grew numb. The raw power of faith—trusting God's promises when I couldn't see, hear, or feel Him—became my lifeline.

This was the horizon of my J6 journey. This deployment, with its deepening sorrows, was the cross that Christ had called me to carry. In His timing, for His purpose, I was following His Gethsemane footsteps. And so, in those darkest moments—racked with pain, stripped of strength, totally trapped—I began to form the foundation of my "Patriot Plea":

"Father, please rescue me from this awful place. Please grant me relief—even this very hour. Yet not mine, but Your will be done. May Your kingdom come, and Your will be done, on earth as it is in heaven."

After more than a thousand hours of this torture—"extended supra-isolation," my lawyers later called it—a guard suddenly announced I had "DHO." This meant a Disciplinary Hearing Officer review of the SIS "charges." In theory, it would finally slap a timestamp on the SHU's indefinite license to abuse me.

I was cuffed and dragged to a shower cage, where I begged for a thirty-second rinse after days without basic hygiene. Denied. Instead, they swapped me into a bright orange jumpsuit, shackled my ankles with steel that cut into the tendons, and wrapped my arms and torso in heavy chains. It was as miserable as it was absurd—BOP theater, pretending to "restrain a violent terrorist" as they monkey-walked me across the compound.

They dumped me in a small office with a guard watching while a blithering bureaucrat droned at me over speakerphone. This faceless "judge" recited a pre-scripted litany of policy worship garbage—until suddenly I heard something outrageous:

". . . the inmate waived his right to a staff representative and declined to submit a written statement in his defense . . ."

"Excuse me, what?!"

I was stunned. They were pretending I had been given due process during earlier "interactions" while I was under duress and psychic torture. No one had ever explained this DHO procedure. They were too busy ignoring my reports of a clear BOP staff failure to provide—or even mention—a policy-mandated rulebook. I demanded to state my defense—and the bureaucrat flatly refused to document or consider any of my explanations.

Another scripted show trial. Another death-by-a-thousand-policy-papercuts.

He "convicted" me of all charges and sentenced me to more time in the SHU—as if the thousand hours I'd already endured simply didn't exist. Then he added another three months of restrictions, withholding all forms of contact: phone, email, visits, and commissary.

They had literally disappeared me.

And it was all at the behest of the Biden regime—their *Department of Jihad* against political opposition—as internal documents would later confirm. They even blocked my mother from hearing my voice for over half a year.

What kind of monster does that to a fellow American?

I was livid—and powerless. Guards monkey-walked me back to the SHU as I fumed in silence, slipping once again into the painful oblivion of isolation. Trying to find rationale in the BOP's torturous cruelty was futile. They entrapped me with their own violations, lied about my First Amendment rights, stripped my legal protections—*actively blocking my attorneys*—and thumbed their noses at Geneva standards.

Yet I was still here.

Still rotting in this law-forsaken hole.

Finally, my attorney in New York broke through the blockade. After months of obstruction, I was granted only a few minutes on the phone—after repeating the entire chained-and-shackled frog march routine. Hearing Nick's voice, I burst out in a ramble of desperation:

"Get me out of here, please, dear God!"

He promised to update Dr. Gold and my mother. We had no time—nor was I in any condition—to address my appeal before I was yanked back into the SHU and disappeared once again.

When the DHO "sentenced" me to three weeks of isolation, I asked for "time served"—since I'd already endured *three times* that amount. Denied . . . again. My repeated pleas for a lieutenant or captain to intervene were ignored. My fate evaporated into the black hole of unchecked cruelty.

It was me versus a mindless machine—kept grinding by men who mechanically ignored my plight, becoming links in an unbroken chain of "minor evils."

Men who became mediocre parts of a monster.

After weeks of excruciating delirium, a guard suddenly barked that I had another DHO.

Huh? I was confused.

Severely weakened, I stumbled through another chain wrap and frog march to the lieutenant's office. This time, now that I understood the game, I demanded my right to a staff representative. That simple request caused a reschedule—meaning a fourth round of the frog march absurdity. The next day, my case manager sat in as my rep, then privately apologized afterward. He admitted the bureaucratic bullying was obvious, and that my fight to litigate the BOP's original policy failure was doomed from the start.

That chain of abuses twisted further. SIS hadn't just engineered a narrative of lies—they weaponized them into six separate "charges" across two "indictments." One was based on an August 16 email, never flagged at the time, which they later "criminalized"—but only *after* my August 24 interview with Grant Stinchfield. To make matters worse, the DHO was reviewing the charges in reverse chronological order.

It was impossible to follow, let alone defend, while trapped in SIIU isolation—now extending to a brutal third month. They would continue obstructing me throughout repeated attempts to utilize the "Administrative Remedy" process for reporting abuse—further weaponizing their power to sabotage that very remedy.

Our government has become the literal definition of insanity.

But there was no confusion about this: I was a targeted political hostage. The orders to put me through such abuse came from "all the way at the top"—my case manager's own words. The SIS thugs were sadistically satisfied to play their part, gaslighting me with grotesque contradictions—berating me as "an actual domestic terrorist," then insisting "you're not being politically persecuted," as they persecuted me.

Yes, those were their exact words—and they repeated them with pride.

It is a bizarre and sickening experience to witness employees of your own government—paid with your tax dollars—smear you with lies and insults as they torture you.

The Founding Fathers would be shaking with outrage.

Even as red-pilled as I was, I felt nauseated by the malice of these people—ostensibly fellow Americans—who spent their days inflicting abuse and then went home each night to their families as if this were still the United States of America. That was the grand deception of **The Greatest American Lie Ever Sold**: The pretense of a constitutional republic was only a Matrix illusion, disguising a sinister tyranny. Suited and jackbooted government gangsters like Jason Manning and Agent

Harper were just two of the endlessly multiplied "Mr. Smith" clones, enforcing the Matrix ruse for the TikTok- and Tinder-pilled masses.

The irony was bitter. At my show trial, the FBI special agent robot thug literally read my Matrix metaphors into the record as "evidence." Now I was suffering the very despotism I'd warned about since the beginning of 2020.

Frog-marched back to the demonic animal circus of SHU isolation, I felt myself nearing collapse. There was still no end in sight. My soul ached to speak with Dr. Gold, my closest friend and partner through this war against our own government. They'd cut me off from her and everyone else for three months of hell—and it was tearing at my soul like a grappling hook. Somewhere in the fog of another thousand hours of torment—it stretched longer than I can possibly describe—I begged a counselor into arranging another attorney call. After another humiliation exercise to reach the lieutenant's office in chains and shackles, the counselor asked for my attorney's phone number. I couldn't remember the New York number, so I gave the only number I could remember: my Florida lawyer.

Dr. Gold picked up the call.

I hadn't realized how the simple sound of someone's voice could short-circuit so much pain. She had been tortured by worry. Her relief at hearing my voice quickly turned to alarm as she heard the trauma emanating from my distraught outburst. I was nearly hysterical.

And then, suddenly, the line went dead. She'd taken the unscheduled call while traveling, and TSA agents forced her to hang up.

Just like that, she was gone.

The first jolt of oxygen after three months of suffocation was cut off before I could fill my lungs. I felt my body slammed by a heart exploding into a million shards of aching sorrow, and I broke down with a wail.

It may not seem like an "alpha male" thing to admit—but I've never been afraid to embrace the wild thing that life is, and the full range of emotions that color it. In that moment it felt like all color and courage had bled away. Yet I would later learn those sobs—shaking me like tectonic tremors—were not weakness. They were the seal of the very courage that carried me into, and through, this agony.

"But there was no need to be ashamed of tears, for tears bore witness that a man had the greatest of courage; the courage to suffer. Only very few realized that."

—Viktor Frankl

The counselor paused for me to gather myself, but the tears kept coming. Shackled and frog-marched back to my cage, I felt my spirit collapse.

My mind was reeling.

My world had been reduced to a couple hundred square feet of bleak filth.

My soul was shredded—nowhere to turn, and no one to hear my silent screams as they echoed off the ugly concrete walls, reminding me over and over again:

You are alone.

Every nerve screamed the same lie—I was abandoned, and this suffering was as pointless as it was endless. It was the zenith of Matrix programming, designed to neutralize my agency and convince me to quit.

And then—in the blackness—I found the glitch in the Matrix.

The Gospel *is* the glitch.

The "Good News" that God is truly good meant that I was not alone.

God was with me.

He always will be—even in a black hole of isolation abuse.

The Matrix mirage was a lie.

It was a cruel and clever trick, enticing me to surrender my destiny, to believe my dreams were dead.

I refused.

I couldn't lessen the pain. I couldn't know how long it would last. But I could cling to the one power no tyrant could touch: my identity.

I was a patriot. A child of God. A son of liberty.

I was a freedom fighter in God's army—and courage was His command.

We all know and often quote the Scripture that says, "The truth will set you free."

(Did you know that's inscribed in stone at CIA headquarters? Serious irony.)

But this is only the second half of the most powerful red pill ever prescribed:

"Jesus said to the people who [claimed they] believed in him, 'You are truly my disciples **if** you remain faithful to my teachings. **<u>And</u>** you will know the truth, and the truth will set you free.'"

That's when the religious "experts" pushed back:

"But we are descendants of Abraham," they said. "We have never been slaves to anyone. What do you mean, 'You will be set free'?"

Jesus replied:

"I tell you the truth, everyone who sins [i.e. violates God's natural law] is a slave of sin."

—John 8:31–34

"**And** you will know the truth . . ."

Because: "Control Theory."

Step 1: *God exercised control and created.* He made the world, imbued it with Natural Law, and declared it good. Within it, He created humans "in His image"—endowed with the divine superpower of *self-control.* And then, because He loves us and wants the best for us, He commanded us to "remain faithful to my teachings" and "remain in my love."

Step 2: *We exercise self-control.* We choose His law—not by force, but because we *trust* that it will reward us with victory and peace. In that obedience we begin to truly *know* the truth—not as theory, but alive in our hearts; it becomes the blood carrying spiritual oxygen to our soul.

Step 3: *God exercises control and completes us.* As we choose faithfulness, He transforms us from the ruined state we've all reached as a consequence of sin—the universal rebellion against Him.

It is this *knowing* the truth that liberates souls.

In that moment of desolate pain, I saw the truth: even here—caged, aching, drained—nothing could sever me from Christ. No walls, no handcuffs, no torment or trick could separate me from the love of God. And His call was clear: Remain faithful. Pursue virtue. Hold fast to courage.

Because victory was already written.

I called on God constantly—curled in a fetal position of pain, praying for strength as I grew weaker by the day. Hour after hour dragged me across endless jagged tracks, a freight train condemned to circle forever.

Then, during the last few days of the year, a rumor slipped through from a sympathetic guard. Congressman Matt Gaetz had grilled BOP Director Colette Peters in a hearing on J6 persecution. On camera, Gaetz demanded answers about my treatment and requested to visit me at FCI Miami. Peters played dumb. She smiled for the cameras, assured Gaetz there was no abuse and he was welcome to visit, then waited for the media to leave.

And the BOP pulled a classic gangster con.

Just before his visit, in the dead of night, a guard shattered the silence and yanked me from my cell. I was shoved in a van and disappeared without a trace. When Gaetz arrived, the BOP had already erased me from the scene.

I sat shackled in the dark with a van full of inmates, a migraine crawling through my skull. At the transfer center, we sat motionless for hours. My requests for water and medication were ignored.

Later, U.S. Marshals loaded us onto a DOJ airliner. Bent over in pain from an untreated migraine, a policy-mandated "medical officer" asked what was wrong. I told him. He shrugged and said there was nothing he could do.

Tylenol was too much to ask.

But the policy goddess was worshipped, and the bureaucratic box was checked.

I was forced to writhe in anguish for twelve excruciating hours of transit before being dumped into another isolation cell somewhere in the middle of the country, hidden from the scrutiny of Congressional investigation. Days later I was hogtied again, this time with a sadistic twist: the "black box."

A steel clamp locked over the chain between my cuffs, turning it into a rigid bar. No flex. No relief. Shoulders wrenched up and neck straining, the cuffs tore into my tendons, radiating spasms of pain with every bump of the road. This device drove me to near-insanity during another twelve-hour transport of total agony.

It was torture. Plain and simple.

A device designed for terrorists, used on a political prisoner.

The transit ordeal—infamously known as "diesel therapy"—finally came to a close on a bus rolling through the Louisiana countryside. It was a long way from any place I'd ever called home.

Outside the window, acres of farmland stretched under a quiet sky. Even drowning in pain, I caught the echo of promise in those fields— whispers of the destiny I was suffering to redeem.

When the bus finally pulled into the razor-wire compound of *FCI Oakdale*, I found myself in another barren BOP landscape of decaying souls. After a shocking four months of isolation torment, I had been released from the SHU . . . only to be locked up in another higher-security prison. Here, I would discover a little relief, a lot of perseverance, and a new way of calculating the cost of my pain.

. . . and how the hope of victory might yet be forged from that sacrifice.

Chapter 18

TRIUMPH IN SUFFERING

Winning has replaced liberty as the quintessential American value. That's a profound shift—with serious consequences—even if the distinction is often lost in the haze of moral relativism. The Gadsden rattlesnake, once coiled above the cry *Don't Tread on Me*, has slithered into near extinction. Patriots still clinging to the "God and guns" of an older era are now smeared by government fiat as "domestic terrorists." Meanwhile, generations are raised under a new creed, wearing the trademark swoosh of self-gratification: *Just Do It*. Our society's pledge of allegiance has become "just win, baby."

Winning is everything.

Winning makes you happy.

Winning is all that matters—if *you* want to matter. And there lies the Team Lunacy perversion of a divine law of nature: we all crave significance because *we are built to pursue a purpose.*

But what is that purpose, really? And what should it be, if happiness is the goal? We know the answer proclaimed by magazine covers and social media influencers, now woven into every fiber of our "athleisure" existence: our purpose must be the comfort, relevance, and affirmation we see paraded on television. The elites are declared winners because they possess the prize of wealth and status. But are they truly happy? If we're honest, we know the disappointing answer to that question as well.

And we rarely ask the deeper question: Is winning the same thing as victory? It clearly isn't the same as liberty. The cost of today's winning is social servitude. The price we pay for those Instagram likes is a contract of compliance with the dogma of a WOKE religion. To be a winner, we must become a slave to the master of affirmation. A master sets all the terms—defining the words, giving the orders, deciding who eats and how much.

If this sounds like communism, congratulations—you learned something your peers missed in history class. But the real master driving communism, fascism, technocratic statism, and every form of totalitarian control is the counterfeit morality of the ruling class—spawned in the ivory towers of academia, corporate media, and bloated government.

This is the Team Lunacy psyop known as "the Matrix."

As we see in the film, people believe the programmed illusion that they are their own master, even as they're enslaved by that very program. Driven by this priority to win at all costs—*the ends justify the means*—we've paid dearly to secure affirmation, chaining ourselves to the fickle masters of fame and fortune. Meanwhile, we squander the real treasure we were meant to invest: virtue—the capital created by choosing the right "means" for a righteous "end."

That raises another uncomfortable question: is the "end" of being happy the same as being satisfied? In chasing the comforts and approval promised by a "win," we've forfeited virtue and any real victory—enslaved in a vicious cycle of addiction and affliction. Driving this death race is the Team Lunacy lie that there is no God, and therefore no master but yourself. The satanic irony is that this lie tricks you into surrendering your God-given sovereignty over appetite and emotion. Claiming to be your own master ends only in slavery to impulse. Many of today's so-called winners are, in truth, losers: they've given up liberty ("Everyone who sins is a slave to sin," John 8:34) and betrayed their destiny, exchanging purpose for a life of short-sighted hedonism that now owns and controls them.

A true victor is different. A victor activates sovereignty: mastering their animal hunger, ruling their spirit, and pursuing triumph—with virtue—over obstacles to fulfill their true purpose.

What, then, is that purpose?

If you can discover the answer to this deepest of dilemmas, you become a true champion. Dreams can be a preview of our purpose—an amazing, Technicolor movie trailer of the story we're meant to live. "It is your destiny, Luke," the Jedi master reminds us.

Destiny must be at the heart of our purpose. But what is destiny? And how do we interpret those Technicolor previews in the wreckage of so many shattered dreams and broken hearts?

This was the climactic question I'd been wrestling with through every chapter of this strange story—and I wondered if I'd lost the upper hand as I stumbled off the prison bus, dazed and hurting, into the mindless misery of FCI Oakdale. Entering this next hostage compound, the stench of spiritual decay was pungent. Guards blurred into a haze of apathy and cruelty, no more dignified than the inmates they herded.

Imagine a junkyard, trampled by careless employees shoving broken parts around in circles, killing time and punching their taxpayer-funded ticket to a supercharged salary for the "maintenance" of abject misery. Not a pretty picture.

The place reeked of casual cruelty and recycled disrespect, thick as the Louisiana swamp humidity.

After hours of box-checking and policy worship, I was finally about to step onto the yard—but got pulled into a large closet.

I was suddenly faced by an SIS agent.

Gulp.

But this one was more "McDonald's manager" than "militia tough guy."

He said they didn't know the details of "*whatever happened back in Miami*," but Oakdale didn't want any trouble from congressmen actually doing their job—or anyone else for that matter—and stressed, "*Just make sure you're not doing no podcasts.*"

Translation: the First Amendment isn't listed in the policy, and BOP policy is the only sheriff in town. As a concession, Oakdale SIS seemed to imply that political persecution wasn't listed either—and they weren't looking for extracurricular activity.

Considering the debacle in Miami, this was a hopeful sign. The trend continued as I entered my assigned unit, R-2—I kid you not, "the force was with me"—and found two men around my age waiting to greet me.

"Ahh, hey, you're John Strand, right? The January Six guy? We've been waiting for you!"

"Uh—yeah, guilty as charged," I chuckled, surprised my reputation preceded me even here.

From "famous on Instagram" to "famous in prison," I wasn't sure whether to laugh or groan. But I was grateful for the enthusiastic welcome. Trent and Stone quickly became family in a dark world. Stone, tall and mischievous, carried an easy confidence. Trent, who shared my Los Angeles connection, was reserved and compassionate, thoughtful beneath a melancholy surface. Together they were an odd couple— with constant brotherly bickering—and they included me with levity and respect.

They wasted no time asking the standard icebreaker: "Who do you run with?"

This time I was ready. "I run with Trump!" I fired back—and the legend grew, along with the laughter.

They saw quickly that I was a real political prisoner, not a criminal. My clean record, education, and work ethic marked me as a misfit in prison culture. "John Strand's library" became their running joke as we cobbled a bookshelf from cardboard to hold the hundred-plus volumes—their eyes nearly popped out of their heads—mailed by my family and supporters nationwide. Their amazement grew as I spent ten hours a day reading and writing at a communal table, soon dubbed "John Strand's office."

Still blocked—shamefully—from all phone, email, and visitation, I leaned on my new brothers as guides. They explained "prison politics"—a hierarchy enforced by racial segregation, layered with hostility toward "rats" and "chomos," and managed by informal leaders called "speakers." Particularly strange: In a bathroom shared by nearly two hundred men, we were expected to use only one of every three shower stalls—for "privacy."

We were goldfish in a concrete bowl, but okay.

Regardless, I thanked them for translating this foreign culture. But with patience, I shared my own worldview: Every inmate, before anything else, was an American citizen—and more fundamentally, a human created by God. That conviction drove me to treat all with dignity and respect, even while acknowledging this was their "star system" in a galaxy far, far away—not mine.

I wasn't here to settle in. I was here as an ambassador—by hostage proxy—representing the Republic and the biblical virtue it was founded on.

Over time, my roommates and others came to respect my ethics. I practiced the virtues I spoke of, especially wisdom and humility, which proved lifesaving in an environment of depravity. Often I had to surrender what was logical or fair—small liberties in daily interactions—to avoid escalation. Flexibility was a discipline, and survival depended on it.

But I was human. I made mistakes. Trent, Stone, and a few others graciously helped me navigate missteps and defuse tension before it exploded.

Even so, conflict was inevitable. Prejudice and spite were rampant among staff and inmates alike. One flashpoint came when an older physician I respected—ostracized as a "rat"—sat across from me in the dining hall. The table was "white guys only." I hadn't invited him, but I wasn't about to shun him either. I spoke with him briefly, then left moments later.

That quiet act of tolerance caused an uproar.

Within minutes, a self-appointed "speaker" from the "white guys" confronted me, furious I'd "allowed" a rat at "our table."

I let him vent—then calmly repeated my principles: respect, dignity, equality, liberty. I wasn't going to abandon them.

He wasn't satisfied. He kept huffing.

Stone stepped in, easing the tension and promising to explain the "rules" to the doctor respectfully. Later, the physician and I agreed to keep our talks in the unit's common areas.

Still, the episode cut deep. Hatred was so ingrained it seemed unbreakable. Yet it only steeled my resolve—to soldier on with courage in the "Red Pill Revolution," armed with #TeamReality truth and the love of Christ, even here on the Dark Side.

Oakdale had its small mercies. R-2 was a rare open-dorm unit with four-man rooms—concrete cubicles with wide openings to the common area. No glass, no doors. The noise was constant, but the freedom mattered more: no locks, and showers available any time. In a place built to crush self-determination, that sliver felt like oxygen.

Even the food was slightly better. Still slop, shoveled down in ten minutes, but at least edible compared to Miami. My real upgrade came from Trent and Stone, who won me over with black-market cuisine.

Inmates have mastered the art of making appetizing meals in a trash can—literally. Commissary staples—gas station-grade prepackaged meats and cheeses along with dehydrated beans, rice, and condiments—were mixed with "extras" swiped from the staff kitchen. Sly theft by inmates with kitchen jobs fueled a constant black-market trade. This was bagged in liners and boiled in a trash can with a makeshift electrical coil called a "stinger," cobbled together from scrap parts "repurposed" by inmates with building maintenance jobs. Primitive, ingenious—an economy of survival.

After more than half a year without unhurried family meals—and I'm Italian, so that's no small loss—I was almost delirious with gratitude to share these tasty moments with the guys. A favorite came on my birthday—which I most certainly did not announce. But these boys did their research, and surprised me with Oakdale's finest: prison strombolis.

Mamma mia!

Flour tortillas glazed with honey and spice caramelized into a crust, stuffed with sausage, chicken, pepperoni, cheese, and pickled hot peppers.

Mangia!

It wasn't gourmet, but it was a meal and celebration fit for prison royalty. It was brotherhood.

I set my intention to embrace this community with humility and grace, and that contrast drew curiosity. It led to deeper discussions about virtue and biblical truths. Most inmates had buried virtue beneath a glacier of bad choices and destructive consequences. But as we talked, I saw cracks form—and a few drops of melting resistance.

Trent noticed my morning Bible habit and asked for the same *One Year Bible*. Soon he was reading the daily passages himself and asking questions about verses he'd never seen. It was an answer to prayer— that God would redeem this suffering for His glory, bearing fruit not only in me but in others.

★ ★ ★

Despite small mercies, the reality remained: I was a political hostage in a federal prison, run by a multibillion-dollar misery machine. The Oakdale grind mirrored Miami as dejected "human parts" shuffled between cages wrapped in miles of razor wire. Hostile guards watched your every move, eager to "catch you" in some petty violation. The BOP, for instance, monetizes your captivity by selling condiments at the commissary—but bans you from bringing them into the dining hall, where you actually need them. So every inmate smuggled in salt and hot sauce.

"Backward" doesn't even spell the half of it.

With stunning irony, the BOP effectively criminalizes the normal use of the very items they sell you. Team Lunacy at its finest.

The constant surveillance was crushing. Anxiety never receded, driving constant exhaustion. The stench of decaying human spirit lingered everywhere—coming equally, if differently, from both staff and inmates. This was a meat locker for the living dead.

Respect was not just absent but forbidden. Guards barked, bullied, and sneered as if we were vermin. Senior staff were just as guilty as the guards. Their contempt was systemic, deliberate.

It's hard to explain how corrosive this becomes to your spirit over time.

A never-ending nightmare.

Inmate culture was no better. Profanity made up half their daily speech. The "spiritual static" of noise, filth, and depravity battered the mind. Prison wasn't just punishment—it was a culture of criminality, a corrosion of virtue and purpose. Like any ecosystem, it reflected the nature of its inhabitants. And their origins often looked a lot like . . . prison.

Here, vice was both the price and the currency. Drug use and trafficking, gambling, trash TV, gossip, objectified women—all stewed together in a cauldron of spiritual sewage. No wonder men joked about being "institutionalized." They had made prison their home, because it was the only home they'd ever known.

One of humanity's deepest needs is to belong. God designed marriage and family to satisfy that need, forming the foundation of society. But those pillars have collapsed. Broken homes leave men desperate, and they reach for substitutes: gangs, drugs, crime, prostitution. The dysfunction that dumped them here becomes the chaos they cling to.

This is no accident. It's the engineered outcome of fractured families, chronic dependency, and political exploitation. The rot traces back to the "Great Society" unleashed by the devil known as Lyndon Baines Johnson.

The prison system maintains this cycle, keeping corrupt elites in power over a permanent class of "customers" forced to buy the oppression government is selling.

Yet another *Artificial Aristocracy* scam.

Prison proved the biblical "farmer's principle": "What a man sows, that he will also reap." We think of prisoners as the losers of society—and the guards certainly treat them that way. But in truth, they are the prize of a culture that worships winning over virtue—that values comfort over liberty.

The staff were no more winners in this equation than the inmates were losers; the only thing separating them was a uniform—and the cruel abuse it authorized. *Casual cruelty* wasn't casual in effect. Repetition normalized it, crushing men into a downward spiral of demoralization (*I don't matter*), demotivation (*There is nothing I can do*), and dehumanization (*I'm not worth saving*). The prison system sows cruelty and disrespect; it reaps corruption and decay.

Jeffrey Tucker of the Brownstone Institute described this exact progression in an *Epoch Times* editorial I read from my prison dorm—while watching it unfold in front of me. These toxic staff encounters left me physically sick and mentally poisoned, desperate to disinfect my soul. Systemic stupidity only made it worse. Nothing exposed this more than the frequent "shakedowns."

The abrupt announcement filled me with dread: "Everyone out!" We had sixty seconds to grab a book before being herded into the rec cage while guards tore through our living quarters.

And when I say "shakedown," I mean it more literally than you can imagine.

Returning to the unit was like walking into an earthquake zone—books torn, papers scattered, our lockers dumped everywhere. An army of tantrum-throwing toddlers couldn't have made a bigger mess.

Actually, that's about what it was.

These thugs routinely confiscated every pillow in the building. Mind you, the BOP doesn't provide or even sell pillows, leaving inmates to toss and turn until desperation drives them to craft makeshift "contraband" solutions—which are just pillows. But the BOP's sadistic logic demanded even that modest comfort be snatched away—because God forbid a man get a decent night's sleep.

The entire mindset was abysmal.

And this was a monthly ritual.

Stupidity mixed with inconsistency was about the only thing you could count on—and it bred deeper disrespect and psychological decay. I jotted down one of a hundred examples that captured the absurdity perfectly:

March 6, 2024

Today brought another head-shaking lesson in BOP tyranny. They're "phasing out" tennis because of "PR concerns" that taxpayers are funding, quote, "*luxury activity*" for criminals. Never mind that nobody's complaining about the rampant drug trade fueled by corrupt staff. What a farce.

I needed exercise free of injury from rougher prison sports—especially with BOP "health care"—so I valued tennis. Another inmate and I planned to play wherever possible. But Oakdale's sole court was available for tennis only one hour each morning, otherwise hijacked for basketball. Our requests for an adjustment were laughed off: *"You're lucky the BOP hasn't banned it altogether!"*

After two closures that week, today looked promising. A guard barked, "Ten-minute move! . . . but NO REC! Rec yard's closed." With an instinctive face-palm, we asked if it would open later. The guard shrugged sympathetically, "I have no idea why they wouldn't open it—makes no sense, it's beautiful out!" We gave each other the universal "Backwards On Purpose" shrug of exasperation.

Ten minutes later I heard a guard yell "Rec move! Rec is now open!" We rushed out and installed the net—a tedious process Oakdale forced us to repeat every time we presumed to use the tennis court for . . . tennis. An hour later, the senior guard—a middle-aged woman with false eyelashes and a matching attitude—blew a whistle. We stopped, dismantled the net, and returned the equipment while a surly orderly bellowed about waiting on us—because, of course, he was a very busy man, locked up in the same outdoor cage as the rest of us.

Yet another face-palm.

The female guard intercepted us, arms crossed, and launched into a tirade: this was our *second* time being "late." It was still ten minutes before the hour, and *at least* ten minutes before the next move. We bit our tongues and nodded passively, waiting for her to move on—but she escalated, threatening to revoke our tennis privileges altogether.

I reminded her politely that the last time she complained, it was because we hadn't heard her recall. Today we obeyed instantly. It didn't matter.

A classic petty tyrant, she forced *me* to explain to *her* that what she actually expected—demanded—was that we stop and pack up *before* the magical moment she decided to blow her whistle. But no one had ever explained that before. And yes, of course, ma'am, going forward we will make sure to pack up *in advance* of your summons . . . because God forbid we follow a schedule and delay your aimless loitering at a locked gate.

Backwards On Purpose, at your service.

Prison was a slipknot—cinching tighter the more you tried to push or pull in any productive direction, choking off ambition. It punished initiative.

A fresh assault of bureaucratic lunacy came, courtesy of Mr. Jason Manning, like a revenge nightmare. He was still burning taxpayer dollars to *block* my attorneys from fixing the government's failure to complete my blank PSI. This left a sacred box unchecked—the horror!—to confirm that yes, in addition to my college experience, I did in fact graduate high school with a diploma. But the box wasn't checked—so my diploma didn't count.

One day, my name appeared on the daily callout sheet of mandatory appointments. I was ordered to the education building at 9:00 a.m—squandering my most productive work hours. Well, it couldn't be helped—and I figured it would be another stupid one-time waste. I'd show up, do the policy dance, and get back to my grind.

If only it had been that simple.

When I showed up, a stony-faced classroom guard called roll for a GED class.

"Excuse me? I went to college. I already have a diploma."

Apparently, I missed the "Policy Goddess" course in college—I wasn't going to win this debate. Until they "verified" it, I would be punished if I failed to attend the class "if you're on the list."

I was on the list again the next day.

I asked my case manager for help. He shrugged: "That's up to Education." The supervisor told me to "Submit a copout," which I did. The next morning, my name vanished from the list. Thank goodness—or so I thought.

I thought wrong.

A few days later I was abruptly summoned to the lieutenant's office—oh boy.

The GED guard had written me up . . . for "prison truancy." It would be funny if it weren't prison.

I was not amused. Worse, I was confused. I hadn't missed any callouts. The lieutenant took down my brief "statement of defense" and said my unit manager would likely resolve it. Still, my stress spiked. I was sweating and furious. This reeked of petty entrapment and targeted harassment.

Stone told me to grab the physical callout sheet—proof I wasn't listed. I handed it to my unit manager, begging him to intervene and end the nonsense. He also shrugged: "I can't interfere with another department."

Ridiculous. When they *want* to fix something, they do.

Meanwhile, I was "back to square one."

The next day, I confronted a different supervisor.

"What exactly do you need"?

"Have your family mail a copy of your diploma."

"Just a Xerox?"

Apparently, that would satisfy the policy goddess. Oakdale harassed me every day for weeks until my family scrambled to locate a copy. The supervisor waited a full week after receiving it before finally replying to the electronic request she instructed me to submit at the start of this circus—diploma received.

So that was it, right? Box checked, goddess appeased?

Of course not.

No, this pathetic bureaucrat *rejected my diploma*: "This is not an accredited school." This was false—I was homeschooled, and my diploma was issued by a licensed umbrella school. She knew I attended college and obviously graduated high school—yet she chose to continue the harassment, stubbornly upholding this absurd charade for no reason but spite and stupidity.

Which pretty much sums up the BOP.

I'll spare you the hundreds of mundane miseries—recalling them still makes me gag. After another miserable incident on the tennis court, I abandoned the yard altogether. I ignored most of the prison moves, avoiding staff and inmates as much as possible. I even gave up going to meals to avoid the dining hall surveillance and oppression.

Talk about losing your appetite.

Every encounter was another sting—venom pooling into a sludge I couldn't escape. It poisoned my focus, choked my creativity, and made breathing feel like a burden. As I absorbed this manufactured misery, my heart grew heavy with the sheer evil of the American prison system. It was clear this wasn't a system in need of "reform." It was a nightmare—an evil machine that required a complete rethinking of justice itself.

The pain of my own injustice cut deep. But deeper still was the nation's quiet compliance: millions cowering in silent service to the poisonous narrative of ***The Greatest American Lie Ever Sold***. The weight of this continuing fraud choked me with anger and sorrow.

It was a red pill signal. Focusing to see from God's viewpoint, I began to share His grief. The devastation of a world rejecting His design was no longer theory—it pressed like a vise on my chest.

One of the most profound moments came during a solitary session of worship and prayer. I pleaded not just for strength to endure the misery, but for insight. *Why, Lord, are you letting this drag on so long?*

The response came like a whisper, almost audible, nearly knocking me over:

Because I want you to feel what I feel. To know my anguish each time my children reject goodness and choose sin—destroying the beauty I created for them.

Our sin hurts God. Not metaphorically, but viscerally—an agony to the author of everything good and beautiful.

I was in awe.

Somehow, it made perfect sense.

Tim Keller, a New York City pastor and author of *The Reason for God*, once wrote that **anger is energy spent defending what you love**. While anger often becomes harmful, that's an indictment of *what you love*—not the anger itself.

At its core, anger is the passionate defense of your deepest loyalty.

And that brings us back to priorities:

"'You must love the Lord your God with all your heart, all your soul, and all your mind.' This is the first and greatest commandment. A second is equally important: 'Love your neighbor as yourself.' The entire law and all the demands of the prophets are based on these two commandments."

—Matthew 22:37–40

Righteous anger flows from rightly ordered love, restrained by self-control. Love without justice is hollow. And both hinge on devotion to God. Where He is not first, liberty dies.

So there was no doubt: The attacks on truth and freedom were stirring a holy outrage.

My isolation abuse felt like psychological waterboarding. Oakdale was more subtle, but still suffocating—like breathing through a clogged straw. Freedom is oxygen to the human spirit—and I was starving for it.

Sifting through scraps I scribbled on during my isolation, I found this:

"To be free is to live, and that freedom is the oxygen we breathe. Captivity is the suffocation of the soul. Prison is an endless fortress of legalized slavery, stripping not just liberty but decency—diminishing his dignity, degrading his respect, denying his purpose, destroying his spirit."

I remembered the prosecutors at my trial mocking a private text where I said "live free or die," insisting I meant it.

Well, I did mean it. And now I had lived it—experiencing a "dying of the soul" as I was cut off from freedom and human connection. It still lingered, now at a slow burn.

The suffering was unequivocally terrible—but now becoming clear that it was *for a purpose*.

And purpose brought me to this point: serving as a political hostage in *The Divided States of America*. I was bearing the weight of a dark consequence I had long known was real—but could now measure in sweat and tears. The expanding suffocation of liberty and virtue—driven by an unseen Galactic Empire—is the dire threat most people miss.

The "Red Pill Revolution" needs a Remnant—now more than ever.

Prison as punishment or deterrence—and certainly as a form of redress for victims—was an absurd cruelty. Not only ineffective, but corrosive—just another exploitative government scam. More importantly, it was fundamentally unethical by the standards of God's Law.

The Torah offers a complete model of criminal justice—and prison is conspicuously absent. Most crimes require financial restitution to repair a victim; violent offenses also merit corporeal or capital punishment. The further a society drifts from the death penalty, the more crime and murder it invites. True justice restores the victim and delivers corrective pain to the offender—pain that leads to repentance and the restoration of dignity *for both parties* . . . because true justice is rooted in *love*.

Prison is the antithesis of this—it is a fortress of hatred.

Still, love is not painless—in fact, quite the opposite, as we all come to learn.

And that made me start to wonder: Are we getting this "pain" thing all wrong?

It was here at Oakdale that I finally opened a book I'd long meant to read: *Man's Search for Meaning* by Viktor Frankl. "He who has a *why* to live for can bear almost any *how*" was his favorite Nietzsche quote, and it buttonholed my survival of the SHU. Frankl survived three years—about the length of my prison sentence—in a Nazi concentration camp, a hell on earth far more torturous than mine. Yet his insights felt uncannily familiar: the cruelty, the suffering, the struggle first to endure, then transcend human depravity.

> ". . . it is not the physical pain which hurts the most; it is the mental agony caused by the injustice, the unreasonableness of it all. . . . The most painful part of beatings is the insult which they imply."
>
> —Victor Frankl

I knew that agony well. The same attack on dignity pulsed through the BOP.

Frankl wrote that prisoners drew strength from memories of their family:

"... my mind clung to my wife's image, imagining it with an uncanny acuteness. I heard her answering me, saw her smile, her frank and encouraging look. Real or not, her look was then more luminous than the sun which was beginning to rise. . . . I understood how a man who has nothing left in this world still may know bliss, be it only for a brief moment, in the contemplation of his beloved."

—Victor Frankl

My eyes burned as I read, remembering my delirium in the SHU. I had experienced the very visions Frankl described, clinging to survival with invisible whispers of encouragement from my loved ones. Resolve washed over me even as I lay slumped in a desolate corner. Their smiles pierced the gloom of despair with the warm hope of tomorrow's sunrise. My love for them burned in my blood, powering an amazing Technicolor connection, unseen on the surface but vivid through the prism of pain.

That connection did more than sustain—it strengthened me. My greatest agony ignited a deeper desire to serve family and country, forged by that crucible of suffering into a current of explosive power that coursed through every fiber of my being. To say I knew bliss at this realization was no overstatement. I had discovered purpose for my pain: a brightened flame of joy and gratitude for the soul fire of the American spirit.

And even more profound, I realized this connection mirrors the intimate relationship God longs to have with each of us.

Frankl revealed one of life's deepest treasures: the secret to suffering. It appears only when we focus the lens of our heart—*red pill vision*—to see beyond pain into spiritual reality.

"In a position of utter desolation, when his only achievement may consist in enduring his sufferings in the right way—an honorable (virtuous) way—man can, through loving contemplation of the image he carries of his beloved, achieve fulfillment. . . . Love goes very far beyond the physical person of the beloved. It finds its deepest meaning in his spiritual being, his inner self."

—Victor Frankl

Frankl wrote at length about this "inner life."

"The consciousness of one's inner value is anchored in higher, more spiritual things, and cannot be shaken by [the horrors of suffering]. But how many free men, let alone prisoners, possess it?"

—Victor Frankl

The answer to his question?

Those who have chosen the red pill—who rise to the call of duty and eternal destiny. That spiritual dimension is where purpose is born, where dreams take shape, where victory becomes possible. It's the glitch in the Matrix, the doorway to the ultimate questions: *Who am I? Why am I here?*

The secret to suffering is the secret to life.

For what is suffering if not the crucible moments that love and fate have meant for us to meet? Some of our pain may stem from our own choices, but much of it does not—and all of it brings a nexus of possibility.

Fate is that part of life we cannot control—as chapter one reminds us. Suffering is not meaningless. It poses a question, and that leads to the heart of our purpose: an opportunity to act.

(Like I said—you're an actor!)

This opportunity reveals your "Jedi patriot superpower": the capacity to _activate the proper response_. That's "the force" residing in your divine self-determination. No matter how cruel the circumstance, no matter how dark the demon, no enemy force across the Galactic Empire can strip your power to choose. A righteous warrior covered by the virtuous armor of God _cannot_ be defeated. They can either choose to persevere on the path to victory—or surrender.

> ". . . everything can be taken from a man but one thing: the last of the human freedoms—to choose one's attitude in any given set of circumstances. . . . Every day, every hour, offered the opportunity to make a decision . . . whether you would or would not submit to those powers which threatened to rob you of your very self—your inner freedom. It is this spiritual freedom—which cannot be taken away [but can be surrendered]—that makes life meaningful and purposeful. If there is a meaning in life at all, then there must be a meaning in suffering. Without suffering and death, human life cannot be complete."
>
> —Victor Frankl

That "prism of pain" crystallized the deepest red pill revelation of all: the meaning of life is found in responsibility—making the decision to answer the questions that life is asking us. And the key to victory is **virtue** as we pursue that purpose.

It is through virtuous **means** _alone that we fulfill our destiny of a victorious_ **end** (James 2:14–20).

And, as always, the Galactic Empire twists this truth into the Team Lunacy creed: "Just Do It"—the ends justify the means.

But true victory is never about shortcuts. If we really want to win— if we want to secure freedom—we must face the hard choices in front of us, and _we must make the right choice._

Fyodor Dostoevsky—a Russian philosopher also forged in persecution—hit the bullseye: "There is only one thing that I dread: not to be worthy of my sufferings."

Victor Frankl echoed that:

"The way in which a man accepts his fate and all the suffering it entails—the way in which he takes up his cross—gives him ample opportunity . . . to add a deeper meaning to his life. He may remain brave, dignified, and unselfish. Or, in the bitter fight for self-preservation, he may forget his human dignity and become no more than an animal. Here lies the chance for a man either to make use of or to forgo the opportunity of attaining the moral values that a difficult situation may afford him. And this decides whether he is worthy of his sufferings or not."

—Victor Frankl

I knew that struggle. The pain, the injustice—it all demands an answer. But here's the Maverick paradox: meaning isn't lost in suffering—it's found there.

"What was really needed was a fundamental change in our attitude toward life. We had to learn . . . that it did not really matter what we expected from life, but rather what life expected from us. We needed to stop asking about the meaning of life, and instead to think of ourselves as those who were being questioned by life—daily and hourly. Our answer must consist, not in talk and meditation, but in right action and in right conduct. **Life ultimately means taking responsibility** to find the right answer to its problems. . . . Sometimes the situation in which a man finds himself may require him to shape his own fate by action. . . . Sometimes man may be required simply to accept his fate, to bear his cross. Every situation is distinguished by its uniqueness, and

there is always <u>only</u> one right answer to the problem posed by the situation at hand."

—Victor Frankl

And so we return to our chapter one challenge:

"Will you fight for what's right?"

More specifically—will you fight for what's right ***when it hurts***?

Will you choose the "only one right answer" . . . when that answer leads to suffering?

"When a man finds that it is his destiny to suffer, he will have to accept his suffering as his task—No one can relieve him of his suffering or suffer in his place. His unique opportunity lies in the way in which he bears his burden."

—Victor Frankl

Frankl explains another *Maverick Paradox*, exposing the Matrix glitch within the WOKE/NIKE creed of "winning happiness":

"But happiness cannot be pursued; it must ensue. One must have a reason to "be happy." Once the reason is found, however, one becomes happy automatically. As we see, a human being is not one in pursuit of happiness but rather in search of a reason to become happy . . . through *actualizing* the potential meaning inherent and dormant in a given situation."

—Victor Frankl

This exposes the Marxist lie, "you'll own nothing, and you'll be happy."

Ownership is responsibility.

". . . life always offers us a possibility for the fulfillment of meaning . . .

as long as we are still conscious, we are each responsible for answering life's questions. This should not surprise us once we recall the great fundamental truth of being human—being human is nothing other than being conscious and being responsible!"

—Victor Frankl

He also said we find meaning in the way our actions impact others "because the fact of being is always more pivotal than the word." We all know the saying—*actions speak louder than words*. But the deeper insight is that **purpose must extend beyond ourselves**.

". . . the true meaning of life is to be discovered in the galaxy rather than within man or his own psyche, as though it were a closed system . . . being human always points, and is directed, to something or someone other than oneself—be it a meaning to fulfill or another human (or supernatural) being to encounter. The more one forgets himself—by giving himself to a cause to serve or another person to love—the more human he is and the more he actualizes himself. What is called self-actualization is not an attainable aim at all, for the simple reason that the more one would strive for it, the more he would miss it. In other words, self-actualization is possible only as a side effect of self-transcendence."

—Victor Frankl

ZAP

[Matrix glitch]

Whoa! This was the golden key to victory: chasing happiness guarantees misery, while serving others produces joy. My mother faithfully preached this during my battles with depression—urging me to expand my red pill vision and refocus on others. Christ Himself gave us the supreme example:

"I have loved you even as the Father has loved me. Remain in my love. When you obey my commandments, you remain in my love, just as I obey my Father's commandments and remain in his love. I have told you these things so that you will be filled with my joy. Yes, your joy will overflow! This is my commandment: Love each other in the same way I have loved you. There is no greater love than to lay down one's life for one's friends."

—John 15: 9–13

Tears splashed the page as it dawned on me. In my obedience to carry this cross of suffering as a political hostage, I had laid down my life for my American brothers and sisters, and for the cause of liberty.

That act didn't erase the pain. But it gave the pain purpose—a "Red Pill Revolution" of both mind and heart.

Frankl outlined three ways to find meaning: by creating or serving, by experiencing or loving, and by the attitude we take toward unavoidable suffering.

And one seems to lead into the next.

The demands of life lead to work, and accomplishment brings satisfaction—but it deepens when our work benefits others, when we love them. Through achievement and relationships, we encounter suffering—and that becomes a forge of *sanctification.*

"But God's discipline is always good for us, so that we might share in His holiness. No discipline is enjoyable while it is happening—it's painful! But afterward, there will be a peaceful harvest of right living for those who are trained in this way."

—Hebrews 12:10–11

Merriam-Webster offers several definitions of *discipline,* but one cuts through: "control gained by obedience or training." Recall the second challenge from chapter one: *using our limited control to reach limitless victory.* We cannot defeat the Galactic Empire alone—but we can choose to take up God's power.

We can choose to be the hero of our own story.

"We must never forget that we may also find meaning in life even when confronted with a hopeless situation, when facing a fate that cannot be changed. For what then matters is to . . . transform a personal tragedy into a triumph, to turn one's predicament into a human achievement. When we are no longer able to change a situation, we are challenged to change ourselves."

—Victor Frankl

We are challenged to take control—to wield "the force" of our Jedi patriot superpower, to choose the "only one right" choice in every crucible moment.

When we do, God's power flows through us—the real source of the force. It wins battles no enemy can overcome, and carries us toward a destiny no darkness can overrun . . . and that is where we find the real triumph in suffering.

CHAPTER 19

RETURN OF THE MAGA ZOOLANDER

Hollywood makes for a strange hometown in modern times. A glittering veneer of glamour and fantasy bubbles on the surface of a deep reservoir of dreams and nightmares. The frothing waves of a million transient souls surge through the city on currents of imagination and addiction, love and pride, creativity and corruption, virtue and vice. Of course, some would scoff at the suggestion that any virtue still survives in the City of Angels, now hijacked by demons and deviants. But I believe there's a remnant still swirling beneath that surface—artists and tradesmen carrying on the noble themes Tinsel Town once etched into our hearts. Despite the overwhelming degradations of WOKE witchcraft and Team Lunacy propaganda, classic Hollywood can still channel eternal truths: humanity's unquenchable thirst for love, purpose, and triumph.

And one of its most beloved themes is the comeback.

America loves a comeback story—the more impossible the odds, the better. Our national obsession with professional sports strikes this chord with infectious clarity: legendary fourth-quarter gridiron miracles backed by roaring crowds, echoed by classic films replaying the tale. And the theme runs beyond athletics to every form of human struggle.

We've always had a heart for the underdog—rooting for the little guy in a cage match; urging a Jedi apprentice to cross sabers with a menacing dark monster; gasping as a hacker transforms into Neo, bending bullets in a clash with an army of murderous clones. We thrive on overcoming the impossible, and we yearn for the triumph of the individual. This ethic is etched into the American soul—an echo of the fiery ethos that burned in the hearts of those patriots who defied the tyranny of the British Empire and fought the American Revolution. From the frozen brink of defeat, they rallied to declare the immortal promise of 1776, that all men—especially the underdog—are destined for, and worthy of, being free, with equal opportunity to pursue their own comeback dream. That hopeless resistance pulled off one of the most consequential comebacks of all time, forging an intrepid national spirit of boundless hope and courageous compassion.

Two and a half centuries later, it appears to be little more than a naive Hollywood fairy tale. What happened?

Our present American tragedy—the abysmal state in which comfort has become our god and cowardice our form of worship—is a clear and ominous sign that our once-intrepid national spirit has not only waned but nearly vanished. It is a devastating abdication of Americanism itself. This is the point where we finally confront the answer to that trendy, propaganda-fueled question: "When was America ever 'great'?"

Here's the thing: America is not merely a place; it's a promise— and a promise is only as great as the truth and goodness that secure it. America is not a result; it is a relentless pursuit of our destiny, a triumph in suffering that can only be found on the pathway of virtue. Virtue is the beating heart of our promise to protect life, liberty, property, and equality—and it is the erosion of this virtue that leaves America less than great, drifting toward the destruction of tribal hatred, hedonism, and despotic greed.

A dire and disheartening place to be.

It is with stupendous irony that we realize our greatest existential threat is, in fact, a form of climate change—not the ridiculous weather scam peddled by Team Lunacy, but a *climate of comfort and compliance,* melting our bedrock of courage, duty, and independence. This WOKE climate shift has unleashed a series of destructive storms battering every pillar of our society:

- **Compassion** has been perverted into an excuse for strategic chaos—erasing borders and flooding us with crime, terrorists, deadly drugs, and a locust swarm of illegal aliens devouring a middle class already staggering under inflation, obscene taxation, and suffocating regulation.

- **National debt** has exploded with our addiction to government dependency—weakening our currency and our sovereignty, greasing the rails to the inevitable demise of "Our Democracy™."

- **Foreign policy** has morphed into genocidal money laundering, licensed by the state to plunder its own people.

- **The DOJ** has become a despotic dragon—corrupted by greed and arrogance, armed with enough arcane laws to criminalize anything and the firepower to destroy anyone.

- **Our children,** the most vulnerable among us, are now sacrificed on the blood-stained altars of abortion and "transgender" medical mutilation—worship given to the murderous goddess of "choice."

- **The sacred trilateral family**—traditional marriage of a man and a woman, with God-given authority over their children— has been demonized as hateful discrimination, concealing a deliberate strategy to dismantle the cornerstone of civilization.

- **Cancel culture** has metastasized into mob rule—shielding ivory tower lunacy while silencing the independent thought needed to resist Marxist sabotage.

The damage is extensive, even catastrophic. But still—revival remains possible.

It is incumbent upon us, We the People—and especially *The Remnant*—to recognize this moment for what it truly is: a call to action. The boundless hope of the American spirit can and *must* be revived. And revival comes only through the (re)activation of **Uncomfortable Courage** and legitimate compassion.

That is the challenge set before us: the Great American Comeback.

The Hollywood Maverick in me dared to dream this comeback was possible—and more than that, dared to believe I might be destined to play a role in it. That dream first sparked in 2020, when I dropped the Red Hat selfie and MAGA manifesto that set my career and my entire life ablaze with Team Lunacy hatred. Those flames ignited when I made "the only right choice" at the nexus of duty and opportunity— recognizing that no one else could fulfill my destiny.

I had to choose faith and fortitude. I had to take courageous action.

The battle, as you've seen, has been brutal—and absolutely worthwhile. That, I suspect, will be the question most often asked upon my release:

Was it worth it?

Do you regret refusing the plea?

Not for a single second.

It was worth every moment of misery—because it transformed me. It deepened the alchemy of virtue in my heart and amplified its power, as the battle rages on . . . and I prepare to begin my comeback:

Return of the MAGA Zoolander.

The fires of persecution still burn. They've torched my career and my reputation—but they've failed to singe my spirit or consume my soul. That furnace forged my character into the burnished bronze of a

Braveheart warrior, as I lived out the truth of William Wallace's immortal words in that film:

> "Run, and you'll live . . . at least a while. And dying in your beds, many years from now, would you be willing to trade *all* the days, from this day to that, for one chance—just one chance—to come back here and tell our enemies that they may take our lives, but they'll never take OUR FREEDOM!"

After a year of relentless suffering as a political hostage of the Obama-Biden regime, I've had over three hundred daily opportunities to prove that declaration: by choosing, in each moment, to embrace my identity as a free man. I am a child of God, created for freedom, and liberated from the bondage of sin by the blood of Christ.

That is a freedom no prison or pain can ever restrain.

But I've also had the opportunity to prove what that freedom *is for*.

Prison is a case study in WOKE "freedom"—an open license to sin, which only becomes slavery to vice. The inner freedom I claimed here in government captivity is the Jedi patriot power that brings true liberation.

Freedom is the fuel that powers the pursuit of our destiny—*and our destiny is to be free.* In other words, freedom is not just the means to an end—it *is* the end!

> "When St. Paul says that 'it is for freedom that Christ has set us free' (Galatians 5:1), his formulation indicates that freedom is not, most fundamentally, a means by which one achieves an external goal. It is not first a power or an ability. Instead, it is itself an end. In fact, properly understood, it is *the* end of man; freedom is ultimately what we are set free *for*."
>
> —D. C. Schindler

It's critical to note the contrast between true freedom and today's counterfeit WOKE morality.

Real freedom mirrors Control Theory: We hold the agency to **acknowledge** God—who is good; we **activate** our pursuit of Him; and we **accept** the fruit of our choices and the character we've cultivated. Real freedom has a purpose, and therefore a responsibility. It is meant for building virtuous relationships.

The purpose of freedom is to pursue the good.

But the enemies of the good have devised a clever distortion—defaming virtue as a restriction on liberty. WOKE wisdom insists that freedom means unrestricted choice: whatever you want, whatever *you* decide is good . . . because WOKE wisdom has declared that God is dead. You are the god of your life, and anything you choose is good—because *you* chose it.

What they've done here is divorce Step 2 from its rightful place in the Control Theory sequence. They tell you to "Just Do It" and promise you'll win—while distracting you from the prize you have won.

The fatal flaw in this WOKE promise is the fruit: They claim you're free to choose whatever you want *and* free from the consequences—that you can be free from the cost of your choices. But this is lunacy.

We all know that "money doesn't grow on trees"—fruit does.

"Free" does not mean without cost; it means without chains.

A free man can step off a cliff—but gravity still collects.

God is not dead—and freedom is not free.

True freedom is opportunity. WOKE freedom is debauchery.

"The fruit of the righteous is a tree of life, and he who wins souls is wise."

—Proverbs 11:30

Now, if the proper purpose of freedom is to pursue the good, it follows that we must understand what good is—and that is the crux of the conflict in our galactic War of the Worlds.

> "[COVID] has set the question of the common good into relief. For the sake of that good, states across the U.S. have shut down all businesses and public events deemed 'non-essential.' But how do we determine what counts as essential? Even to attempt to answer that question, we first have to ask: essential to what? Essential to mere survival, or essential to humanity? Essential to existence or to full human flourishing? . . . One would presume this threat to general welfare would force a reckoning with the fundamental questions liberalism does not like to ask; questions concerning the nature of things—in this case, the nature of the common good, of the political order, or man, and of everything in between. What good, in fact, is the state charged with protecting?"
>
> —D. C. Schindler

Suddenly, the abstract crystallizes into absolute. These are questions of control.

In his letters, my brother Michael shared a powerful insight: because the "modern morality" of WOKE wisdom insists that truth, goodness, and beauty are all relative—"you have your truth, and I have mine"; "beauty is in the eye of the beholder"—the only goal left is the expansion of possibility. Unrestrained narcissism, sanctified as freedom.

"All that's left to do," he wrote, "is to expand possibility [unrestricted choice] as a good—indeed, the good—in itself. It becomes all about clearing away barriers to that end, and so, predictably, we see courts declare that individuals have the 'right' to abortion, pornography, gay marriage, etc. We can expect this list of pseudo-rights to keep growing [boys invading girls' sports and private spaces, children mutilated by barbaric TRANS surgeries], since that's the only direction to go, as the system is currently structured—and as liberty is currently defined."

To define liberty is the only way to defend it.

"We are fond of talking about 'liberty,' but the way we end up talking of it is an attempt to avoid discussing what is good. We are fond of talking about 'progress'; that is a dodge to avoid discussing what is good. We are fond of talking about 'education'; that is a dodge to avoid discussing what is good. The modern man says, 'Let us leave all these arbitrary standards and embrace unadulterated liberty.' This is, logically rendered, 'Let us not decide what is good, but let it be considered good not to decide it.' He says, 'Away with all your old moral standards; I am for progress.' This, logically stated, means, 'Let us not settle what is good; but let us settle whether we are getting more of it.' He says, 'Neither in religion nor morality, my friend, lies the hope of the race, but in education.' This, clearly expressed, means, 'We cannot decide what is good, but let us give it to our children.'"

—G. K. Chesterton

This is not just a clever critique—it's a stunning indictment.

And tragically accurate.

We have indeed been giving more and more of "it" to our children—especially since the Marxist upheaval of the sixties. That infection metastasized through schools and universities, then seeped into media and politics. Together, they saturated society with a sinister WOKE religion.

The result has been catastrophic. Our civilization has been slowly poisoned by the erosion of the good, dissolving the very foundations of human flourishing.

We've been sabotaged by the systemic erasure of God.

Michael went on to point out, "the word 'republic' means a *res* which is public; *res* refers to some actual, objective thing, around which society is oriented and to which it is ordered."

This is a simple concept—of profound importance.

"Diversity is our strength" is a Team Lunacy lie, because diversity without a unifying center is not a strength—it's a dangerous road to chaos and destruction.

> "The safety of a republic depends essentially on **the energy of a common national sentiment**; on a uniformity of principles and habits; on the exemption of the citizens from foreign bias, and prejudice; and on *that love of country which will almost invariably be found to be closely connected with* **birth**, **education, and family**."
>
> —Alexander Hamilton

Our republic is called the "United States of America"—but what exactly unites us? What objective reality are we anchored to?

My fellow Americans, it is nothing less than our national identity that is now in peril. The fate of our republic has marched to the precipice of irreversible tyranny—despite its constitutional clothing. A sovereign republic of free people—for that is the vanguard of liberty—cannot function without a *res*: a heartbeat of shared principle and purpose. That is what pumps the oxygen of freedom through our national veins and brings *e pluribus unum* to life.

MAGA must be more than a movement—it must be a spiritual revival.

A "Red Pill Revolution."

MAGA is the resuscitation of a nation in cardiac arrest—and J6 was a historic defibrillator, shocking our national heartbeat out of paralysis, waking us from a coma of apathetic comfort. In that moment, we proved that America still has a pulse—but it is weak, and her enemies continue to poison her from within. We must infuse her with an antidote to save her from certain death—and the antidote is the Red Pill of absolute truth.

Now is the time for Uncomfortable Courage.

Now is the moment to ignite the Great American Comeback.

But we cannot pull off a comeback without first defining—and unifying around—what it is we are coming back *to*.

What is the principle and purpose that once electrified a melting pot of dreamers—uniting them into the land of the free and the home of the brave? What was the source of that hope that powered a five-thousand-year leap into the greatest nation on earth?

What is the grand American promise?

A pledge is a promise—so it seems the American "Pledge of Allegiance" would answer this question: ". . . with liberty and justice for all."

But liberty to do what? And justice according to whom?

As always, the middle gets messy and becomes meaningless without the beginning. We often rush to recite that legendary line, forgetting the foundation underneath.

We must sit before we stand, so we know what we're standing *on*. Only then can we step forward in the battle—and win.

"I pledge allegiance to the flag of the United States of America, and to the Republic for which it stands, one nation under God, indivisible, with liberty and justice for all."

So the *res* of our Republic—the objective reality around which we were ordered, the unity that made us indivisible—was this:

One Nation under God.

Translation: WE WERE ALL ON TEAM REALITY.

Liberty meant freedom to pursue the good—the only path to lasting happiness. Justice meant equal treatment according to God's Divine Order. This reaches back to the Roman statesman Cicero (those maverick Italians!), who articulated *Natural Law* almost a century before the crucifixion and resurrection of Christ.

That is some ancient Red Pill action.

Now, if we're really going to take this Red Pill—seeking true enlightenment, reclaiming our national identity and purpose—then we must go back to the beginning.

The beginning of everything.

We must discover what our source—that is to say, *who* our God—is, and what *He* says about identity and purpose.

"In the beginning the Word already existed. The Word was with God, and the Word was God. He existed in the beginning with God. God created everything through him, and nothing was created except through him. The Word gave life to everything that was created, and his life brought light to everyone. The light shines in the darkness, and the darkness can never extinguish it.

"God sent a man, John the Baptist, to tell about the light so that everyone might believe because of his testimony. John himself was not the light; he was simply a witness to tell about the light. The one who is the true light, who gives light to everyone, was coming into the world. He came into the very world he created, but the world didn't recognize him. He came to his own people, and even they rejected him. But to all who believed in him and accepted him, he gave the right to become children of God. They are reborn—not with a physical birth resulting from human passion or plan, but a birth that comes from God."

—John 1:1–13

The power condensed in this Scripture is staggering—but let's unpack a few keys.

First: God is not "alone."

Before creation, before time itself, the one true God existed *with His Son*. He existed in *relationship*—intrinsic to His nature—and it's echoed in His creation of man as conscious, relational beings: male and female.

"Word" here is the Greek *logos*—the origin and boundary of reality. *Logos* refers to both Scripture and Jesus: the only begotten Son of God, who *is* God ("The Word was God") and yet is *with* God in relationship ("The Word was with God").

How can this be?

It's the greatest of mysteries—illuminated by another divine mystery: marriage. That magical fusion of two hearts into one love is an exquisite echo of God's relational essence: "a man shall cleave to his wife, and the two become one flesh" (Genesis 2:24). Two distinct individuals, yet united physically, emotionally, and spiritually into a sacred whole: a unique catalyst for intimacy, fulfillment, and human flourishing.

> "The man who finds a wife finds a treasure, and he receives favor from the Lord Yahweh."
>
> —Proverbs 18:22

Another key from John 1: God—through His Word (the Bible) and His Son (Jesus)—is the source of light.

That is, *revelation that produces enlightenment.*

This light is what enables us to "believe" (Step 1: Acknowledge) and "accept" (Step 2: Activate) as described in verse 12. We can choose to know God, His Word, and His son Jesus for who He is—and yield to His authority in the Divine Order.

That alignment leads us to receive (Step 3: Accept) "the (re)birth that comes from God"—which gives us the "right to become children of God."

That is our identity—the starting point of our purpose.

Our purpose, ultimately, is to *be in the family*. This leads to worship—the rightful prioritization of God in the Divine Order. And that Divine Order is the key to everything—reflected in "the laws of nature and of nature's God."

"In the beginning God created the heavens and the earth. The earth was formless and empty, and darkness covered the surface of deep waters. And the Spirit of God was hovering over the surface of the waters. Then God said, 'Let there be light' and there was light. And God saw that the light was good."

—Genesis 1:1–4

This opening of the Bible has shaped all of Western history.

Dennis Prager, in *The Rational Bible*, underscores why:

"Because the world was created by God, God exists independently of the world. God is therefore not part of nature. We do not worship trees—because trees are created, not creators. We worship the Creator of trees. Unlike the other religions of the ancient world, biblical religion never worshipped nature. Another reason not to worship nature . . . is that nature, unlike God and human beings, is amoral. That is why we think of a [murderer] as evil, but we don't think of an earthquake or a hurricane, which may inflict far more suffering and destruction, as evil. God is good. Man can be good and/or evil. Nature is neither."

Another insight from Genesis: the importance of order:

"Genesis describes the original state of the earth as *tohu* and *vohu* (Hebrew), translated here as 'unformed and void' . . . God's work was not only creating and making, but **composing order out of chaos**.

Genesis 1 is about Divine Order as much as it is about Creation. God is the Maker of order and distinctions. Order and distinctions are fundamental characteristics of a biblical worldview. . . . God distinguishes between light and dark, day and night, land and water, and humans and animals. . . . God distinguishes between man and God, good and evil, man and woman, the holy and the profane, parent and child, the beautiful and the ugly, and life and death. **Preserving God's order and distinctions is one of man's primary tasks**. But, like the unformed chaos of Genesis 1:2, undoing God's order and distinctions is the natural state of man."

That last line rings especially loud today. The WOKE "mission: insanity" is an assault on God's order and distinctions—as we see in the deceptively named "Pride" movement. This has metastasized into radical TRANS ideology—a rebellion against reality itself.

As Prager warns:

"The battle for higher civilization may be characterized as the battle between biblical distinctions and the human desire to undo [them]. As Western society abandons the Bible and the God of the Bible, it is also abandoning these distinctions. I fear for its future, because Western civilization rests on these distinctions."

—Dennis Prager

Suddenly, the chaos and destruction unleashed by BLM Inc., TRANS Inc., and the like reveals itself as a coordinated strategy—with a deadly aim. America is the front line in this war, where every battle ultimately comes down to Team Reality versus Team Lunacy: God and His Divine Order versus "No God!" and the chaos that follows.

Cicero saw it long ago: These rebels are not just at war with society—they are at war with themselves. They're rebelling against their own higher nature, tearing their souls apart by "fleeing" from the destiny created for them by their maker. They shred their own soul—and burn the pieces in hellfire.

It is a fate far worse than death—but they demand it, and they refuse to be deterred.

They refuse to be saved from themselves.

In contrast to the chaos of WOKE witchcraft, when we observe the creation and instruction of God, we find incredible beauty, goodness, and hope.

> "Such repetition of the phrase 'God saw that it was good' can only mean the Bible considers it very important. . . . That the world God created is good gives all of us who believe in the Bible a reason for optimism, even when our life is troubled. Ultimately, this world is good, and good will eventually prevail (here or in an afterlife).
>
> God took pleasure in seeing how well His work had turned out. This is also a human teaching moment. . . . Humility means knowing your strengths but not allowing them to make you arrogant. Rabbi Chazon Ish . . . said, . . . 'Humility means that a person realizes his true worth.'"
>
> —Dennis Prager

Humility is the firm grasp—held without arrogance—of our dignity as sons and daughters of a good God.

> "Then God said, 'Let us make man in our image, to be like us. They will reign over the fish of the sea, the birds in the sky, the livestock, all the wild animals on the earth, and all the earth.' So God created the man in His own image. In the image of God He created them; male

and female He created them. Then God blessed them and said, 'Be fruitful and multiply. Fill the earth and govern it. Reign over [it all].'"

—Genesis 1:26–28

Here at the dawn of humanity, God has already established "His Democracy." Man is designed to be self-governing: **fruitful, responsible, free**. God instituted *true* liberty: not profane license, but sacred opportunity paired with responsibility.

"God grants man dominion over the animals and all of nature because man is a higher being. He alone is created in God's image. And though obviously a physical being, he is, like God, outside of nature (he has a soul). *Nature is not sacred; human life is.* God intended for man to dominate the natural world ("they shall rule") . . . the world was created for human use. This biblical instruction . . . opened the way to finding cures for diseases. It is no coincidence that the Western world essentially developed modern medicine . . . the first requirement is to understand that human beings must learn how to conquer nature—conquer, not pray to natural forces (like rain gods) or try to propitiate them. People in our time romanticize nature, perhaps not realizing—or not wanting to realize—that either humans rule over nature or nature will destroy humans."

—Dennis Prager

Scripture gives us a clear understanding of God's character and His foundational principles for humanity.

"I am Yahweh your God, who rescued you from the land of Egypt, the place of your slavery. You must not have any other god but me. . . . You must not . . . worship them, for I . . . am a jealous God who will **not tolerate** your affection for any other gods."

—Exodus 20:1–6

Red Pill alert: Do not be misled by modern distortions of "tolerance." More on this later.

"'For I know the plans I have for you,' says the Lord *Yahweh*. 'They are plans for good and not for disaster, to give you a future and a hope. In those days when you pray, I will listen. If you look for me wholeheartedly, you will find me. I will be found by you,' says the Lord *Yahweh*."
—Jeremiah 29:11–4

"Should we sacrifice our firstborn children to pay for our sins? No, O people, the Lord *Yahweh* has told you what is good, and this is what He requires of you: to do what is right, to love mercy, and to walk humbly with your God."
—Micah 6:6, 8

"One of [the Pharisees], an expert in religious law, tried to trap Him with this question: 'Teacher, which is the most important commandment in the law of Moses?' Jesus replied, '"You must love Yahweh your God with all your heart, all your soul, and all your mind." This is the first and greatest commandment. A second is equally important: "Love your neighbor as yourself." The entire law and all the demands of the prophets are based on these two commandments.'"
—Matthew 22:35–40

The directive for mankind—and the purpose he craves—is to know God and to commune with Him.

God is **relational, distinct, orderly** . . . and **fundamentally good**.

He is also the original Artist, scripting a cosmic drama on the stage of human history. It turns out, God also loves a comeback story. The Gospel is His epic masterpiece. And the key to our *Great American Comeback* is to understand the stage we're standing on . . . to seize the role we were created to play . . . and to act the supernatural script of our Almighty Playwright and Director.

Yes, we are real-life characters, and our Director has granted us extraordinary freedom to improvise our lines and movements. But every great actor understands the importance of taking on the essence of their character. And they know the necessity of following the story's scripted outline in order to deliver a performance that ultimately satisfies.

With Red Pill clarity, we can see the stage, and we know what first made America great: **our national covenant**—a foundational promise to be *One Nation under God.* Our guiding principle was "indivisible, with liberty and justice for all." And our shared purpose was the pursuit of divine destiny—becoming virtuous, truly free people.

In my cell, a political hostage within the *Divided States of America,* I drafted a "Declaration of American Revival" to restore that singular principle and purpose. I believe the truest expression of MAGA is *Make America **Godly** Again.*

This alone gives us a shot at the Comeback.

WE ARE ONE NATION UNDER GOD

God is the Reality of the Higher Power We Must Recognize and Respect

We the People of these United States of America are united first and foremost by those truths we hold to be self-evident: that all men are created equal; that they are endowed by their Creator God with certain unalienable rights; that among these are life, liberty, and the pursuit of eternal destiny; and that the exercise of all rights and their corresponding responsibilities are guided by Natural Law: "the laws of nature and of nature's God."

If we do not acknowledge this higher power, then man becomes the only conscious form of power. By definition, this makes man take the place of God—and this is the goal of socialism and communism.

Socialism and communism are rooted in a categorical rejection of God and His authority, making corruptible men the ultimate authority and inevitably forfeiting our rights—life, liberty, and property—to the power of the State. These Marxist systems have been widely practiced and proven catastrophic throughout world history.

America will *never* be a socialist country; America will never be a communist country, because we know that murder and stealing are wrong—the gravest of evils. America is more than a place; it is a promise that life will be protected, that property will be respected, and that the murder, theft, and godlessness of socialism must be rejected. America is not a race; it is the noble ideal that all men are endowed by God with equal rights which cannot be given or rescinded, only recognized and defended. Our rights remain secure only while we respect the One who entrusted them—and only as we exercise them with virtue in line with His Natural Law.

The only thing necessary for evil to win is for good men to play it safe—assuring their rights dissolve into the total safety of a prison-state. Therefore, as free citizens of America, vanguard of liberty for the world, we must stand and dare to proclaim:

We *are* one nation under God—and thus, we shall remain.

Can you imagine the impact of a rising wave of citizens signing this declaration—then staking their lives, fortunes, and sacred honor on its promise?

Can you feel the tectonic force?

Can you hear the golden tones of that supernatural melody?

Can you envision strongholds of greed and corruption torn down, barriers of hatred broken, and the hopes of the heartbroken lifted?

Like I said . . . a hopeless romantic and a "consummate dreamer."

This pledge is the bedrock of our national comeback. And the first half of that cornerstone phrase is just as vital as the second: "One Nation." Throughout this book, we've traced the fractured contours of our present *Divided States of America*—a reality in stark contradiction to our pledge, and a serious obstacle to its revival.

Most of us know the phrase: "A house divided against itself cannot stand." Or as the apostle Luke records it:

> "Any kingdom divided by civil war is doomed. A family splintered by feuding will fall apart. . . . Anyone who isn't with me opposes me, and anyone who isn't working with me is actually working against me."
>
> —Luke 11:17, 23

There is no "Switzerland neutrality." The binary is unavoidable—every human takes either the red pill or the blue pill. This may sound like doom for America—but in fact, it's the crucible for our revival:

> "I have come to set the world on fire, and I wish it were already burning! . . . Do you think I have come to bring peace to the earth? No, I have come to divide people against each other!"
>
> —Luke 12:49, 51

Yet we also remember the angels at Christ's birth:

> "Glory to God in highest heaven, and peace on earth to those with whom God is pleased."
>
> —Luke 2:14

Peace *is* the ultimate destiny of man—but it comes only after division between those "working with me" and those "actually working against me." Between good and evil. Between Team Reality and Team Lunacy.

Those are the teams.

That is the division.

And in every moment, that is our decision.

Locked up at FCI Oakdale, I reflected on the lessons learned and the discipline forged through my deployment. I began to pray and prepare for my release.

And I continued to do what I always do: dare to dream.

What could my comeback look like—and why does it matter?

Our lives are relational. Each choice ripples outward with eternal consequence. The butterfly effect is real. And America's comeback must begin with her citizens—one by one.

The Republic belongs to its people—they are the stakeholders in that enterprise.

So I took stock: the resources God had provided, my present circumstance, and the future only He knew. Then I prayed for clarity in this reconfigured dreamscape.

I was still a musician—the spirit of "Love, Liberty, Rock & Roll" still pulsing, and new anthems echoing in my mind. And I still had a top-notch producer and bandmate for a brother. . . .

I was still a model—with a *Rolling Stone* nickname and visions for a cultural renaissance of "Triumphant Masculinity."

I was still an actor and filmmaker—Hollywood blacklist notwithstanding—with an alternative media market paving new avenues for virtuous content.

I was still a writer, now an author, and a social media voice. And I was still the Creative Director at America's Frontline Doctors and GoldCare.com, leading the health-and-wellness revolution.

And now, I was also a hostage-proven political prisoner, dedicated to exposing **the Greatest American Lie Ever Sold**. I would become a leader of the WeAreJ6.com mission to deliver Restorative Justice.

Needless to say, I had a lot going on.

Whatever shape my *Return* takes, boredom is not on the agenda. And I was aching to reunite with my family and rejoin my coalition of patriot colleagues.

A Jedi patriot comeback was starting to light up my horizon with renewed hope.

The cruelty of my persecution—directly ordered by the Obama-Biden regime—included being cut off from contact with my family for an inexcusable *three-quarters of a year*. Not until March 2024, after furious intervention from two brave Congressmen—Matt Gaetz of Florida and Clay Higgins of Louisiana—did the embargo break. At last, Dr. Gold was able to keep her promise. Soon after, my parents and sisters followed, spending two whole days with me in the Oakdale visitation room.

That was the spark of my comeback.

The moment I saw my best friend face to face, and hugged her after so many months of torment and aching loneliness—was priceless.

As we caught up and made plans, I learned Dr. Gold and my legal team had been working relentlessly: advocating for my rights, documenting abuses for civil litigation, and advancing my appeal. My appellate attorney had scored a huge win: securing a writ of certiorari from the U.S. Supreme Court on §1512. He called it "shooting the moon," given the political firestorm. The outcome was still pending then, but by June 28 the Court's *Fischer v. United States* decision would vindicate me.

I was innocent—a political hostage of a weaponized government.

We were confident about the full appeal of the remaining charges. There was no evidence of *mens rea* or *actus reus*—I had done nothing beyond peaceably fulfilling a professional duty. I would never give up until securing complete exoneration—something the entire world had assured me was utterly impossible. The Supreme Court win meant I would be released from wrongful imprisonment before the make-or-break election of 2024. More importantly, it meant God was rewarding *Uncomfortable Courage*—blessing my refusal to swallow the poisonous plea. I felt in that moment a prophetic stirring of "The Remnant." The call to spiritual arms—a clarion Patriot Plea—was now ringing in my heart.

Almost as if she heard it too, Dr. Gold suddenly interjected with a jolting question:

"Are you interested in running for public office?"

My soul did a double take. Somehow, I realized I'd already asked myself that question in the silence of my deployment—and answered it.

"Yes. Yes, I am."

The words leapt out—both instinctive and deliberate. I heard an almost audible *click* of my Red Pill vision snapping into focus. I recognized the landscape of this decisive moment—I had been here before.

"Uncomfortable Courage" was calling. Again.

Of course I'd been asked the question before—many times. It began in high school when I volunteered for Kevin Lundberg's state senate campaign, and picked up again when I torched my Hollywood career with a Maverick barrel roll into public support for MAGA.

My standard reply—both to myself and those asking—was some

version of: "I'm committed to the freedom fight, but I'm better suited to the culture war and the media space." Fair enough . . . but that didn't exactly answer the question—because the question wasn't really "Do you want to run for public office."

It was: "Our nation is in peril—so who is going to step up?"

When duty calls, it is for you to answer.

That call had found me before—when I sacrificed my dreams in 2020 to fight the "Red Pill Revolution," and again in 2022 when I came to Naples, Florida. Neither choice was easy or convenient. But there is a higher purpose than simply chasing preference. And there is a higher calling to serve your country, rather than always expecting it to serve you.

Freedom is purchased and preserved by those who answer the call.

Dr. Gold and I hadn't discussed this particular summons before, but we both knew what part of the movie we were in. We were at war—and the #TeamReality ranks were decimated.

Our nation's "Artificial Aristocracy" of corrupted ruling-class elites had completely hijacked the Republic into a Matrix illusion. The real Republic was gasping for air. Only spiritual CPR—Courage and Principles based in Reality—could revive it. When someone stops breathing, you don't wait for the doctor. You jump in and try to save a life.

President Trump is right, as he often is, when he says: "We are a nation in decline."

The danger was clear and present. And I was the "next man up" that Steve Bannon described—as I read his interview transcript in a prison cell:

". . . the reason we got in this situation was establishment Republicans that were controlled opposition. The only thing these people understand is smash mouth. Now, you have to play within the Constitution and the rule of law. But we . . . now understand that this is a war to the death, right? We *have* to win this. . . . And I keep saying it's next man up. You can't lean on Trump. You can't lean on Tucker, you can't lean on Bannon. . . . This is a populist revolt. You have to step up and do it yourself. . . . You have to understand we're in a political war and information war, and you've got to start fighting like you're in a war. . . . we just commemorated the eightieth anniversary [of D-Day] . . . half of them didn't get up to the bulwark on the beach. They were gone. . . . The only reason they got off that beach is next man up. American history is built upon next man up. . . . You'll lose the people at the front of the phalanx. You got to pick up the armor. You got to pick up the spear and do it yourself. This is going to be a very good exercise for us."

—Steve Bannon

It's almost like we took the same Red Pill.

"You've got to start fighting like you're in a war" . . . because you are.

And if you don't fight across the full spectrum of reality, you will be crushed. We are now on the brink of losing the free republic that Ben Franklin warned we might not keep:

"Perhaps [we] have lived with this miracle too long to be properly appreciative. Freedom is a fragile thing, and it is never more than one generation away from extinction. It is not ours by inheritance; *it must be fought for* and defended constantly by each generation, for it comes only once to a people. Those who have known freedom and then lost it have never known it again."

—Ronald Reagan

I have known this freedom to the fullest. I do not intend to lose it. And I will give nothing less than my full fury to defend the innocent, expose the darkness, and protect the life and liberty of those I love.

Reagan's warning highlights a profound truth: Because freedom is fragile, its defenders must be the opposite—"anti-fragile." A patriot defends their nation, and persecution only hardens their resolve.

God was forging that strength in me through this J6 journey—and for a purpose.

We reviewed the political landscape, and there was no doubt: Congress was compromised—riddled with corruption and cowardice that threatened the *Comeback* mission. After the Butler assassination attempt—which I watched on a prison TV—President Trump's third victory was nearly sealed. But that victory alone wouldn't save the Republic. He would need true patriots in Congress to follow his lead and carry the fight.

Waging the "Red Pill Revolution" inside Congress would be quite the irony. I was a political hostage because of the government's historic crimes there on January 6. It was a bold and intriguing thought.

My mission would be clear: challenge the runaway freight train of federal power. Slash spending. Shrink Washington—literally and figuratively. Restore constitutional governance—starting with a nearly lost First Principle: the "vertical separation of powers" called Federalism.

But first, another deception loomed: the weaponization of "separation of church and state."

J6 is **The Greatest American Lie Ever Sold.** But that lie grew in poisoned soil.

We've been told that because America guarantees religious liberty, government must purge religious expression—that faith is impermissible in the public square.

This legal sorcery has twisted our cherished "freedom *of* religion" into a fatal "freedom *from* religion" with the lie that religious liberty demands a secular state.

But secularism *is* a religion—one the Founders flatly rejected.

"The God who gave us life, gave us liberty at the same time . . . the hand of force may destroy, but cannot disjoin them."

—Thomas Jefferson

"Of all the dispositions and habits which lead to political prosperity, Religion and morality are indispensable supports. In vain would that man claim the tribute of Patriotism, who should labor to subvert these great Pillars of human happiness, these firmest props of the duties of Men and citizens . . . reason and experience both forbid us to expect that National morality can prevail in exclusion of religious principle."

—George Washington

The Founders' rejection of secularism was as unequivocal as their claim in the Declaration, that all men are created equal, endowed by their Creator with unalienable rights. They knew—because it is logically inescapable—that we couldn't have unalienable rights without a supreme source who created them. That's why, in the Declaration's closing, they appealed to the "Supreme Judge of the world for the rectitude of our intentions."

Abraham Lincoln, a devout Christian, recognized this foundation and its enduring power:

"All honor to Jefferson—to the man who . . . had the coolness, forecast, and capacity to introduce into a merely revolutionary document, an abstract truth, applicable to all men and all times . . . a rebuke and a stumbling-block to the very harbingers of re-appearing tyranny and oppression."

—Abraham Lincoln

The Founders respected a plurality of religious practice, but they also knew no society can survive without a fixed moral authority—a standard accessible by both reason and revelation:

> "We want not, indeed, a special revelation from heaven to teach us that men are born equal and free; that no man has a natural claim of dominion over his neighbors . . . These are the plain dictates of that reason and common sense . . . confirmed . . . by . . . the sacred oracles [Scripture] . . . and that they come from Him 'who hath made of one blood all nations to dwell upon the face of the earth. [Acts 17:26]'"
>
> —Reverend Samuel Cooper

A secular state denies God as the supreme authority. That makes the state itself the authority—and gives it power to grant or revoke rights at will. This is the very despotism the Founders loathed and swore to resist. Nearly all were devout men of virtue and conviction. They would be outraged to see their sacrifices to *protect* faith twisted into weapons against it.

Speaking of "separation," let's separate fact from fiction.

The phrase "separation of church and state" appears nowhere in the Constitution. Its true origin? Scripture. In Exodus, God gave the Ten Commandments, then established the first republican form of governance, with distinct offices: Moses leading civil affairs, Aaron as high priest over spiritual matters. Separate—but unified under God.

King Uzziah broke that boundary in 2 Chronicles 26—"he became strong, his heart was so proud that he acted corruptly"—arrogantly entering the temple to usurp the priest's role.

God struck him with leprosy on the spot. Uzziah died in disgrace.

God never demanded a "secular kingdom" or godless government. He didn't forbid worship, prayer, or open faith in public life. What He condemned was government seizing control of the church—dictating which religious practices were allowed.

That temptation has plagued rulers across the ages. And every time, the result was the same: religion exploited to justify conquest, expand state power, and suppress freedom. That is what the separation doctrine was meant to prevent—not free expression of faith. Not public calls to virtue and piety.

The early American leaders understood this. They confirmed it. For them, separation—or more precisely, division—of Church and State was never about excluding God. It was about protecting the Church from government control.

"The separation of the Church from the State did not mean the severance of the State from God, or of the nation from Christianity."
—Bishop Charles Galloway

"I have lived, Sir, a long time, and the longer I live, the more convincing proofs I see of this truth—that God governs in the affairs of men. And if a sparrow cannot fall to the ground without His notice, is it probable that an empire can rise without His aid? We have been assured, Sir, in the Sacred Writings, that 'except the Lord build the House, they labor in vain that build it.' I firmly believe this."
—Benjamin Franklin

"Religion is the basis and Foundation of Government."
—James Madison

America was built by men of faith—to protect faith itself. That's a fact our enemies hope you'll forget.

The American founders were vigilant in protecting both public and private religious practice from state control—because they'd suffered that tyranny themselves. Many colonists fled to the New World after King Henry VIII declared the Anglican Church the state religion in the sixteenth century. Those who practiced *according to their own conscience* were persecuted, often brutally.

So the architects of the Constitution built specific religious protections:

"Congress shall make no law respecting an establishment of religion, or prohibiting the Free Exercise thereof."

—The First Amendment, U.S. Constitution

"Notice that the Establishment Clause prohibited the State from enforcing religious conformity, and the Free Exercise Clause ensured that the State would protect (rather than suppress, as it currently does) citizens' rights of conscience and religious expression. Both clauses are prohibitions only on the power of Congress, not on religious individuals or organizations. This was the meaning of 'separation of Church and State' with which Thomas Jefferson was intimately familiar, and it was this interpretation that he repeatedly reaffirmed in his writings and practices, not the modern perversion of it."

—David Barton

In 1853, the U.S. Senate confirmed this intent:

"The First Amendment was not designed to weaken or diminish religion, but to prevent the establishment of a national religion, and that it did not prohibit individuals **or states** from expressing religious convictions."

—U.S. Senate Judiciary Committee report (1853)

In 1833, Supreme Court Justice Joseph Story agreed:

"The clause speaks of 'an establishment of religion.' What is meant by that expression? It referred, without doubt, to that establishment which existed in the mother country [Britain]. . . . They intended, by this Amendment, to prohibit 'an establishment of religion' such as the English Church presented, or anything like it."

—Justice Joseph Story

The following year, the U.S. House of Representatives spelled it out:

"What is an 'establishment of religion'? It must have a creed defining what a man must believe; it must have rites and ordinances which believers must observe; it must have ministers of defined qualifications to teach the doctrines and administer the rites; it must have tests for the submissive and penalties for the nonconformist. There was never an established religion without all these."

—U.S. House of Representatives. *Report on the Religious Aspect of the United States Government*

Let's be absolutely clear: **America is—and must remain—a Judeo-Christian nation**. That doesn't mean a coercive "national religion." It means our national identity and moral framework are rooted in the Judeo-Christian ***worldview***.

Every human lives by a worldview. And a sovereign league of those individuals—for that is what a republic is—must unify around a common understanding of this framework.

That is precisely what the American Founders achieved with the Declaration of Independence. It is the *res*—the central reality—of our republic. They articulated a consensus of self-evident truths rooted in biblical principles, shared by Jew and Christian Gentile alike, that formed the foundation of Western civilization.

Today, much is made of the term "Christian Nationalism." It's often a smear intended to mischaracterize patriots who seek a national revival of our founding Judeo-Christian values, painting them as radical zealots demanding religious submission.

Speaking for myself, let me be clear: **I am an unapologetic American Nationalist**. Nationalism is the balanced center of the real power spectrum. To the left is Globalism—which is tyranny. To the right is tribalism and anarchy—which is the tyranny of chaos.

I reject tyranny in all forms, and I will fight against it on all fronts.

At the same time, **I am an unapologetic follower of Jesus Christ**. That makes me a Christian—so if you want to call me a "Christian Nationalist," that's on you.

American Nationalists who know their history will appreciate the value of our Christian heritage—and they will support its revival whether or not they share the faith themselves. The critical irony is this: the Judeo-Christian worldview is the only civilizational cornerstone that provides both a universal objective standard—the necessary anchor to what is good and evil—*and* legitimate ***tolerance*** of cognitive and religious liberty.

History has proved this, again and again, in blood and ashes.

G. K. Chesterton put it bluntly in *Orthodoxy*: "The first effect of not believing in God is to believe in anything." Yes, it's true: the WOKE battle cry of "tolerance" and "inclusion" is just another DoubleSpeak delusion. Because without a fixed moral standard, "tolerance" means whatever those in power say it means.

As always—it's a control thing.

This question of ultimate control must be answered before any political platform can be taken seriously. A candidate who won't answer it is either clueless—or corrupt.

"Return of the MAGA Zoolander" isn't just a Hollywood line. It's the comeback God has called me to—for my life, my family, and my country. And it's not about personal vindication.

Not revenge—revival. The revival of true constitutional government. **Returning Power to the People**.

That was my battle cry in 2020. Now it's my mission, forged in the fires of COVID, rigged elections, and J6 persecution—as I draw up a game plan for *The Great American Comeback*.

First rule of any comeback: Know the game. What are we playing? What are the rules? What defines the field? And who are the two teams?

Don't fall for the Team Lunacy pump-fake; a pure "democracy" is **not** the game. We are fighting—for keeps—for the revival of the American Republic.

The Declaration and Constitution are the rulebook, grounded in scriptural revelation. The field of play is the physical and digital, intellectual and spiritual gridiron connecting the minds and hearts of the Republic's stakeholders—its citizens.

On one side: Team Lunacy—led by the *Artificial Aristocracy*, aiming a kill shot at individual sovereignty.

On the other: Team Reality—led by *The Remnant*, patriots of Uncomfortable Courage rallying a comeback strike.

And that strike is the "Red Pill Revolution."

This "Team R" is the People's Party—and it is not measured by Republicans or Democrats. It is anchored in **Reality** itself. #TeamReality is marked by enduring, noble convictions:

- Strength over safety
- Freedom over fear
- Love over laziness
- Duty over despair

This is the character required to win—and the contest is life-or-death.

Shall we begin?

To launch the comeback, we need a *starting line*—the premise we all stand on:

ALL PEOPLE ARE DIVINELY DESIGNED TO BE SOVEREIGN INDIVIDUALS

We also need a *finish line*—the "end zone" that defines victory:

ALL PEOPLE ARE SET FREE AND SECURED TO PURSUE THEIR DESTINY

Once the game, the teams, and the target are clear, we need a "government game plan." Policy will fill out the playbook, but first let's establish some *"Keystone Principles"* for operating a People-powered government.

NUMBER 1: "NAME THE GAME"

What is government even *for*? What exactly is the objective?

The purpose of legitimate government—the sole reason it exists—is to **PROTECT PEOPLE'S RIGHTS**.

The road to hell is paved with good intentions. We are dangerously close—with tyranny disguised as "safety" and "equity." As a government *of the People, by the People, for the People*—which is the true meaning of *democracy*—we must guard against any deception that lures us down that road.

Every policy, law, executive action, and judgment must serve a simple test: does it protect the unalienable rights of *the People*?

NUMBER 2: "TAKE THE PLEDGE"

What is the grand American promise?

"Who" and "what" are We intending to "be" and "do"?

We must unite in our national covenant: **WE ARE ONE NATION UNDER GOD**.

That's not religion—it's reality. Our rights come from God—and no state can revoke them. This *res* of our Republic is the foundation of liberty

NUMBER 3: "MAKE THE PLAY"

Who actually throws and catches the "ball" here?

Every citizen must engage in their government, because **YOU ARE RESPONSIBLE FOR YOUR OWN SUCCESS**.

Freedom is a full-contact sport. We all know "a chain is only as strong as its weakest link." To Make America Great Again, we must realize America is only as great as the strength and service of her citizens. Our nation will rise or fall based on the stewardship *you* contribute. That is the duty stamped on the other side of the liberty coin we've promised to invest in our people.

Remember: As a citizen, you are an equal percentage partner in the American enterprise—a democratic constitutional republic—and **there are no silent partners in democracy**.

Also remember: "Free" doesn't mean without cost—it means *without chains*.

The entire point of a People-powered Republic is to unleash the awesome industry and ingenuity of the American citizen—and to reap the rewards of peace, prosperity, joy, and satisfaction that come as we cross that finish line of being truly "set free and secured."

So now that we've strapped on the keystone fundamentals—are you ready to huddle up, snap the ball, and begin this comeback drive?

Are you ready for some freedom football?

More importantly—are you willing to step up to the line as a citizen-player?

Will you answer the call and join the fray as a warrior in this "Red Pill Revolution"—to set the captives free and truly manifest our national destiny?

Are you ready to become a patriot?

CHAPTER 20

A PLEA FOR PATRIOTS

Remember *The Patriot*?

Imagine what might have transpired between father and son "when the cameras weren't rolling," with an allegorical twist—and how it might inspire a future challenge.

"Your country needs you."

Gabriel Martin spoke softly, his words firm. A quiet plea—but in his father's ears it struck like a war drum.

Benjamin Martin had dodged the fight against British tyranny, even in the wake of America's international bombshell—the signing of the Declaration of Independence. He stayed home, clinging to neutrality while imperial oppression spread. He found cover in the complaints of weaker men who doubted the cause of liberty, twisting Scripture to sanctify their cowardice: "Everyone must submit to governing authorities."

But Benjamin knew the Word in full—and he knew this excuse was a fraud. His real reason was darker: a dread of violence. The blood he had spilled years ago still haunted him. Now those demons had circled back to strike his son.

He had ignored the summons of the militia, hoping other men would carry the fight somewhere else. So Gabriel went alone. And now his son lay before him—bloodied and gasping for breath. Benjamin knelt at his side, tending the wounds, bracing for the anger he'd earned—for abandoning his son and his country.

But Gabriel didn't lash out. He reached for his father's hand, met his weary eyes, and whispered again:

"Your country needs you."

Benjamin could feel each pounding beat of his heart in the stillness, as though it might explode from his chest at the silent scream burning in Gabriel's eyes. That simple plea carried the weight of a nation—urging him to rise, to answer the call of duty.

It was the clarion cry of a country desperate for men to stand, to shoulder the burden of defending liberty—not just for themselves, but for their children and their countrymen. In the tension between duty and despair, Benjamin was caught in a war within his own heart. Had he not bled enough? Were six years of bloodshed—and the loss of his wife—not enough to prove his patriotism and satisfy the debt? Did he not owe something now to his children . . . to himself?

Was there no end to the brutal suffering and death?

The Bible says to "train up" and "direct your children onto the right path, and when they are older, they will not depart from it." Benjamin had trained his sons to be righteous and fearless—and now Gabriel was living it. Even in pain, he chose courage. This defiance stirred his father's spirit, urging him to reclaim that same virtue—and rejoin the righteous revolution that depended on good men confronting evil.

Benjamin closed his eyes and squeezed his son's hand, swept into a flashback—a recent talk with his sister-in-law, Charlotte, surrogate mother to his young children. He had confessed his guilt to her, haunted by demons from his past. The duty of protecting family warred with his principles, even as British atrocities mounted.

Recent images were burned into his mind—young men from the

hometown of Anne Howard, Gabriel's fiancée, hanging lifeless from ropes in the town square. Their bodies swayed in grim warning: Bend the knee to King George—or else. The memory made him shudder.

Charlotte touched his shoulder gently, sensing the torment beneath his silence.

CHARLOTTE: You have done nothing for which you should be ashamed.

BENJAMIN: I have done nothing. And for that, I am ashamed.

His eyes snapped open, breaking the trance. He wiped a cold sweat from his brow, swallowing the bitterness of shame. Then he turned back to Gabriel—and in his son's eyes, he saw it:

Hope. Fierce and undying love. Faith.

It was an unspoken invitation to rise—to choose Uncomfortable Courage in the most sacred of moments: **Now**.

Now was his chance to reconcile the past and answer the present. And it was a holy gift from God—along with "*your country,*" which once again "*needs you*" in its defense.

The moment hardened in him—then shattered at the sound of horses.

Gabriel frowned, sitting up with a wince. Benjamin raised a finger to his lips and moved to the window, slipping past wounded British soldiers who lay in uneasy slumber—men he'd been nursing back to health beside their American counterparts. He peered out at his driveway—and froze.

Colonel M. Garland Tavington.

Black dread surged through him. This was the butcher who'd executed Anne Howard's townsmen as a grotesque display—a man who despised virtue, and the God who commanded it.

"Where's the insurrectionist?" Tavington bellowed, yanking his stallion to a hard stop, papers raised in the air. "Where's the traitor who dared enter His Majesty's Capitol with this seditious speech? Bring him out, or I'll burn this house to the ground—with every man, woman, and child still in it!"

Before Benjamin could reach the door, Gabriel was already there.

"I am the patriot you seek to defame, Garland Tavington. Before God, and the men He has blessed with this land and the freedom to govern it, I am innocent—and I have nothing to hide. Take me and do as you will. But spare the wounded and the children behind me—they are no threat to you."

"Ha!" Tavington sneered, slashing a signal to his FBI SWAT team.

They fell on Gabriel with fury, dragging him away in chains. Torches crashed through the front windows. Flames roared to life.

Benjamin screamed. "STOP! Your own soldiers lay wounded inside—and the children are innocent! For God's sake, have mercy!"

"Mercy is reserved for better men, traitor!" Tavington jeered, hatred twisting his face—until his eyes shifted past Benjamin, to the porch.

Thomas.

Benjamin's second son.

Barely a teenager, he worshipped his brother, begging to join him in the militia. And now he charged forward, wielding his father's rifle, fearless.

"NOOO!" Benjamin's scream tore from him, helpless. Time slowed as Tavington raised his pistol and fired.

The crack split the air.

Thomas fell—lifeless in the dirt.

M. Garland Tavington wheeled his stallion, thundering away with his soldiers in a cloud of dust and curses. They left Benjamin kneeling in the dirt, cradling his boy's limp body.

Tears streamed down his face as he lifted his eyes to heaven, desperate for a miracle . . .

. . . but the miracle of Thomas's life was gone.

Patriots are not born—they are forged.

Citizens can be born—though not every birth on American soil grants that status. The modern myth of *birthright citizenship* is a lie. And no one becomes a patriot without first becoming a true citizen.

But what makes a citizen legitimate? What does it really mean to be an American?

These are basic, unavoidable questions. If we ignore the answers, we lose the Republic—and liberty with it. America is more than a government. It's a declaration of God's design for mankind. Without allegiance to that design, we perish.

"Give me liberty or give me death" is not an opinion or a preference—it is a red-pilled recognition of reality.

So the question now becomes: *"How then shall we live?"*

What are we going to do with this knowledge?

Congressman Bob McEwen taught me that "wisdom is the proper use of knowledge." The Bible says, "The fear of Yahweh is the beginning of wisdom." My brother Michael suggested that "Wisdom is integrated knowledge"—integrated with its context, built on bedrock.

Scripture is the bedrock.

Now, before you dismiss that as "religious" and scroll back to TikTok, dare to dream of something more. Imagine a profound unity among mankind. A vision of the ages.

Recall the back cover of this book: *You Are the Hero of Your Own Story.*

Only you command your own mind—choosing to acknowledge or ignore revelation; to accept or reject the case I've set before you.

Perhaps you'll be surprised by my next statement—but of course it's true, and rightly so: You don't have to be a Christian to be a true American citizen.

Ironically, that's true not *in spite of,* but *because of,* the fact that America is—by principle and history—a Judeo-Christian nation.

Why?

Because Christianity, rightly understood and lived, is the strongest conduit of true tolerance—because tolerance, like anything else legitimate, must be anchored in reality.

As a Judeo-Christian nation, the United States guarantees every citizen absolute freedom of conscience—including full religious liberty in belief and practice.

Red Pill alert: Tolerance does *not* mean "accept everything," because that would include accepting evil—and evil is intolerant of good.

Real tolerance is respect for that which is not yours, but which has an equal right to be. All people have an equal right to their own opinions—but not to their own facts. We should tolerate and respect those we disagree with—but refuse to accept lies and the destruction they unleash.

And so, in recognizing that Christianity is not a prerequisite for citizenship, my argument comes in two stages—a "Plea within a Plea."

The outer stage, the broader Plea, is for every citizen, whatever their worldview. It is for all who desire—and I will argue are obliged—to become patriots.

The inner stage, the deeper Plea, is for those daring souls ready for an extra-strength dose of the Red Pill—Christians who resonate with that peculiar frequency of *The Remnant*.

And so, once again, Morpheus—and now MAGA Zoolander—stand before you in gleaming black leather and Matrix-piercing sunglasses to ask the question that really matters: Are you ready?

Well, then—let's dive in.

First, the question almost no one asks anymore: What makes a true citizen?

Let's start with the word itself.

"Citi-" is the root of *city*, extending here to *country*—a physical place with borders, an identity, and a legal system that governs its existence. Without those, it's just a hill, valley, or field.

"-Zen" means an inhabiting member. A *citizen*, then, is a legally established member of a sovereign nation.

Membership means you *belong*. That necessarily means others do *not*. Membership requires shared interest and mutual agreement. It also carries a cost—an exchange. Rights and privileges are granted to members, but responsibilities are required in return.

Americans love to talk about *rights*. But how often do we consider the *cost* of citizenship?

. . . and that strange word you keep hearing—*responsibilities*?

Like many, you may have been born inside U.S. borders to parents who were legal citizens—and you might assume your citizenship carries no cost.

You'd be wrong.

As they say: "There's no such thing as a free lunch." Not in a cafeteria, not in a country. Citizens before us paid dearly to secure this Republic. They bought your inheritance with blood.

But every citizen still owes the ongoing membership dues of their citizenship—and that price is their allegiance.

No wonder Team Lunacy fights to silence the Pledge of Allegiance.

In fact, we've done native-born citizens a disservice by dismissing the formal process required of immigrants. By swearing the U.S. Citizenship Oath of Allegiance, naturalized citizens can grasp both the value of their new status—and the solemn duty it carries.

And if we truly have one equal class of citizen—not two   then this oath applies to us all. That realization is deeply instructive.

I hereby declare, on Oath, that I absolutely and entirely renounce and abjure all allegiance and fidelity to any foreign prince, potentate, state, or sovereignty, of whom or which I have heretofore been a subject or citizen . . .

A clean break for the foreign-born. But what do they *take on*?

. . . that I will support and defend the Constitution and laws of the United States of America against all enemies, foreign and domestic; that I will bear true faith and allegiance to the same; that I will bear arms on behalf of the United States when required by the law; that I will perform non-combatant service in the armed forces of the United States when required by the law; that I will perform work of national importance under civilian direction when required by the law; and that I take this obligation freely without any mental reservation or purpose of evasion, so help me God.

Freedom is not free. This oath lays out the cost. Our freedoms are only accessible through the rights—and thus the responsibilities—recognized by that citizenship.

"You get what you pay for" is a truism we cannot afford to ignore. It's simply the modern echo of the farmer's maxim: "Whatever a man sows, that he will also reap." To heed this is wisdom. To dismiss it is folly—and folly is extremely expensive.

Yet America has become a *Society of Fools*, sailing blindly toward shipwreck. Our ignorance of citizenship—and our failure to pay its price—have led us to despise our birthright. We've exchanged liberty and responsibility for a bowl of WOKE soup. Recent generations have cashed in their inheritance, placing all their chips on a desperate gamble for pleasure and the promise of freedom from pain. The bill is coming due—and there will be, as the saying goes, hell to pay.

I urge you to see the peril of this gamble. Decide now, even as you read these words.

Now is the time for unpopular wisdom, and you must plant the seeds of what you wish to eat. You know what's at stake—liberty and justice are under assault. So let's examine the critical elements of our citizenship pledge—and commit ourselves to a relentless pursuit of the duties that preserve our birthright.

The Oath begins with a charge to support and defend the Constitution and laws of the United States of America against all enemies, foreign and domestic.

Let's be clear: You can't support something without touching it. Citizenship demands engagement. "Freedom is a full-contact sport." We have to get our hands dirty and our feet moving. Championships aren't won from the bleachers, but on the field—by players who know the playbook and sweat to execute it.

Dear reader: If you are an American citizen, this means you. And yes, it means getting involved in "politics." Because **you can't have self-governance without getting yourself involved in . . . the government.**

This is basic.

And it means more than just voting every few years—though a shameful number don't even do that. At a minimum, citizens should review the Declaration and Constitution against current events. Know your state and federal representatives. Contact their office. Speak with your city or county officials. Connect with your precinct leaders and join your local GOP committee.

That's how "Our Democracy™" actually becomes *ours*.

And let's settle the democracy disinformation. The Founders knew the end game of pure democracy, which is why Ben Franklin warned we had a constitutional republic—*if you can keep it.*

"We are forming a Republican Government. Real liberty is never found in despotism or in the extremes of Democracy."

—Alexander Hamilton

"Democracies have been found incompatible with personal security or the rights of property; and, in general, been as short in their lives as they have been violent in their death."

—James Madison

"Remember, democracy never lasts long. It soon wastes, exhausts, and murders itself. There never was a democracy yet that did not commit suicide."

—John Adams

"A simple democracy is the devil's own government."

—Dr. Benjamin Rush

Here's the distinction: In America, **Democracy is the verb; the Republic is the noun**.

We engage in democracy—but we are sworn to support and defend a constitutional republic.

"Democracy is what we do; Our Republic™ is what we do it for."

Let's also admit: You can't "support and defend" something without risk. Freedom is dangerous—and that's the point. It means you're alive. "*He who hesitates is lost*," and he who surrenders to fear is already dead. America has proven we are safer when we are braver.

This charge applies to everyone—not just lawyers and soldiers. Every citizen must rise to the call of duty. Democracy is a team sport.

Still, let's not rush past the core of the Oath:

What exactly are we supporting and defending?

What are we swearing to "bear true faith and allegiance to"?

THE RULE OF LAW.

Why is this so important?

Because *everything* comes down to control. And ***sovereignty*** is a claim of authority—but based on what?

The binary is inescapable: **God or No God**.

Sovereignty is only legitimate when rooted in something real and just. Either we appeal to the higher authority of God—by whom "all men are created equal"—or we claim sovereignty by human will alone, through the raw force of power. That raw force becomes tyranny—or anarchy, the tyranny of chaos.

This is "the rule of men."

America rejected tyranny and the rule of men because it is evil. It violates the moral imperative of equality the Founders called *self-evident*. They declared "one people" must assume "the separate and equal station to which the Laws of Nature and of Nature's God entitle them."

They appealed to a higher authority to justify both individual and national sovereignty.

Our Founders declared all men are "endowed by their Creator with certain unalienable rights," and that "to secure these rights, governments are instituted among Men, deriving their just powers from **the consent of the governed**."

American citizens hold a legitimate claim to individual sovereignty. They don't bow to rulers. They don't owe allegiance to any man. They are governed by law—valid only when it reflects Natural Law and is administered by a government of their own choosing.

This law—not a ruler, not a regime—is the object of their "true faith and allegiance."

Red Pill alert: This is where the Romans 13 distortion gets exposed.

The Constitution is our "golden rule"—the standard we use to measure and maintain our rights. It is the spine of our Republic: the guardrails of justice and equality, the shield protecting life, property, and opportunity. This is the priceless treasure we must support and defend against all enemies, at all costs.

Because it is by this golden rule we rise and fall together—One Nation Under God, with an eternal hope of liberty.

The Constitution is valid because it rests on sovereignty—and America's sovereignty exists only by virtue of the legal document that birthed it:

the Declaration of Independence. That charter asserted the consent of the governed, establishing the moral and legal basis for the nation.

The Declaration *is the legal preface* to the Constitution. They are inseparable.

This pairing—the Founders' genius guardrails to bind down tyrants and protect the rights of the People—is what we swear to support and defend "against all enemies, foreign and domestic."

Red Pill alert: Domestic enemies are far less visible than foreign adversaries—which makes them far more dangerous.

"Eternal vigilance by the people is the price of liberty, and . . . you must pay the price if you wish to secure the blessing. You have no longer any cause to fear danger from abroad; your strength and power are well known throughout civilized nations. . . . It is from within, among yourselves—from cupidity, from corruption, from disappointed ambition, and inordinate thirst for power—that factions will be formed and liberty endangered. It is against such designs, whatever disguise the actors may assume, that you have especially to guard yourselves. . . ."

—President Andrew Jackson

Jackson exposed the Deep State two centuries ago.

So let's be frank: Are we truly supporting and defending the Constitution against her enemies? Because that is the cost of citizenship—the price that must be paid to preserve our freedom.

But what defines a constitutional enemy?

The answer: any person or power that threatens the rights of *the People*, which the Constitution was written to protect.

By that definition, we face a vast horde of enemies.

A cancer of corruption has spread through every branch of government—violating laws, betraying voters, abusing trust.

But there is another strain of this "American Cancer": our own ignorance and apathy. Too many citizens ignore abuses that don't appear to touch their own lives. That cowardice of self-interest was called out by Dr. Martin Luther King Jr.:

"Injustice anywhere is a threat to justice everywhere. We are caught in an inescapable network of mutuality, tied in a single garment of destiny. Whatever affects one directly, affects all indirectly. . . . Anyone who lives inside the United States can never be considered an outsider."

"*. . . tied in a single garment of destiny.*" Almost like a "Technicolor coat of our dreams." And those dreams are threatened when we let injustice stand. Because the cancer of injustice is never dormant—it expands. Always. Until it strikes #YouNext.

And the danger is not only from unjust laws, but selective prosecution—the Soviet police playbook, which the Reverend also condemned:

"One has not only a legal but a moral responsibility to obey just laws. Conversely, one has a moral responsibility to disobey unjust laws. I would agree with St. Augustine that 'an unjust law is no law at all.' Now, what is the difference between the two? A just law is a man-made code that squares with the moral law or the law of God. An unjust law is a code that is out of harmony with the moral law.

"Sometimes a law is just on its face and unjust in its application. For instance, I have been arrested on a charge of parading without a permit. Now, there is nothing wrong in having an ordinance which requires a permit for a parade. But such an ordinance becomes unjust when it is used to maintain segregation and to deny citizens the First Amendment privilege of peaceful assembly and protest."

—Martin Luther King Jr.

Let me be extremely clear: Martin Luther King Jr. would be appalled by the double standard weaponized against conservative protesters.

He would be disgusted by the race-baiting and hate-mongering of Barack Obama, Joe Biden, and their media accomplices. And he would be horrified by the brutal atrocities inflicted on J6ers and their families.

And let me assure you, he would be doing something about it.

Because Martin Luther King Jr. was a patriot.

And patriots are not born, they are forged—in the fiery furnace of the "irate minority" standing for unpopular truths against a wayward majority. Forged in fierce conflict—advancing uncomfortable truths against an *Artificial Aristocracy*. Forged by righteous action in the face of overwhelming opposition.

Patriots are citizens who have been tempered in the crucible of civic responsibility—living in "true faith and allegiance" to a power higher than themselves. A sacred devotion to "One Nation Under God." That sacrificial service ennobles them into **the heroes we need to be free**.

And that crucible is calling—for citizens to stand and be counted, to fight back against this tyranny among us—to be forged by fire into American patriots, ready for the task that liberty has assigned.

Do not ask if you have what it takes—the breath in your lungs is the answer.

Do not suppose another will serve in your place—your birthright belongs to no other.

Do not give fear a foothold—this is the time of testing.

It was *for such a time as this* that God prepared you—to advance His kingdom and establish justice in the land.

A *citizen* enters a covenant with his country—a bond of brotherhood, an oath of loyalty to his national family.

And a *patriot* is one who fulfills that promise: a father to that family, who answers the present and anticipates the future. A citizen-soldier who stands in the breach where duty meets destiny, and who rises to the challenge of "*setting brushfires of freedom in the minds of men*." That is what makes a man a patriot. And those are the men and women we desperately need in this moment of crisis.

A nation of citizens without patriots is an empty promise and a hollow country—poised to collapse at the advance of tyranny.

. . . and our American tyranny is here.

We stand in a moment of peril—here in the shadow of freedom, cast by the ominous darkness of *The Divided States of America*. We stand today only because of the forged character and daring action of the Founding Fathers. They earned us the chance to pursue our destiny. Those men knew who they were—an unshakeable identity. They were children of God, and sons of liberty. They knew their rights. And they dared to fulfill their duty.

They fought and bled so that we might live.

Sam Adams, "the Father of the American Revolution," gave a prophecy:

"The liberties of our country, the freedom of our civil Constitution, are worth defending at all hazards; and it is our duty to defend them against all attacks. We have received them as a fair inheritance from our worthy ancestors: they purchased them for us with toil and danger and expense of treasure and blood, and transmitted them to us with care and diligence. It will bring an everlasting mark of [SHAME] on the present generation, enlightened as it is, if we should suffer [our liberties] to be wrested from us by violence without a struggle, or to be **cheated out of them by the artifices of false and designing men.**"

—Samuel Adams

The duty is clear. The challenge is ours.

Now is the time for Uncomfortable Courage—now is the moment for citizens to become patriots.

And here's the truth: J6 is the artifice of false and designing men. **The Greatest American Lie Ever Sold.**

The domestic enemies we are sworn to oppose have hijacked our Republic, weaponizing a staged entrapment. Crooked Joe is only a frail puppet of the Biden Crime Family—all of whom serve the same corruption. The nation is infected with an *American Cancer,* spawning endless tyrannical tumors.

We the People must cut this Cancer from the Republic—and that surgery must start *within our own hearts*. Andrew Breitbart famously said, "Politics is downstream from culture"—and culture is downstream from the wellspring of the human heart.

As Jesus said:

"It is what comes from inside that defiles you. For from within, out of a person's heart, come evil thoughts, sexual immorality, theft, murder, adultery, greed, wickedness, deceit, lustful desires, envy, slander, pride, and foolishness. All these vile things come from within; they are what defile you."

—Mark 7:20–23

We've come full circle from chapter one: it's time to take control—of our wellspring.

And the key to proper control is VIRTUE.

The Founders knew their daring experiment in self-government would collapse without a virtuous populace. They warned us plainly:

"I thank God that I have lived to see my country independent and free. She may long enjoy her independence and freedom *if she will*. It depends on her virtue."

—Samuel Adams

"Our Constitution was made only for a moral and religious people. It is wholly inadequate to the government of any other."

—John Adams

James Madison, architect of the Constitution, made it clear only fools would expect it to function without virtuous citizens:

"Is there no virtue among us? If there be not, we are in a wretched situation. . . . To suppose that any form of government will secure liberty or happiness without any virtue in the people, is a chimerical idea [translation: it's lunacy]. **If there be sufficient virtue and intelligence in *the community*, it will be exercised in the selection of these men; so that we do not depend upon *their* virtue, or put confidence in our rulers, but in *the people* who are to choose them**."

—James Madison

Sam Adams was nobody's fool. He saw through the Matrix illusion:

"If we would most truly enjoy [liberty], let us become a virtuous people; then we shall both deserve and enjoy it. While, on the other hand, if we are universally vicious and debauched in our manners, though the form of our Constitution carries the face of the most exalted freedom, we shall in reality be the most abject slaves.

"A general dissolution of principles and manners will more surely overthrow the liberties of America than the whole force of the common enemy. While the people are virtuous they cannot be subdued; but when once they lose their virtue they will be ready to surrender their liberties to the first external *or internal* invader. How necessary then is it for those who are determined to transmit the blessings of liberty as a fair inheritance to posterity, to *associate on public principles in support of public virtue*."

—Samuel Adams

Clearly, Sam Adams played for #TeamReality. He knew the entire point of the American experiment was to rule ourselves—and that self-government is impossible without virtue. But many people today don't even know what virtue is—or worse, they openly despise it.

This is no accident.

What use does an *Artificial Aristocracy* have for virtuous citizens capable of thriving independently?

"Only a virtuous people are capable of freedom. As nations become corrupt and vicious, they have more need of masters."

—Benjamin Franklin

Thomas Jefferson reminded us: "Virtue is not hereditary."

And Ronald Reagan knew that freedom—itself a virtue—is "not passed through the bloodstream." Freedom is "not ours by inheritance; it must be fought for and defended constantly by each generation."

Virtue does not happen by accident. It isn't easy—or comfortable. Surgery never is. But it is necessary—if we are to cut out the rot of indulgence, pride, and cowardice from our hearts.

And that is the only way to give virtue a healthy place to grow.

We've spoken about virtue, and called for courage with urgency. But what is courage, exactly?

It is not the absence of fear—fear serves a vital purpose when guided by truth. Nor is it aggression, bravado, or fleeting emotion. If it were merely a feeling, it would be unreliable. C. S. Lewis nailed it: "Courage is not simply one of the virtues, but the form of every virtue at the testing point, which means at the point of highest reality."

A real Red Pill sage, that Lewis.

We've spoken about the courage required to confront evil and defend Our Republic™. But the deeper truth is this: *courage is most critical in confronting* **yourself**. The rebellion against God buried in every heart is painful—sometimes terrifying—to face. Yet we must choose that uncomfortable bravery to master ourselves, exercising humility and grit. We must rule our own spirit and control the lower "animal" nature, submitting to the higher nature God designed us for.

This is the essence of self-government—the foundation of a virtuous citizenry capable of reviving a nation.

God made this clear at the dawn of humanity:

> "'Why are you so angry?' God asked Cain. 'Why do you look so dejected? You will be accepted [also translated 'your face will be cheerful'—you'll become happy] if you do what is right. But if you refuse to do what is right, then watch out! Sin is crouching at the door, eager to control you. But you must rule over it and be its master.'"
>
> —Genesis 4:6–7

Now is the time for that "spiritual surgery."

We've spoken of enlightenment and love as the antidote to ignorance and hate. But modern politics has counterfeited love into lies—packaged as "care," sold for votes, traded for obscene wealth and permanent power.

The problem is, **they keep lying—*and you keep listening***. And that's because they're telling you what you want to hear.

So here's the uncomfortable truth: our society is addicted to comfort and pleasure—and terrified of pain. But pain has a purpose: it keeps you alive.

Pastor Rob McCoy explains that biblical leprosy wasn't primarily a skin disease—it was a nerve disorder. Lepers couldn't feel pain.

Sounds like a blessing, not a curse—right?

But here's the catch: Without pain, the body ignores danger. A stubbed toe or scraped arm goes unnoticed . . . until infection, then amputation, then death.

Addiction is our modern leprosy. It deadens the soul, numbs the pain, and enslaves us in a living death.

We've become a society of broken and bitter souls, stampeding toward a utopian mirage—camouflaging the cliff of catastrophe. You can't ignore this stampede any more than you can wish it away—because you are caught in the middle of it.

This is the part of the movie where Neo finally sees the system for what it is—and must choose.

And as we witnessed in The Matrix . . . he had very little time to make that choice.

My "Patriot Plea" is simple—but audacious. It is nothing less than an ultimatum for our Republic. A clarion call for the heroes we need to be free. And that hero is **you**.

You—and only you—can be the hero of your own story. That story is part of the American story, a shimmering thread in our national Technicolor dreamcoat, MLK's "single garment of destiny." And a hero is one who chooses to do the right thing *when it hurts*—when others shrink back. A hero embraces the pain.

When I served in the Civil Air Patrol, our boot-camp T-shirts bore this motto: **Pain is Temporary; Pride is Forever.**

National pride is the joyful confidence and unwavering commitment we give to a righteous cause. And there is no calling more noble than American liberty.

The glory of that cause is indeed eternal.

The seeds of that glory are within us—suspended in our thoughts, dormant in our hands. All that remains is for those seeds to sprout . . . when we seize the duty set before us. This is the nationalism we truly need: fearless, righteous American pride.

I have a dream that *today* our people will rise and become a nation of heroes who "do justly, love mercy, and walk humbly with their God"—especially when it's uncomfortable.

I have a dream that *today* our citizens will become patriots who know their rights *and* their responsibilities, and demand fidelity to both.

I have a dream that *today* we will revive Martin Luther King's dream: liberty, meritocracy, integrity—so the *Divided States* might once again be united as One Nation Under God, indivisible, with liberty and justice for all.

What are we waiting for?

Will anyone reading these words join me and *dare to dream*?

Dreams are prophecies of potential—glimmers of destiny. And building destiny is the work of patriots. My plea is for you to see you've been designed to become a "patriot superhero." Even Spider-Man's uncle understood: "With great power comes great responsibility." Do you realize? You hold the greatest power on earth: self-determination—*Cognitive Liberty*. The sovereignty to rule your own mind, direct your own actions, fulfill your divine purpose.

Thus, with great *liberty* comes great responsibility. We must exercise it with supernatural strength if we hope to keep it, along with Franklin's genius Republic.

Understand this:

It will not be easy.

It will not be painless.

It will not be cheap.

But that is what makes it necessary to count the cost and invest in this great American enterprise.

We stand once again at the gates of "The American Crisis":

"These are the times that try men's souls: the summer soldier and the sunshine patriot will, in this crisis, shrink from the service of his country; but he that stands it now deserves the love and thanks of man and woman. Tyranny, like hell, is not easily conquered; yet we have this consolation with us, that the harder the conflict, the more glorious the triumph."

—Thomas Paine

And I share another dream—to realize Dr. Viktor Frankl's vision:

"Freedom is only part of the story and half of the truth. Freedom is but the negative aspect of the whole phenomenon whose positive aspect is responsibleness. In fact, freedom is in danger of degenerating into mere arbitrariness [i.e. Team Lunacy] unless it is lived in terms of responsibleness. That is why I recommend that the Statue of Liberty on the East Coast be supplemented by a Statue of Responsibility on the West Coast."

—Viktor Frankl

The "Statue of Responsibility" is, indeed, "just what the doctor ordered." And I will strive to bring it forth—because the American dream is only made possible by stewarding the rights and resources God entrusted to us. That is how to fulfill those three great commands to "fill the earth and govern it," to "rule over sin and be its master," and to "make disciples of all the nations."

The purpose of freedom is to pursue the good—and that pursuit is the only path to glory.

Picture with me, once more, how the characters in *The Patriot* might have responded in the context of our themes here in this book. I imagine it like this:

"Your country needs this church."

Benjamin Martin's voice rang through the South Carolina chapel with quiet force, his resolve casting an eerie stillness across the room. Whispers rippled through the pews—but the implications hit like a cannon blast.

An American patriot had just mixed politics with religion. That Molotov cocktail tossed in a sanctuary was sure to ignite.

"This is no place for politics!" someone shouted.

"God has established the Crown! Doesn't Paul command us to submit to governing authorities?" another cried.

A mother's voice pierced the din:

"Did we not flee England to worship in peace—without politics? Must we now send more sons to die?"

And beneath it all, an unspoken concern: slavery. South Carolina's wealth depended on it. King George backed the slave trade, blocking every colonial effort to end it—because slavery made politicians very rich.

Some things never change.

Politics, religion, and the cost of liberty had collided in that chapel. Once reluctant, Benjamin Martin had been transformed by the killing of his son Thomas at the hands of M. Garland Tavington. That cruelty snapped him into action—as a father, and as a patriot.

After Gabriel was dragged off in chains by Tavington's SWAT team, Benjamin unearthed his weapons, armed his two younger sons, and led a furious rescue. With deadly precision, they ambushed the British squad—striking with cold precision, killing all but one. The lone survivor reported back in terror that his squad had been slain by "the Ghost of retribution."

It's rumored it was an orange ghost—but that's unconfirmed.

Now, seated with Colonel Harry Burwell, Gabriel, and other militia, Benjamin had been listening as Reverend Oliver preached from the New Testament:

"But my life is worth nothing to me unless I use it to stay the course and finish the work assigned me . . . I have been faithful . . . for I didn't shrink from declaring to you the whole purpose of God."

He looked up. "What does the Apostle mean by 'the *whole* purpose'?"

The question hung in the stillness.

The Reverend continued:

"Be on guard for . . . the flock, among which the Holy Spirit has made you *overseers*—'providers and protectors'—to shepherd the church of God which He purchased with His own blood. I know that after my departure savage wolves will come in among you, not sparing the flock . . . Therefore be on the alert! . . . I showed you that by working hard in this manner you must help the weak."

The directive was clear. Christian service must be active in the physical world—defending the innocent from evil.

Benjamin could hold back no longer. He rose, gripping the pew.

"Your country needs this church."

The congregation erupted in protest until Reverend Oliver hammered his pulpit and nodded for Benjamin to continue.

"You heard the Reverend. We are providers and protectors to guard the flock—like a father to his children. Brothers: St. Paul calls us to be patriots! To 'work hard and help the weak.'

"Does God not speak through His prophet Isaiah? 'Give up your evil ways. Learn to do good. Seek justice. Help the oppressed.'

"And does He not condemn wicked governments? His prophet Micah says: 'You hate justice and twist all that is right. You are building Jerusalem on a foundation of murder and corruption. You rulers make decisions based on bribes . . . because of you . . . Jerusalem will be reduced to ruins!'

"But God also raises a Remnant, to revive the assembly of the righteous, the church of God's people—to rebuild a nation of free men and women. For He says, 'Then the remnant . . . will take their place among the nations. They will be like a lion.'

"And through Amos, He makes clear what is required of legitimate authority: 'Hate evil and love what is good; turn your courts into true halls of justice,' and, 'Away with your noisy hymns of praise! . . . instead, I want to see justice roll down like waters, an endless river of righteous living.'"

Reverend Oliver broke in with a warm chuckle. "Benjamin Martin, you'll put me out of a job, preaching like that."

"Good!" Benjamin shot back. "Because I've got a new job for you—in the Continental Army!"

The room tensed as Benjamin continued.

"Brothers, you know the injustice rising among us. God has called us to defend the innocent and fight against evil. I only regret that I held back from fighting until evil came to my door—and struck down my son.

"But Thomas never hesitated. He was the better man."

A tear traced his cheek. He steadied himself.

"So come—let us repent of selfish cowardice and petty bickering. Let us raise up a Remnant in this hour of need. It is God's church that must burn bright as a light to the nations, and your nation needs you to stand and fight for her independence!

"Your country *NEEDS THIS CHURCH*!"

Benjamin pounded the pew three times, each strike punctuating his final words. The chapel exploded—cheers mixed with cries of *"Treason!"* A wave of townspeople crossed the aisle to stand with the militia. Other voices shouted warnings about South Carolina's "separate interests" and the risk of ruin.

Colonel Burwell raised his hand and boomed a command for silence:

"This is not a war for the independence of one or two colonies, but for the independence of one nation."

A loyalist challenged him: "What nation is that?"

A parishioner quickly shouted back the answer: "An American nation!"

The loyalist exclaimed this was treasonous, but the claim of independence had taken hold. Shouting broke out—then a gasp.

The Reverend stepped down from the pulpit and walked toward the militia.

REVEREND OLIVER: A shepherd must tend to his flock. And at times . . . fight off the wolves.

That was the tipping point. The townspeople roared in unity. Men rose to enlist, answering the call to join the greatest freedom-fighting force the world has ever known: the U.S. military.

Benjamin allowed a faint smile, grateful for the Reverend's courage and the new recruits.

Gabriel beamed with pride—for his father, his church, and his country. He sensed something was stirring.

Something historic. Something glorious.

He clasped the shoulder of his friend Occam, a freed slave fighting beside him. They shared a prophetic exchange, as Gabriel mused that a victory by the American rebels would have enormous repercussions.

GABRIEL: They call this the New World. It's not. It's the same as the old. But we have the chance to build a new world. A world where all men are created equal under God.

The dream to build a new world where all men are created equal under God—the MAGA dream—was a vision of inspiration and consequence.

But dreams are tricky things.

What is the line between dream and delusion? How do we discern the true pulse of this vision, to secure the Great American Comeback?

It demands a special kind of soul-searching: a "peering through the looking glass."

Alice in Wonderland was a reasonable girl hoping for a peaceful tea party—until strange revelations caught her eye. She glimpsed enchanting mysteries and the gleam of an impossible destiny.

So she took the potion to see more, and kept going—deeper and deeper.

Are you ready to dive all the way down the "rabbit hole"?

Whether it is curiosity or Christianity that drives you to "take the leap," I believe "the net will appear." Whatever your worldview, you cannot ignore the power of certain history and prophecy.

Borrowing St. Paul's words but speaking for myself: **I am not ashamed of the Gospel of Jesus Christ.**

"For it is the power of God at work, saving everyone who believes—the Jew first and also the Gentile. This Good News tells us how God makes us right in His sight. This is accomplished from start to finish by faith. As the [Old Testament] scriptures say, 'It is through faith that a righteous person has life.'"

—Romans 1:16–17

Asking me to deny the power of the Gospel is like asking a suffocating man to deny the power of oxygen as he begins to breathe. I may not see it with my eyes, or fully grasp its process in my mind—but I absolutely know it's there. To live reborn by the spirit of the risen Christ is to freely breathe again. I cannot recant the Gospel which I have tasted, nor can I deny its power to "set the captives free" and preserve for all mankind the unalienable gift of liberty.

Jesus Christ, the promised Messiah, is the "only hope" for all humanity—our rescue from the Galactic Empire of evil that dominates this present darkness. And His Church channels this hope for the freedom and salvation of the nations.

America has long carried that mantle of "last greatest hope"—true only so long as she championed Christianity and the true tolerance it teaches. Our Founders knew this:

"Christianity is the only true and perfect religion, and that in proportion as mankind adopt its principles and obey its precepts, they will be wise and happy."

—Dr. Benjamin Rush

"Almost all the civil liberty now enjoyed in the world owes its origin to the principles of the Christian religion. . . . The religion which has introduced civil liberty is the religion of Christ and His apostles, which enjoins humility, piety, and benevolence; which acknowledge in every person a brother, or a sister, and a citizen with equal rights. *This is genuine Christianity,* and to this we owe our free constitutions of government."

—Noah Webster

Samuel Chase—signer of the Declaration and Justice of the U.S. Supreme Court—wrote this in the Maryland General Court's 1799 opinion in *Runkel v. Winemiller*:

"Religion is of general and public concern, and on its support depend, in great measure, the peace and good order of government, the safety and happiness of the people. **By our form of government, the Christian religion is the established religion**; and all sects and denominations of Christians are placed upon the same equal footing, and are equally entitled to protection in their religious liberty."

His articulation is specific: The government did not establish a religion—the government was built upon the previously established

Judeo-Christian worldview and the Christian faith, which the Founders all accepted as a predicate to the entire American project. The historical record, for any who care to look, is overwhelming: Christianity—and specifically the Church in America—was the heartbeat that birthed our Republic. And when that heartbeat faltered, the nation stumbled.

In fact, the Founders' experiment nearly failed before it had fully taken flight. By the early 1700s, colonial churches had declined into lifeless apathy. Public virtue decayed, and self-government nearly collapsed.

Until . . . the Gospel was preached again with power.

Jonathan Edwards and George Whitefield ignited "the Great Awakening," starting in 1734, rekindling repentance and sparking explosive growth in the Church.

The American spirit of liberty was supercharged—because liberty, rightly understood, is the power to pursue God and His "Good News." This is the only pursuit of happiness that can ever reach its destination.

> "The enjoyment of God is . . . the only happiness with which our souls can be satisfied . . . earthly friends are but shadows; but God is the substance . . . These are but streams, but God is the ocean."
>
> —Jonathan Edwards

That Awakening led directly to the greatest wave of Uncomfortable Courage the West had ever seen. Patriots rose, suffered, and persevered to establish the Republic we must now revive—in Jesus' name.

If critics wish to smear this as "Christian Nationalism," so be it. They are only warring against the truth of our Judeo-Christian history—of true American nationalism.

And history, like Christian prophecy, has an undefeated record.

The fatal flaw in most "religion" is the attempt to sever the sublime power of liberty from its source—meaningless without the beginning—by claiming we can earn heaven on our own. Most people believe they're "good enough" for God.

They are deceived.

God _is_ love—which means He does not lie, because love _is_ truth. And the truth is: no man—except Jesus—is good enough. "Everyone has sinned; we all fall short of God's glorious standard" (Romans 3:23).

If we're honest with ourselves, that is painfully obvious.

We all have "the Dark Side" warring within us. To err is human. But God is perfect, and cannot tolerate evil whatsoever. That would be a permanent tragedy—except for the climax of the Gospel. Our Savior steps in to rescue us from the eternal death we've chosen—_if_ we now choose to accept His rescue by faith. Only then is liberty reconnected to its divine source, powerful for good works and virtuous character.

This principle of faith answers the question "What about those who lived before the time of Christ?" Abraham acted by faith in God's plan for human salvation—and that was credited to him as "righteousness."

Another way to think about this: Dr. Frankl taught that happiness cannot be secured by chasing it—it must _ensue_ from the pursuit of purpose. Likewise, salvation cannot be "chased" with our own effort. First, we _acknowledge_ our sin, which condemns us by God's perfect standard—perfect, because He is good. Then we must _activate_ our faith in His grace through the redemption of Christ's sacrifice—and true faith is proven by the action it produces. Only then can we _accept_ the ensuing salvation He purchased for us.

The fatal flaw in many Christians is the tendency to _misdirect_ our sublime power away from its divine purpose—"hopeless without the end"— by chasing our own desires above "the whole purpose of God." This brings us back to the paramount question of priorities: what do we worship as _preeminent_—above even the prominence of our own opinions?

What is the "whole purpose" of God?

In *The Patriot*, our "Patriot Preacher" Benjamin Martin shouted it in that South Carolina chapel:

God desires righteous living.

God calls us to seek justice—in all things.

God commands us to rule our own spirit, submit to His authority, know the truth, and be set free—so that we may love and serve others.

Christians: THIS MEANS HERE AND NOW.

Jesus warned we will have to account for the "talents" God gave us to invest (Matthew 25:14–30).

Jesus taught us to pray: "Thy will be done on earth as it is in heaven."

St. James did *not* tell us to ignore or flee from evil—he told us to "*resist* the devil, *and he will flee from you.*"

And St. Peter gave clear instructions on how to use our liberty:

"The end of the world is coming soon. Therefore, be earnest and dis-ciplined in your prayers. Most important of all, continue to show deep love for each other. . . . Cheerfully share your home with those who need a meal or a place to stay."

—1 Peter 4:7–10

"So humble yourselves under the mighty power of God, and at the right time He will lift you up in honor. . . . Stay alert! Watch out for your enemy, the devil. He prowls around looking for someone to devour. *Stand firm against him*, and be strong in your faith."

—1 Peter 5:6–9

Christians: Avoiding conflict with evil is not "tolerance"—it is sin.

"Remember, it is sin to know what you ought to do and then not do it."

—James 4:17

"*People may be right in their own eyes, but *Yahweh* examines their heart. *Yahweh* is more pleased when we do what is right and just than when we offer him [ceremonial displays].*"

—Proverbs 21:2–3

"*If you fail under pressure, your strength is too small. Rescue those who are unjustly sentenced to die; save them as they stagger to their death. Don't excuse yourself by saying, 'Look, we didn't know.' For God understands all hearts, and He sees you. He who guards your soul knows you knew. He will repay all people as their actions deserve.*"

—Proverbs 24:10–12

Christians: The Bible explicitly equates life and liberty. The J6 patriots have been "unjustly sentenced to die"—some for decades, many for years *pretrial without due process.*

This is an abomination.

Why are we silent? Why are we absent?

We will be called to give an answer—and no one escapes the courtroom of heaven.

When the people of his time asked Jesus to "prove" himself, he quoted Psalm 82 to show two things: He was the promised Messiah, and his obedience to the Father was the ultimate proof of His identity. So it must be for all God's children.

"*The people surrounded him and asked, 'How long are you going to keep us in suspense? If you are the Messiah, tell us plainly.' Jesus replied, 'I have already told you, and you don't believe me. The proof is the work I do in my Father's name. But you don't believe me because* you are not my sheep. My sheep listen to my voice; I know them, and they follow me. I give them eternal life, and they will never perish. . . .'

"Once again the people picked up stones to kill him. Jesus said, 'At my Father's direction I have done many good works. For which one are you going to stone me?' They replied, 'We're stoning you not for any good work, but for blasphemy! You, a mere man, claim to be God.' Jesus replied, 'It is written in your own Scriptures that God said to certain leaders of the people, 'I say, you are gods!' And you know that the Scriptures cannot be altered. So if those people who received God's message were called 'gods,' why do you call it blasphemy when I say, 'I am the Son of God'? After all, the Father set me apart and sent me into the world. Don't believe me unless I carry out my Father's work'"

—John 10: 24–37

And what is "the Father's work"? Scripture answers without ambiguity:

"How long will you hand down unjust decisions by favoring the wicked? Give justice to the poor and the orphan; uphold the rights of the oppressed and the destitute. Rescue the poor and helpless; deliver them from the grasp of evil people . . . I say, 'You are gods'; you are all children of the Most High."

—Psalm 82: 1–6

"Speak up for those who cannot speak for themselves; ensure justice for those being crushed. Yes, speak up for the poor and helpless, and *see that they get justice.*"

—Proverbs 31:8–9

"*See that they get justice*"—don't just wish for it or preach about it. Pursue it *until you see it actually happen.*

"This is what *Yahweh* says: Be fair-minded and just. Do what is right! Help those who have been robbed; rescue them from their oppressors."

—Jeremiah 22:3

The American people have been robbed blind by an *Artificial Aristocracy*. God declares this unacceptable. God calls it evil. And He commands His people to rectify it.

"Our people must learn to do good by meeting the urgent needs of others; then they will not be unproductive."

—Titus 3:14

God cares about *all* the needs of His people—including physical and spiritual concerns.

"All Scripture is inspired by God and is useful to teach us what is true and to make us realize what is wrong in our lives. It corrects us when we are wrong and teaches us to do what is right. God uses it to prepare and equip His people to do every good work."

—2 Timothy 3:16–17

And James seals the case:

"What good is it, dear brothers and sisters, if you say you have faith but don't show it by your actions? Can that kind of faith save anyone? Suppose you see a brother or sister who has no food or clothing, and you say, 'Good-bye and have a good day; stay warm and eat well'—but you don't give that person any food or clothing. What good does that do? So you see, faith by itself isn't enough. Unless it produces good deeds, it is dead and useless. . . . You can say you have faith, for you believe that there is one God. Good for you! Even the demons believe

this, and they tremble in terror. How foolish! Can't you see that faith
without good deeds is useless?"

—James 2:14–20

The uncomfortable truth is this: The American church has become
overwhelmingly useless. With no rudder and no spine, it drifts in a
drugged stupor—caught in the wake of a secular *Society of Fools*, headed
for shipwreck on the jagged shores of sin.

So the question confronts us:

Are we part of the problem—or pursuing the solution?

Buckle up your spiritual seatbelts.

Christians: Are you not citizens of a sovereign nation, placed here
by God until He calls you heavenward? And if your home is the United
States of America—a republic founded on biblical principles more than
any other nation in history—do you think that's an accident, or a gift
of no consequence?

"Whatever is good and perfect is a gift coming down from God our
Father, who created all the lights in the heavens. He never changes or
casts a shifting shadow."

—James 1:16–17

Is there any earthly gift greater than American citizenship—where
human dignity is recognized, liberty and property is protected, and
religious freedom is secured? Yet we have despised that birthright and
abandoned our duty. We have slept while wolves ravage the flock. We
have heard the cries of the persecuted and oppressed—yet we remain
silent and still.

We should be ashamed.

You say, "America is no longer just; it is wholly corrupted." True. But whose fault is that? Who abandoned their post? Who fled the gates?

It is the Church that is missing in action.

It is Christians who have retreated and surrendered the field.

"He who separates himself seeks his own desire, he quarrels against all sound wisdom."

—Proverbs 18:1

"Do not be overcome by evil, but overcome evil with good."

—Romans 12:21

You say, "The Church is no place for politics." But what is politics, if not the guardianship of law by which we should live? For we are a nation of laws, not rulers. And what is "the Church," if not the body called to "be equipped for every good work" and to "make disciples of all the nations"? Is not the whole earth the Lord's? Should pastors not teach the whole counsel of God without fear of man?

Christians: Government is not "for politicians" any more than church is "for pastors." If you are a Christian, you are a citizen-heir to God's kingdom—and there are no "retirees" in heaven. You have a specific role in the church, with a divine duty to perform it. That duty is sacred—it is not optional.

And if you are an American, you are an equal partner in the American Republic—and there are no silent partners in democracy. You have a specific role in the nation, with a patriotic duty to perform it. That duty is sacred—it is not optional.

The excuses are many, and the path is wide that leads to distraction—and destruction. "There is a way that seems right to a man, but in the end it leads to death." We must recover "the whole purpose" of our mission—engaging it with "Red Pill" vision and perseverance. God rescued Israel from the tyranny of Pharaoh and delivered them to the Promised Land—then commanded them to "be strong and courageous" and drive evil out of the land. That command has no expiration date. The mission is not over until God ends the war.

Christianity is not for the faint of heart.

It is a full-contact sport. It is a full-spectrum theater of war: physical and spiritual, individual and national. That's why Scripture, prayer, and the heritage of the Founders are not electives—they are survival gear.

We are more than 'actors' in this life drama. We are builders. The kingdom of God is not a veneer painted over a broken world. It is the totality of heaven and earth, beginning here and now with God's foundational commands:

Be strong and courageous.

Rule over your own spirit.

Fill the earth and govern it.

Make disciples of all the nations.

BUILD MY KINGDOM.

And yet, you say Christians don't belong in politics? You say we should "submit" to the wholesale corruption and violent weaponization of government against the people? You say Romans 13 commands our obedience to tyrants, even as their moneychangers desecrate our temples of justice and steal the sacred gifts of God?

No! A thousand times no!

That Romans 13 perversion must be torn down. Paul commanded submission not to government, but to *authority*. And what did we declare allegiance to as U.S. citizens?

THE RULE OF LAW.

Have we already forgotten why that matters?

Christians are commanded to master themselves—and no one else. We must submit to the supreme authority of God's Divine Order. Any law, ruler, or government that does not "square" with that Natural Law is illegitimate.

It is a fraud.

It is a perversion.

It is a constitutional enemy—and it must be named, exposed, refuted, and opposed, come hell or Merrick Garland.

Paul elaborates in that verse: "For rulers are not a cause of fear for good behavior, but for evil." Can any sober Christian—or any honest American, for that matter—claim this describes our current rulers?

"How foolish can you be?" God asks in Isaiah 29:16.

Paul was referring to legitimate rulers—those who punish evil and protect the innocent.

> "What sorrow for those who say that evil is good and good is evil . . . they take bribes to let the wicked go free, and they punish the innocent . . . so their roots will rot . . . that is why *Yahweh*'s anger burns against His people. . . ."
>
> —Isaiah 5:20

The Apostle Peter confirms our true allegiance:

> " . . . for the King has sent [his government officials] to punish those who do wrong and to honor those who do right."
>
> —1 Peter 2:14

> "But Peter and the Apostles replied, 'We must obey God rather than any human authority.'"
>
> —Acts 5:29

We must obey God, and we must pursue the good—in government and everything else. The Founders affirmed this biblical truth in our national birth certificate:

> "... that whenever any form of government becomes destructive of these ends, it is the right of *the People* to alter or to abolish it, and to institute new government. . . . it is their right, it is their duty, to throw off such government, and to provide new guards for their future security."
>
> —The Declaration of Independence

Notice: "it is the right of the People"—and not only that—"it is their duty." Not with violence or anarchy, but with sober resolve, to "provide new guards."

And who must provide these new guards?

We the People.

Remember: Every right requires a duty. And the duty belongs to you.

Now for the big questions: *When*, and *how*, should *the People* throw off an illegitimate government—and provide new guards—so they may prosper?

> "Unjust laws exist; shall we be content to obey them, or shall we endeavor to amend them, and obey them until we have succeeded, or shall we transgress them at once? Men generally, under such a government as this, think that they ought to wait until they have persuaded the majority to alter them. They think that, if they should resist, the remedy would be worse than the evil. But it is the fault of the government itself that the remedy is worse than the evil. *It **makes** it worse.*"
>
> —Henry David Thoreau

Indeed—it instigates a J6 Fedsurrection. It wages war against citizens by lynching hundreds of Red Hat deplorables and devastating their families. Yes, the government makes it worse.

Much worse.

"Why is it not more apt to anticipate and *provide* for reform? Why does it not cherish its wise minority? . . . Why does it not encourage its citizens to be on the alert to point out Its faults, and do better than it would have them? Why does it always crucify Christ, and excommunicate Copernicus and Luther, and pronounce Washington and Franklin rebels?"

—Henry David Thoreau

If Martin Luther King Jr. had "waited until they persuaded the majority," would civil rights ever have advanced? If the "Sons of Liberty" had waited for more than 3 percent to join the militia in 1775, would we even have a country?

Americans: The time for excuses and empty promises is past. We must end our compromise with corruption. One day our children, and their children, will look back on this very moment of decision between cowardice and courage, and they will ask us:

"How did you plead?"

Christian or not, I believe we all can agree: Now is the time—and the Church is the place.

Why is this true? Because we still must answer the *how*.

Violence is certainly not the "how." I have never condoned nor called for political violence, and I never will. The Founders endured it so their children would not have to. But when the People abandon duty, violence rushes in to fill the void. That is why we must act—before corruption makes it inevitable.

So, how do we "throw off the corrupt" and "provide new guards"?

History and prophecy give the blueprint: We must dare to dream.

"Where there is no vision, the People are unrestrained, but happy is he who keeps the law."

—Proverbs 29:18

"If My people, who are called by My name, will humble themselves and pray, and seek My face, and turn from their wicked ways, then I will hear from heaven, and I will forgive their sin, and I will heal their land."

—2 Chronicles 7:14

The dream of liberty and justice for all is God's dream. It is the rainbow illuminating that single garment of mankind's destiny. And God's dreams are always built through His chosen people.

His greatest dream is that every soul would exercise their free will correctly, to accept His eternal marriage proposal—to become the bride of Christ.

That is the Church.

The uncomfortable truth is that His Church has grown adulterous and cold. As a result, the nation built by that Church has fractured into "The Divided States of America." We are now in a spiritual stampede toward a permanent divorce from God. Complete disaster is the only possible outcome.

I believe—and I've written this book to plead—that the only hope to save America is the rise of "The Remnant," that reserve of Jedi patriot warriors ready to embrace the pain; God's people, "who are called by My name." It is those who renew our covenant with this nation—a promise we will keep: to humble ourselves and pray, to seek God's face, to turn from our cowardice and selfish ways.

And in response, He will heal our land—as we work together to revive His Church and build His kingdom "on earth as it is in heaven" . . .

. . . right here in the USA.

The title of this chapter serves two purposes. I'm making a plea *to* you: stand up, take action, and carry out your citizenship. But I'm also modeling a plea *for* you to echo—the deeper plea of *The Remnant*: humility, constant prayer, and radical repentance.

We are meant to seek God's "face"—searching to discover His personality, His character. And Jesus promised: *if we seek Him, we will find Him.* As we pray, we pursue *agreement*—that is, harmony—with God's dreams as we journey through this life.

Wherever we find "disagreement"—attitudes or actions that don't align with His Divine Order—we must repent:

Stop. Turn around. Come back into alignment with His will.

This isn't a one-time decision. It's a daily practice. Jesus showed us the way—and the Holy Spirit whispered a reminder to me in the terrible blackness of my isolation:

"Heavenly Father, your name is Yahweh—and you call me by name as your child. You are good, always and forever, and you are in control.

"Right now, I see *this* problem. I feel *this* anger, or fear, or sorrow. I have *this* question or desire, and I want *this* answer or deliverance.

"But God—I love you, and I trust you.

"So I ask: *Not my will, but yours be done—on earth as it is in heaven.*"

Simple words—but they carry miraculous power. It lays the bedrock we can stand on to pursue our dreams, disciple the nations, and build the kingdom. It anchors us in life's most fundamental truths:

God's identity. Our identity. God's authority.

From there, we step into real partnership with our Father—learning to embrace His Word, prioritize His will, and welcome His presence. The result is growth, joy, and unshakable purpose.

Let this "Patriot Plea" fill you with confidence:

You *can* find purpose.

You *can* find triumph in suffering.

And—here's *the Great American Comeback*—when we unite as the reignited Church of Christ, as One Nation Under God, we have real hope.

Hope to revive the American Republic.

Hope to save our nation.

Now, God doesn't promise America will be saved. But He commands us to pursue that mission—with virtue—seeking His divine assistance, partnering with Him in the effort, and trusting Him with the outcome. John Quincy Adams coined it perfectly: *"Duty is ours; results are God's."*

Yet Paul tells us to "run the race in such a way as to win." Duty isn't going through the motions. Jesus said we should be "shrewd as serpents and harmless as doves." Wisdom calls us to be honorable, strategic—and effective.

So begin every battle with the *Patriot Plea*. And remember this: Faith is not wishful thinking. When I say, "Dare to Dream," I mean bold, righteous confidence. "The wicked flee when no one is pursuing, but the righteous are bold as a lion" (Proverbs 28:1).

If courage is doing what you know is *right* despite your fear and pain, then faith is holding fast to what you know is *real* despite what you may not see.

"Faith shows the reality of what we hope for; it is the evidence of things we cannot see" (Hebrews 11:1).

"This hope is a strong and trustworthy anchor for our souls" (Hebrews 6:19).

And speaking of courage—what's the call that always comes before? BE STRONG.

Strength isn't just for soldiers. It's God's command to all of us. And strength isn't wished into existence—you have to train for it, with discipline. Physical and spiritual. Weakness—when it results from our failure to engage—is sin (James 4:17).

But fear not: "I can do all things through Christ who strengthens me" (Philippians 4:13).

The future belongs to those strong enough to endure, courageous enough to act, and humble enough to know only God can deliver the win.

Another principle to remember comes from the curiously delightful children's book, *If Everybody Did*. And yes—everybody should read it.

It reveals the curious power of the **micro-decision**.

Every day, we make countless choices. Most slip past unnoticed, dismissed as trivial. But that dismissal is a subconscious calculation—limited by our tiny view of time and consequence. We fail to realize: our priorities are revealed by our choices—even the micro ones.

When we begin to justify cowardice in microscopic degrees—or neglect gratitude and respect toward others—we are rehearsing misaligned priorities. We are aiming to miss and training to fail. And we deceive ourselves if we think micro-mistakes only carry micro-consequences.

Our spiritual mathematics leave much to be desired.

As Paul wrote: "Do you not know that a little yeast leavens the whole lump of dough?"

This brings up another politically incorrect virtue: **purity**.

"So let us celebrate the festival, not with the old bread of wickedness and evil, but with the new bread of sincerity and truth" (1 Corinthians 5:6–8).

God is pure in every aspect of His character. The more we prioritize His standard above our own opinion, the stronger and wiser we become. The spiritual alchemy of suffering is a process of purification, refining us into the burnished bronze of patriot warriors.

The Lord Yahweh is a master builder—and We the People are His workmanship.

Every day is a gift—an incredible opportunity, magnified by the historic gift of the American Republic. We have a duty to support and defend it.

As we prepare for the next swiftly approaching nexus of duty and opportunity, we can target three objectives in the "Red Pill Revolution":

1. <u>Enlightenment:</u>

   Take the Red Pill daily. Scripture is God's medicine—our "daily bread." It is the primary conversation He wants to have with you. Study the Bible. Study the Declaration, the U.S. Constitution, and your state constitution. Study *The 5,000 Year Leap* and the Federalist Papers. And study accurate history, relentlessly. Because "In times of change and danger, when there is a quicksand of fear," history and prophecy show us **how**.

2. <u>Engagement:</u>

   Faith without works is dead. God gave you life so you could live. Strap on your spiritual armor and get on the battlefield. Every citizen should stay connected with their state and federal representatives, maintain relationships with local officials, and actively participate in their county caucus—because that's where the real citizen-work of government is done. It's your job. No one else can do it for you.

   Join your local Republican Party and become a precinct captain. Join America's Frontline Citizen Corps at AFLDS. org. Get a membership at GoldCare.com. Support bold partners like Turning Point USA. No matter what your circumstance, God has an assignment for you. It will take faith. It will be uncomfortable. But victory is waiting on the other side of obedience.

3. <u>Encouragement</u>:

God saw that it was not good for man to be alone. We were made for relationships. *"As iron sharpens iron, so one man sharpens another."* Following your relationship with God, your family comes first. Then your local church. ***Go to church***. "Let us not neglect our meeting together, as some people do, but encourage one another, especially now that the day of His return is drawing near" (Hebrews 10:25). And don't just fill a seat—*engage*. Embrace the role God has given you in the church along with the civic role He's given you in your city, county, and state.

Here's the truth: **Tomorrow is always one day out of reach—and it's not promised to any man**.

"This is the day that the Lord has made; I will rejoice and be glad in it" (Psalm 118:24).

Now is the time you've been waiting for.

Now is the answer to the question life is asking.

Now is the only chance you are guaranteed—to impact your family, your nation, and your destiny.

Each answer you give to *now* forms an eternal thread in your dreamcoat—shimmering within that single garment of destiny. God is weaving together a grand eternity we cannot imagine—the greatest story ever told.

At the beginning of this story, we mentioned that love would be critical to reaching the end.

And indeed—it is.

Love is the final answer to every question ever asked.

But we must know, and live, the answer to what love truly means.

President Trump gave a wise reminder after surviving an assassin's bullet: Love is laying your life down to lift up those you truly care about. It is the most powerful force that exists—but you can't buy love, or steal it, or even create it on your own. You can only receive it from its Source—and freely give it away.

God alone is that source.

My friends, America is not finished. And neither is your role in her revival. Our most thrilling scene is yet to come. The lesson of our *Patriot Plea* journey is this:

The key to everything is the script of reality.

That means we must discover, and never deviate from, **The Truth**. And the most astonishing truth is this: Almighty God has written and directed this grand story of humanity . . . just for you.

You are His hero.

And **Now** is the time for you to become a hero of the American story—and to "live free or die," because . . .

Now is temporary—Freedom is forever.

AFTERWORD

The Road Less Traveled

I met John Strand in the middle of a civic psychosis.

Los Angeles in 2020 was a pressure cooker of fear, propaganda, and performative obedience. I was still practicing emergency medicine then—one of the physicians who had spent decades treating actual emergencies—now being applauded every night at 8:00 p.m. by neighbors banging pots together because CNN told them doctors were warriors and everyone else were plague carriers.

Yet I was also one of the very few willing to say publicly what millions silently suspected: the "public health" being imposed on Americans was political theater draped in a white coat.

John was not a doctor. He was something rarer in those months: a sane man in an insane world. He saw instantly what most people still refuse to see—that beneath the masks and mandates was a battle not over a virus, but over truth itself. When I founded America's Frontline Doctors, he was one of the few people who understood the mission without translation. This actor-model-artist threw himself into medical freedom work—creative director, strategist, communicator. And when hostility came—and it came in abundance—he did not waver.

People often misread John at first glance. He is handsome, stylish, attentive to detail—a man who appreciates beauty in a world drowning in chaos and ugliness. But if you stop there, you miss the point entirely. You miss the steel in his spine.

Thomas Jefferson once wrote, "In matters of style, swim with the current; in matters of principle, stand like a rock." John is the rare man who embodies both halves of that sentence. His style may be adaptable, but his principles are immovable.

January 6 revealed the measure of John Strand in a way nothing else could. The federal government charged us identically—same events, same prosecutors, same machinery, same plea offer designed to make the nightmare stop. We stood at the same crossroads and the government dangled the same bargain before us: recite our narrative and we'll let you go. I am the one person who knows exactly what John Strand faced, and I can attest—without qualification—to who he is when the full force of government pressure bears down.

My path, as brutal as it has been, did not include walking into prison in a designer suit—as if to say, *this is who I am and they will not change me*—to serve nearly three years. It did not include spending four months in isolation, waiting for a Supreme Court decision that ultimately vindicated his refusal to lie. If you have read *Selective Persecution*, you know I spent sixty days in prison and eight days in isolation. I described it as accurately as I could, but even that description is inadequate. Multiply that experience by a factor of fifteen. If even I cannot imagine it, I can assure you, you cannot.

John lived it. And he lived it without regret. Without bitterness.

The Decision Revealed the Man

Character is what a person does when there is no rescue coming.

John took the road less traveled—the road our Founders' took—the road they hoped would never disappear from this country. He chose trial. He chose the harder path, not because it was strategic, but because it was right. People wonder how such a decision is even possible.

It is possible only because the moral architecture was already there.

Everyone counseled John to take a plea. Everyone agreed there was no ethical conflict in complying with a corrupt judiciary.

John never wavered—not for a moment, not for a millisecond.

His decision caused him no stress. He did not lose a minute of sleep.

He never regretted it—not before prison, during prison, or after prison.

James Madison said, "It is in our lives, and not our words, that our religion must be read."

John did not speak his faith—he lived it.

He did not talk about courage—he practiced it.

He did not theorize about liberty—he sacrificed it—to preserve his sacred honor.

You cannot fake that. You cannot perform it. You cannot purchase it.

And you certainly cannot pressure a man like that to abandon it.

Why This Matters for America Today

I know something about standing alone against institutions that expect obedience. I know how the federal machine uses fear, indictment, reputational destruction, and coercion to break people. That experience gives me a vantage point from which to say something few others can say with the same authority: John Strand is incorruptible.

There is no amount of pressure—legal, social, financial, political—that can make him say what he does not believe. That is the rarest trait in American public life, and the one we need most.

John's imprisonment was a tragedy—but also a revelation. In a world where so many negotiate their principles for comfort, John demonstrated something that should be the minimum qualification for anyone who hopes to lead others: an unshakeable moral core.

Before intelligence, before charisma, before experience, the first question should be: *Will this person stand like a rock when the pressure comes?*

John Strand already has.

As he steps into public leadership, Americans will recognize something unusual—almost unprecedented in modern politics: John Strand's character has been tested and proven before entering public life. His ability to withstand corruption is not theoretical. He has already refused the easy road. He always will.

America has no shortage of politicians. What it lacks are men of character.

America needs more men like John Strand—men whose principles are as unwavering as their style is impeccable; men whose faith is legible in their lives, not merely their words; men who understand that the road less traveled is still the only road that leads anywhere worth going.

I am writing this Afterword not to praise John, but to tell the truth about him.

To tell you why the Founding Fathers would have recognized him instantly.

To tell you why they would have counted on him.

And to tell you why America will be stronger if more men follow his example.

John Strand is proof that courage is contagious, truth is resilient, and character—real, tested character—still has a place in American public life.

**—Simone Gold, MD, JD, is the founder of
America's Frontline Doctors, CEO of GoldCare.com,
and author of *Selective Persecution*.**